EUSTACE MULLINS

THE RAPE OF JUSTICE
AMERICA'S TRIBUNALS EXPOSED

ⒸMNIA VERITAS®

EUSTACE CLARENCE MULLINS
(1923-2010)

THE RAPE OF JUSTICE
AMERICA'S TRIBUNALS EXPOSED

1989

Published by
OMNIA VERITAS LTD

ⓄMNIA VERITAS®

www.omnia-veritas.com

© Omnia Veritas Ltd

For

JANE KATHARINE MUSE MULLINS

"the mother makes all things possible"

FOREWORD

I n my travels throughout the United States, I have found that the first complaint of our citizens is the sorry state of our legal system. They do not complain that the laws themselves are onerous, but rather that their administration is almost universally unfair and unjustified. I have even heard farmers arguing with each other at their markets, each protesting with inverted pride that "Our county has the crookedest lawyers and judges in this state," only to be met with the fervent response from a farmer representing another county, "Oh, no, our lawyers and judges are a lot crookeder than the ones in your county!"

Americans recognize that we must have laws, and that we must abide by them, otherwise life would become intolerable. The problem is that law-abiding citizens are usually greeted in our courts with disbelief that anyone still obeys the laws in this nation, and two, that a legal system which is operated by and for criminals has no greater enemy than the law-abiding citizen.

The first purpose of law has always been "Salus Populi," the safety of the people. I write this in a building which has five locks on every door. Twenty-five years ago, the doors were never locked. We hardly knew where the key to the front door was kept. With hundreds of other citizens in Washington during its tropical summers, I went to a nearby park to sleep in the era before air conditioning. Today, no one in his right mind would close his eyes in a Washington park, either by day or by night. It is rightfully known as the "murder capital of the world," rather than as the capital city of the United States of America.

This situation has been created, not by the negligence of the police, who are working harder than ever, but by the legal system, which abruptly denied the previous basis of our legal system, "Salus Populi," in 1933, with the advent of President Franklin Delano Roosevelt, who adopted the Marxist concept that the legal system was being used unfairly to defend property. Because of the Communist decree that all property was now the property of the state, the legal system need no longer defend crimes against personal property. This was soon extended to crimes against persons. The doctrine of compulsory equality meant that no citizen was entitled to wear a gold watch or to live in a large home. Other citizens who wished to deprive them of their excess property, even at the cost of their lives, were looked upon with approval by the legal system. If they injured or killed too many citizens in their exuberance, they might be confined for a short time, but they were soon released to continue the Marxist campaign of "levelling," that is, of reducing all citizens to a common level of fear and despair. This goal was first achieved in the Soviet Union, when Wall Street bankers financed the "noble experiment in compulsory equality." Soviet Russia was reduced to a giant concentration camp, a Gulag in which tomorrow might be worse than today, but it would surely be no better. The United States has travelled that same road with remarkable speed, constantly accelerating the techniques which force our citizens to new levels of personal depth and degradation.

Under this Marxist system, our citizens have found that the legal system is now something quite apart from "the law," that is, the fixed doctrine under which we live. A law is a fixed power. In contrast, the administration of the law today is a fluid power, in flux, and subject to outside influences, mainly the power of money and its concomitant political influence. When an American citizen comes into court today, he is not faced with the power or the majesty of the law. To his dismay, he finds that this force is no longer present. Instead, he finds that he is facing the power of money, and the power of political influence.

Traditionally, the scales of justice are depicted as awaiting the weight of the evidence. A preponderance on one side or the other will tip them to a just conclusion. Indeed, this is the ideal to which we still aspire. Unfortunately, it is rarely found today in our courts. If an attorney finds that the weight of evidence is tipping the scales against his client, he immediately employs one of the myriad techniques of "civil procedure" to have that evidence declared inadmissible, to have his opponent's witnesses impeached or found incompetent, and to mount a counterattack of his own to tip the scales back to favor his client. This technique is called "practicing law." Like any other skill, it is honed by constant practice, but this skill depends heavily on its practitioner's willingness to employ any subterfuge on his client's behalf. It is as though a football game were being played during which the players were allowed to commit any unsportsmanlike or illegal act in order to gain a point, with the umpire (that is, the judge), actually cooperating in and officially approving the illegal conduct. In legal parlance, this has a name; it is known as "professional courtesy," because the judge, like the lawyers, is also a member of the bar.

ACKNOWLEDGMENTS

I extend heartfelt thanks to the staff of the Library of Congress, the curator of the John W. Davis Collection at the Law Library of Washington and Lee University, and most especially, to the staff of the Law Library of the University of Virginia (and indirectly, to Thomas Jefferson, who sponsored this splendid university) for their painstaking cooperation in making this research possible. My sincere appreciation to Bill M. for his valuable guidance in the preparation of this book, and to my correspondents throughout the United States who have sent crucial material for my research.

CHAPTER 1

LEGAL ANARCHY

I n perusing articles in the nation's press concerning the present practice of law, one can only ask whether the lunatics have finally taken over the asylum. Consider the following; a mother is ordered confined to jail for many months by a judge because she refuses to obey a court order from a judge who demands that she turn over her infant daughter to a divorced father. The mother refuses, because she states that the father has sexually abused the child, a statement reinforced by medical evidence. After twenty-seven months of confinement, she is still in prison, but has never faced a jury or been convicted and sentenced for any offense.

Another mother, in the state of California, is sent to jail because she refuses to turn over her fifteen year old son to her husband, a homosexual, and his lover. A judge in Boston appoints himself the Superintendent of Schools because he disagrees with the manner in which the city's schools are being operated. Another judge, in Yonkers, New York, fines the city one million dollars a day for "racism" because its inhabitants, who have fled in terror from the drug-crazed streets of Manhattan, now refuse to turn their neighborhoods over to the very criminal influences from which they had fled. They had been found guilty of the crime of "white flight," of seeking a more stable area in which to bring up their children. In American courts today, "white flight" is accepted by judges as prima facie evidence of guilt of the crime of "racism." Rather than extremes, these stories are to be garnered from the issues of any metropolitan daily newspaper. However, in more mundane court cases, which do not merit attention by the press, the ruling presence of what can only be described as madness (perhaps the peculiar delusions and madnesses of crowds), provides endless examples of equally horrendous examples of the rape of American justice and its perversion at the bands of the mob. The guillotine is omnipresent in our courts, where our modern Madame Desfarges sit knitting on the front row. Here again, the blade drops, not on the heads of criminals, but on those who have been found guilty of being productive, law-abiding citizens of these United States of America.

Consider the following; a plaintiff sues for damages incurred in an automobile accident, after the person at fault has steadfastly refused to make any payment. The opposing counsel finds an elderly black alcoholic who will support the defendant's claim that the plaintiff was responsible for the accident. However, during his deposition, the alcoholic states that he is unable to identify either the plaintiff or his vehicle. Realizing that they have a credibility problem, the defendant's lawyers suddenly have their witness committed to an insane asylum the day before the trial. (He has been an inmate on previous occasions). The plaintiff demands that this witness be produced before the trial can proceed. The judge has no option but to comply. The alcoholic is brought in from the insane asylum under armed guard. His testimony is crucial to the defense, but the jury must now consider its source. Before this farce goes much further, the judge hastily saves the day for the defendant by declaring a mistrial.

At the second trial of this cause, the judge thoughtfully requests the plaintiff to bring his car to the court building, so that the jury can examine it and decide who was at fault. The plaintiff welcomes this opportunity to let the members of the jury look at his car. They file out and solemnly inspect the car, noting that its two right front doors have been smashed in, where the defendant's front bumper struck it three years before. The jury returns to its deliberations, and after eight minutes, files back into the courtroom to deliver their verdict that the plaintiff had backed his car into the front bumper of the defendant, smashing in the two doors on the righted side! The fact that this feat defies all the laws of physics carries no weight with them. Verdict for the defense.

Developments of this type illustrate the theory of morphic resonance. Morphic resonance is the process by which the past becomes present within morphic fields. The rape of justice is an excellent illustration of the process by which the transmission of causal formative influences becomes evident through space and time. The memory within the morphic fields is cumulative, so that things become increasingly habitual and more acceptable through repetition. This is apparent in much of our legal system, where the most outrageous testimony and judicial decisions are made to seem reasonable and acceptable. This illustrates the operation of morphic resonance conceived by an evolutionary spirit, becoming impressive nonmaterial fields of influence extending through space and continuing in time. Because they are localized within the systems which they organize, they turn the cosmos into a growing organism. However, the processes of morphic resonance need not be devoted entirely to formulae of insanity or unreason; they can just as easily be influenced by reason and human intelligence, instead of irrationality. This process was in force during the creation of the American Republic, when the finest minds among the American pioneers conceived the Constitution as the vehicle in which to enshrine their reason.

Even among these Founders of the Republic, there was no overweening optimism that what they had created would be immune from later abuse. Samuel Adams may have expressed the concerns of his peers when he wrote in 1789,

> "I have always been apprehensive that through the weakness of the human mind often discovered in even in the wisest and best of Men, or the perverseness of the interested, and designing, in as well as out of Government; Misconstructions would be given to the federal constitution, which would disappoint the Views, and expectations of the honest among those who acceded to it, and hazard the Liberty, Independence and Happiness of the People. I was particularly afraid (sic) that unless great care should be taken to prevent it, the Constitution in the Administration of it would gradually, but swiftly and imperceptibly run into a consolidated Government pervading and legislating through all the States, not for federal purposes only as it professes, but

in all cases whatsoever: such a Government would soon annihilate the sovereignty of the several States so necessary to the Support of the confederated Commonwealth, and sink both in despotism."

Adams did not envision the judiciary as the vehicle of this despotism, but his colleague, Thomas Jefferson, who was aware of the perils inherent in a central banking system as well as in a consolidated judiciary, wrote in 1821,

"It has long, however, been my opinion, and I have never shrunk from its expression ; that the germ of dissolution of our federal government is in the constitution of the federal judiciary: an irresponsible body (for impeachment is scarcely a scare-crow.) working like gravity by night and by day, gaining a little today and a little tomorrow, and advancing its noiseless step like a thief over the field of jurisdiction, until all shall be usurped from the States, and the government of all consolidated into one. To this I am opposed; because, when all government, domestic and foreign, in little as in great things, shall be drawn to Washington as the center of all power, it will render powerless the checks provided of one government on another, and will become as venal and oppressive as the government from which we separated. It will be as in Europe, where every man must be either pike or gudgeon, hammer or anvil If the States look with apathy on this silent descent of their government into the gulf which is to swallow all, we have only to weep over the human character formed uncontrollable but by a rod of iron, and the blasphemers of man, as incapable of self-government, become his true historians."

Modern governments rule by a simple formula, by convincing the masses that they are able to exist by the labor of others. In return for this "free" existence, they agree to "cooperate" in helping the "government" crush anyone who dares to speak out in favor of our traditional liberties. Frederic Bastiat, the French philosopher, pointed this out when he said, "Government is the great fiction through which everybody endeavours to live at the expense of everybody else." Note the crucial word "endeavours." The sub humans, that is, the gray men, the mattoirs, those who admit they are unqualified to compete in the games of modern life, sink back into the morass from which they emerged, a morass which is variously labelled, Communism or other dictatorships. In the United States, the gray men have found a unique defender, the court system.

Although many Americans express concern, but little else, about the growing crime problem, few of us understand that most crimes are committed in our courts. If a criminal commits an illegal act, this constitutes a crime. However, when he is taken to court, our legal system then becomes an integral part of the criminal process. The crime of which the criminal stands accused is nothing to the crimes which are now committed in the name of a "legal system." During the course of an ordinary legal action, whether it be criminal or civil, from three to ten additional crimes are usually committed. These crimes, in most instances, particularly if two attorneys are engaged, one as plaintiff and one as defendant, consist of subornation of perjury, suppression of evidence, intimidation or silencing of witnesses, conspiracy to obstruct justice, and denial of the rights of the injured party.

Because of the crimes committed against them by the legal system, the American people have been for many years engaged in a desperate war, a war to the death. Their mere survival in this war is an amazing and almost unbelievable historical event, because most of us have no inkling that we are in the midst of a great war. We believe that war is a situation where two countries formally engage each other in battle. In fact, during the past five thousand years of recorded history, most wars have been internal, or civil wars. Very few of them are wars fought against an external enemy.

Civil wars obscure the issues at stake, but the result is the same, the survival of the fittest. It is still a war of the fit against the unfit, even though the unfit manage to survive by creating alliances, by keeping the issues in the dark, and by dividing and conquering their historic foes. Although the results of this great civil war may result in a temporary advantage for one side or the other, the issue remains unresolved until one side has succeeded in ending the conflict by totally exterminating the opponent. The unfit are resolved that they will be the victors, and that the fit will disappear from the pages of history. The fit rarely have a clue as to what is at stake, that is, their very survival, and in most cases, they massacre each other at the clever instigation of the unfit.

A further amazing aspect of this impasse is the fact that once the fit do disappear, if indeed they are exterminated, the unfit themselves, unable to exist without their parasitic dependence upon the fit, will also disappear from history. Humanity, as a brief happenstance of history, will be forgotten. This paradox is explained by the ample evidence of the psychological aspects of the unfit - that they are perpetually mired in their self-hatred, and that the goal of their earthly existence is to end in their destruction. If this is their goal, one may well ask, why don't they go ahead and end it? They cannot do so until they have fulfilled what they see as their historic mission - to exterminate the fit everywhere on earth before they go down to their own long sought self-destruction. This dilemma is rooted in the hatred, misery, greed and envy which characterize the existence of the unfit upon the earth, from which they can never escape, despite any ameliorating effects of improvement or civilization.

Rather than face this stark dilemma, most of the unfit prefer to ignore it, turning their attention to some ephemeral excuse for not facing reality. It is another paradox that the fit, so able to compete and to excel in any field of life, have but one condition which continues to place their very existence in peril, their refusal to face reality. From birth, they are brainwashed to deny their fitness, and to cast about for some area of weakness which will enable them to believe that they really belong with the unfit. It is this brainwashing which enables the unfit to constantly recruit able allies from the fit. Although the educational and religious systems are constantly maintained "in form" to achieve this objective, it is the legal system which remains the final arbiter of the unfit in their war against the fit.

The present writer has appeared in American courts for some forty years, arguing his cause in every court except the Supreme Court of the United States. I have ignored the Supreme Court, because it is geared to handle only the pleadings of special interests. The individual has no chance to appear before this court. It is a waste of time and money for an individual to prepare and submit a brief to the Supreme Court. If he can enlist the support of one of the special interests, who see in his plight some opportunity to advance their own cause, he has a chance, albeit a slim one.

During these forty years of court appearances, a record which exceeds that of most practicing attorneys, this writer has seen elderly judges turn off their hearing aids, and sit dreaming of their mistresses, while apparently following with intense interest the droning protestations of attorneys and their paid witnesses. Many of us would be alarmed, thinking that if the judges are not listening to the testimony, justice is not being served. In fact, this creates no problem. In most litigation, the case has been decided long before the trial actually begins. This charade is necessary in order for the attorneys to collect their enormous fees, and to convince the ignorant litigants that they have indeed had "their day in court."

It is difficult to be critical of the judges for not bothering to listen to days and months of testimony in litigation, because experts believe that up to ninety per cent of all evidence given in American courts is perjury. The judges may have other impairments which interfere with their proper absorption of vast amounts of manufactured and coached testimony. This writer has appeared before judges who were widely known for their "quart a day" habit, a necessary preparation for sitting long hours on the bench. Although most of us might be affected by such daily consumption of the best Southern bourbon, here again, there is no real effect upon the judge's rendering a decision, as this has been decided before he took his first drink of the day, nor is there any question of his impartiality. His verdict usually favors a merchant or a professional man over a complaining customer.

There is also no real abridgment of the citizen's access to justice. He does have access to justice, but it is his misfortune that he is totally in the dark as to what kind of justice is available. He has been brainwashed to believe in the impartiality of the law, the application of Constitutional principles in our courts, and the absolute integrity of our legal system. At no time is he ever advised by his omnipresent "counsel" that the Constitutional "law" in which he retains such a childlike belief, touching in its very innocence, has long since been replaced by the "law merchant" that is, the law of commerce. This will be explained in greater detail in a later chapter, but for the moment, let us suppose that the citizen comes back with

"Well, what's wrong with the law of commerce? It is also a vehicle of integrity, is it not? Doesn't it maintain principles of equality and fair play, and honest dealing?"

Certain aspects of the law merchant are acceptable-the merchant asks a price, and the buyer pays it. There is a warranty on the goods, debts should be paid and so on. However, there are disturbing ramifications to the law merchant. First, it is always international, although it may be applied nationally. Second, it recognizes no national boundaries, or any national obligations. The United Nations, a law merchant entity, had made this clear. For instance, under the United Nations Treaty, the crime of treason against an individual cannot be successfully prosecuted. Alger Hiss had to be prosecuted for the crime of perjury, rather than the crime of treason, because he was protected by our acceptance of the United Nations Treaty (which he himself had written!). He was convicted of lying about his thefts of government documents, because he could not be convicted of turning them over to the Communists. Subsequent espionage cases in the United States have been prosecuted by the same subterfuges, with varying results. Many of the convictions have been obtained by relying upon military regulations and their violation. Nevertheless, no American judge is willing to make the pronouncement in open court that we can no longer prosecute the crime of treason, although this is generally acknowledged throughout our judicial structure.

Judges and lawyers are always aware that they are proceeding according to the principles of the law merchant. Litigants are never informed of this crucial fact. Citizens who confidently cite their Constitutional rights in court are amazed to find that the judge becomes furious, and threatens them with severe punishment if Constitutional principles are brought up again. This is our hidden code of justice. It is not a secret code, because it is no secret that our courts function on the principles of the law merchant. However, it is concealed from the citizens, hence it is a hidden code. When the citizen objects that his Constitutional rights are being violated by this foreign procedure, he is curtly informed that "You just don't understand how we do things here."

The law merchant principles guide the outrages committed by agents of the Internal Revenue Service against American citizens. Americans know that they are guaranteed the right of trial by jury, and cite the Seventh Amendment to the Constitution in support of that guarantee. However, the law merchant recognizes no right of trial by jury, nor does it recognize any "rights" of individuals. There are no rights; there are only adherence to the principles of the contract between the parties. The Internal Revenue Service would be violating its own principle, the principle of the law merchant, to allow trial by jury. For this reason, the Tax Court does not allow jury trial. The sitting judge is the only person who can render a decision.

Another vexing aspect of Internal Revenue operations are the continual demands that personal records and papers be produced for their "inspection." They cannot know how much of your property to seize until they have made an inventory of it. This IRS custom was drafted by Lenin in his crucial program "The Threatening Catastrophe," in 1917. He laid down the dictum that "concealing income" would result in the confiscation of assets. Not only did this program ensure his success in setting up a Communist dictatorship in Russia; it also became the guiding principle of our Internal Revenue Service. The actual basis of the IRS operations is the Communist principle that ownership of private property by an individual is a crime. An individual who owns private property or assets of any kind, cash, bonds, etc., not only is committing a crime against the Communist State by owning said property he commits an even more serious crime by not making a Jesuitical "confession," admitting that he owns said property which he has concealed, and that be thereby loses his rights to it. It is confiscated by the state. In essence, most "judgments" by IRS agents consist of the confiscation of all assets of the accused; not merely the "tax" owed, but all other assets as well, in penalties interest, fees and other "assessments." Thus Nikolai Lenin has established his dictatorship over the citizens of the United States.

American citizens are expressly relieved of any obligation to turn over their personal records to government agents, according to our Constitution. However, the compulsory maintenance of records, and the compulsory producing of them in a controversy, is an essential feature of the law merchant. Without the keeping of adequate records, recording transactions and payments, commercial life would be very difficult.

Therefore, the law merchant compels the keeping and production of records, a command which is now mandatory throughout our legal system, not only in tax controversies, but in all litigation, despite the fact that Constitutional law states that said records are the inviolable private property of the individual. However, the law merchant overrides this protection by defining as a "merchant," anyone who engages in any commercial transaction, whether as a buyer or as a seller. Thus every citizen, engaging in commercial transactions on a daily basis, is classified under our present legal system as a "merchant," and thus subject to the precepts of the law merchant.

Once the law merchant had become the dominating factor in our legal system, just after the Civil War, lawyers began to demand the production of personal papers and documents. However, this did not become endemic until after the Second World War, when individual nations which had attempted to establish national boundaries for their commercial law, and had become identified as "fascist" nations because of that precept, had gone down in utter defeat, and the international commands of the law merchant had become the law of all nations. Court orders are routinely issued by judges for the "production of documents," ignoring all Constitutional protection against such orders. These orders also become the instrument for destroying an opponent, because an order to produce documents can run into millions of dollars in costs. Such costs are always ignored by our judges, because "justice must be served"-no matter what the cost to the parties. This meant that litigation, which had once been the trial of issues of fact, that is, the conflicting stories of the opposing litigants, now became a process of "discovery," meaning that a race was on to discover which party would run out of money first, and then go into default.

The present writer has endured many such assaults upon his personal rights. He was stripped of all the earnings from his historic work, the first history of the Federal Reserve System, when a conniving "philanthropist," who had guaranteed him all proceeds from the sales of the book, embezzled all of the income from sales. With no other recourse, this writer was forced to sue him. He was then served with a federal court order by the philanthropist's attorneys, to produce all of his income tax returns, expense disbursements, and other financial data for the previous thirty-five years, although he had been involved with the philanthropist for only two years. Being unable to comply with this federal court order, this writer was then informed he could either go to jail for an indeterminate period, possibly life, since the records could not be produced at any time in the future, or he could sign a quitclaim, which he did. The embezzler kept all of the proceeds from the book, aided and abetted not only by a federal judge, but by the precepts of the law merchant.

Most Americans, being informed of this amazing outcome, would exclaim, "That's impossible! They can't do that!" Of course they can't do that, under Constitutional law. However, such a court order is routine under the law merchant. At the time of this imbroglio, this writer had seen references to the "law merchant," but naively supposed that it referred to the Uniform Commercial Code. 1strode into court, prepared to defend my complaint on Constitutional principles. Instead, I was quickly ground down by the wheels of our legal Juggernaut, the law merchant. At no time was I informed that our modern day Benedict Arnolds had turned the court (our West Point fortress of our rights) over to the English foe, or that I was now standing on the property of the Bank of England. However, in future trials, I will be prepared. I will begin by requesting the court to identify each legal procedure used in the trial, as to whether it is authorized by the Constitution, citing the pertinent Article, or whether it is a procedure of the law merchant, again identified by the pertinent code. The judge has but one defense - to cite me for "contempt of court" each time I raise this question. Otherwise, he will have to answer my request.

CHAPTER 2

THE ORIGIN OF LAW

The law under which we live, that law which is now so liberally construed, altered, misinterpreted, and bent to private ends by members of the legal profession, has always been intended, from its earliest records, as a fixed power. The word "law" in its pristine meaning, is recorded in its Old English roots, "Lauh," or "Laucht," meaning "laid" or "fixed." This in turn was earlier derived from the Aryan "logh," also meaning fixed, and in the Teutonic root, "lag," meaning, "to lie in a fixed manner," and evenly. In Latin, it was "lex," or law, and in Old French, "loi" a word similar to the earlier Aryan logh.

In previous civilizations, the law was not only regarded as a fixed power; it was deemed to originate in the heavens, and in godly rule. We find in the Cairo Museum a nineteenth century B.C. papyrus, the "Hymn to Amen-Ra":

"Rail to thee, Ra, Lord of Law;
father of the gods; maker of men."

Civilized nations have generally acknowledged that the ultimate source of the law and its authority is the will of God, as it was codified in scripture. In Isaiah 2;3, "The law shall come forth from Zion." In Micah, 4;2, "The law shall go forth from Zion." Isaiah 5I declares, "Thus saith the Lord; Hearken unto Me, ye that know righteousness, the people in whose heart is My Law; fear ye not the reproach of men. Neither be ye afraid of their reviling. For the moth shall eat them up like a garment, and the worm shall eat them like wool; but My Righteousness shall be forever, and My Salvation from generation to generation."

Sir William Blackstone, in his Commentaries, a primary source in the English common law, states a profound belief in the origin of law: "When the Supreme Being formed the universe, and created matter out of nothing, he impressed certain principles upon that matter, from which it can never depart, and without which it would cease to be." Blackstone's observation, offered as an article of his faith, has been remarkably verified by the modern discovery of DNA, the gene structure which controls our actions. The law, then, is not only the law of God, the law of men, and the law of our people, but it is also the law of nature, the very law which binds our physical being. This explains the multitude of "psychosomatic" illnesses which plague millions of people, and which stern directly from the perversion of law and the rape of justice. In my book of health, "*Murder by Injection,*"[1] I quoted the great scientist, Morley Roberts, on "Malignancy and Evolution," "Malignancy is the diversion of energy from high differentiation into the proliferation of low-grade epithelia which can endure irritation but only differentiate with difficulty. May we go further and even say that the common tendency to malignancy is the result of sociological refinements which ask for a higher role for epithelia?" In short, Morley Roberts is asking whether the widespread cases of cancer are not due to sociological factors, which demand that we alter our genetic makeup in order to proliferate low-grade epithelia. The courts have led the way in this "crusade," punishing the healthier and more productive members of society in favor of "the deprived, the homeless, the malformed. "This has been accompanied by the systematic debauching of our monetary unit through international central bank manipulation, as I pointed out in "*Secrets of the Federal Reserve,*"[2] impoverishing the healthier, productive members of society. The subsequent ruin, in turn, has resulted in the weakening of our immune systems, creating the

---

[1] Published by Omnia Veritas Ltd.

2

phenomena of AIDS, cancer, and many other degenerative types of illnesses.

The first codifications of law recorded in civilization acknowledged the importance of law to our human systems. Noah enjoined his sons to observe justice, to cover the shame of their flesh, to bless their Creator, to honor their father and mother, and to refrain from iniquity and uncleanness. These principles were later refined into the form in which we know them, the Ten Commandments. Man's very existence was predicated upon his obedience to the Law of God. Tradition maintains that this law was formulated as a verbal acknowledgement of the covenant between God and His People. It entailed consideration from both parties, and thus was a legal and binding contract according to the established principles of law. However, this Covenant did not encompass all of the known population of the world, but merely that group known as God's People, the People of Israel. As chronicled in Genesis, the first book of the Bible, Man, that is, Adam, was ruddy of complexion. This ruddiness was the conscious reminder of his dedication to upholding the Law of God. Whenever he transgressed this law, he would blush, in conscious acknowledgement that he had been disobedient. The blood would rush to his face, in a visible blush, as the mark of his disobedience and the reminder that he must fulfill the Law.

Because of this dedication, Adam had an immortal soul. His son, Enoch, differed from Adam because he was mortal. Henceforth, God's Law would deal with the mortality of His People. God later blessed the seed of Isaac, because "Abraham obeyed My Charge and kept My Commandments and obeyed My Law." Among Isaac's sons, a term later shortened to more popular usage as "Saxons," was Jacob, whose name was later changed to Israel. Since that day, Israel has been the chosen People of God. Isaac's sons, the Saxons, brought God's Law to the nations of the world, as they emigrated and settled in other lands. This law was codified by the jurists of England, principally by Coke and Blackstone, as the English common law. It was later transformed, after having been brought across the Atlantic Ocean by English colonists, as the Constitution of the United States. The Founding Fathers were acutely conscious of their precepts and their mission. Samuel Adams, the main instigator of the struggle for American independence from England, declared, "We have come here to establish our Israel."

The history of civilization has always been marked by the clearly defined milestones of codified law. In 2250 B.C., the Code of Hammurabi was promulgated "to establish law and justice in the land." We have also been greatly influenced by the codes of Roman jurisprudence, which were administered as the ruling code of the world for some thirteen hundred years. Kent's Commentaries, the principal legal textbook for American lawyers throughout the nineteenth century, notes, Vol. 1, p 556, "The great body of the Roman or civil law was collected and digested by order of the Emperor Justinian, in the former part of the sixth century It exerts a very considerable influence upon our own municipal law."

The Roman jurists developed the principle of "jus naturale," that is, a code of laws which reflected the laws of nature and the natural order. In his Commentaries, Blackstone expands upon this "law of nature." "Law of nature-the Will of his maker is called the Law of Nature, being coeval with mankind, and directed by God Himself as a course superior in obligation to any other. It is binding over the globe in all countries and at all times; no human laws are of any validity, if contrary to this."

Blackstone also writes that "Revealed Law is only scripture. Upon these two foundations, one, the law of nature, and two, the Law of Revelation, depend all human laws; that is to say, no human law should be suffered to contradict them." This is in strange contrast to our present day legal system, in which the rape of justice daily contradicts both the Law of Revelation, and the law of nature.

Because it was developed over a period of many centuries, Roman law had ample time to respond to the emerging problems brought on by its historical growth. Founded by Romulus in 753 B.C., Rome became a Republic in the year 509, after the expulsion of the Etruscan kings. In 450 B.C., the Laws of the Twelve Tables were formulated. The earliest Roman law was the Jus Quiritium, developed by the Quirites, who were the First

Families of the Republic. As patricians, the Quiritian Law was developed primarily to protect their families and their property. These families were known as gentes, or the clans. Their descendants have since been known to history as "gentlemen," as contrasted to the less distinguished masses, or plebs, as the freedmen, or non-gentiles, were known. The Latin "gentilis" meant belonging to the same clan or gentes. In those European nations which developed from these Roman antecedents, the gentes' descendants were known by the sobriquet "gentilhomme" in France, and as "gentlemen," later, aristocrats, in England.

The privileges arrogated by the First Families, the gentlemen, became a source of constant criticism and contention from the plebs. In fact, ancient Rome soon developed into the two groups which have remained fairly constant for three thousand years, the older families, which held the majority of property, and the masses. In the twentieth century, they are usually known as Republicans, and Communists.

The essential difference between the two classes was that the patricians, or gentlemen, knew who their parents were, and the plebs, who paid little attention to such niceties, did not. Because of their family records, the patricians were able to band down their property to their heirs, while the plebs, even if they prospered, had no family records with which to protect their holdings. This fundamental distinction led to the demands of the plebs that the government intervene to support them, demands which, some twenty-five centuries later, led to the Communist Manifesto, and Karl Marx's demand that all inheritance be abolished. In the United States, this precept of Communism was enshrined in punitive inheritance taxation and income taxes.

The Quiritian Laws in ancient Rome served to protect the family lines of the patrician families, and to provide inheritances for their descendants, their rightful and acknowledged heirs. Property and inheritance laws have been a basic part of our laws since that time. Roman law was divided into the *fas jus* and the *boni mores*. By fas was understood the will of the gods. The scholar Breal derives this word from the Greek "oeuis," meaning, the divinely inspired word, the laws given by heaven for earth. Jus also derived from the Sanskrit *ju*, to join, bond or unite, meaning the family bonds and ties which transcended the mortality of man. This was later interpreted as the *jos* or *jaus* of the Vedas, and the jaes or jaos of the Zend-Avesta. *Boni mores* was an essential ingredient of the maintenance of the patrician family; it meant dutiful service, respect, chastity, and fidelity to the law of contract, the law of the family.

The stern family discipline of the Roman patricians, which enabled them to continue their family lines, was steadily battered by the rapidly multiplying plebs, whose mathematical proliferation and willingness to endure a lower standard of living resulted in their greatly outnumbering the patricians. Under this pressure, the great landed estates were broken up into smaller, individually held parcels of property, as the gentes, or clans, began to disintegrate. Heretofore, strict laws had governed the ownership of property in Rome. Heredia, that is, plots of land within the city proper, had been granted to the heads of the gentes, the leaders of the patricians. Our word heredity derives from this custom, referring to the passing on of these plots of land to the heirs of the patricians.

Emboldened by their increasing numbers, the plebs began to demand more and more "rights" for themselves. The issuance of the Twelve Tables marked a watering down of the original Jus Quiritium. This process was greatly enhanced with the *Jus Civile*, at the establishment of the Republic. Our "civil law" derives its name from the outcome of the centuries long struggle between the patricians and the plebs, when the plebs insisted upon a law which granted them more privileges, as "civil" laws. In 471 B.C., the plebs celebrated their final triumph, with the establishment of the "tribunes," as the expression of their newfound political power. Thus the patrician age in Rome lasted a scant three hundred years, a short period in the long history of Rome. Nevertheless, much of the power and organization of Rome continued to be based on the stern precepts of its founding patricians, just as much of the protection afforded to its citizens in the United States by the Constitution had been laid down by the stern precepts of our own Founding Fathers. Even today, our lawgiving bodies are frequently referred to as "tribunats," as recognition of the triumph of the plebs in Rome in 47I B.C.

In 445 B.C., Caious Canuleius led the final assault of the plebs against the entrenched privileges of the patrician families. He wrested from them the source of their continuing power, the protection of their blood lines. By very stringent and exclusive marriage bans, they had managed to preserve their blood lines by prohibiting marriage with a plebe. Canuleius now succeeded in overcoming this ancient prohibition. From that time on, plebs were allowed to marry into the patrician families.

Rome was now "democratized." With this democratization came the inevitable diminution of the powerful blood lines which had so encouraged the ascendancy of Rome. Rome, in the time of the passage of a mere three centuries, had already begun her downhill road to decline. With the new democracy came increasing power and growing complexity of the Roman legal system. Cicero was led to publicly denounce the well-known practice of bribing jurors. By the end of the fourth century, B.C., Ammianus Marcellinus protested that "We see the most violent and rapacious classes of men besieging the bouses of the rich, cunningly creating lawsuits. Doors are now daily more and more opened to plunder by the depravity of judges and advocates who are all alike."

We could remind Marcellinus of the old saw that "The more things change the more they remain the same." Certainly his complaint could be echoed in any American city today. At the present time, our economy is imperiled by the burgeoning merger and acquisition activity among the large corporations, as they prey upon and swallow up each other. Corporations were well known in Roman law; the provisions for the establishment of corporations had been copied from the laws of Solon. Private companies were entitled to stay in business as long as they did nothing contrary to the public law. This precept was soon ignored. Both Augustus and Julius Caesar were forced to dissolve the corporations, because their machinations created widespread faction and discord among the people. It was during this crisis that a schism developed which has remained fairly constant to the present time, the schism between the civil law, which was designed to protect the public, and the law merchant, or the law of commercial activities, which was designed solely to protect

THE RAPE OF JUSTICE

the merchant. Although civil law takes into consideration the rights of the individual, commercial law only recognizes the stipulations of the contract, however this might infringe upon the rights of the citizen. Also, commercial law was pragmatic in its origins, having developed strictly from mercantile operations, whereas civil law ostensibly was based upon religious precepts and the Law of God.

By 467 A.D., Roman civil law, overtaken by historical developments, had reached the end of its legal authority. In 476, the Roman Catholic Church sought to resuscitate the power and authority of the ancient Roman law through its worldwide operations, with the present-day version of the Roman Empire headquartered in the Vatican, in Rome. The Roman Senate re-emerged as the Vatican's College of Cardinals. In contrast to this development, England became the repository of the ancient law of Isaac's sons, or Saxon law. Three branches of this law were established there; the Danes brought Dane Lag, the Danish Law, to England; the West Saxons brought the West Saxon Law to England; and the ancient Britons had their traditional Mercan-Lage, or Mercian Laws. King Alfred the Great codified the English common law in 872 A.D., as the Dooms of Alfred, taking his inspiration from the Covenant of Moses. By this upholding of the contract with God, Alfred assumed the title of "Great," becoming the representative of the People of Israel.

Blackstone notes that "The common law of England is generally founded in Biblical principles." Alfred the Great began his Dooms of Alfred with the Ten Commandments. In the eleventh century, Henricilus Bracton blended the English common law with the Roman law, as it had been revised in the Justinian Code of 533 A.D. This became operative in England as a Christian version of Roman law. Hugo Grotius, a lawgiver whom one of our Founding Fathers, James Madison, called "the father of the modern code of nations" firmly believed that God's law was superior to human laws. This view upheld Cicero's earlier contention that a law of the state which was in contradiction of natural law could not be viewed as law.

The Anglo-Saxon common law developed in three distinct steps: first, as the common law; second, as Equity; and third, as

Parliamentary enactments. Each development represented a further watering down and perversion of the original Teutonic or Anglo Saxon precepts. In the United States, we have followed a similar path. American law began as Constitutional law, the enshrinement of the ancient Teutonic strictures which protected the rights of the individual from powerful lords, which today we call the State. Commercial legal requirements then gradually took over as equity law or the law merchant, continually subduing Constitutional precepts of law, a process which was typified by the thirteenth, fourteenth and fifteenth amendments to the Constitution of the United States. These amendments controverted the original intent of the Constitution, as Congressional or Parliamentary enactments, which were and are legislative powers delegated to the law merchant. Included in these developments are the Federal Reserve Act, the Internal Revenue Service code, and the National Recovery Act of the Roosevelt Administration. The latter was overturned by the Supreme Court, as obviously being unconstitutional. However, the Federal Reserve Act and the Internal Revenue Service have never been challenged before the Supreme Court. The principal feature of the ancient Teutonic law, from which our common law derives, was "veragelt," a legal principle which established the payment of compensation for death or injury. Also known as "manngold," it evolved into the term "wergeld" under Saxon (or Isaac's sons) law. The amount of wergeld was always stated in schillings. After William the Conqueror invaded England and established the power of the "Black Nobility" there (see *The Curse of Canaan*,[3] by Eustace Mullins), the nation was once again divided into two classes, the foreign lords and the native born population. The natives became known as borders, or villeins. A "border" was a villain of the lowest rank, who held his cottage only at his lord's pleasure, and only if be produced sufficient income to the lord to justify his continued presence. This became known as the legal principle of Bordlands Anglice,

---

[3] Published by Omnia Veritas Ltd.

governing the land held by a border in tenure under Anglican law, which was also known as villeinage.

The fundamental change in legal authority in England after the Norman Conquest eliminated many of the principles of the ancient Anglo-Saxon law. However, it continued to be the basis of the legal system, because it was so firmly rooted in long recognized Roman and Saxon precepts. These precepts could be traced all the way back to Alaric the Goth Visigoth, who issued laws for his Roman subjects well before Justinian. His code was known as the *Breviarium Alarici*, or the *Lex Romana Visigothorum*. In England, Alaric's precepts were preserved in the *Lex Salica*, circum 500 A.D., in the Dooms of Ethelbert, of 600 A.D., and in the *Lex Saxonum*. However, legal historians often choose to ignore these precepts, preferring to attribute the development of the common law to Henry of Bratton, whose name was later corrupted to Bracton. He died in 1268 A.D. These historians claim that "legal memory," that is, the record of our legal system, can only be traced through written precepts to the coronation of Richard I in 1189. Bracton served King Henry III for many years, as the model for Henry's justices. His legal work was based upon the treatise of Azo of Bologna, who is remembered as "Master of all the masters of the laws." Bracton, in turn, served as the model for the most illustrious name in English common law, Sir Edward Coke.

Sir Edward Coke (1552-1634), was born of an old Norfolk family, which traced its lineage back to William of Coke of Dedlongton, in 1206. Coke not only managed to codify the English common law in his Institutes; he was also embroiled in most of the major political disputes of his time. He was born to the lord of the manor of Milkham. At the age of nineteen, he began the study of law in 1571 at Cliffords Inn at the Inner Temple in London. He completed his studies some seven years later, in 1578, and was called to the bar on April 20 of that year. His first marriage, in 1582, was a fortunate one. He married Bridget, the daughter of John Poston of Suffolk. She brought him a dowry of thirty thousand pounds. After her death, he made an even more advantageous second marriage, choosing Lady Elizabeth Hatton, granddaughter of the great Cecil, Lord

Burghley. The Burghley family, the Cecils, were one of the three ruling families of England. Coke's political future was now assured. His first marriage had brought him money; his second marriage, power. He had now become privy to the small inner circle of the men who actually ruled England.

Coke had won Lady Elizabeth despite the fact that, as a very desirable partner, she had been actively pursued by two of England's most powerful lords, the Earl of Essex, and Sir Francis Bacon. Essex was rumored to be the lover of Queen Elizabeth; Bacon, a founder of the Rosicrucian Society, maintained secret alliances with Freemasons throughout Europe. In his continuing quest for power, he was able to draw upon these sources for support. He also became Coke's principal rival in seeking the influential post of chief justice of the common pleas. Again, Coke won the post. As the protege of Lord Burghley, he was named Chief Justice of the King's Bench in 1613. In this office, he had the pleasure of prosecuting another former rival, the Earl of Essex, in 1600. Later, he was the prosecutor of Sir Walter Raleigh in 1603; in 1605, be prosecuted the perpetrators of the Gunpowder Plots.

When his daughter married the elder brother of the Duke of Buckingham at his wife's home, Oatlands, Coke further cemented his growing political alliances. Throughout a long legal career, Coke dedicated himself to completing his monumental work on law, first published in 1628 as Coke's Institutes; it was also known as Coke on Littleton. Subsequent volumes of this work continued to appear until 1644. Coke's work remains the fondamental treatise on law, although it is seldom taught in American law schools. After the triumph of equity, the system of the law merchant, in our system of jurisprudence, Coke and Blackstone's works were relegated to remote shelves in the rare book rooms.

The lasting influence of Coke's work may be attributed to its firm grounding in both Roman and Anglo-Saxon law. Coke returned to the principles of the ancient Jus Quirites, when he divided the people into two classes, the nobility and the commonality. This was a restatement of the earliest legal division in Rome, the patricians or the gentes, and the plebs. Coke began his work with the statement,

> "Reason is the life of the law; nay, the common law itself is nothing but reason" He continues with a Latin maxim, "neminam oportet essem sapientorem legibus; no man (out of his own private reason) ought to be wiser than the law, which is the perfection of reason."

Coke also commented in the Institutes that "the common law of England is called right, sometimes common right, and sometimes *communis justitia.*" He dwelt on the principle of ligeance, or a *ligando,* that is, the quality of allegiance as "the highest and greatest obligation of duty and obedience." With this precept, he had returned to that stern sense of duty which had guided the patricians of Rome and the establishment of the Roman Empire. It was just such a sense of duty which guided our Founding Fathers, and such leaders as General Robert E. Lee.

These basic qualities of Coke in his work later made a great impression on the imprisoned poet Ezra Pound, who had been shut away without trial because of his obedience to such a stern sense of duty. Coke also spent much of his later life as a political prisoner. During his years as a prisoner, Pound was able to study the entire work of Coke, which had appeared in four parts: 1. The reprint of Littleton's treatise on tenure, which was to serve law students during ensuing centuries as their first textbook; 2. the text of various statutes of the Statute de Donis, and other statutes to Magna Carta to James I; 3. criminal law; 4. the jurisdiction of the different courts of law. He later published his further studies of the law, Coke's Reports, which appeared in thirteen parts.

Despite his powerful political patrons, Coke frequently found himself under attack by his many enemies. On Feb. 26, 1620, be delivered an important speech on the problems of the scarcity of money, a statement which increased the number of his enemies by the number of those whose fortunes were made by trading in money. After much study of the problem, be found that the scarcity of money could be traced to seven causes, which be enumerated as:

1. the turning of money into plate;

2. the use of gold folia in gilding;

3. the undervaluing of silver;

4. the East India Company "who intercept the dollars and other moneys that would otherwise come into the Kingdom and bring in for it nothing but toys and trifles;

5. the excess of imports over exports;

6. the French merchants for wine carry forth 780,000 pounds per annum and bring nothing but wines and laces and such like trifles;

7. the patent for gold and silver lace and thread which wastes our bullion and coin and hinders the bringing of it into the kingdom."

Much of Coke's definition of the problem facing his nation four centuries ago is applicable to the plight of the United States as we approach the twenty-first century. We too are plagued by an excess of imports over exports. We import not only wine and lace, but oil and many other expensive products. Coke's emphasis on the necessity of maintaining the nation's supply of bullion echoes the preoccupation of our Founding Fathers, when they inserted into the Constitution the specific provision that lawful money should consist of gold and silver. However, it was Coke's open criticism of the activities of the East India Company which caused him to undergo the most severe pressures. This company represented then, and for many years afterward, the secret government of the British Empire. With full knowledge of this power, Coke refused to hold his tongue, when more prudent men would have remained silent. The passion for justice which ruled his life was not confined to the courtroom, but was applied to every realm of life. Chambers Encyclopaedia notes that "from 1606, Coke stood as the champion of national liberties, opposing any illegal encroachment of both church and crown." He openly criticized the Spanish marriage of King James I, who married a Catholic. This marriage resulted in a civil war, the end of the Stuart dynasty in England, and the Glorious Revolution.

King James I responded to this criticism by sending Coke to the Tower of London. The imprisonment lasted for nine months; Coke was released in August of 1622. While he was in prison, his enemies sought to close in on him. Five different lawsuits were filed against him. He won them all. He was called up by government agents four times for lengthy examination "on state interests" with no incriminating results. His chambers were repeatedly ransacked; again, no evidence against him was found. Nevertheless, his private papers were seized and brought to the council to be searched. His victorious emergence from these trials later caused him to refer to his "seven great deliveries while in the Tower" (Holkham Ms 727).

For the remainder of his life, Coke remained under suspicion. In 1631, King Charles I gave the order that his papers should be secured (SPDP S.P.D. CLXXXILI 490) lest he be an influence on the people. However, Coke continued to denounce any interference by the Crown with the liberties of Parliament. He opposed King Charles I's demands for additional subsidies for the Crown; he continued to speak against illegal taxation; and he denounced the King's favorite, the Duke of Buckingham. For these reasons, his career as a citizen of England was as illustrious as his career as a jurist and as a legal scholar. After his imprisonment in the Tower of London, he was secluded in his home in Stoke Poges. On the news that he was seriously ill, a King's Warrant had been prepared (S.P.D. CCLXXIL 65), and an envoy, Sir Francis Windebank, was sent to Stoke Poges to seize Coke's personal papers. These effects were kept by the government for seven years. Many of his most important manuscripts disappeared; even his will was never returned to his heirs. They had to assign his belongings without the benefit of his testament. Sir Edward Coke died at Stoke Poges on September 3, 1634. His personal story is typical of the treatment of a great man by envious and lesser rivals, who knew how to abuse their governmental powers. Many years later, one of his descendants, Thomas Coke, was finally named Lord of Holkham; his present heir is known as the Viscount of Coke.

Sir Edward Coke's long and fruitful life embraced the years of the British Empire's greatest power, which had been attained under Queen Elizabeth, from 1558 to 1603. James I followed, from 1603-1625; Charles I from 1625 to 1649. Coke had entertained Queen Elizabeth at his home in Stoke Poges in 1601.

During that visit, he presented her with gifts worth at that time more than one thousand pounds. Coke's patron, Lord Burghley, was Elizabeth's secretary of state. Whether because of or in spite of his illustrious patronage, Coke never hesitated to challenge Elizabeth's successor, King James I. Coke's successful impeachment of Sir Francis Bacon was widely interpreted as a direct attack upon the authority of King James, and the king himself believed this was the case. Coke had stood before the King, citing Bracton to his face, "The king should be subject to no man, but to God and the law." After King James' death, his enemies circulated the claim that he had been a homosexual, a slander which has been traced to but one originator, Anthony Weldon, who had been excluded from court circles. As a consequence of this exile, he developed a pathological hatred of the Stuart family. He first penned the story about King James in 1650, twenty-five years after James' death. Antonia Fraser, a prominent historian, attributes the slanders to the fact that James had begun to suffer from early senility, years before his death, causing "peculiar unorthodox behaviour." In support of King James, historians cite cardinal facts of his life; that he was the first in history to unite the feuding tribes of Scotland into one nation; the man who united Scotland and England; and the man who encouraged the propagation of the Bible in the language of the people; the King James version of the Bible.

Coke's impeachment of Sir Francis Bacon not only caused King James to imprison him; it also brought down upon him the wrath of the rapidly growing Masonic movement throughout Europe. Freemasons and their shock troops, the Illuminati, have continuously sought to wreak their sinister program on the people through control of the legal system. To lose the chief justice of England was a serious setback to their plans. In retrospect, we can only wonder that he was not executed, as the death penalty was a frequently employed punishment of political offenders. Apparently the Cecil connection was too great, and Coke was allowed to die quietly at his home. The Dictionary of National Biography honors him with an effusive memorial, "in his mode of stating what he believes or wishes to believe, he often reaches a perfection of form, exhibiting that freedom from flabbiness and that careful use of terms which is essential to a good legal style."

Legal historians have pointed out that perhaps never before or since has one man made so much law. He denied the right of the king to judge cases personally, or to give jurisdiction to ecclesiastical courts at the expense of the courts of the common law. He asserted that it was unlawful to give a commission (such as a royal commission) the power to hear and determine offenses which should be heard in the ordinary courts. Such practice robbed the citizen of the protection of established law. Coke maintained that no martial law which was executed by military law should be carried out without following the common law process. He brilliantly expounded the common law, simultaneously defeating Sir Francis Bacon's project to codify the law, a tactic for which Bacon had apparently been engaged by his Masonic conspirators. Coke thus gave us an exposition of the common law which has spread it throughout the English-speaking world. Coke laid down in Peacham's case (1615) that it is contrary to law to ask the judges separately before trial in a pending case to give their opinions in camera and ex parte. This practice has become a growing abuse in the American legal system. It was Sir Edward Coke, standing alone, who denied the right of the king to delay or stop proceedings in the common law courts. Coke further denied the right of the King to make law by proclamation.

Coke's monumental Institutes fixed the common law for the next three centuries, and established its supremacy over the Church, the Admiralty, the Star Chamber, and the code system of law which was propounded by Sir Francis Bacon. Coke also established its supremacy over the royal prerogative, through his insistence upon grand jury indictments, jury trial protection against unlawful searches and seizures (from which he himself was not protected), protection against double jeopardy, and the right of habeas corpus. It seems impossible that one man could have done so much, and thus he remains an inspiration to all who share his passion for justice. Few Americans today are aware of Sir Edward Coke's influence upon our Founding Fathers. Our historians ignore Coke's great feat in backing the Petition of Right of 1628 in England, which directly challenged the ascendancy of King Charles I. King Charles not only ignored the Petition of Right; he continued on his arrogant course while his popular support steadily eroded. He was executed in 1649. The Petition of Right later became a major factor in the drafting of our Declaration of Independence and the Constitution's Bill of Rights.

The rivalry between Sir Edward Coke and Sir Francis Bacon continued to affect the history of England long after both were gone. Ironically, it was Coke's challenge to the Crown as an absolute monarchy which resulted in the limited monarchy which we find today in England. His challenge exposed the vulnerability of the absolute monarchy, a situation which was eagerly exploited by a group of bankers in Amsterdam. They financed Oliver Cromwell and his Puritan forces' military takeover of England, resulting in the execution of King Charles I. When Cromwell's death without a suitable heir led to the collapse of this dictatorship, and the restoration of the monarchy with King Charles II, the Amsterdam bankers used their financial skills to cause unrest and economic chaos in England. After King James II succeeded Charles, the resulting problems proved too much for him, and he was forced to leave the throne, being succeeded by William of Orange, the Amsterdam bankers' choice, who became King William III. This event is known historically as "the Glorious Revolution."

The Glorious Revolution is a historical event which is little noted in the United States. It refers, not to our own successful American Revolution, but to the even more momentous revolution of 1688 in England. No historian has noted that the history of the world since 1688 has been directed by the consequences of the Glorious Revolution, which not only ended the attempts of the Vatican to recover its extensive landed holdings in England which had been seized by King Henry the Eighth, but also resulted in the establishment of the Bank of England and its espionage service, Great Britain's notorious SIS, the Secret Intelligence Service, which in turn set up our own Central Intelligence Agency, under the name of Office of Strategic Services, during World War II.

The Glorious Revolution not only made possible the chartering of the Bank of England, which was to become the world's most influential central bank; it also opened the door for the subsequent usurping of the English Crown by the Illuminati in 1714, when George I, Duke of Hanover, ascended to the throne of England. Since that date, the English monarchy has been prominent in the world machinations of the Freemason movement. The Amsterdam bankers had first subdued the English Crown when they financed Oliver Cromwell's rule of England as a Calvinist dictator, controlling England as Lord High Protector from December 1653 to September 1658, when he died. After Charles II, King James II succeeded to the throne. A Stuart who had converted to Catholicism in 1670, James married a Catholic, Mary of Modena, in 1673, and launched a campaign to rescind more than one hundred years of Protestant rule in England, by returning the nation to the fold of the Roman hierarchy. However, this goal was strongly resisted by the great majority of the English people, who were Protestant, and had no wish to return to submission to Rome. At first, James' crusade was not taken too seriously in England, because he had two daughters who had been baptised as Protestant. However, he now had a son and heir who was baptised as a Catholic, ensuring that the throne of England would descend to a Catholic prince. It was this birth which provoked the Glorious Revolution against him.

A small group of English aristocrats, led by the "Kingmaker," the Duke of Devonshire, with his associate, the Duke of Marlborough, sent a cypher letter to William at the Hague, inviting him to take the throne of England. William had married James' daughter, but his claim could only be exercised legally at the demise of James and his Catholic heir. James further angered the English people in June of 1688, when he jailed seven bishops in the Tower of London. Their offense was that they had refused to read his latest proclamations about religion from their pulpits. The bishops were then tried by a jury, and were acquitted on all counts.

At the time of the Glorious Revolution, King James had an army of 40,000 men, led by carefully chosen officers, all of whom were Roman Catholics. The challenger, William of Orange, had only 13,000 men. To compound his problems, his fleet was blown off course and missed their landing spot. The Duke of Devonshire hastened to their rescue, and received

William's daughter, Princess Anne, at his castle. James was then informed that despite his superior numbers, his troops would not obey their Catholic officers, and he had little chance of succeeding against the invaders. He abdicated to France. His abortive attempt to make a comeback in Ireland also met with defeat. William was now King William III, the King of England. He signed a Declaration of Rights on February 13, 1689, which ended the king's power to suspend the deliberations of Parliament or to dispense with its laws, which had been the goal of Sir Edward Coke's mission. Coke's Petition of Right had now become the law of the land. England has been a constitutional monarchy ever since. The official release of the British Information Service, the propaganda arm of England, states that

> "the United Kingdom is a parliamentary democracy with a limited constitutional monarchy. Government is carried on by Her Majesty's Government in the name of the Queen, who reigns but does not rule. The Queen is an integral part of Parliament."

The Declaration of Rights of 1689 was followed by an even more powerful contract between the English monarchy and the people of England, the Act of Succession of 1701. This Act specifically barred the Stuarts from ever again claiming the throne. The Act further placed the Hanover line of Germany, which was waiting in the wings, in the direct line of succession. It specified that all future monarchs must belong to the Anglican Church, the Church of England. It specifically barred Catholics from the throne. Later monarchs received the title of head of the Church of England. Other clauses of this Act secured parliamentary supremacy by requiring that the monarch must go to Parliament each year and request his annual stipend. The royal household now existed at the pleasure of Parliament, which controlled its purse strings.

In 1694, King William III chartered the Bank of England. Since that date, there has never been another revolution in England. A history of civil wars and revolutions against the throne had come to an end. A privately owned central bank, the Bank of England, now controlled the issuance of money, which had formerly been a royal prerogative. The throne's goodwill was secured by the assignment of a large number of shares to the royal family.

The sudden access to fonds provided by the Bank of England ushered in a great flowering of English culture and international prestige. The Bank's monetary manipulations created enormous fortunes for its shareholders, and great estates were built throughout the countryside. The fortunate few who had invited William to take the English throne, and who had subsequently been invited to become charter subscribers to the Bank for 10,000 pounds each (the equivalent of ten million dollars in today's currency), made certain the success of the Glorious Revolution. One of these chosen few, the Duke of Devonshire, was appointed Lord High Steward of England by King William, given a seat on the Privy Council, named Steward of the Royal Household, and given the coveted award, the Most Noble Order of the Garter. After William's death, his daughter, now Queen Anne, continued the Duke's appointment as Steward of the Royal Household.

Queen Anne married Prince George of Denmark. Although seventeen children were produced, they all died. Anne was extremely self-indulgent, and was plied with rich foods by her solicitous staff. She became very fat, and endured poor health because of her excesses, which finally caused her death. Once again, the throne of England was a matter of contest. Historians have suspected that Queen Anne's overindulgences were deliberately encouraged by some of her staff, to ensure that there would be no heir to the throne. She ruled from 1702 until her death in 1714.

The successful claimant who replaced Queen Anne was the Elector of Hanover, in Germany. Although he was merely the head of a small principality, the Elector was descended from Henry the Lion (1129-1195). Henry the Lion, Duke of Saxony, was the only son of Henry the Proud, and was a prominent member of the Guelph dynasty. At that time, the fate of Europe was contended for by two opposing forces, the Guelphs, representing the new "Black Nobility," and descended from the Canaanites, or Phoenicians (see Mullins' *The Curse of Canaan*), and the Ghibellines, who represented the ancient Teutonic Knights and the ruling dynasty of Europe. Frederick of

Barbarossa, a member of the Hohenstaufen family, was head of the Ghibellines during the time of Henry the Lion. Henry the Lion persuaded the Hohenstaufens to make peace with the Guelphs, (known as Welfs in that area of Europe). Henry, whose capital was Brunswick, a city later to figure importantly in the development of the Illuminati movement, married Matilda, daughter of Henry II, King of England. The Hanovers later came into possession of the Gospel Book, a twelfth century manuscript from the Abbey of Helmarhausen, which sold it to the King of Hanover in 1861. In 1983 the family put it up for sale; it was purchased by a consortium of German interests in 1983 for eleven million, nine hundred and twenty-thousand dollars.

The Hanover family had spent some twenty years diligently preparing their claim to the throne of England. Their official genealogist and historian was one of the most well-known scholars in Europe, Gottfried Wilhelm Leibniz (1646-1716). Leibniz had been secretary of the Rosicrucian Society in Nuremberg in 1667. He then moved to Frankfort, where he was employed by the Elector of Mainz from 1676 until his death in 1716. Not only did he serve the Brunswick family loyally as their historian; he was also a lawyer, and served them as a judge and administrator. His massive work, Codex Juris Gentium Diplomaticus Hannoverae, not only traced the descent from Henry the Lion, who had married into the British royal family; it also documented the later developments. Elizabeth, one of King James I's Protestant daughters, had married Frederick the Fifth, the Elector of Palatine. Their daughter, Sophie, married Ernest Augustus, the first Elector of Hanover. Although Sophie was not a claimant to the English throne, having died before Queen Anne, her son, who was now Elector of Hanover, was able to overcome the other claimants by the sheer weight of Leibniz' tremendous amount of research. Thus Leibniz, secretary of the Rosicrucian Society, not only brought the Hanovers to the throne of England; with him came the fraternity known as the Freemasons.

Because of these mystical connections, Leibniz, who founded such esoteric systems as economic science, and many other branches of physical science, was a close correspondent with his fellow Rosicrucian, Sir Francis Bacon in England, the historic

THE RAPE OF JUSTICE

opponent of Sir Edward Coke. Bacon, subsequently given the title of Baron Verulam, authored a book, "The New Atlantis," which describes the purpose of the House of Solomon. Nicolai, among others, has ascribed to this celebrated romance the origin of Masonry in its present form. Leibniz was at the very heart of the new intellectual movement of the eighteenth century, a spirit of liberalism and humanism which has been traced directly back to the ancient cult of Baal (*The Curse of Canaan*). He was a major influence in the development of legal doctrine, reaffirming doctrines of Christian natural law which originated in the Golden Renaissance of the fifteenth century. His writings shaped the thinking of Benjamin Franklin and Thomas Jefferson in their phrasing of the Declaration of Independence and the Constitution of the United States. In addition to providing intellectual inspiration for the American Revolution, Leibniz's writings also became the inspiration for the Industrial Revolution. It was his influence which led Benjamin Franklin to establish the American Philosophical Society. Franklin served as colonial Postmaster General, and carried on a worldwide correspondence. He went to England in 1757; the following year, be worked with Matthew Boulton Jr. on electricity, metallurgy, and the harnessing of steam power. Josiah Wedgwood, the potter, and Boulton's personal physician, Erasmus Darwin, organized a group which duplicated the aims of Franklin's Junto in Philadelphia, the organization being known as the Junto of Birmingham. It was later known as the Lunar Society. Through its influence, Manchester by the year 1790 had become a major industrial power. Boulton built the massive Soho Works, the first great manufacturing plant. It used water through a system of canals and steam power. The Soho plant became well-known as the headquarters of the Lunar Society.

With Leibniz' able assistance, the Elector of Hanover became George I, King of England, in 1714. He spoke no English, and stubbornly refused to learn a single word. Only German was spoken at the royal court in London. He ruled from 1714-1727. George II ruled from 1727-1760, and George III, whose name figures so prominently in American history, ruled after 1760, placing him in the crucial role of provoking the American colonists until they erupted in revolution. He was succeeded by

William IV in 1830. In 1837, the granddaughter of King George III, Victoria, became Queen. She married Prince Albert of the German province of Saxe-Coburg Gotha, whose family name was Wettin. During the First World War, this sounded suspiciously German, and it was legally changed to Windsor, the name by which the present royal family of England is known.

The Glorious Revolution unleashed many currents in history which remain strong today. The European battle between the rival forces of Protestant and Catholic was exacerbated by the ascension of William of Orange in 1688. For more than a hundred years, the historical enemies, England and France, had been at peace. William changed this arrangement, by joining the League of Augsburg against France, which resulted in seven wars between England and France between 1689 and 1815. The alliance of France with the rebelling American colonists was but one minor aspect of this longstanding struggle. One legacy of this rivalry is the present contretemps between Protestants and Catholics in Ireland. The Protestants proudly wave banners depicting their great patron, William of Orange. William's participation in the League of Augsburg was but one aspect of the growing conspiratorial work of the Masons. The League was essentially a Masonic foreign policy apparat which was determined to destroy the traditional balance of power between the reigning monarchies of Europe, finally displacing them by setting up their own World Order (see *The World Order*,[4] by Eustace Mullins).

In effect, Leibniz and his fellow intellectuals, with the ascent of George I in 1714 to the throne of England, became the secret powers behind the throne. In 1717, it was announced that Freemasonry was officially revived in England. From this base of power, Lord Sackville was dispatched to Italy in 1733 to set up Freemason lodges there; in 1735, Lord Derwentwater was sent to Paris to organize a Grand Lodge. The result was the

---

[4] Published by Omnia Veritas Ltd.

THE RAPE OF JUSTICE

destruction of the monarchy in those nations. Through the secret forces which led to revolution, England was finally able to dispatch its great rival, France, and to end her claims to world power. The new order was announced at the Congress of Vienna in 1815, when the triumphant Masons, led by the banking power of the Rothschilds, dictated their terms, not only to France, but to the other nations of Europe. Financed by the monetary power of the Bank of England, enforced by the British Navy and the worldwide intrigues of the Secret Intelligence Service, the Masons were well on their way to fulfilling their historic goals.

Leibniz' accomplice, Sir Francis Bacon, had paved the way as the apostle of the new humanism in England. He thus imposed on this nation his interpretation of the ancient rites of Baal, the cult of Canaan, and the predecessors of Europe's Black Nobility. He was one of the founders of the Rosicrucians, the Knights of the Rosy Cross, and the group known as the Free and Accepted (Speculative) Masons, who had departed from the function of the Masons as a craft organization. Scholars have identified much of Bacon's work as reflecting the Rosicrucian Manifesto.

Under the Hanovers, the Freemasons were able to step up their own monopoly of secret societies in England. On the 12th of July, 1798, an Act was passed in Great Britain, known as the Sedition Act, for the Suppression of Secret Societies. In his definitive work, *The Brotherhood, the Secret World of the Freemasons*, Stephen Knight complains that the Masons have never complied with the stringent requirements for listing their members under this Act. However, he seems unaware that the Act specifically exempts the Freemasons from compliance. Its language reads,

> "And whereas certain societies have long been accustomed to be holden in this kingdom, under the denomination of Lodges of Freemasonry, the meetings whereof have been in great measure directed to charitable purposes; be it therefore enacted, that nothing in this Act shall extend to the meetings of any such Society or Lodge which, shall, before the passing of this Act, have been usually holden under the said denomination, and in conformity to the rules prevailing among the said Societies of Freemasons."

In effect, this Act banned all secret societies except the Freemasons.

Such a powerful ban reflected the active participation of the now reigning family of England, the Hanovers, in the lodges. From 1782-1790, the Grand Master of England was His Royal Highness Henry Frederick, Duke of Cumberland; from 1791-1812, His Royal Highness George, Prince of Wales, who subsequently became King George IV; from 1812-1842, His Royal Highness Augustus Frederick, Duke of Sussex, son of King George III. The Duke of Sussex united the rival lodges, the Ancient and the Modern, into a single potent force. Thomas Howard, the Catholic Duke of Norfolk, had been Grand Master in 1730 despite many Catholic edicts issued against membership in the Freemasonry movement. Several Earls of Strathmore have also been Grand Masters of England. A Strathmore married the Duke of York, later King George V, and is now Queen Mother of England.

A century after the passing of Sir Edward Coke, another great legal scholar appeared in England. Sir William Blackstone published his monumental Commentaries in 1765. Blackstone continued and expanded Coke's work, by further defining the language and the principles of the common law. In Book I of his Commentaries, be lays down the three absolute rules of civil liberties: one, the right of personal security; two, the right of personal liberty; and, three, the right to private property. Blackstone divided the law into the rights of persons and the rights of things, private wrongs as opposed to civil or public wrongs, and crimes and misdemeanours. In Section 2 of his Commentaries, be writes that "Ignoranti juris, quod quisque tanatur scire, neminem excusat. Ignorance of the law is no excuse, because who can ignore God's will." This became the present day legal maxim, "Ignorantia non excusat legem; ignorance of the law is no excuse." This was further qualified by the presence of fraud, or a mistake in fact, as "Ignorantia facti excusata."

Sir William Blackstone was born in 1723. He was called to the bar in 1746, and was named Solicitor General to the Queen in 1761. Like his predecessor, Sir Edward Coke, be also had a powerful benefactor, Prime Minister Sir Robert Walpole, who named him to the prestigious foundation of the Charterhouse School, and to Oxford's exclusive Fellow of All Souls. The Commentaries appeared in four volumes, the first brought out in 1765, and the other three volumes appearing over the next four years. He made fourteen thousand pounds from the sale of the Commentaries, an enormous sum for that age. The Commentaries also proved to be a great influence in the legal doctrines of the United States for the next century. They were finally supplanted by a native product, Kent's Commentaries, as the basic textbook for American lawyers.

Calvinism, a stern branch of Protestantism which had originated in Switzerland under the aegis of a French leader, Calvin, had played an important role in the winning of England from the Catholic Stuart dynasty. Oliver Cromwell had been an ardent Calvinist, as was the eventual victor over the Stuarts, William of Orange. After the American Revolution, an adept combination of Calvinist and Masonic influences was brought to bear at the Constitutional Convention. Although the principles of Sir Edward Coke had been a contributing influence to the writing of the Declaration of Independence, and survived in the Bill of Rights, which was a belated addition to the Constitution, the convention itself was dominated by Episcopalians, that is, for all intents and purposes, by a branch of the Anglican Church, and by a strong Jesuit presence. However, the guiding principles of the convention were laid down by Freemasons, many of whom were also members of the other dominant groups. Bradford notes that Daniel Carroll represented the State of Maryland at the convention. He was the brother of the Archbishop of Baltimore, and was a Mason, as well as a Catholic.

The convention purported to draft the Constitution as the final protector of the rights of independent citizens against any oppressive force of government. However, as we have previously noted, the Bill of Rights was added, not as an afterthought, but as a device to ensure the adoption of the Constitution. Much of the work of the convention was mere window dressing to conceal its real purpose, which was to establish a strong central government with legal authority to provide repayment of loans made to the

Americans by British financiers, principally those who were also stockholders of the Bank of England. The new government was also commissioned to insist upon the repayment of mortgages to British lenders, which the post-Revolution courts, notably led by George Wythe, a drafter of the Constitution, and called the father of our legal system, duly demanded from the debtors. On July 9, 1778, meeting in Philadelphia, Congress had approved the Articles of Confederation, which then became the ruling body of law for the young nation. These articles established the principles of states' rights, and effectively ruled out the possibility of a strong central government, a federal power. When the Constitutional Convention met in Philadelphia on May 27, 1787, its secret agenda was to emasculate the Articles of Confederation, and to authorize the establishment of a strong federal government. The delegate who was entrusted with the task of carrying out this secret mission was Edmund Randolph. During the previous year, Randolph had been elected Grand Master of the Masonic Lodges of Virginia. His father, a leading Tory, and King's Attorney, had returned to England at the outbreak of the American Revolution. He never returned to America.

Edmund Randolph opened his plan with an unexpectedly strong attack on the Articles of Confederation. He claimed that "the confederation fulfilled none of the objectives for which it was framed." He then listed a number of objections to the Articles, among them,

> "It is not superior to state constitutions. Thus we see that the confederation is incompetent to any one object for which it was instituted. Our chief danger arises from the democratic parts of our constitution."

Although one might have expected cries of outrage from the defenders of liberty who were present, none were made. In fact, most of those assembled were of like mind; the few who might have objected preferred to remain silent and go along with the crowd. Randolph's proposals received strong and concerted support from his fellow Masons at the convention. He then worked out a Constitution which largely scrapped the Articles of Confederation, and replaced it with a Constitution which authorized a strong centralized federal government. A cloak of concealment was thrown over this creation by the hasty addition of a "Bill of Rights," intended as a sop to those who otherwise would never have voted for ratification. Well-hidden within the basic framework of the Constitution were Masonic plans and authorizations for a national judiciary power, which would exercise final authority in disagreements between the branches of government, while the national executive power was given little opportunity to enforce the Bill of Rights.

During the first few years of the Republic, the national judiciary was discreetly quiet. The Supreme Court met in a basement room, and appeared to be little more than an ornamental power within the government. However, it asserted itself sharply when John Marshall became Chief Justice of the Supreme Court. He had recently succeeded Edmund Randolph as Grand Master of the Virginia Lodges, which have played a major political and judicial role ever since. Marshall made his first bold bid in 1803, in the well-known case of Marbury v. Madison. Marshall's court ruled that the judiciary has the power to strike down any law. The legal background of Marbury v. Madison was that it was a brazen exercise in partisan politics. The case became a *cause célèbre* after James Madison, the Secretary of State, worked far into the night, hastily signing commissions for members of the Federalist Party on his last day in office. On the following morning, Thomas Jefferson came in as the new Secretary of State. Because Madison was a stalwart of the opposing Federalist Party, Jefferson threw Marbury's commission into the wastebasket, even though Madison had signed it. Marbury then brought suit to claim his due appointment as a justice of the peace. Chief Justice Marshall, who was also a leading member of the Federalist Party, ruled in favor of the plaintiff, and awarded Marbury his commission, a decision delivered along strict party lines. Marshall's decision created the precedent for the supremacy of the federal power.

On September 3, 1807, Marshall delivered another famous ruling, in U.S. v. Burr, as reported by Mr. Ritchie. He declared that "the laws of the several states could not be regarded as rules of decision in trials for offences against the United States, because no man could be condemned or imprisoned in the federal courts under a state law." This legal decision came about because of Marshall's role as "one of the usual suspects." For many years, Aaron Burr had been one of the most active Masonic conspirators in the new Republic. He had plotted to set up a separate and independent republic in the states bordering the Mississippi River. When Burr was charged with treason for this plot, he was defended by his attorney, Edmund Randolph, a former Grand Master of the Lodges of Virginia. Sitting as judge in this important case was Justice Marshall, who was then Grand Master of the Lodges of Virginia. The decision was a foregone conclusion, because Masonic law decrees that a Mason must always rule in favor of a fellow Mason, due to his "obligations."

Despite the success of Edmund Randolph and his fellow Masons in writing a Constitution which gave the federal government supremacy over the states, many legal authorities continued to cast doubt on the validity of that power, until the Civil War silenced forever the Americans who still opposed a strong federal power. In Sturges v. Crowninshield, 4 S Wheaton 193, the Chief Justice of the United States observed that

> "the powers of the states remained, after the adoption of the Constitution, what they were before, except so far as they had been abridged by that instrument."

During the nineteenth century, the available legal textbook for American lawyers was Kent's Commentaries. In Book I, p. 490, Kent commented on the Marbury v. Madison decision. "The question, said the Chief Justice, was whether an act repugnant to the constitution can become a law of the land. The powers of the legislature are defined and limited by a written constitution. But to what purpose is that limitation if those limits may at any time be passed? The distinction between a government with limited and unlimited powers is abolished if those limits do not confine the persons on whom they are imposed, and if acts prohibited, and acts allowed, are of equal obligation. If the constitution does not control any legislative act repugnant to it, then the legislature may alter the constitution by an ordinary act. The theory of every government with a written constitution must be, that an act of government repugnant to the constitution is void."

What Kent does not deal with here is the power of the judiciary to reverse itself on national issues, as has repeatedly occurred. The Supreme Court today declares that an act is not repugnant to the constitution. Tomorrow it rules that the act is repugnant to the constitution, and is void. No safeguard exists that the court cannot be subjected to varying influences which bring about these stunning reversals on decisions.

Kent further observed, in Lecture XVILI,

"The limitation of state power or sovereignty would exist in only three cases: where the terms granted an exclusive authority to the union; where it granted in one instance an authority to the union, and in another prohibited the states from exercising a like authority; and where it granted an authority to the union, to which a similar authority in the states would be absolutely and totally contradictory and repugnant."

The American Republic had the benefit of a written constitution, plus the well-established precedents of the English common law. The legal basis of the common law was firmly established in England, one source being "The Laws of England," sec. VI, chapter 31, which stated, "Be it therefore enacted etc. that the common law is, and shall be, in force in this government, except such part (pertaining to the provinces) laws of England are the laws of this government." At that time, America was a province of the British Empire. Kent notes in Book I of the Commentaries, p. 514,

"The common law includes those principles, usages and rules of action applicable to the government and security of persons and property, which do not rest for their authority on any express and positive declaration of the will of the legislature."

The Laws of North Carolina, chapter 5, which were enacted in 1785 by this free state, declare, "An act to enforce such parts of the statutes and common laws as has been heretofore in force and use here, and the acts of assembly made and passed when the territory was under this government of the late proprietors and the crown of Great Britain." C. J. Pearson says that "The laws of our state rest for a foundation upon the common law of England."

However, the Supreme Court, in 8 Peters 658, stated, "It is clear there can be no common law of the United States (only constitutional law)."

The authority of Constitutional law has been steadily eroded in the United States by the growing dependence upon the law merchant, and the consequent violation of individual rights of American citizens. This development flies in the face of James Madison, who wrote the Fifth Amendment to the Constitution. Madison stated that power must come from the people; "the government has only such powers as the people delegate to it through a social covenant, the Constitution which is derived from God's Covenant with man. This derivation limits the power of the process of law and the powers of government.

This covenant cannot be contravened as it is 'the law of nature and of nature's God.' "The natural laws written by Madison and the other Founding Fathers laid down the separation of powers of the legislative, executive and judicial branches of the government and the nexus imperium, the law of checks and balances, safeguards which are now largely being ignored and contravened by the judiciary through the adept usage of admiralty law and jurisdiction of the law merchant. In modern times, the law of checks and balances has been redefined by the Speaker of the House of Representatives, Jim Wright (who has since resigned), "We (the Congress) will write the checks and the people will have to provide the balances."

CHAPTER 3

A PLAGUE OF LAWYERS

I n his "Institutes," Sir Edward Coke defines a lawyer as "one who is set in place of another." In the early years of the American Republic, many of the Founding Fathers were either lawyers or trained in the practice of law, as part of their classical education. As a result, we have maintained the fiction that lawyers themselves are personages of unimpeachable probity, so much so that in the rare occasions when a lawyer absconded with a widow's funds, it was a moment of great shock. Such occurrences have now been relegated to the era of old W. C. Fields' comedies; the lawyers no longer abscond with the widow's funds. They merely transfer them to their own bank account and then send the widow an enormous bill for "services rendered." Charles Dickens gave us the most memorable portrait of a lawyer's techniques in his rendition of Uriah Heep; servile, insinuating, and once he has taken your funds, overbearing and demanding. Dickens also posed the great problems endured by those who found themselves delivered over to the hands of lawyers, in his rendition of the case of Jamdyce v. Jamdyce, a legal struggle which went on for generations, beggaring the clients but enriching the lawyers. Unfortunately for Americans, Jamdyce v. Jamdyce has proved to be the model on which our legal profession has modeled itself; our courts are filled with similar struggles, the least of which may come to a decision in a mere five years.

The Rand Foundation recently completed a study of our legal profession, finding that soaring legal costs accompany delays in getting to trial, which now reach an agonizing eighteen months, on the average. The Rand noted that half of the $30 billion annually spent on lawsuits goes to lawyers. Fifteen billion a year, much of which is created by deliberately prolonging the time and expense of litigation, goes to the lawyers for shuffling a few papers. Their expenses rarely entail more than five per cent of this amount: consequently, hundred dollar power lunches, fifty thousand dollar a year memberships in country clubs, and many other perquisites must be pursued in order to sop up the excess cash.

When an American citizen hires a lawyer, he enters the office of the practitioner under the now defunct image of the profession as that closely akin to one's physician, into whose bands one delivers the vital question of one's personal health; or of one's minister, who will be glad to cooperate in one's eternal salvation. However, just as the physician is likely to give you a new drug whose side effects will be worse than what is affecting you, or that the minister will divert your financial contribution to some tart in Harlot's Alley, the lawyer may prove to be even more devastating. Few people realize that an association with a lawyer may turn out to be the most dangerous step you can take, possibly resulting in the loss of your home, job, family and life's savings. They have no idea that lawyers often engage in one or more of the following practices during a single case of litigation-subornation of perjury; conspiracy to obstruct justice; and flagrant violation of the Constitutional rights of the opposing party.

Perjury, that is, false swearing under oath, is one of the most prevalent practices in our courts, not only by witnesses, but also by lawyers, who often coach witnesses to repeat carefully directed and totally false testimony. I once appeared with an attorney in a traffic case in New Jersey, which went on for about five hours in a stuffy small town courtroom (no air conditioning). At the end of the case, the judge, who ruled against us, informed the attorney that of all the testimony heard that evening, his was the most incredible! Subornation of perjury, that is, going over the prospective testimony of a witness, and instructing him what not to say or what he should say, is the linchpin of our present courtroom drama, the adversary system of justice. Two pit bulls are released into the arena, to tear at each other until one sinks into death. This system has little to do with justice, but much to do with power, profit, and augmentation of fees. The practice arose because a lawyer who did not know what his witness might say on the stand would be sitting on a keg of dynamite, wondering when it would go off. Many cases, which have been arduously prepared, have been lost in a twinkling when a witness goes beyond the scope of a question, and volunteers further information which destroys the client's case.

For this reason, lawyers rely heavily upon pre-trial depositions, or pre-trial discovery. Once these are typed up and presented to the court, they are set in stone, removing the fear that the witness will volunteer extra information or alter his testimony. Like Congressional speeches which are daily reprinted in the Congressional Record, the testimony may be subjected to intensive editing, alteration and deletion, all without any notice to the witness or the court. The altered deposition is then presented to the court, after a lawyer's extensive changes, as "sworn testimony"! Should an error be exposed, it would be blamed on the court reporter.

The other tools of pretrial discovery are written interrogatories and requests for admission, both of which are also answered under oath. The interrogatories constitute one of the greatest abuses of parties. They were sometimes expanded to as many as fifty or even one hundred questions, some of which were so artfully phrased that the party who answered question 18 would be asked it again in question 74 so that in answering it, he would totally contradict his answer to question 18. Interrogatories are always identified as "continuing in nature"- that is, First Set of Interrogatories, followed by Second Set, ad infinitum. Some courts now limit the number of questions in a single interrogatory to twenty or thirty, but no correction of the abuse of "continuing" interrogatories is contemplated.

As I have repeatedly pointed out in Motions for Protective Orders against Depositions to the court, pretrial discovery is actually "pretrial trial." The lawyer actually conducts the hearing with himself sitting as judge and jury, with no actual judge being present. Judges have been universally hostile to my motions and have always denied them, indignant that a "layman" would question one of the most profitable and arrogant practices of the legal profession. I identified them as "bills of attainder" which are absolutely forbidden by the Constitution, being too naive at that time to understand that the law merchant or admiralty procedures of our courts ban any and all Constitutional protections of citizens. Pretrial discovery is also modelled after the ancient Star Chamber procedures; the subject of the deposition is summoned to a room where he is placed under oath, with the understanding that anything he says may be used against him. As Roy Cohn has pointed out, discovery has become the bread and butter of the legal profession. Previously forbidden by both common law and the Constitution, it is now the sacred cow of our legal procedures. Legal authority Emily Gouric pointed out in an article in Albemarle Magazine, July, 1989, that lawyers in the state of Virginia have been able to engage in this profitable practice since the early 1970s. She quotes Robert Taylor as stating, "Discovery takes a great deal of interest out of trial practice," further pointing out that it prolongs cases fivefold and makes them much more expensive.

Although we may think that the proliferation of lawyers and their willingness to abuse everyone is something new, an affliction peculiar to modern civilization, we have only to turn to the scriptures to find these warnings,

"Woe unto you, you masters of the law! you snatch the keys of knowledge. "And Jesus said, Woe unto you, you masters of the law! You heap great burdens on the sons of men, yea, loads by far too great for them to bear Woe unto you, you masters of the law! You snatch the keys of knowledge from the bands of men; You close the doors; you enter not yourselves, and suffer not the willing ones to enter in. His words provoked the Pharisees, the lawyers and the scribes, and they, resenting, poured upon him torrents of abuse. The truths he spoke came like a thunderbolt from heaven; the rulers counselled how they might ensnare him by his words; they sought a legal way to shed his blood."

This gospel offers striking insights into the practices of the legal profession, not only in the time of Jesus, but even more so today. We should not honor this profession by calling it the "practice of law," but rather, as the subversion of the law, and the rape of the law, the all-too-familiar methods by which God's law is subverted and perverted by dedicated and professional criminals. Note the dictum, "the rulers counselled how they might ensnare him by his words." I have just identified this conspiracy as pretrial discovery. Further, "they sought a legal way to shed his blood." This too is the goal of our legal practices.

To protect American citizens from just such abuses, the Founding Fathers added certain guarantees, which they termed "the Bill of Rights," protective measures which had been cited by Sir Edward Coke earlier in his Petition of Right, and which had long been envisioned by enlightened European scholars. Of these rights, none is more important than the Fifth Amendment, which was personally authored by James Madison, the prohibition of self-incrimination. However, the legal profession has boldly circumvented this guarantee through pretrial discovery. They attempt to force a party or a witness to provide statements which will destroy his testimony and his case. "The rulers counselled how they might ensnare him by his words." In so doing, "they sought a legal way to shed his blood." What does this mean? It means precisely what it says. They sought a *legal way* to shed his blood. When you go into an American court, the legal profession seeks a legal way to shed your blood. No technique associated with this goal is too vicious or too base to be excluded from the arsenal of the lawyer, even though its barely concealed purpose, openly approved by the judge, is to shed your blood. This may seem rather coldblooded, or even unchristian, to the intended victim, who fails to recognize his dilemma. The court is the reincarnation of the ancient Roman arena, where the Christians are present only because they are to be thrown to the lions. Their struggles provide amusement for wealthy but bored spectators. The court has adopted the old Roman rule of absolute impartiality, extending compassion to none in the arena, whether plaintiff or defendant. Each of them is to be equally tom and mangled until only shreds are left on the teeth of the lions. The doctrine of "legal immunity" is also an important part of the Roman games, as our courts may more properly be known. The cheering audience sits high above the arena. No lion is strong or agile enough to leap into the seating, and present a threat to the spectators. Judges, lawyers and the jury can safely watch the torment of the victims without fearing for their safety. Not a drop of blood will splash onto their silken robes. This is justice.

Our jurisprudence demands that we hire an attorney to represent us, because the legal system has grown so complex that only a highly skilled practitioner is qualified to present our case. There is some truth to this claim, but it is far from the whole story. In fact, civil procedure as it is practiced in our courts can be learned in a few hours. We are speaking now of the basic practices. The ramifications of our civil procedure are in fact infinite; the present writer has contributed his modest addition to it by observing that under our present legal system, any case is in fact endless and can be continued ad infinitum, depending on the extent of funds of the rapidly impoverished parties to the action. This writer has found most attorneys not only unqualified, but unfamiliar with many aspects of legal practice, a discovery made when I repeatedly filed motions which attorneys, both in private practice and employed by government agencies, had no idea how to answer or to argue. Their way out of this dilemma was one on which they have relied constantly during this writer's forty years of practice in the courts; they simply have the judge deny the motions without argument.

The layman will exclaim, "But that's impossible! The court's duty is to hear and to resolve all motions of the litigants." In a perfect world, this would be true. The dodge by which they ignore it is one of the most treasured privileges which judges have granted to themselves. It is called "judicial discretion." The first line of defense for the judges is "judicial independence." No one can influence a judge, because he is absolutely removed from any possibility of influence, whether family, financial or political. His second line of defense is "judicial immunity." This is the claim that when a man puts on the black robe of ancient physical and ritual sacrifice of victims, dating from the time of the cults of Babylon, he is placed beyond any criticism or retribution, and removed from any liability for violations of morality, national loyalty, or religious concepts. As I stated in a letter to the press October 12, 1985.

"The present practice of "judicial independence," "judicial discretion" and "judicial immunity" is intolerable in a free society. A judge is simply a monitor or policeman who sees to it that the statutes are observed. No one can be "immune" from the consequences of his actions in a law-abiding society. " In a previous letter, October 10, 1985, I had noted that "For twenty-five years I have filed suits in area courts in which the evidence in my favor was stricken or ruled inadmissible, while the evidence against me, including hearsay from mental patients and patients with brain damage, was admitted. I have sued four attorneys, all of which suits were dismissed on demurrers (insufficient cause of action) which is barred by the Federal Rules of Civil Procedure. I went to the U.S. Attorney with a list of forty-two consecutive motions I had filed, all of which were denied, while motions against me were perfunctorily granted. I later learned that this fellow was a political crony of "our crowd." I never heard from him to this day."

Of the three unholy practices of judges, the doctrine of "judicial discretion" is the most pernicious and the most frequently encountered. Briefly, this means that the judge has the option of personally ruling for or against any motion without going into its legal merits. He may also ignore it altogether by "taking it under advisement." This means that he postpones his decision for months, or even years, leaving the case in limbo. His fellow members of the legal profession, the opposing lawyers, eagerly accept this denouement, because their meters will continue to run throughout the period of the judge's monumental wrestling with the merits of the motion, until he finally reaches his decision. In truth, little or no such "wrestling" ever takes place. The judge merely buries the motion until the agonized screams of the victims force the lawyers to request that he deliver his opinion.

But what does all of this have to do with justice? asks the gentle reader. The answer to that question is in the title of this book. It is not titled "In Praise of Justice" or "The Merciful Qualities of Justice." It is only with which this writer is concerned, that is, those who are forced to submit to indignities for the pleasure and profit of others. Force, as in rape, is the backbone of all legal practices. Every order handed down within the confines of an American courtroom is delivered with a backup of force. Armed bailiffs stand on guard in the courtrooms, not merely to intimidate those appearing, but also to arrest, incarcerate, or even to beat or kill anyone who challenges what is taking place. The attorney whom you hired is a willing participant to this force. He never informs you, when he bands you his bill, that he is bound as "an officer of the court." You pay their fees, but the lawyers' primary obligation is to the court, that is, to the legal system and the practices for which it stands. A wit commented that the Pledge of Allegiance for lawyers should read, "I pledge allegiance to the legal profession and to the criminality for which it stands."

Sir Edward Coke's definition of a lawyer as "one who stands in the place of another" takes us back to a more open type of justice. In earlier civilizations, differences between citizens were settled by trial by combat. The dissenters might fight to the death, or until one was disinclined to continue. The triumph went to the battler who was left standing. Our boxing matches follow the same principles. The winner is the one who is still standing, or who has outpointed his opponent throughout the bout. The victors emerge, not only as champions, but also as leaders. This led to the hiring of "champions" to stand in for those not able to enter the lists or who obviously had no chance of winning. This is the *raison d'être* for the hiring of attorneys today. Your lawyer is a "hired gun" who will go up against the fastest gun in the West, in your stead. The legal profession maintains that you have no chance of winning in our complex legal system; therefore, you must hire a champion, an attorney, to appear in your place.

In some forty years of court appearances, I have never found myself in a legal situation in which an attorney would have been better able to represent my interests than I could do for myself. The reality is that no attorney can "represent" you. As an officer of the court, he can plead or "pray" your case before the court; in other words, be intercedes with the imperial presence of the court in your behalf. He "prays" that the lions may be called off before you are tom to bits. He beseeches the court not to award damages or penalties against you which are several times greater than your total assets, but to exercise mercy and reduce them to a sum only slightly greater than your entire net worth.

This explains why the patron saint of lawyers is Saint Matthew. In Matthew 5:40, be counsels, "And if anyone would go to law with thee and take thy tunic, let him take thy cloak as well." This is not merely an exhortation to turn the other cheek, but rather, to allow the attorney, who is making off with your tunic, to turn back and appropriate your cloak as well. For this reason, I have advised my audiences for many years that the ancient adage, "A man who represents himself in court has a fool for a client," must be brought up to date with the admonition that "A man who hires a lawyer is a fool."

Few Americans experience any qualms at turning over the most intimate details of their personal and financial lives to a lawyer, yet the risks should be apparent to anyone. For years I have counselled anyone who plans to meet with or consult a lawyer to take adequate precautions. The first precept is "Never discuss any details with a lawyer over the telephone." In one case which dragged on for three years, the opposing counsel, one of the most influential and highly paid lawyers in the state, repeatedly demonstrated that be believed he was dealing with a fool, by calling me unannounced at my home in the afternoons, and trying to obtain verbal commitments from me about various legal maneuvers in which we were engaged. I filed a complaint against him with the court. The judge never took any action, but it did stop the telephone calls. In almost every action in which I have been a party, I have had to file repeated motions with the court, complaining about the illegal procedures followed by opposing counsel, Motions for Reprimand. To date, none of these has ever resulted in a reprimand.

The second precept which I offer is that you should never go alone to a lawyer's office. In recent years, books on legal problems have suggested that you obtain a signed agreement with your lawyer, agreeing on costs, etc., before engaging him to represent you. This would have been unheard of a few years ago, and is rarely requested even today, because few lawyers would sign such an agreement. They would piously inform you that such an agreement would place too great a limitation on their ability to represent your case. The lawyer wants only a blank check from you, not an agreement before his meter starts running.

He will eventually fill in the blank check with the sum of your net worth. Also, when you go to an attorney's office, you would be wise to bring a relative or a trusted friend with you. I have taken as many as eight people into judges' chambers for motions hearings, or into a lawyer's office for a required appearance. In every instance, the judges and lawyers have not dared to voice any objection, or to ask, Who are all these people? It is also wise to tape record any conversation with an attorney. Here again, most attorneys would object to this, as it places them on notice that you do not trust them, and automatically places limits on the amount of damage they will be able to inflict. A fatal mistake made by many citizens is their naive belief that because a lawyer is a relative, a close friend, or a longtime neighbor or country club member, he can be trusted. In fact, you would probably be safer with a stranger handling your affairs, as thousands of widows and orphans could attest. Lawyers trade upon such associations as relationship, membership in a religious or a fraternal organization, or any human contact which they can use to "bring in the business." The *Washington Post* recently noted that "an ambitious associate can generate profits to a firm of $200,000 per year on gross billings of $300,000." Note these figures. They indicate that two-thirds of the billing is net profit to the firm, with costs amounting to one-third of charges. The Post noted that large D.C. law firms pay associates with two to four years' experience $85,000 to $100,000 per year, in the salary range of the attorney general of the United States. Partners of large law firms bill clients at $225 per hour, while associates' charges are $125 per hour. A typical eighty partner firm pays a mean income per partner of $360,000 per year on $938,000 of gross revenue, which means that the firm must gross $29 million annually, or $80,000 for every day of the year. Merely organizing the file and indexing documents in a lawsuit can cost from $2500 to $5,000, while the drafting and filing of a complaint costs upwards of $10,000. No wonder people sneer, "Sue me," knowing that few people can afford such expensive justice, regardless of the merit of their complaint. A single motion before the court will cost from $5,000 to $30,000. The present writer sometimes filed as many as three motions at a time, during a period of maintaining eight or more cases in state and federal courts. None of the motions were the one or two paragraph motions such as those filed by opposing attorneys. My motions ran from five to ten pages of documented legal arguments, with ample quotations from precedents and legal authorities. I discovered that the judges rarely bothered to read these motions, much less allow them to be argued in court. I routinely filed interrogatories or answered the opponent's interrogatories, which the Post states costs $5,000 for each answer. Oral depositions are billed at $1,500 to $2,000 per day per partner, with half that fee charged for the ever present associate, plus $300 to $500 per day for the court reporter and costs of the written transcripts. Litigation only a few months old can already have accrued costs of from $50,000 to $100,000, with little or no progress being made towards a solution.

In my forty years of practice, lawyers' fees for the work I did for myself, would have been billed at more than five million dollars. To nip the growing tendency for citizens to appear as their own attorneys, lawyers have been urging the Internal Revenue Service to compute the legal costs of litigation for persons representing themselves, and then to tax the full amount as accrued income. To date, the IRS has not acted on the proposal.

One of the legal profession's dirty little secrets is the frequent abuse of women by lawyers. Features have repeatedly been run on such magazine type programs as "60 Minutes" about sexual exploitation of women who find themselves alone in a lawyer's office. Here again, I must emphasize the danger of going alone to any lawyer's office, whether you fear rape or not. You can expect to routinely take place, whether physical rape occurs or not. A woman who has been through a trying experience with her husband, and who has reluctantly decided to seek a divorce, is already distraught. Many attorneys are quick to take advantage of a woman who is already facing serious emotional difficulties. Before she knows it, she is athwart his desk and undergoing an examination which she never anticipated. One commonwealth's attorney was finally removed from office, after a series of complaints from outraged women, over a period of years, forced reluctant officials to abandon their coverup and to take action.

Legal observers conjecture that perhaps only ten per cent of such incidents ever result in a formal complaint. First, the victim realizes that despite the unwelcome nature of such attentions, she is dependent on this lawyer to salvage some funds or property from her collapsing marriage. She has already established dependency, merely by going into his office. If she storms out and goes to another lawyer, voicing her complaint about his behaviour, the lawyer, because of "professional courtesy," is obliged to call his colleague and ask if the charges are true. His peer will drop a hint that the lady in question shows serious signs of being "disturbed"; she may wind up with no one to represent her.

The iconoclastic writer, Robert J. Ringer, has inveighed forcefully against the destructive influence which lawyers inflict in the business world. He states that "the proper time to lock Legalman in his cage is when you are serious about closing a deal." Like most of us, be learned about lawyers the bard way, after they repeatedly prevented the closing of deals on which he would have netted millions of dollars. He defines Legalman as "the omnipresent defender of the nonexistent problems of people" and as "one of the players in the game of business who got into the park by sneaking under the fence, then took it upon himself to assume the role of head skimmer."

In some forty years of documenting the greatest crimes which have been committed against the American people, I discovered that in every instance, at the very heart of each of these events, like a malignant virus, were the lawyers. John T. Flynn, writing in the New Republic, May 22, 1935, chronicled Professor William Douglas's address to a convention of lawyers in Durham North Carolina, as follows:

> "It is sad but true that the high priests of the legal profession were active agents in making high finance a master rather than servant of the public interest. They accomplished what their clients wanted accomplished and they did it efficiently, effectively, and with despatch. They were tools or agencies for the manufacture of synthetic securities and for the manipulation and appropriation of other people's money. In

doing this, they followed the traditions of the guild. They never took seriously the nature of their public trust."

The New Republic further commented on these statements,

"These great law firms have guided their greedy and acquisitive clients through the mazes of trickery that the financiers had not the wit to travel alone. No cause seems too reprehensible for the lawyers to gild with their own sadly tarnished respectability."

When you suggest a course of action to a lawyer, the usual response is, "Oh, you can't do that." This response is almost automatic, because it is incumbent upon every lawyer to discourage any client from striking out on his own strategic course. He must place his destiny totally in the bands of the lawyer, no matter how incompetent that attorney may be. Also, they are very reluctant to guarantee results from any course of action. In his heyday, financier J. P. Morgan complained that no matter what he proposed, lawyers would tell him he could not do what he wanted to do. Morgan said, "Mr. Elihu Root is the only lawyer who tells me how to do what I want to do." The result of this compliance was that Elihu Root became the preeminent lawyer on Wall Street. Financiers flocked to his offices when they discovered that no matter what manipulations they could devise, Root was capable of coming up with a legally acceptable formula to allow them to get away with it. He finally became the patron saint of America's corporations, when he worked out the strategy of setting up tax exempt foundations for millionaire entrepreneurs who wished to preserve not only their money, but also their power.

J. P. Morgan later chose Elihu Root to set up the agitprop operation, the League to Enforce Peace, in 1916. Its purpose, notwithstanding its seemingly pacifist title, was to involve the United States in World War 1. It later took the name of "Carnegie Endowment for International Peace," headed by Alger Hiss, who later went to prison for committing perjury, when he lied about his handing secret documents to Soviet agents. After World War I, Root became the honorary chairman of the newly established Council of Foreign Relations, which had been set up as the

American branch of the Rothschild policy group, the Royal Institute of International Affairs, in London.

Elihu Root is also remembered as the man whom President Wilson sent to Russia in 1919, with twenty million dollars in cash to bail out the collapsing Bolshevik regime. This money was taken from the one hundred million dollar Special War Fund which Congress had appropriated for President Wilson's use. The record of the expenditure of this twenty million dollars by Root's Special War Mission to Russia is recorded in the Congressional Record, Sept. 2, 1919, as authorized by Wilson's private secretary, Joseph P. Tumulty.

However, it is Root's role as the legal mastermind of the chartering of the influential tax exempt foundations which has laid his dead hand upon the throat of all living Americans. In 1909, he drew up the legal charter of the Carnegie Foundation, as its principal incorporator. His fellow incorporators were Frederic A. Delano, son of China's most famous opium dealer; Cleveland H. Dodge, of the National City Bank, and financier of Wilson's presidential campaign; and the longtime Rockefeller henchman, Daniel Coït Gilman, who had been trained by the German Illuminati in devious techniques of subversion. Gilman also incorporated the Russell Sage Foundation, and other vital undercover operations. Elihu Root then incorporated the Carnegie Endowment for International Peace in 1921. His assistant, Philip Jessup, ran the CEIP after Alger Hiss was sent to prison.

The epitome of the great corporation law firm is the Wall Street firm of Sullivan and Cromwell. Its founders' background provides ample proof of the ruthless nature required if one is to succeed in this bandit profession. The Cromwell who founded the firm, William Nelson Cromwell, was publicly denounced on the floor of Congress as "the most dangerous man in America!" This description was not the prose of some reckless demagogue; it is to be found in a document published by the Congress of the United States, a 736 page volume, "The Story of Panama" the House Hearings on Panama in 1913. "In September, 1904, during the absences of Secretary Taft from Washington, Mr. Cromwell, a private citizen, practically ran the War Department. John F.

Wallace, Chief Engineer of the Panama Canal, testified before the Senate Committee on Feb. 5, 1905, 'Cromwell appeared to me to be a dangerous man.' "

In these Hearings, Congressman Rainey was quoted as follows:

> "The revolutionists were in the pay of the Panama Railroad and Steamship Corp., a New Jersey corporation. The representative of that corporation was William Nelson Cromwell. He was the revolutionist who promoted and made possible the revolution on the Isthmus of Panama. At that time, he was a shareholder in the railroad and its general counsel in the United States - William Nelson Cromwell - the most dangerous man this country has produced since the days of Aaron Burr - is a professional revolutionist."

And you thought lawyers were dull! Congressman Rainey used language which we might expect to describe Leon Trotsky or Al Capone; however, he was talking about the founder of the most august law firm on Wall Street. And what has been the history of this firm since the passing of its notorious founder? Cromwell trained and produced a protege who outstripped his predecessor, the famous John Foster Dulles. A relative of the Rockefeller family, Dulles was closely linked with international espionage groups headquartered in Switzerland and England. He can be described as the architect of the Second World War, as well as the man who singlehandedly issued the orders which precipitated the Korean War. At the Paris Peace Conference in 1919, the senior partner of the J. P. Morgan Company, Thomas Lamont, wrote, "All of us placed great reliance upon John Foster Dulles." History proved that that reliance was not misplaced.

In 1933, when a victorious but penniless Adolf Hitler needed funds to build his Nazi regime, his personal banker, Baron Kurt von Schroder, arranged a private conference with Hitler at the Schroder residence in Cologne, Germany. Attending this meeting as representatives of Kuhn, Loeb Co. and other Rothschild interests were John Foster Dulles and his brother, Allen Dulles, who later founded the Central Intelligence Agency. The bankers, through their emissaries, guaranteed Hitler the funds to install his Nazi government. However, this did not mean that they were

Nazis, or friendly to the precepts of Nazism. They were bankers who were making a sound investment in a coming event, the Second World War.

Whatever one's feelings might have been towards Adolf Hitler, there was no escaping the fact that without him, there could be no Second World War. The Governor of the Bank of England, Sir Montague Norman, whose financial manipulations precipitated the Great Depression of 1929-1933, was one of the first bankers to acknowledge this situation, and to advance Hitler funds from the Bank of England.

During the 1920s, John Foster Dulles brought to Sullivan and Cromwell as clients the blue chip firms of Wall Street J. P. Morgan Co., the National City Co., Dillon Read, W. A. Harriman Co., and Brown Brothers, which later merged to form the firm of Brown Bros. Harrimans. Dulles' instant stature as the senior partner of the nation's most influential law firm reflected a truism of the profession, that the senior partner of such a firm is merely the one who has the greatest credibility. His word will not be challenged, his authority will not be denied, and when be exerts his influence on behalf of a political candidate, a church, a university, or any institution, funds will be raised and the goal will be reached. Behind this facade of respectability are the facts; that such senior partners have been and are deeply involved in the greatest international swindles and acts of treason throughout the twentieth century. They attain the rank of senior partner precisely because they have the talent of telling the most outrageous lies with the highest degree of credibility, whether they are launching a securities issue or the campaign of a candidate for the presidency of the United States.

John Foster Dulles ensured his place in history by sending a telegram from Tokyo to President Truman, "If it appears that the South Koreans cannot repulse the attack, then we believe that U.S. force should be used." It was this telegram which Truman used as his authority to plunge the United States into the Korean War. The use of the imperial "we" by Dulles notified President Truman that the most important leaders of the World Order wanted this war; he had no choice but to obey. Dulles was rewarded for this extraordinary act by his appointment to one of the nation's most influential posts, the presidency of the Rockefeller Foundation. Ostensibly a "charitable" organization, from its inception the Rockefeller Foundation was planned by John D. Rockefeller and his legal adviser, Elihu Root as a business operation using extraordinary means. It is more properly described as a "syndicate," which was the term Roget used to describe a trust. Roget further describes a syndicate as a cartel, or a monopoly, which also is an accurate description of the Rockefeller Foundation. The purpose of the foundation's charter was to perpetuate a corporation in perpetuity by removing it from any threat of a takeover by other interests. In a world in which everything is for sale, the shares of a corporation are the most saleable item of all. This means that no matter how profitable and powerful a corporate entity you may build, it can be bought out from under you by anyone who can raise the necessary funds. It was Elihu Root's brilliant contribution to the future downfall of American industry that a tax exempt foundation would forever remove the possibility of any outside force capable of buying control of the corporation. Standard Oil, the Rockefeller Oil Trust, placed its controlling shares in the Rockefeller Foundation in 1913. They remain there today, insulated against any outside threat. The foundation gave Standard Oil an enormous financial advantage over its competition, as Congressman Wright Patman, chairman of the House Banking and Currency Committee, pointed out in remarks before Congress. While it could not be swallowed up by any other company, it could proceed uninterrupted on its course of swallowing up or dominating its rivals. This impregnability also made possible its profitable cartel agreements with monopolistic firms in other countries, such as its historic 1926 agreement with I. G. Farben in Germany to control the world's chemical business.

In "*The World Order*[5]," I painstakingly traced the background of the officers and directors of the Rockefeller Foundation from

[5] *The World Order - Our secret rulers – A study in the hegemony of parasitism*, Omnia Veritas Ltd, www.omnia-veritas.com.

1913 to the present day. Very few of these directors had any background in charitable work; however, most of them had very impressive backgrounds in such "humanitarian" endeavours as chemical warfare, international espionage, munitions manufacture, cartel agreements, and so forth. On the whole, charity was lacking in their resumes.

Although society has been, on the whole, over-respectful of lawyers in recent years, mindful of their power and their ability to inflict grief on their critics, diligent investigation discloses a few rare expressions of doubt in national organs of the media. Harper's magazine, October, 1976, featured an article, "A plague of Lawyers," by Jerome S. Auerbach. He notes that the Constitution of Carolina declared it "a base and vile thing to plead for money or reward. " The states of Massachusetts and Rhode Island prohibited lawyers from serving in their colonial assemblies, a striking contrast to today's situation, as we find that ninety per cent or more of state legislatures are now members of the legal profession. The historian Crevecoeur described lawyers as "weeds that will grow in any soil that is cultivated by the bands of others; and when once they have taken root, they will extinguish all other vegetation around them."

The historian, Ferdinand Lundberg, wrote in Harper's, April 1939 about "The Priesthood of the Law," in which he described "the Purchase of the law." Lundberg quoted a historic case, Gebhardt v. United Railways of St. Louis, Mo. 1920, in which the decision noted that "the law does not make a law office a nest of vipers in which to hatch out frauds and perjuries," a withering comment on the legal practices which had come to light in this case.

The Saturday Evening Post, Dec. 2, 1933, noted in an editorial that "When the Attorney General of the United States finds it necessary, in addressing an anti-crime conference, to refer to 'unscrupulous lawyers who aid and abet crime (the historic "mouthpiece" Ed. Note), criminals and employing every artifice in their defense, the public cannot fail to realize that in the relation between lawyers and crime it faces a problem at once peculiar and ominous.' The Attorney General went on to say that 'there is reason to believe that in many localities a certain number of lawyers are in touch with and regularly employed by the criminal element, being the scavengers of the bar We find connivance and connection between lawyers and crime, with its concomitants of jury fixing, bribery and perjury.'"

One of the most astounding examples of legal conspiracy in America is described in the exhaustively detailed book, "Senatorial Privilege," by Leo Damore, Regnery 1988. The nation's leading journals have resolutely ignored this documented work. Damore relates the amazing story of a phalanx of lawyers, sworn to a Mafia code of Omerta, or silence, which formed around Senator Edward Kennedy in a conspiracy to obstruct justice shortly after the body of a young woman, who was said to be pregnant, was found in his abandoned car. The District Attorney in this case, Edward Dinis, later publicly denounced the jury system in the state of Massachusetts as "absolutely discriminatory," and "a systematic denial of justice throughout Massachusetts." He also attacked the scandal ridden probate court system as "a little-known citadel of judicial patronage and favoritism operating in an atmosphere of intimidation." The Chappaquiddick incident, as Kennedy's escapade came to be known in the national press, not only destroyed Kennedy's chances of being elected President; it also destroyed the journalistic career of Roger Mudd, who was already accepted as the coming heir to Walter Cronkite. When Mudd interviewed Kennedy on September 29, 1979, he asked the fateful question, "Do you think, Senator Kennedy, that anybody really will ever fully believe your explanation of Chappaquiddick?" Kennedy made the equally fateful answer that he found his own behaviour "beyond belief." The liberal phalanx vowed to get Mudd for having exposed their champion in the lists, and he was subsequently dumped by the network in favor of Dan Rather.

This writer was exposed to the true character of the legal professionals early in a writing career. An attorney accompanied me on an afternoon outing along the Garden State Parkway in New Jersey. Enjoying the openness of the newly completed superhighway, I was tooling along in a new Hudson at a comfortable ninety-five miles per hour, when I was surprised to see a black Chrysler draw up beside me. The young trooper motioned to me to pull over. When we stopped, the attorney I hastily drew out his card and handed it to the trooper. He took one look at it, said "Okay," but added plaintively as he drove away, "But try to hold it down, will ya?"

This same lawyer asked me to accompany him to a courthouse in a small town, ostensibly to do some legal research. When we went into the deserted record room, he asked me to wait by the door in case the somnolent clerk wandered in. I stood there while he calmly ripped out several documents from the files and walked away. I expected that we would be seized and sentenced to serve at least ten years, but we walked by the clerk, nodded a brief "Thanks" and were on our way. I later learned that it is customary for lawyers to "delete" records in this manner, to alter entries, or to prepare substitute pages which are then inserted in the files to replace the genuine ones. Whatever is on paper can be forged or destroyed-this, I discovered, is an unwritten motto of the legal profession.

On October 5, 1988, the *Washington Post* headlined a feature on lawyers, "LAWYERS ON DRUGS CREATE PROBLEM WRAPPED WITH LEGAL, MORAL QUESTIONS." The gist of the story was that cocaine was becoming an increasingly serious problem among the lawyers practicing in our nation's capital. One attorney admitted to the press that he frequently represented his clients in court while he was high on cocaine, stating that while he was under the influence of the drug, he felt "like nothing could go wrong." Another addict, Richard Winters, said, "The thing that is really tragic in the legal system is this concept of the officer of the court as a superhuman. This is what keeps a lot of lawyers who are addicts, either alcohol or substance abuse addicts-locked up in their closets and unable to say, Christ, I have a problem, somebody please help me."

The same issue of the *Washington Post* recounted the story of an immigration attorney accused of preparing documents for illegal aliens designed to defraud the immigration service. In her documented work, "The Trial Lawyers," Emily Gouric chronicles some of the successful techniques of the nation's most famous attorneys, among them Howard Weitzman, who won acquittal for John DeLorean on charges of conspiring to distribute cocaine, by first filing some fifty procedural motions, including Freedom of Information requests. Weitzman knew that the judge would probably deny all or most of them. This process is informally known as "exhausting the court." It is well-known among lawyers that judges have a very short attention span; by flooding them with a mass of procedural motions, the lawyer can usually beguile the judge into a state of passivity, allowing him to proceed with a strategy for the defense of a client who is probably guilty. It is a truism of American justice that only the guilty can afford a really good lawyer. The innocent must content themselves with someone from the third or fourth echelon, who has a discouraging record of lost cases.

Gouric also describes the tactics of the famed Texas lawyer, Richard "Racehorse" Haynes, who represented Fort Worth millionaire T. Cullen Davis in his notorious Smith and Wesson divorce, as Texas style divorces are known. She also gives us Arthur Liman, who was featured in a TV series, "The Moscow Show Trials," as the North hearings before Congress were later described. Liman had been a protege of Nelson Rockefeller in an "investigation" of the Attica prison riots and killings. He is a partner in the Wall Street firm of Paul, Weiss, Rifkind, Wharton and Garrison. Liman's clients include takeover tycoon Carl Icahn, Lazard Freres, the investment bankers, and Pennzoil, which won a ten and a half billion dollar judgment against Texaco. Despite his role as chief counsel of the Iran-Contra Hearings, Liman recently stated on the op-ed page of the Richmond Times Dispatch, "We do not have political trials in this country." This will come as news to Col. Oliver North.

Outraged clients find that in most states, it is impossible to find a lawyer who is willing to file a suit against another lawyer. Theoretically, lawyers have no more immunity against lawsuits than anyone else; in practice, membership in a bar association, a law firm, or a Masonic lodge usually prevents or discourages any lawyer from taking a case against another lawyer, no matter how flagrant the offense may be. This was demonstrated to me in the case of the wife of a wealthy entrepreneur. Unknown to her, be had built up a billion dollar operation. After he decided that his new wealth required him to have a companion whom he could flaunt in public, be began to spend most of his time with his mistress. The wife sued for divorce, hiring a lawyer who, for reasons never revealed, placed himself on the side of the wealthy and influential husband. She stated that her lawyer summoned her to his office for a conference with her husband's lawyer. Her attorney then requested that she sign a stack of seemingly "routine" papers in their presence. Hidden deep within the stack was a document which stated that she hereby relinquished all claims against any of her husband's property. She read it and refused to sign it, even though her own attorney had conspired to get her to do so. Although she was unaware of the ways of the business world, she was not stupid. Nevertheless, she did not fire her lawyer, but allowed him to represent her through the divorce procedure. The layman finds that it is extremely difficult to fire a lawyer for cause, due to court procedures which are designed to protect the legal profession, another little-known aspect of our mediaeval legal system. You discover, as I did, that you cannot fire your lawyer, your attorney of record, as he is known to the court, without the permission of the court. What this entails is that you must find a lawyer to represent you in an appearance before the court, in which you request or pray the court to allow you to discharge your previous lawyer and hire this one. The procedure requires that you hire an attorney to file a motion that you wish to fire your first attorney; this motion is then argued before the court. Had she been appearing as her own lawyer, she could have done this herself, but few people are willing to risk everything in our arcane legal system by such an appearance. After hearing the motion, the judge then can exercise his "judicial discretion" as to whether he should allow you to fire the lawyer who has been selling you down the river. Such a motion is usually granted, with the stipulation that you must be sure to pay the fees of the lawyer who was misrepresenting you, as well as the fees of the lawyer who is now representing you.

This unfortunate lady wound up with a mere $20,000 settlement from her husband; the lawyer claimed this was all he could get from him. Her husband then called her up, to taunt her as follows: "You didn't know I was a millionaire, did you?" she was enraged to find that he was indeed worth millions, which would now be lavished on his mistress. She immediately resolved to sue her lawyer for malpractice. She told me that for months she travelled the entire state, trying to find a lawyer who would sue the attorney who had robbed her. She was always given the standard response, "You have already accepted the settlement through your attorney. There is nothing I can do to help you." I informed her that I had been aware for years that no lawyer in this state, as well as in most states, will take a suit against a fellow lawyer. The bar association claims it will hear complaints from civilians against a lawyer, but in actual practice such complaints are promptly buried, never to be exhumed.

I informed this lady that I had sued a number of lawyers in this state, acting as my own attorney. All of these suits were promptly thrown out by complaisant judges on the technicality known as "demurrer," legally making a claim that there is insufficient cause of action, but in reality, in legal jargon, saying, "So what?" The entire texts of my complaints against these lawyers had been copied verbatim from the statutes. One judge grinned at me as be chidingly remarked, "You know, Mr. Mullins, no one can expect to win every suit." I could have risked a contempt citation by replying that I would like to win one in forty years of pleadings, but I said nothing. I had already reported this selfsame judge for dismissing almost fifty consecutive motions without argument, only to find that the federal attorney was one of his old pals. That complaint was buried, along with most of my other legal pleadings. I obtained some small satisfaction from these lawsuits against our sacrosanct legal profession, when one of the lawyers came up to me at the door of the judge's chambers, whining that during the last two years, my suit against him had caused his malpractice insurance to double. Small victories are better than none at all.

The filing of lawsuits against lawyers by disgruntled, betrayed and cheated clients remains one of the great untapped oilfields of jurisprudence in the United States. On November 5, 1986, the Wall Street Journal carried a front page story about one "maverick" lawyer, Edward Friedberg, who has tapped this field, and found it a very profitable one. Friedberg, a lawyer practicing in Sacramento, California, gleefully sues his colleagues when clients inform him of their malpractice. The statement that this is an untapped oilfield is proven by Friedberg's assertion that eighty per cent of his malpractice cases against other lawyers are settled before trial. Only seventeen per cent ever go to trial. The reason was obvious; the lawyers were guilty, and they did not dare to face a jury. Friedberg says he has a great advantage in suing lawyers, and forcing them to take the stand in their own defense.

"Jurors bate lawyers. We rank just above used car salesmen. Besides, lawyers are lousy witnesses. They talk too much, and they are arrogant."

Despite Friedberg's enormous financial success-he wins million dollar awards for his clients in these malpractice suits, and takes one-third, plus expenses, for his contingency fee-no champion of the public has dared to enter the lists in other states. Certainly, other lawyers are aware of the thousands of cases begging to be filed for legal malpractice, but the profession has closed ranks. It is not merely professional courtesy - it is the fear that the entire profession will be imperiled, and perhaps destroyed, if the public was allowed to go into court with the amply documented cases of malpractice. The state bar associations and the Masonic lodges will never permit their members to do what Friedberg has done. Once the extreme cases of malpractice, negligence, and conspiracy to obstruct justice begin to be argued in the courts, the profession is doomed.

The lady whose divorce case was previously cited, like most clients, was unaware of one legal tactic which is always devastating to the cause of the litigant. This tactic is called "an advisory meeting" with the attorney for the opposing client to discuss the ramifications of the case-how long it will take, what sort of pretrial discovery is contemplated, and, most important, how much each of them can milk his client of before bringing the case to its predetermined conclusion. Such conferences, known as "ex parte," that is, without the parties, and without their knowledge or consent, may include meeting with the judge to privately discuss the case. Ex parte is one of the most flagrant abuses of the present day legal profession, and is strictly forbidden by law. A few indictments for this practice have surfaced in the last decade, but the chances of a lawyer being prosecuted for engaging in ex parte discussions are still closer to his chance of being struck by lightning.

By statute, private citizens are forbidden by law from filing any paper with a court, unless they have previously filed the case themselves, thus notifying the court that they are attorney of record, and are representing themselves. In recent years, emphasis has been placed on filing "in propria persona," as a proper person, rather than as attorney pro se, the theory being that one thereby escapes being tainted as an officer of the court, or of being subjected to the jurisdiction of the court. However, anyone who enters a courtroom is presumed by the sitting judge to be under the jurisdiction of his court, and those who deny it can protest all the way to their serving of a six month sentence for "contempt of court."

The language of the statutes forbid any clerk of the court to accept any paper for filing unless it is submitted by a licensed attorney, or a person representing himself. You may have a document which you believe will help your case. If your lawyer decides not to submit it to the court, you have no recourse. Your attorney will try to pass it off as irrelevant, although it could win your case. The problem is that your attorney has already agreed with the opposing counsel to watch you wash away down the drain. You must accept his decision, because the public education system carefully trains you to accept whatever a professional man tells you, without protest. Your doctor will tell you that vaccination is good for your child; your banker will tell you that the Federal Reserve System is not privately owned; and your lawyer will tell you that he has your best interests at heart.

In recent years, public statements have surfaced which question the competency of American lawyers. Chief Justice Berger of the Supreme Court stated that "American lawyers are incompetent." President Jimmy Carter warned that "ninety per cent of our lawyers serve ten per cent of the people," which is probably a break for the other ninety per cent of would be clients. Nevertheless, American lawyers show no incompetence in conspiracy to obstruct justice, conspiracy to suborn perjury, or their "ex parte" meetings during which they agree to sabotage their clients for the common weal. This writer has observed for forty years that American lawyers are extremely competent in carrying out the abuses of the public which have enriched them throughout the twentieth century. The American Bar Association issued a carefully weighed statement that "it has long been aware that the middle seventy per cent of the population is not being adequately served by the legal profession." This may be a warning to the profession that our lawyers are overlooking seventy per cent of the available market. The almanac shows some 651,000 members of the legal profession in the United States, including judges. Of this number, the American Bar Association has enrolled some 335,000 members. In theory, the American Bar Association is merely another professional group, whose function is to promote the practices of its profession. In fact, the principal function of the ABA, its state units, and its local bar associations, is to form an impenetrable phalanx for the protection of its members from punishment for their transgressions against the public. These transgressions include not only offenses committed against individual members of the public, but also crimes by lawyers against the public weal and the common good. Many decisions obtained by lawyers through malpractice of their profession serve not only to injure individuals, but all members of the public as well. Anyone who has ever filed a complaint against a lawyer with a local bar association can testify that the complaint is met with thunderous silence. Once filed, it is never to be heard of again. Public commissions have repeatedly verified this claim by releasing their findings. Former Justice of the Supreme Court Tom Clark headed a commission, which, after an eighteen month study of the legal disciplinary system, published its findings that "the prevailing attitude of lawyers towards disciplinary enforcement ranges from apathy to outright hostility. Disciplinary action is practically nonexistent in many jurisdictions." We are given an official conclusion that there are few, if any, areas in the United States where a citizen can obtain any satisfaction after making a complaint against an attorney. The Clark Commission noted that ninety per cent of complaints against lawyers are dismissed without any person bothering to investigate the alleged facts. If you live in Sacramento, you might be able to hire Edward

Friedberg to handle your complaint against an attorney, if there is sufficient damages involved. As for the rest of the United States, you can save yourself a stamp by not writing to the local bar association.

Outrage over the known abuses of the legal profession caused New York legislators to set aside $840,000 to fund disciplinary proceedings against lawyers. However, the disposal of these funds was left entirely to the discretion of the private New York City Bar Association, which has sole authority to hire or fire all employees entrusted with the handling of disciplinary actions against lawyers. As could be expected, the $840,000 was turned into another boondoggle for the lawyers, providing salaries for their relatives, with the understanding that they would do absolutely no work on the job.

One of the more colorful opponents of the legal monopoly is Andrew Melechinsky, the founder of the Constitutional Revival movement, which is headquartered in Fairfield, Connecticut. In his literature, Melechinsky forcefully states, "Yes, Virginia, there is a conspiracy. The driving force of that conspiracy is the bench/bar monopoly." A man who is willing to stand behind his beliefs, Melechinsky regularly patrols court buildings, wearing a large badge which reads, "Lawyers, Judges and Politicians Are Scum." Note that he does not qualify this statement. It does not read, "Some Lawyers, Judges and Politicians Are Scum." His characterization is all-inclusive. As an editor, I carefully analyzed his statement. I found that despite the most stringent editing, nothing could be either added to or subtracted from it to make it more direct. Melechinsky also pickets courthouses and law schools, bearing a large sign, "The court system is utterly corrupt." One does not do this sort of thing in free America without consequences. Melechinsky has been thrown into jail, but his vast knowledge of Constitutional procedures always secures his release. There should be a Melechinsky patrolling every courthouse in the United States, but so far he has carried on his crusade alone.

Texas journalist Molly Ivins, an iconoclast herself, offers some explanation as to why Melechinsky describes our professional legal talent as scum. A lawyer named Heard was to have been named the next president of the Texas Bar Association. At the height of his campaign, he was picked up during a police raid on a nude modelling studio. The Bar Association reluctantly chose another candidate as president. Other prominent attorneys make the news on charges usually found only in the supermarket weeklies such as the Star. Marvin Mitchelson, who invented the concept of "palimony" for the discarded lovers of Hollywood movie stars, was charged with professional misconduct after complaints originated from actress Julie Newmar and Eleanor Revson, of the cosmetics family. The complaints included charging excessive fees, failing to place a client's funds in trust funds, an allegation of moral turpitude, and that he had allegedly refused to pay one million dollars for jewelry bought in Switzerland in April, 1987. The two pieces of jewelry, from the collection of the late Duchess of Windsor, had been auctioned in Geneva. The AP story, dated Dec. 6, 1988, noted that the bar association now had more than twenty complaints against Mitchelson, which would be handled at a disciplinary hearing. On Jan. 15, 1989, Mitchelson was ordered to pay interest and attorneys' fees on the one million dollars from April, 1987, when he took possession of the jewelry, although he had claimed that the money was not due until Oct. 21, 1988. His fellow California lawyer, Melvin Belli, known as the King of Torts, was written up in the Wall Street Journal as an exile from his twenty-five room San Francisco mansion, a local tourist attraction, after a court order was obtained by his wife. Now legally separated, he lives on a one hundred and five foot yacht. Although his staff has now been reduced to thirteen attorneys, Belli estimates that he has won more than $350 million in damage awards for his clients. In 1985, he lost a malpractice suit, resulting in a $3.8 million judgment against him.

Six more malpractice suits have been filed against him in San Francisco Superior Court. However, this has not discouraged his clients. He currently has one thousand cases pending, or seventy for each lawyer on his staff. He also faces Tax Court proceedings in which the government is asking for up to three million dollars on a transaction involving his San Francisco law office building. Belli vows revenge, threatening a lawsuit for malicious prosecution. Because he sold the building to his children in 1981, the government wants up to three million dollars in gift taxes, stating that the sale was invalid because no money changed bands, nor was a written contract drawn up when the sale supposedly took place. Belli's fame as "the King of Torts" was built on his mastery of courtroom drama. He pioneered "demonstrative exhibits," such as bloodstained bandages, gory pictures, and other materials which shocked the jury members into making large awards. If there is one word which describes the activities of the legal profession, that word is bribery. However, this practice is less important in the poorer areas of the nation than the equally effective force of intimidation. Bribery reaches its apogee in the large cities, and among the major law firms, which handle multi-million dollar cases. In small towns, money rarely changes bands, because the legal system fonctions on political influence, fraternal ties, and the ubiquitous club laid along the rear of the neck. There is a certain "noblesse oblige," that is, I owe you and you owe me, or "one band washes the other." The latter was the favorite saying of an attorney with whom I worked for several years.

Few legal bribery cases are ever brought to the attention of the public. However, one such case, involving the august Wall Street law firm of Cravath, Swaine and Moore, exposed the activities of one of the firm's senior partners, Hoyt Augustus Moore. In the early 1930s, Moore was legal counsel for the giant Bethlehem Steel Company, a J. P. Morgan enterprise. This firm, in the course of its monopoly, tried to take over a competitor in the wire rope field, a practice supposedly forbidden under the stringent terms of the Sherman Anti-Trust Act. It seemed that a federal judge, Judge Albert W. Johnson, would uphold the decision against Bethlehem Steel. However, Johnson, wishing to appear a reasonable man, let it be known that for a token payment of $250,000 (the equivalent of five million dollars in 1989 funds), he could be persuaded to withdraw his objections to the takeover. In later testimony before a Congressional committee, Counsellor Moore stated that "this amount is not excessive and not objectionable." Payment was delivered forthwith. Despite his public acknowledgement that he had committed the crime of bribing a federal judge, Hoyt Augustus Moore continued his distinguished legal career for some twenty-five years after the event. In 1959, he retired at the age of 88. Not only did the New York Bar Association ignore his admission of a crime; Judge Johnson was later elected president of his bar association! He later was indicted for bribery and conspiracy, but be won acquittal, after his co-conspirators refused to testify in the case.

In September of 1978, Mahlon Perkins Jr., the senior partner of another sacrosanct Wall Street law firm, Donovan Leisure (it had been founded by General Wild Bill Donovan, a World War I hero who later organized the Office of Strategic Services under British auspices during World War II, later reorganized as the present Central Intelligence Agency) pleaded guilty to lying under oath when he stated that he had previously destroyed certain documents that his opponent in an antitrust lawsuit had obtained court orders that he produce. Not only did Perkins lose the case; a verdict of $81.5 million was rendered against his firm. Perkins was sentenced to serve one month in prison, but the bar association refused to take any action against him. If the bar associations can ignore crimes of this gravity, how could anyone believe that they would take action on the complaint of a private citizen?

Indictments against leading members of the legal profession could be cited for many pages; these will suffice to make the point. The fact remains, however, that the greatest damage they have inflicted has been the betrayal of the nation through their activities in international conspiracies. We have cited John Foster Dulles; although he is the most notorious of the conspirators, he has not lacked for emulators on many lesser levels. The Wall Street Journal has noted that his firm, Sullivan and Cromwell, seems to have lost much of its clout, and its important clients, in recent years. No doubt it requires a partner capable of similar intrigues before its enormous fees are renewed.

Present legal practice, in the experience of the present writer, consists almost entirely of the game known as "Let's Make a Deal." The result of this practice is that few lawyers today have a working knowledge of legal strategy, or even of the requirements of writing a simple motion. Early on, in my appearances in our courts, I discovered that I was creating consternation in the ranks of these "nonpracticing lawyers," because of the scope and length of my legal briefs. Because of my many years of training and practice as a researcher and writer, I had no objection to spending many hours reading such legal tomes as the United States Code or the *Corpus Juris Secundum*, books which my opponents rarely opened. As a result, the judges were hard put to deny my motions in the face of the feeble efforts of their distinguished colleagues. However, this never prevented them from doing so. Their only hope was that after persistent rejection on every level of the courts, I would run out of funds, or I would become discouraged and go away. In fact, I stayed on to see just how corrupt the system actually was. It was a fascinating experience.

The most tried and true technique of exhausting the opposition, that is, by wiping out their financial resources, did not work in my case. I was not paying the expense of a large law firm, or of a single lawyer, to handle my work. My greatest expense was typing paper and ribbons, perhaps ten dollars a month. This expenditure enabled me to keep six or eight cases going in state and federal courts. However, my best efforts were usually torpedoed through the legal technique of "discovery." Briefly stated, discovery entails an order from the court that you turn over all documents and evidence of your case to your opponent, so that he will then have the weapons to fight you. The opposing lawyers sift through all of your documentation, extract all the evidence favorable to you, and have the judge declare it "inadmissible." At the same time, all evidence favorable to their side will automatically be ruled "admissible" by the judge. In forty years of court practice, I never saw this practice overlooked, nor did I ever see it fail to produce a decision against me.

Discovery also requires prolonged appearances in pre-trial depositions, providing answers to lengthy questionnaires, known as Written Interrogatories, and answers to Requests for Admission. If these procedures fail to destroy you, the court then goes to Order for Production of Documents. Usually, this means that the court orders you to produce your great grandfather's passport and similar papers which have not been seen by anyone for many years. Failure to do so results in immediate court sanctions, including indefinite jail sentences until the documents are produced. The discovery techniques, on which present legal practice depends, constitute, first of all, a trial of the case by the opposing lawyer without benefit of judge or jury, and second, a bill of attainder against the party who is ordered to appear. Bills of attainder are strictly prohibited by the Constitution of the United States, yet every judge to whom I made this notice ignored it. At that time, I did not understand that the admiralty law of England has superseded the Constitution in American courts. Bills of attainder are not prohibited in admiralty law.

Roy Cohn, reputed to be a fierce opponent in a courtroom, writes in his autobiography, "In a Hall of Fame example of the tail wagging the dog, discovery has become the be all and end all of trial practice. Years are spent in 'discovering' the other fellow's case, in the privacy of conference rooms in brilliantly decorated law offices paid for by clients who are supposed to be getting a fair shake for their money and instead are all too often getting a shakedown by lawyers who would not know how to try a case before a jury if their lives depended on it. Depositions, it's called, and all it does is finally support incompetents who are afraid to show up in court."

Cohn glosses over the fact that discovery is more often employed to destroy the opponent before trial, through protracted expense and abuse. The Wall Street Journal noted that by September, 1988, the Wall Street firm of Drexel, Burham and Lambert had spent some $140 million to defend itself against charges of violations of securities laws, a cost which included $40 million for copying one and a half million pages of documents. The firm finally settled out of court, agreeing to pay $650 million in fines for charges which it might have been able to disprove in court, after paying legal costs of double the amount of the fine. The Department of Justice case against the giant American Telephone and Telegraph Company was also a lawyer's dream, involving the payment of hundreds of millions of dollars in legal costs, which you, gentle reader, wound up paying through increases in your telephone bills. As you may have suspected, the Department of Justice, the largest law firm in the world, specializes in creating such lawsuits for the benefit of lawyers everywhere. This explains F. Lee Bailey's cryptic comment on "the cold fear associated with being a defendant in an American court." M & N Associates, in a poll taken in 1968, found that 68% of American citizens did not believe they could obtain a fair trial in any American court. The famed lawyer, Gerry Spence, in his most recent book, "With Justice for None" writes that "The truth is that there is no justice in any court for the American people."

Libel suits also remain a fertile field for lawyers, as the judgments and legal expenses have no limits. When two liberal writers of the New York school, Lillian Hellman and Mary McCarthy, went to court against each other, the results were disastrous for both. Hellman had a long record as an habitual liar. After she married Hollywood script writer Dashiell Hammett, she took all the income from his work, refusing to allow his children by a previous marriage to receive any funds. However, it was her reputation as the most outrageous liar in a profession not noted for its dedication to the truth, which caused her fellow liberal, Mary McCarthy, to speak in exasperation during a nationally broadcast interview on the Dick Cavett show, characterizing Hellman as "a holdover tremendously overrated, a bad writer and a dishonest writer." she followed this denunciation of Hellman, which might be excused as legitimate literary criticism, with an actionable statement when she concluded, "Every word she writes is a lie, including and and the."

After brooding over McCarthy's statement for a few moments, Hellman called her lawyers. In February, 1980, Mary McCarthy had to defend herself in a libel suit. Despite the fact that she had long been a darling of the literati, and bad had many best sellers, she soon found her savings decimated by legal expenses. Her New York attorneys charged her $35,000 for filing one motion in this case. (I sometimes filed three and four motions in a single day, but I had no comparable expenses). The case dragged on, as cases do when one has expensive New York lawyers. Lillian Hellman died in 1984, before the case came to trial, a considerable relief to Mary McCarthy. It is a truism of the legal profession that one never can predict what a jury might do; the usual award in libel cases of this type is one dollar, but punitive damages, which are aptly named, and which are pure admiralty law, can amount to millions of dollars.

The famed unpredictability of juries has now given rise to a new art, the art of jury selection. It is an art, because the final framing of the painting depends entirely on which jurors the lawyers have selected. One might call this the fine art of stacking the jury; although jury stacking is theoretically illegal, this has never prevented anyone from trying it. Members of a jury usually base their final decisions on factors of race and sex, or on the way a defendant, if she is a woman, does her hair. This is understandable when we consider that after days or months of listening to conflicting testimony, most jury members have not the faintest clue as to which party is in the right. In recent decades, juries made up entirely of poor, black Democrats in District of Columbia criminal cases have routinely voted for the conviction of white, middle class Republican White House staff members in political show trials. The Watergate trials were the apogee of this process, which reached a new wave with the conviction of most of Ronald Reagan's White House staff in recent years. Reagan's closest associates, among them Michael Deaver and Lynn Nofziger, were found guilty on vague charges by black juries, who were perhaps expressing their resentment at having had to endure three hundred years of slavery in the United States. At any rate, the crimes of which they were accused were beyond the scope of these jurors, whose daily lives were filled with the necessity of surviving in a murderous, drug saturated environment. The Moscow show trial of Colonel Oliver North continued this brave tradition. Even the *Washington Post* was driven to comment on the possibility of injustice because "the entire jury was composed of another race." Even the *Washington Post* forbore to mention "the race that dare not speak its name"- the reader was left to conjecture whether Col. North was being tried before a jury of Chinese, or perhaps Indians.

Our legal system is usually described as "the adversary system." The two opposing clients come before the court for an impartial judgment by either a judge or a jury, or by both. In practice, the court room adversarial system creates rancor and hostility on both sides. It precludes processes and solutions which are potentially satisfactory to both litigants, because it is more profitable for the attorney to keep them at each other's throats. Each attorney assures his client that he is certain to win, therefore the case must be prosecuted all the way through the court. Instead of arbitration, or dispute resolution, which would be much cheaper and more satisfactory to the litigants, they are deluded into going for a total victory. The lawyer gains everything and loses nothing by urging this path. If his client loses, he will try to persuade him to appeal this "unjust" decision. The result is more fees for the attorneys and for the courts.

Early in my legal experience, I was astounded when a lawyer with whom I was then associated gave me one of the keys to a successful legal practice-an attorney will often lose your case on purpose, so that you can then be persuaded to file an appeal. We were in court when I noticed that the defendant's attorney had failed to call a key witness to testify. This witness's testimony would have won the case, which was then lost. "Why didn't the lawyer call that witness?" I asked my associate. "Oh, that's routine," he assured me. "He wanted the guy to lose the case, so that he could file an appeal. It's only business."

This was my first revelation about how our legal system really works. I have never forgotten it. Perhaps this was what Oliver Wendell Holmes, the patron saint of modern lawyers, meant when he said, "The law has nothing to do with justice, under a trial by battle system in which the goal is victory not justice." He went on to say that the lawyer can permissibly employ a host of stratagems and tricks to obscure the truth, manipulate witnesses, and pander to the jury and the judge on the basest motions. The philosophical justification for the adversary system is the claim that the opponents are "evenly matched." This is never true, but it remains the favorite myth of the adversary system. In 1906, the legal authority, Roscoe Pound, described it as "the sporting theory of justice." Jerome Frank declared that "Of all the possible ways to get at the falsity or truth of testimony, none could be conceived that would be more ineffective than trial by jury. The client and the counsel have different personal agenda."

Frank strikes at the root of the matter when he notes that client and counsel have different stakes in the trial. The client wishes to preserve his property and his liberty. The counsel wishes to keep the cash flow coming into his office.

Dr. Richard Gardner noted in a letter to the *New York Times*, June 18, 1989, that "After 25 years of experience working primarily as a court appointed impartial examiner (primarily in custody litigation but more recently in child sex-abuse litigation), l am convinced that the adversary system is not only an inefficient way to ascertain the truth, but is the cause of significant psychiatric disturbance in all those unfortunate enough to be subjected to its procedures."

Trial by jury, which was demanded as a right in our Declaration of Independence, and which is now guaranteed by our Constitution, is now threatened, not as a principle, but as a method which has been corrupted by the machinations of our legal system. Jury trial has been diminished by the tactics of the "adversarial" lawyers, and also by the carefully loaded "instructions" which the judge delivers to the juries. As I pointed out earlier, all evidence favorable to my case was routinely ruled inadmissible by judges, while all evidence against me was routinely admitted. How can any jury be expected to reach a fair decision under such circumstances? Even if I had been allowed to present the evidence in my favor, the judge would have neutered it by his loaded instructions to the jury.

Since the courts prevent anyone from adequately representing himself in litigation, we return to the important factor of the quality of one's legal representation, when a citizen employs an attorney. The late Roy Cohn, who died of AIDS, became the nation's most renowned lawyer on the strength of his political and ethnic affiliations. He represented such important clients as the Mafia, the Catholic Church, and members of the nation's wealthiest families. These clients were attracted to him, not merely by his legal abilities, but by his reputation for ruthlessness. His underworld clients included such notorious gang leaders as Sam (the Plumber) Cavalcante, Carmine Galanto, Tom and Joe Gambino, and Fat Tony Salerno. However, in a revealing study of Cohn's legal abilities, Nicholas von Hoffman states that Cohn's clients seldom received the legal quality they were paying for. He turned over most of his legal work to a cadre of poorly paid law students and recent graduates. Cohn himself had little time for the dreary work of preparing legal briefs, because he spent most of his hours in a mad search for pleasure. He "flung roses riotously, riotously, with the throng." He paid for as many as a half-dozen five hundred dollar a night callboys to accompany him on his yacht on a single outing. All of these "expenses" were charged against his legal fees, on which he paid no taxes. To maintain his alternative lifestyle, he often charged outrageous fees in cases which were nothing more than legal shakedowns. In August of 1978, he sued Henry Ford II, claiming that Ford had looted the company of $750,000 in tribute extorted from a food concessionaire. The information had come to Cohn from a disgruntled former Ford employee. The charge was thrown out because Cohn had neglected to file it in the proper jurisdiction. When he threatened to refile the case, Ford gave him $100,000 in "legal fees" to drop the case. Cohn was later disbarred for taking $100,000 in "loans" from a wealthy client. He continued to flit from night club to night club in his Rolls Royce, maintaining his headquarters in a luxurious Manhattan townhouse.

During these years, most of Cohn's legal abilities were squandered in efforts to survive special task forces from the New York U.S. Attorney, Henry Morgenthau, task forces from the Department of Justice in Washington, and task forces from the Internal Revenue Service. The wasting of many millions of dollars in taxpayers' funds in the prosecution of Cohn was not based on moral objections, because of his homosexuality and his reputation as a "Mafia mouthpiece," nor was it based upon the fact that he was Jewish, because many of his opponents from government agencies were themselves Jewish, notoriously Henry Morgenthau. The battle against Cohn was waged because he had early on taken a turn to the right, unlike most of his Jewish colleagues. He played a crucial role in the prosecutions of atomic spies Julius and Eshel Rosenberg, and in the prosecution of Alger Hiss. He also became Senator Joe McCarthy's chief of staff in McCarthy's short-lived and doomed anti-Communist crusade.

Cohn represented the "neoconservative" group among American Jews, who were headquartered in the Trotskyite group, the League for Industrial Democracy, a Rockefeller sponsored operation. These Jews were vociferously anti-Moscow, because of Stalin's murder of Leon Trotsky in Mexico City, and they were unanimously in support of the State of Israel. Cohn was adopted by such rabid "anti-Communists" as George Sokolsky and columnist Walter Winchell, and frequently dined with them at their reserved table at Table Fifty in Manhattan's Stork Club. Other favored visitors to this table were J. Edgar Hoover and his consort, Clyde Toison, and Frank Costello, then head of the New York Mafia families. It was the execution of Julius and Ethel Rosenberg which caused the diehard Stalinist Communists in the U.S. government to vow revenge against Roy Cohn. Special "Get Cohn Squads" routinely sallied forth from the Department of Justice, the Internal Revenue Service, and various state U.S. Attorney's offices. Much of the ensuing harassment and publicity succeeded only in bringing additional clients and fees to Cohn's offices. Prospective clients concluded that with all that government opposition against him, Cohn couldn't be all bad. Cohn was able to get away with these practices for many years, because he had early learned the precepts of surviving in this nation under our present legal system, that is, the difference between de jure, a confession which carried the force of law, and de facto, or mere gossip. Most of the charges against Cohn were based on mere gossip, the FBI "raw files" obtained from informants who in every instance had a special interest in "getting Cohn." The FBI files were replete with items about the altar boys and handsome young priests whom his close friend, Cardinal Spellman, brought to the nightly outings on Cohn's yacht. In his frantic efforts to destroy Cohn, U.S. Attorney Morgenthau subpoenaed many of Cohn's clients before grand juries. The Department of Justice routinely offered special deals to criminals who would testify against Cohn, bargaining to have criminal charges against them dropped if they would aid the Department to "get Cohn." These witnesses usually refused to cooperate, because they were more afraid of Cohn and his associates than of the Department of Justice. Roy Cohn was an exception in the present legal profession because he was theoretically of the right, whereas most attorneys are pronouncedly loyal to the left. On July 22, 1988, the National

Review noted that Queens President Claire Shulman had refused to deliver her scheduled address to the graduating class of the City University of New York Law School, because they insisted on the playing of the Communist anthem, "The Internationale," as the theme of the ceremonies. The school authorities had simultaneously banned the playing of the American anthem, "The Star Spangled Banner," and the display of the United States flag at the school ceremonies, because they would be "a distracting influence." Indeed, their display might have caused a riot among the fiercely Stalinist Communist law students. Notwithstanding the official ban, a few students risked their future careers and their diplomas by waving small American flags during the ceremonies, thereby guaranteeing they would not be hired by the Department of Justice or any other government agency.

The fact that many American attorneys are dedicated Marxists of the Stalinist Communist persuasion, as opposed to the Trotskyite Tel Aviv Communist faction, does not prevent, but rather encourages them, to charge their clients as much as possible. As individual venture capitalists who are actually Marxists, they delight in charging their middle class conservative American clients, who are usually businessmen, the only group of Americans who can actually afford to hire an attorney, tremendous fees for relatively little work of dubious value. The political allegiance of these attorneys has been epitomized in a new philosophical program of legal studies called "Critical Legal Studies." This philosophy of revolution claims that all current American law is "the instrument of capitalist oppression," and that it must be "deconstructed" by a Stalinist conspiracy within the legal profession. This philosophy had found its apogee in the Legal Services Corporation set up by the U.S. government under the Stalinist Democratic Party. Its funds were promptly cut from $321,000,000 to $241,000,000 in 1981, when the Reagan counter-revolution, led by the Trotskyite faction of the Communist Party, swept into office in Washington. The Legal Services Corporation had been set up with the objective of providing legal aid to families too poor to afford an attorney, a group which encompassed most of the population of the United States. However, the young lawyers hired by the LSC found family legal matters such as divorce and custody too boring and too far removed from their Stalinist Communist loyalties. They began to concentrate on suing other government agencies, on housing and welfare disagreements.

Critical legal studies found its natural home in the halls of Harvard Law School, which has been traditionally Marxist since its dominance by a Viennese immigrant, Felix Frankfurter, early in this century. Frankfurter was publicly denounced by President Theodore Roosevelt as "a dangerous revolutionary," a recommendation which caused his cousin, Franklin Delano Roosevelt, to appoint him to the Supreme Court. Today, Frankfurter's heirs at Harvard Law School are engaged in a bitter internecine struggle, in which two groups of diehard Marxists, outspoken enemies of the American Republic one and all, have engaged in a civil war. The Marxists who are attempting to do away with traditional legal studies and replace them with the Critical Legal Studies program, in a campaign to do away with "bourgeois law," are opposed by the old line Marxists who have dominated the school since the days of Felix Frankfurter. The CLS advocates claim that the present legal system must be "liberated," so that it will no longer operate on behalf of property owners, but only on behalf of the "oppressed," with its goal as the ultimate "redistribution" of all privately owned property. The "Crits" argue that law professors should exchange their jobs every six months with janitors, a basic goal of the Maoist Communist philosophy. Jeffrey Hart characterizes the goals of the Crits as "the ministrations of vermin," although they offer eloquent testimony to the present insanity of the American legal system, and may thereby serve a useful cause.

The extreme pro-Marxist bias of the American legal profession may be explained by simple business necessities. A Marxist state which inflicts endless 1984 decisions on the people requires frequent hiring of lawyers in efforts to survive the diktat of the State power, and to defend one's person, one's liberty and one's property from Marxist seizure by the government. Once the state has become totally Communist, the need for personal representation apparently vanishes. This is made obvious by the fact that in the entire Soviet Union, there are only 27,000 professional lawyers, as compared to some 675,000 in the U.S. Communist lawyers in the Soviet Union are members of the privileged classes, with membership in the Communist Party, and living as members of the Nomenklatura, the special class which enjoys a lavish life style while most of their Russian subjects live in misery and poverty. These "advocatura" are organized under statutes of the USSR, whereas, according to the Great Soviet Encyclopaedia, "In bourgeois states, lawyers join professional organizations only to defend their own private interests." This definition ingenuously ignores the fact that Soviet lawyers are also preeminently concerned with their private interests.

The Nomenklatura classification of American lawyers is most evident in the District of Columbia, where one in every seventeen residents is an attorney. In contrast, the state which has the most lawyers, Massachusetts, has only one lawyer for 212 residents; in more rural states, the figure drops to one in six hundred residents. The high ratio of lawyers in the District population is explained by the fact that the national government offers easy pickings for the parasitic greed of the legal profession. Arriving in the District as a Congressman, a lawyer may later be defeated for office, but this will be but the beginning of a more prosperous career as a lobbyist, or as a highly paid government bureaucrat whose decisions will involve billions of dollars. Current lobbyists in Washington earn about $700,000 per year, with another $500,000 in perks such as chauffeured limousines, two hundred dollar dinners, and a choice of expensive male or female prostitutes. The current American Medical Association lobbyist and a few other pleaders for special interests are paid about one million dollars a year, with an equal amount in personal expenses. The Internal Revenue Service chooses to look the other way at these events taking place on its own doorstep, preferring to reserve its most dire punishments for newspaper boys, scrubwomen and waitresses. Those in the upper echelons of remuneration usually have little to fear from the IRS. When billionaire Ross Perot was advised to hire former IRS Commissioner Sheldon Cohen, he was able to save fifteen million dollars in taxes on his stock profits. Cohen lobbied a special tax bill through Congress for Perot, as is frequently done, and Perot laughed all the way to the bank.

Because of their relative affluence, one might expect that American lawyers would be stolid, middle class conservatives. However, their incomes are largely dependent upon the existence of a ruthless Marxist state power in Washington and in the various State capitals, as evidenced by the Critical Legal Studies group at Harvard, and by the bias of the younger lawyers hired at the Department of Justice in Washington. The Legal Services Corporation diverted most of its funds to such leftist groups as the American Civil Liberties Union and its favorite projects, among them Planned Parenthood, Safe Sex, the Sonoma County Sanctuary Movement, and other approved Marxist organizations. In September, 1988, the Legal Services Corporation mounted a well-financed campaign to force HUD to turn over foreclosed homes to the homeless. The resulting forced delays in sales cost taxpayers more than five hundred thousand dollars, and opened the door to widespread corruption in HUD. The chaos created by the LSC agitation created opportunities for many sellers of foreclosed HUD homes to bank the proceeds in their own bank accounts; most of it will never be traced, Although a few HUD officials admit to embezzling millions of dollars, much of which they claim they turned over to the "poor," Although they acquired yachts, expensive homes and other assets in the process.

The Legal Services Corporation, like so many of the governmental aberrations which plague the nation, was the personal project of a single member of Congress, Senator Warren Rudman of Vermont, in whose view the agency could do no wrong. A current critic of the agency, Clark Durant, insists that the agency should fulfill its designated mission of helping the poor, and that it should cease to fund leftwing think tanks to do away with laws on monogamy, lobby for a negative income tax, that is, government payments to those who pay no tax, and prompting the socialization of housing. Durant also outraged the American legal profession when he proposed that the Legal Services Corporation could stretch its budget by hiring paralegals to do much of the work performed by its staff of lawyers, such as the writing of wills, deeds, and leases.

The headquarters of the Marxist bias among American lawyers has been for many years the American Civil Liberties Union, whose existence and exposure played a dominant role in the 1988 campaign for the Presidency of the United States. The goals of the ACLU are succinctly stated in "The Red Network" ; "it is directed by Communist and Socialist revolutionary leaders... it works untiringly to further and legally protect the interests of the Red movement in all of its branches Red strikes, Atheism, sex freedom, disarmament, seditious 'academic freedom,' and 'freedom of speech' for Communists only." Although it was an outgrowth of the American Association for the Advancement of Atheism," and thus continuously battles any religious symbolism in any aspect of American life, it has always been first and foremost an agency of the Communist Party. The U.S. Fish Report notes that the ACLU had provided bail for Communist defendants in a strike in Gastonia, N.C. during which the chief of police was murdered. 'The Civil Liberties Union was active from the beginning of the trouble in the cases both at Marion and Gastonia.' The N.Y. State Lusk Report says: 'The American Civil Liberties Union, in the last analysis, is a supporter of all subversive movements; its propaganda is detrimental to the State. It attempts not only to protect crime but to encourage attacks upon our institutions in every form.' The U.S. Fish Committee report officially stated, Jan. 1931, 'The A.C.L.U. is closely affiliated with the communist movement in the United States, and fully 90% of its efforts are on behalf of communists who have come into conflict with the law the main function of the A.C.L.U. is to attempt to protect the communists in their advocacy of force and violence to overthrow the government, replacing the American flag by a red flag and erecting a Soviet Government in place of the republican form of government guaranteed to each State by the Federal Constitution.' Among its most active members are the aforenamed Felix Frankfurter and George Foster Peabody. A director of the Federal Reserve Bank of New York, Peabody exemplified the close affiliation of some bankers with the most violent aims of the Bolshevik movement.

A recent issue of the ACLU's 576 page Policy Guide lays down the party line to be followed in specific context; Policy 318, "it opposes work requirements at government-assigned tasks as a condition of eligibility for welfare on the grounds of fairness, dignity and privacy." However, the ACLU offers no objection to the excesses of the Internal Revenue Service when it breaks into homes and offices to seize assets from private citizens in order to finance the "welfare state." As a proponent of "redistribution of income," the ACLU cheers when ruthless government agents seize the private assets of American citizens to finance its Marxist state. On foreign policy, the ACLU is succinct but undeviating, "Abolish all covert operations." The fact that most of the CIA's covert operations throughout the world have been on behalf of leftwing groups, rather than in opposition to them, carries no weight with the A.C.L.U., whose policies are generally adopted word for word by the Stalinist fanatics of the Democratic Party. A.C.L.U. members quail at the mention of the horrible phrase, "national security," because national security is the antithesis of the A.C.L.U. program for a world Communist government. Its members are often found engaged in active acts of treason, whether turning over secrets to foreign governments, or destroying the living standards which make life bearable within the geographical limits of the United States. Policy No. 92 states that "the ACLU opposes tax exemptions for religious bodies," a policy which originated in its other incarnation as the American Association for the Advancement of Atheism. However, the A.C.L.U. does not oppose the large tax exempt foundations which contribute millions of dollars to the A.C.L.U. budget. Policy No. 242 urges that "ail criminals except those guilty of such crimes as murder and treason, be given a suspended sentence and sent back to the community." In fact, the A.C.L.U. actively intervenes on behalf of murderers and those accused of treason, furnishing legal and financial assistance. Policy No. 242 has become the guideline for most American judges today; they routinely band out suspended sentences, and return the most violent criminals to the community for "work release" and "community service" programs. Policy No. 210 calls for legalization of all narcotics, including 'crack' and 'angel dust,' contending that "the introduction of substances into one's own body" is an inalienable civil liberty.

Despite its historic agenda, the ACLU Policy Book remains unknown to most Americans, even to those taxpayers who continue to be assessed many millions of dollars each year to pay for the frivolous and destructive lawsuits brought against communities by the A.C.L.U. Their target is often local government bodies, thus avoiding the better-financed federal agencies. It was the rumored existence of this agenda which torpedoed the Presidential campaign of Michael Dukakis in 1988. Dukakis seemingly had a clear road to the White House-he had a weak opponent, a fanatically supportive media coverage, the support of the entire government and academic bodies, and absolute support from all minorities, including the homeless and the homosexuals. His campaign was sunk by one photograph of a convicted rapist, Willie Horton, and by the A.C.L.U. agenda which had brought about the release of Horton. Dukakis proudly proclaimed that he was a card-carrying member of the A.C.L.U., thus identifying himself irrevocably in the public mind with Willie Horton. At no time did he ever repudiate the Communist origins of the A.C.L.U., which had its original incarnation on Dec. 18, 1914, as the American League to Limit Armaments, a spinoff from the Emergency Peace Foundation, headed by Communist propagandist Louis Lochner. Its other founders were Jane Addams, of Hull House, later revealed to be a secret member of the Communist Party; John Haynes Holmes, a prominent Communist activist; Rabbi Stephen S. Wise, a rabid Communist apologist; Morris Hillquit, a founder of the Socialist Party and a paid agent of the Soviet Government; and George Foster Peabody, a "capitalist" who sought to implement Lenin's demands for a nationalized bank and "confiscation of assets" for the "crime" of "concealing income," which became the official program of the IRS. It was Peabody who had rescued the tottering Soviet government in 1918 with ready infusions of cash, aided by his fellow directors of the Federal Reserve Bank of New York, William Laurence Saunders, deputy chairman of the bank, who wrote to President Wilson on October 17, 1918, "I am in sympathy with the Soviet form of government as the best suited for the Russian people," and William Boyce Thompson, a financier who announced that he was personally donating one million dollars to promote Bolshevik propaganda in the United States!

Without funds from these bankers, Communism, which has never won an election anywhere in the world, would have died an early death. Every Communist government has been installed by military takeover, a fact which the A.C.L.U. never mentions in its copious socialist propaganda.

The A.C.L.U. continued to be liberally supported by the bankers, because of its dedication to their Soviet ideals. In 1920, it took the name American Civil Liberties Union, under the leadership of Roger Baldwin, an Anarchist Socialist who had already spent a year in jail because of his revolutionary work. Its National Committee now consisted of Baldwin, Elizabeth Gurley Flynn, and William Z. Poster. Both Flynn and Foster later became chairmen of the Communist Party of the United States. A 1943 Report of the California Pact Finding Committee on Un-American Activities concluded that "The ACLU may be definitely classed as a Communist front. At least 90% of its efforts are expended on behalf of Communists who come into conflict with the law." This conclusion was repeated verbatim in a 1931 judgment of a Special House Committee to Investigate Communist Activities in the United States. A Barron's weekly story, August 26, 1968 by Shirley Scheibla concluded that "Careful study of ACLU cases reveals that nearly all the causes it has taken up tend to weaken law and order and the ability of society to defend itself. Some landmark cases give Communists more freedom to destroy the nation from within. Those involving the draft code erode the state's ability to defend itself against armed attack. Other significant ALCU cases diminish the authority of schools and police and the influence of religion."

Typical of A.C.L.U. operations is the New York Student Rights Project. Its director, Alan Levine, told assembled students, "Oppressive institutions give you no right at all to say why you go there, how long you go there, and what you do while you're there. Indeed, you can not exercise the rights the courts have told you have without disrupting the system." The already demoralized school system faces interminable lawsuits seeking "students' rights." Another A.C.L.U. operation, its National

Prisoner Project, was defined in the A.C.L.U. national newspaper, Civil Liberties, issue of March, 1973, "First, get the prisoners out. Next, protection of prisoners' First Amendment activities. Next, reform of pretrial facilities." The A.C.L.U. Women's Rights Projects sponsored the Equal Rights Amendment, a lawyers' dream which would have resulted in every woman in the United States suing every man for her "rights." The A.C.L.U. Death Penalty Project worked to abolish capital punishment in the United States, a goal which was won and then relinquished as the death penalty was reintroduced to stern the rapidly mounting crime toll throughout the country. A.C.L.U. also is the leader in the national campaign for gun control, more properly called "gun seizure." It has long been a truism in Washington that only the possession of some five hundred million guns by American citizens has postponed the Communist seizure of power in the United States. In the Soviet Union, only trusted members of the Communist Party are allowed to own guns. The Massachusetts A.C.L.U. Newspaper, The Docket, stated in its April, 1974 issue on Civil Liberties, "The Civil Liberties Union of Massachusetts favors all bills that seek to control ownership of guns. Where firearms are widely owned, there is a threat to free expression of ideas." The truth is that free expression of ideas is prohibited where private ownership of guns is prohibited, as in the Communist countries.

The A.C.L.U. continues to work tirelessly against all forms of piety and religious observance throughout the United States, such as the singing of "Silent Night" during Christmas celebrations in public schools, the posting of the Ten Commandments in the schools, and the installment of Nativity scenes on public property. A.C.L.U. leaders demand the removal of the words, "In God We Trust" from our coinage, and the phrase, "under God" from the Pledge of Allegiance, Although the entire Pledge of Allegiance remains a favorite target of the A.C.L.U.

For years, the A.C.L.U. claimed to be against all forms of racial discrimination. In 1963, the organization suddenly reversed its longstanding policy, coming out for racial quotas in every field of American life. It abandoned its cry for "equal opportunity," replacing it with "preferential treatment" for its favored minorities. When columnist Pat Buchanan wrote a column exposing some of the A.C.L.U. treachery, its executive director, Ira Glasser, wrote him a vehement letter, accusing him of "McCarthyism, terrorism and slime." How Glasser or anyone else could be terrorized by a mere newspaper column was not explained.

In 1988, the A.C.L.U. finally involved itself in a situation about which the present writer had been complaining for many years, in letters to the press, articles, and books. This is the infamous section of the statutes which establishes severe penalties for anyone who reveals any information of complaints about a judge. A columnist had written about this statute on the editorial page of the *Washington Post* in 1977, suggesting that it was probably unconstitutional, as indeed it is. In 1978, the Supreme Court ruled it unconstitutional, decreeing that the state could not prosecute reporters for reporting "secret judicial investigations." The state Judicial Inquiry and Review Commission routinely received complaints from the public against judges, which were promptly buried. Its director finally admitted that in some fifteen years, only one or two complaints had actually been investigated. Nevertheless, the director of the commission continued to warn all complainants that it was a criminal offense for anyone to talk about his complaint, and that he would be prosecuted!

The A.C.L.U. filed suit on the grounds that both the state code and the Judicial Inquiry and Review Commission violate the First and Fourteenth Amendments protecting free speech and due process. The complaint stated that the law enables concealment of "evidence of substantial misconduct by judges." It took the A.C.L.U. seventy years to discover a statute about which citizens had been complaining for decades. Because of the numerous lawsuits which it generates, the A.C.L.U. functions as the godfather of the American legal profession. Most of these suits are intended to weaken the institutions of the nation, such as schools and churches, but many are so trivial in origin as to create new markets for lawyers where none previously existed. The flood of "job discrimination" and "sexual harassment" lawsuits which engulf our major companies have seriously weakened our

THE RAPE OF JUSTICE

ability to compete in the world economy. Thus the A.C.L.U. has actively worked to promote the rise of Japan, Korea and West Germany in their domination of our auto and appliance markets, while simultaneously encouraging the wave of "mergers and acquisitions," promoting the giant monopolies which the Sherman Anti-Trust Act claimed to have outlawed.

The professional organization by which the lawyers have become the Nomenklatura, or ruling, elite, in the United States is the American Bar Association. This organization selects, and for all practical purposes, elects judges to our courts. It not only "recommends" judges, but also passes on their qualifications, labelling them "able," "mediocre," or "not recommended." The reasons for the latter unfavourable designation remain shrouded in secrecy, but are always based upon political or ethnic prejudices. Rarely does it have any bearing on the character, the training, or the ability of the designate. "not recommended" simply means that the elitists of the American Bar Association have decided to blackball someone who does not fit into their narrow categorization. Such unfavorable decision is always spared anyone who has the necessary qualifications, the most important being membership in a Masonic lodge. The ABA system ensures that a small, dedicated group, existing in an atmosphere of conspiracy and secret goals, can dominate the selection of all judges in the United States. Like most invasions of our rights, the inspiration for the American Bar Association invasion came directly from England. Our Constitution guarantees our citizens equal rights under the law; the British Secret Service has sought to undermine this guarantee by decreeing that the laws of the United States shall be administered by persons who want unequal rights, or special licenses. The Constitution tried to prevent this by expressly outlawing grants of special privilege. The American Bar Association had its inception at a meeting in the summer of 1878 of some seventy-five lawyers from eleven states. The guiding force of the group was Simeon E. Baldwin, a descendant of Roger Sherman, a Governor of Connecticut, and a Justice of the state's Supreme Court. The ABA subsequently underwent three periods in its history: from 1878 to 1902, it was a strictly professional organization dedicated to improving the practice of law; from

1902 to 1936 was its era of national expansion, when it became a genuinely national organization; and from 1936 to 1950, when it became a truly elitist organization, which sought to extend its control over other aspects of American life. It was in 1936 that the ABA adopted a federalized constitution, creating a monolithic organization which was tightly controlled by a small group of elitists. It also founded the National Association of Law Schools in 1900, giving it control of the crucial field of accreditation, and the National Conference of Commissioners of Uniform State Laws, giving it access to the statutes of every state.

The appearance of the ABA as a genuine national force first came in 1909, when a group of British lawyers arrived in Chicago to set up a monolithic organization. They were actively assisted by John D. Rockefeller, who was then setting up the University of Chicago to promote the principles of British Fabian Socialism, with a gift of fifty million dollars. The Illinois legislature then passed a statute that only members of the legal union, the ABA, would be allowed to practice law within that state. With this act, the State of Illinois, for all practical purposes, seceded from the constitutional union of states, by granting special privileges in violation of the Constitution. This statute also set up a class system in the United States. Other states were persuaded to adopt the Illinois statute, California in 1927, and the other states in the 1930s, until the ABA had achieved its goal of national power.

Yale law professor Fred Rodell characterizes the union members of the ABA, the duly licensed and chartered "lawyers" as "purveyors of streamlined voodoo and chromium-plated theology," whose "weird and wordy mental gymnastics" enable them to carry on a "high-class racket." There are now some 180 "approved" law schools in the United States, licensed by the ABA to turn out "approved" lawyers. On graduation, these lawyers are still mere apprentices, because they have been taught little or nothing about how the legal system actually operates, or what a lawyer must do to earn his fees. They are not taught the classics of the law, such as the works of Coke and Blackstone, but they endure months of semantic quibbling about the law of contracts or the meaning of a household. This is to prepare them for the practice of the law merchant.

During some forty years of research into the problems plaguing this nation, the present writer dug down to the strata of a common plateau, which revealed the simultaneous origins of the various forms of criminality infesting the land. It had begun with a small fraternity of international bankers who first fastened their central banking system onto the nations of Europe, and later, in a secret meeting at Jekyll Island, Georgia in 1910, conspired to create a "Federal Reserve System" (which was not federal, had no reserves, and was not a system, but a syndicate). In "*The World Order*" I revealed the tentacles of the financiers which manipulated the governments of the world. I proved that the three professions which were doing the most damage were the bankers, the lawyers, and the doctors. Educators came in a strong fourth. In "*Murder by Injection*"[6] I exposed the medical profession, and in the present work, I expose the legal profession, despite its function as a legal octopus whose tierce squirting of black ink confuses and subdues its prey.

In all of these works, I have found myself dealing with essentially the same families and the same groups, both within the United States and abroad. A recent television expose of a Dr. James Burt, who had for years performed strange sexual operations on his women patients with the knowledge of his peers, carried the official disclaimer of the medical profession from a prominent physician, "Of course the other doctors knew what he was doing, but they wouldn't dare expose him. He might sue them, and no one wants to get involved in that horror which is our legal system." The lush profits from malpractice suits have made the medical field easy pickings for the legal vultures, while discouraging conscientious doctors from adequately treating their patients. The result is intended to be the final socializing of all medical practice in the United States, under the total control of the government.

The ABA carries considerable weight in the operation of the legislative process. The Resolution of the 74th Congress, on Aug.

---

[6] Published by Omnia Veritas Ltd.

27, 1935, of the Joint Resolution Consenting to an Interstate Oil Compact to Conserve Oil and Gas, would not have been possible without the ABA, whose members drafted a Federal Oil and Gas Conservation Act in 1935, subsequently passed as a state law in South Dakota in 1955 and later in other oil-producing states. This drive for "conservation" was intended solely to protect the oil monopoly of the Rockefeller interests and their many subsidiaries. It forbade newcomers from drilling so as to control production and maintain high price levels. This program was originally formulated at the ABA annual meeting in Seattle in July of 1928. An act was written which removed the major oil companies from the control of the anti-trust laws (vol. 53, pp. 72-89). In 1934, the Governor of Texas, who just happened to be the president of Humble Oil, one of Rockefeller's main acquisitions, used this ABA act to call out the National Guard, stopping further drilling by independent producers. Congress was then ordered to draft national approval of this act by the Joint Resolution of 1935.

The ABA maintains a number of active subcommissions which constantly review and redraft laws controlling the daily lives of all Americans. Their recommendations, like their "approvals" of candidates for judgeships, are always accepted by the pertinent Congressional committees as worthy of being drafted into law without changing so much as a comma, yet no citizen has ever elected any member of an ABA commission to national office. Typical of these secret commissions is the ABA's Section on Patent, Trademark and Copyright Law, which was exposed in the Senate Judiciary Hearings of February 3, 1974 under the title, "The Organized Bar: Self-Serving or Serving the Public?"

The Committee found that the incoming chairman of this influential ABA section was Theodore Bowes, a member of a secret ABA operation known as "the Tuesday Group." Bowes was a former General Patent Counsel for the Westinghouse Corp., and a prominent Washington lobbyist in the field of patent law. The "Tuesday Group" was a clique of lawyers which drafted the Scott Amendments, proposals which would exempt many presently illegal patent practices from the antitrust laws. The "Tuesday Group" then persuaded Senator Hugh Scott to introduce them on the Hill. Scott was a Washington politician who enjoyed many of the perks of a prominent political figure. He was able to indulge his penchant for collecting priceless Chinese antiques, a hobby which was beyond the means of most of his colleagues on Capitol Hill. The Judiciary Committee found that other ABA Sections were headed by lobbyists from leading corporations; the chairman of the Environmental Controls Committee of the ABA comes from a large Richmond, Virginia law firm representing Humble Oil, three power companies, three railroads, General Motors, a gas pipeline company and a chemical corporation. He seemed an ideal choice to draft regulations on pollution. The Judiciary Committee further stated, "The Coal Committee (of the ABA) is headed by a lawyer from Consolidation Coal Co; his vice chairman is the lawyer for the National Coal Association; the Oil Committee chairman, the General Counsel of Cities Service and his vice chairman is General Counsel for Humble Oil; the Forest Resources Committee (of the ABA) has a chairman whose law firm represents Georgia-Pacific and Moore Oregon Lumber; the vice chairman's law firm represents U.S. Plywood, Champion Paper etc."

The entire Senate Judiciary Committee report is a fascinating expose of the intrigues in which lawyers engage to protect the profits of their clients, while these firms defraud and injure the American public. The ABA also takes strong public positions on many political issues; the entire organization unhesitatingly endorsed the Equal Rights Amendment in the confident expectation of generating billions of dollars in extremely profitable lawsuits. Indeed, it was the fear of an avalanche of lawsuits which finally caused the ERA to be defeated. This one amendment would have paralyzed an already overburdened court system.

Much like the American Medical Association (which is also headquartered in Chicago), the enormous influence exercised by the American Bar Association lies in its monopolistic practices. It controls the means of entering the profession by controlling the accreditation of law schools, just as the AMA controls the accreditation of medical schools and hospitals. In all but two states, Georgia and California, the would be lawyer must attend an "accredited law school," that is, accredited by the ABA, before permission is granted to take the state bar examination, which is also prepared under the supervision of the ABA. Legislation is now under way in California to end the opportunity for non-accredited students to take the bar exam in that state. The bar exam prevents anyone from practicing law, even though Robert H. O'Brien, chairman of the California Committee of Bar Examiners, admits that the bar exam does not accurately predict the ability of future attorneys. Those who pass are then admitted to the "integrated" bar association, the state monopoly, which has the power to punish any attorney who fails to conform to its stringent controls. For years the state bar associations have operated in open defiance of anti-trust laws, conspiring to fix fees, prohibiting advertising by attorneys, and prosecuting anyone accused of unauthorized practice of law. Competence is not an issue. The bar monopoly can and does prosecute highly skilled legal practitioners, such as paralegals, trust officers, and others whose skills and experience more than qualify them to practice law.

The ABA particularly frowns upon anyone who is labelled a "tax protestor" by the vigilant agents of the IRS, or who criticizes any person or institution of the Establishment. Although the ABA tries to present a public figure of a stern moral entity which prosecutes and punishes any attorney suspected of "moral turpitude," judges publicly known to have accepted bribes have been elected presidents of bar associations. An ABA panel commissioned to look into the disciplinary situation among lawyers in 1970 summed up its findings in one word, "scandalous."

Although few Americans are aware of the ABA and its sinister machinations, its conspiracies affect the daily cost of living for every American. The ABA strongly urges the extension of state powers over the lives and property of every American. Whether one wishes to call this Marxism, or 1984, or Communism, it most definitely is not American, nor is it the Republic for which we stand. For this reason, there is now rising opposition to the ABA and the monopoly which it exercises over the practice of law. In Austin, Texas, Daniel Madison has filed a suit against the ABA, the Texas Supreme Court, the University of Texas Law School, and the Law Schools council for violation of the antitrust laws, and for conspiracy to keep power from nonlawyers. Madison explains his suit with these words, "If you're rich, you can have all the justice you want, but if you are a working class citizen, you may get little or none. That is the system in America." The precipitous decline in American production and export income has been ascribed to many factors, such as poor American workmanship, the strength of the dollar, and other factors. However, only one scholar, Peter Huber, has dared to put the blame where it most plainly lies. In his fully documented work, "Liability: The Legal Revolution and Its Consequences," he tells us that "Tort law was set in place in the 60s and 70s by a new generation of lawyers and judges Some grew famous and more grew rich by selling their services to enforce the rights they themselves had invented." Although a few Americans may have been pleased by the enormous settlements won for them by their lawyers against American manufacturers, the overall result has been devastating. More than thirty billion dollars a year is now spent on such lawsuits, according to recent studies by the Rand Corp., with more than half of this sum going to attorneys as fees. Huber says that the industrial havoc wrought by this practice "accounts for 30% of the price of a stepladder and 90% of the price of childhood vaccines." He writes that an amorphous new jumble of contract and tort law called "contort law" overrules our most important economic freedom, the freedom to make advance commitments and to arrange deals on terms mutually agreeable." Writing in the Wall Street Journal, Sept. 28, 1988, Huber cites the reluctance of insurance companies to write liability coverage at any price, with a concurrent decline in overall safety as new technologies are withheld from the market, and the decline of American competitiveness in foreign markets." He says, "U.S. contort law gives foreign manufacturers an important competitive edge." Huber has found that tort law costs the American consumer $300 billion a year! The overall verdict of Huber's book is that there has indeed been a revolution in liability cases, with the result that in the past thirty years tort law, the law of accident and personal injury cases, has been altered by judges and law professors to make the law "more compassionate," and more anti-business, a logical result of the growing Marxism of the American bench. The results may be seen on every band; in the rapid obsolescence of the "Rust Belt"; the growing deficit of the U.S. balance of trade, and in the growing foreign investment in the United States. In 1988 it had grown to $304 billion, which included 33% of chemicals, 12% of all manufacturing in the U.S., 12% of printing and publishing, and 10% of fiber and textile manufacturing. Huber is not the only one to attribute this tragic decline in American assets to the malignant depredations of our legal profession.

Huber recommends as a first step the repeal of the judge invented collateral-source rule, thus relying on direct insurance of goods and services. It is unlikely that the judges will back down from the dilemma which they themselves have created, or that the insurance companies could afford the vast amounts required for direct insurance coverage. Whatever the outcome, the situation can be traced all the way back to Starkey's apt observation during the reign of King Henry the Eighth, "Everyone that can color reason maketh a stop to the best law that is beforetime devised."

The excesses of tort law are the consequence of earlier abuses by lawyers in the early years of this century. Lawyers usually acted as claim agents for companies facing a damage suit, using their talents to persuade the victim to sign a release on payment of minimal damages. This practice backfired when the lawyers realized that they could make much more money by representing the victim against the companies, extracting huge settlements, of which they took one-third in contingency fees, plus untold "expenses." The practice was little more than ambulance chasing, but it proved very lucrative.

The red lights of the ambulances still prove to be an irresistible attraction to the legal profession. The Wall Street Journal headlined on Sept. 1, 1988, "Texas Bar Rushes to Crash Site to Protect Victims from Certain Lawyers," "Attempting to protect victims' families from solicitations by unscrupulous lawyers, the State Bar of Texas rushed its own lawyers to the site of the Delta Airlines crash at Dallas International Airport." The article noted that "solicitation by lawyers is a crime, usually a misdemeanor, known as barratry."

On Feb. 16, 1989, the Wall Street Journal memorialized "the dozens of lawyers who raced to Bhopal in the days after the accident and later brought the victims' cases into U.S. courts." The mad, mad world aspect of the lawyers' rush to Bhopal was occasioned by the tempting prospect of thousands of clients, when the Union Carbide plant at Bhopal had a gas leak in 1984. The lawyers actually signed up thousands of clients, but were thwarted when the Indian government assumed control of the litigation in 1986. Union Carbide agreed to a $470 million settlement, with payment to the registrar of the India Supreme Court. This apparently left the American lawyers in limbo, as they would have no access to the funds. In tort action, it is axiomatic that the lawyer takes his payments off the top. It is unlikely that India's bureaucracy will be willing to share the loot, most of which will probably never reach the victims. For the "Bhopal flyers" it may be a bitter pill.

Louis Vuitton, the French leather goods manufacturer, developed another new angle on the attorney problem. Instead of continuing to hire lawyers to battle against counterfeiters who illegally put the Vuitton name on their products, Vuitton has now prosecuted more than fifty cases in New York by having judges appoint corporate counsels as special prosecutors. These counsels then launch criminal contempt proceedings against offenders who violate court injunctions against counterfeiting. Because such counterfeiting is now a $5.5 billion a year problem, other manufacturers have followed suit. They have shifted their costs onto the shoulders of a public prosecutor, because they have notified him of the commission of a crime. It is then his duty to prosecute it. However, when the present writer has done this in the past, the government agencies have refused to prosecute. No action has ever been taken on notification of serious violations of law.

The legal profession continues to make its fees from public misfortunes. When the A. H. Robins Co. of Richmond, Va. marketed a faulty intrauterine device, the Dalkon Shield, some

195,000 women who were injured by it filed claims for their injuries. The firm sought protection under the Federal Bankruptcy Act, but eventually set up a $2.4 billion fund to settle the flood of personal injury lawsuits. In Sept. 1988, a confidential report concluded that a major Wall Street law firm, Cadwalader, Wickersham and Taft (as in President Taft), violated conflict of interest laws in an "impermissible appearance of impropriety" by simultaneously representing a committee of Robins' plaintiffs and the five trustees who will be disbursing the billions in settlements. The Cadwalader firm was said to have played the principle role in nominating four of the five trustees. Millions of dollars of potential revenue for the Cadwalader firm are at stake.

The national crisis among the savings and loans banks has been explained by the involvement of lawyers in the longstanding campaign to "deregulate" them. Those same lawyers are now stepping in to write proposals for "resolving" the problems. The Wall Street Journal noted on Jan. 31, 1989 that Thomas Vartanian, the former general counsel for the Federal Home Loan Bank Board, wrote the laws which deregulated the thrift banks. After they went bankrupt as a result of that deregulation, he joined the New York powerhouse law firm of Fried, Frank, Harris, Shriver and Jacobson. The firm earned some twelve million dollars in 1988 by handling 55 thrift mergers. Vartanian's deputy at the FHLBB, Patrick Doyle, also has built up a thriving savings and loan business, at the Washington law firm of Arnold and Porter.

Washington remains the preeminent home base for the lawyer lobbyist, some eleven thousand now holding court there. The dean of Washington tax lobbyists is Charles Walker, whose CEW Associates represents a powerful corporate base, known as the Group of 14. These 14 major corporations include Alcoa, AIT, Bechtel, Champion, Dresser, DuPont, IBM and others, with aggregate sales of $260 billion a year, and employing two million workers. They depend on CEW to handle tax code changes which will affect their profits. Walker came to Washington as the protege of Robert Anderson, Secretary of the Treasury from 1957-1960. Walker became overseer of Congressional relations for the Treasury Dept., later writing the Tax Reform Act of 1969.

He earned a valuable reputation as the man to see if you wanted something done in Washington in the tax field. His firm now makes millions per year. His mentor, Robert Anderson, was not so fortunate. Although he later became president of the American Bankers Association, he was disbarred in New York on Jan. 11, 1989, after conviction on tax evasion of $240,000 from 1983-84, and having operated an illegal bank which cost investors some $4.4 million.

CHAPTER 4

JUDGE NOT

The origin of the word "judge" is found in "juden," or, in Spanish, "juez." In the United States, the judge sees himself, first of all, as the guardian of the present legal system. While carefully cultivating his public image as the epitome of impartiality, he succeeds in letting interested inquirers know that his impartiality may be swayed by certain considerations. For this reason, it is crucial that a citizen entering an American court as a litigant should discard the assiduously cultivated myth of "judicial impartiality. "If you are a farmer, a small business operator, or a wage earner in any type of business, you are already "beyond the pale," as far as the judge is concerned. You have been consigned to the never never land of the hoi polloi-the judge will not let anyone leave his court without being convinced that he is an elitist.

During a national campaign to increase judges' salaries in 1989, it was found that judges, whose salaries range from $89,500 to $115,000 a year, reported average extra earnings from $16,624 to $39,500. An Associated Press survey found that the median 1987 income for a federal judge was from $108,000 to $130,300. In pleading for the pay raise, Robert McWilliams of the 10th U.S. Circuit CT in Colorado, stated that 'Judges' salaries, rather than being geared to the income of the average taxpayer, should be geared to the average of practicing lawyers." However, the Associated Press survey showed that median income for America's 707,000 lawyers and judges was only $45,069, (Census reports). McWilliams apparently was unaware that judges' median income was already more than double the median income for American lawyers. The demand for ever higher salaries is part of the judges' elitist drive. The judge has attended a university; his family had sufficient funds for him to go on to graduate law school and to become a professional man; and he later became a judge because he attracted the favorable attention of even more powerful elitists, who concluded that he would serve to protect their interests in the court. The judge resides in an upper income suburb, owning a home of considerable value in an area of other elitists. He belongs to a country club whose members are strictly limited to elitists. He maintains unadvertised affiliations in one or more religious, fraternal and political groups. Preeminent among such groups is the Masonic fraternal organization. The majority of Masonic members never go beyond the three degrees of the Blue Lodge. They are never informed that the higher degrees are forbidden, under pain of death, to disclose any of the machinations of the higher degrees to any member of the Blue Lodge. This does not mean that members of the Blue Lodge reap no advantages from their membership. On the contrary, they continually receive favorable treatment in the banks, in the courts, and from other businessmen. The courts are preponderantly extensions of the Masonic brotherhood. Most lawyers and judges are fellow lodge members. Preferential treatment is extended to all members of the brotherhood who come before the court.

In our larger cities, most judges are also Zionist collaborators; if inactive Zionists, they have been screened by a Zionist organization and have been found satisfactory. A judge is almost always a member in good standing of one of the major political parties; he is almost never a member of an "independent" political movement. He is usually a member of an established church, if Protestant, usually Episcopalian, although more than half of the judges in the United States are Roman Catholic. He may even belong to some "extremist" organization, as Supreme Court Justice Hugo Black had long been a member in good standing of the Ku Klux Klan. After he had been appointed to the Supreme Court by President Franklin Delano Roosevelt, Black admitted his Klan membership. The leak had come from a Communist ideologue, during the heyday of the capture of the national Democratic Party by the fanatical Stalinist wing of the Communist Party. Klan membership was anathema to these ideologues; only Nazi affiliation carried a greater stigma. Black humbly promised never to go to another Klan meeting, and served on the Court for many years. Political realists in Washington knew that Black's political career had been built on his Klan membership in Alabama. Without it, he could not have been elected to the Senate. Once in Washington, he became a loyal supporter of FDR's most socialist policies, and was rewarded by the Supreme Court appointment. With the Klan affiliation hanging over his head, Black became an ardent supporter of every violation of the Constitution, as a member of the FOR court. The Black episode illustrates the necessity of a judge having powerful political support. Conversely, he need know little or nothing about legal problems or the actual practice of law. He is expected to show unwavering loyalty to the prevalent party line during his service as a judge. Those judges who at some point begin to believe that they are a power in themselves, and who substitute their personal views for the exigencies of the current party line (which varies from day to day, as any practical political stance must do), are the judges whom you read about in the press. They are judges who are impeached for high crimes and misdemeanours, stripped of their office, and sent to prison. This is a very rare occurrence, as the sitting judge is never allowed to forget where his real allegiance lies. The judge exercises supreme power over the parties who stand before him in civil litigation or in criminal actions. He has equal power over the lawyers who stand before him, and be never allows anyone to forget that power. In this regard, the judge is not actually an employee of the city, state or nation which pays his salary. He is the tool of the secret entities who control all aspects of American life from behind the scenes. The servile press has made it fashionable to sneer at anyone who speaks of a "conspiracy," with the implication that anyone who believes there are conspirators is probably mentally ill, and should be secluded for the safety of society. We are often reminded that persons who claimed to have some knowledge of the inner workings of "the conspiracy" have been promptly spirited off to an asylum, where the continuous administration of mind-altering drugs soon convinces him that he was mistaken in his charges. The "agitator" is soon reduced to a helpless, drooling inmate who, whenever he shows signs of recovering his wits, is immediately given a stronger dose of Thorazine, a la KGB.

The fallacy of judicial impartiality could be denied by any practicing attorney. In our larger cities, the practice of "judge shopping" among scheduled members of the bench is a daily occurrence. A lawyer will use any stratagem, not the least of which is the employment of carefully cultivated relationships with clerks of the court, to have a case moved from a judge known to be hostile either to the defendant, or to the type of crime he has committed, or to the lawyer himself. Throughout the legal profession, it is common knowledge that most judges with years of service on the bench are almost universally hostile to anyone who comes into a court without an attorney, and declares his intention of representing himself. The judges are also very hostile to women lawyers, and to blacks and other minorities.

Judge Susan M. Skinner of Lee County, Florida, recently resigned her judgeship, citing sexism and "petty politics" in the judicial system as reason for resigning the judgeship she has held since 1984. She made her letter of resignation public, stating that "I have come to the conclusion that there is more to life than remaining as a part of this judicial system! I cannot envision myself emulating a number of the present judges with their infighting, envy, and dispassionate processing of their cases, nor can I further tolerate the total domination our current court administrator is allowed to exercise over the judiciary." Ft. Myers Fla. News Press, June 16, 1989. Judge Skinner had caused a community uproar when she learned that a defendant had AIDS. She ordered him from her courtroom, saying that she was insulted by his audacity in appearing in court, and she feared he would spread the disease to others in the courtroom. A national public outcry was raised by the powerful homosexual community, and she realized that she would no longer be able to carry out her judicial duties in the atmosphere of harassment and intimidation.

Liberal elements in Washington had sought to replace the older members of the judiciary with blacks and women, a process hastened by President Jimmy Carter, who replaced some three hundred members of the federal judiciary. Some of them have since been indicted, while others have resigned. In 1717, Bishop Benjamin Hoadley informed the King of England, "Whoever

bath an absolute authority to interpret any written laws is truly
the lawgiver to all intents and purposes, and not the person who
wrote them."

Thus it is the judge, rather than the .person who wrote the
laws, who has been transformed from an impartial referee of the
statutes into the creator of the statutes. Judges are now handing
out excessive punishments, with little or no restraint on their
decisions. The Wall Street Journal noted April 28, 1989 that
federal judge Richard Owen had given some defendants one
hundred years in a criminal case, and fifteen years in a tax fraud
case, which was at least five times more severe than most
attorneys thought appropriate. A federal judge ruled June 5, 1980
that the city of Parma, Ohio must provide three hundred units of
low income housing annually. This was described as "the first
federal takeover of a city."

The D.C. Court of Appeals ruled May 10, 1989 that District
of Columbia Superior Court Judge Tim C. Murphy should have
withdrawn from an assault case which had been brought by
federal prosecutors, because at that very time, he was applying
for a position with the Department of Justice. It was ruled a clear
cut violation of ethical rules, Although Judge Murphy defended
his action by pointing out that "I taught judicial ethics for years."

The overweening power of the judge in the American legal
system has increased inversely to the decline of Constitutional
guarantees of individual rights, and the concurrent rise of equity
law. Equity originates from the Latin Aequitas, meaning equality
of justice. Equity is defined by Sir Henry Maine in "Ancient
Law" as "any body of rules existing beside the existing original
or civil law, founded on distinct principles, and claiming
incidentally to supersede the civil law in virtue of a superior
sanctity inherent in those principles, principles stemming from
praetor edicts." This is a reference to the annual proclamation on
administrative law which was added to each year by the praetor,
who corresponded to the lord high chancellor in English law.
Equitable jurisdiction had been established in England by the
reign of Edward m. Equity has exclusive jurisdiction where it
recognizes rights unknown to the common law, such as trusts;
equity has concurrent jurisdiction where the law recognized the

right but did not give adequate relief; and auxiliary jurisdiction when the machinery of the courts of law was unable to procure the new evidence."

Maine goes on to deplore the evils of this double system of judicature. The present writer found early on that when his opponents realized that they could not destroy him in the civil courts, they moved to have the case heard in the equity or chancery courts. At first, I was mystified by this move, although I was soon convinced of its purpose. I doggedly hung on, and was finally able to settle the case on my own terms. The existence of this double system of judicature is a powerful secret weapon, which both judges and lawyers use against the public, giving them a decisive tactic which they can deploy, just when the citizen believes that at last he will finally receive justice in the court.

The abuses of our legal system are the more ironic when we learn that the traditional meaning of the scales of justice is that all things should be in harmony, weighed and establishing an equilibrium between warring opponents. Libra, the sign of the scales, is the seventh sign of the Zodiac, and is ruled by Venus; its jewel is the emerald, which represents the divine blend of colors, the blue of heaven with the gold of the sun. In tarot, the Justice card is represented by a seated and crowned Lord, who is the enthronement of the imperial dispenser of justice, King Solomon. The designation of the scales as the sign of justice was intended to decree that all worlds, and all forms of human nature, should attain a balance. In practice, this ideal has not been achieved. The scales of justice, rather than weighing the evidence presented by the opposing forces, until preponderance occurs on one side or the other, allow the adversary system to force the scales down on one side, justifying a decision in favor of that party. Thus the idea of balance has been abandoned, not only because of the adversary system, but also because the scales of justice, instead of signifying harmony, have been converted into the scales of commerce, in which commodities are weighed to determine their price before the sale. Equity law was a tremendous move in this direction, allowing first the admiralty courts, and then the law merchant, to supersede the common law and in the United States, our Constitutional law. In the law merchant, all law is concerned merely with the handling of economic disputes, and the scales of justice have become the scales of the trader, or the broker.

Because of this development, the office of judge itself became an item of trade, to be auctioned off to the highest bidder. Just as the scales of justice are used to weigh the relative power, influence and finances of the parties, so the judicial robe became a saleable property. Although it is still offered in outlying areas of the nation as a bid for those who hold the reins of power, in the larger cities, it has been reduced to the sole element of price. This can be verified in our most reputable publications, such as the *New York Times*, Oct. 2, 1988. This newspaper featured a lengthy interview with Matthew Troy, who was formerly a pillar of the "system" as a New York City councilman, and a Queens Democratic Party leader. Troy served short prison sentences in 1980, after pleading guilty to filing false income tax returns. He now lectures at universities on the realities of our judicial and political system. Troy says that the public has an idea that politicians are crooked, "and usually they are right." He states that he swapped State Assembly votes for judgeships, that visitors came to his office with briefcases bulging with cash, and that he routinely turned down bribes from reporters and developers. One reporter offered to run favorable newspaper stories about him for a mere $500 a week.

Troy's most important revelation is his recounting of the current price lists for the purchase of a judgeship. "The usual price for a judgeship on the Supreme Court of New York was $75,000, with lower court posts going for $15,000. That was common knowledge that I grew up with." He continues, "A man came to see me, and he put a briefcase on my desk, loaded, absolutely loaded with cash. And be said to me, 'I'd like to be a judge.' I asked him, 'Are you a lawyer?'"

Although money remains the ruling factor, the guiding principle of the legal system remains its allegiance to the Masonic order. In many areas, the local bench is merely a chapter of the Masonic Lodge. Because of the great secrecy maintained by the lodges, no accurate figures can be given as to the number of American lawyers and judges who are members of a Masonic lodge. Of the current total of 707,000 American judges and lawyers, it seems a good estimate that at least 500,000 are lodge members. It could be as high as 90%. Figures have been established for England, in Stephen Knight's best-selling book, "*The Brotherhood*." shortly after publishing this book, which immediately became a best seller, Knight, who was a young man, died suddenly. Interested persons have been unable to obtain any details of his death. Knight states that "the Law Society (the English equivalent of our Bar Association) is one of the most masonic institutions in the world. Ninety per cent of its members are Masons." He points out that this situation itself creates grave inequities, because the Law Society is the final arbiter as to who will receive legal aid and who will be denied it. In practice, a non-Mason has no chance of receiving legal aid in a suit against a Mason.

Knight says that fifty to seventy per cent of all English judges are Masons. This figure is probably close to that in the United States. Lawyers soon become aware that if they expect to have any clients, and if they wish to win cases in court, they must join the Masons, because of most of their client referrals will come from this source. Knight cites the Unlawful Societies Act of 1799 requiring that secret societies could hold meetings only if the names of their members were submitted to the local Clerks of the Peace. He notes that although this law has been on the books for almost two centuries, the Freemasons have never complied with it. However, he failed to consult the text of the Act, which specifically exempts the Freemasons, because the English Royal Family was and continues to be the official patron of English Freemasonry. The lodges were brought to England in 1717 as the result of a conspiracy of many years, which placed the Hanover family on the throne of England. They have been consistently active in and faithful to their Masonic origins ever since that date.

Americans who become involved in the legal mazes of our courts are often astounded by the strange decisions which are handed down by the judges. In nearly every instance, the strange outcome of the case can be explained by the omnipresent Masonic influence. Thus, citizens have no way of knowing that they have been subjected to the arrant assomptions of an Oriental despotism, masquerading under color of law. How can genuine justice be administered if the judge has taken an oath under penalty of death that be must always rule in favor of his brother Masons?

The Masonic Handbook command is as follows (p. 183184),

"Whenever you see any of our signs made by a brother Mason, and especially the grand hailing sign of distress, you must always be sure to obey them, even at the risk of your own life. If you are on a jury, and the defendant is a Mason, and makes the grand hailing sign, you must obey it; you must disagree with your brother jurors, if necessary, but you must be sure not to bring the Mason in as guilty, for that would bring disgrace upon our Order."

The Handbook continues,

"You must conceal all crimes of your brother Masons except murder and treason, and these only at your own option, and should you be summoned as a witness against a brother Mason, be always sure to shield him. Prevaricate, don't tell the truth in this case, keep his secrets, forget the important points. It may be perjury to do this, it is true, but you are keeping your obligations."

It is also important to note that the use of the word "obligations" is a key ingredient of the Masonic code. Most persons, in referring to a moral problem, would use the word "duty," as did the Founders of our Republic; however, a Mason is certain to use the word "obligation" as a code warning to other Masons who may be present that they are now under an overriding order to carry out their obligation to the brotherhood. This obligation means that he must commit perjury in court, he must rule as a jury member in favor of a brother Mason, despite any evidence presented against him, and, as a judge, be must rule for the Mason. As a clerk of the court, or any other court official, he is obligated to alter, steal or destroy any official public records or documents which might compromise a brother Mason. This writer has frequently sent written complaints against Masonic judges and lawyers to U.S. Attorneys. In every instance, the Department of Justice has replied to documented charges of blackmail, theft and extortion, "You should hire a private attorney," meaning that you must find yourself a Masonic attorney and hope that he will handle your case against his brother Masons.

The Masonic Handbook further commands that

> "If you cheat, wrong or defraud any other society or individual, it is entirely your business. If you cheat government even, Masonry cannot and will not touch you; but be very careful not to cheat, wrong or defraud a brother Mason or Lodge. Who ever else you may defraud, live up to your (Masonic) obligations."

It is impossible for anyone to understand the depths of such depravity unless one understands the very origins of the Masonic brotherhood (see *The Curse of Canaan*, by Eustace Mullins). Its morality is dictated by the basic authority, the Will of Canaan:

> "Five things did Canaan charge his sons; "love one another (of the tribe), love robbery, love lewdness, hate your masters, and do not speak the truth."

Canaan had lived out his earthly existence under the Curse of Canaan, a sentence of slavery which was fastened onto all of his descendants. The command to love one another referred only to these direct descendants; it also gave the implied command that they were to hate all other occupants of the earth. They were further commanded to seek out their living by committing robbery, by promoting sexual vice through love of lewdness, and to hate their masters, because they had been condemned to live on earth as slaves. Finally, they were not to speak the truth, a command which launched the tidal wave of perjury which has now inundated our courts. The fact that Masonry stems from Biblical times is shown by its secret password, "Tubal Cain," which memorializes the line of Cain. Cain committed the first murder on earth, when he slew his brother, Abel. Cain's descendant, Nimrod, a demonic power, became the first ruler of the world. His reign was marked by sex orgies and child sacrifice, outrages which caused Shem, the son of Noah, to behead him, and to cut his body into pieces, as a warning to other malefactors. These pieces were sent to Nimrod's priests as a warning to desist from their vile practices and demonic orgies. Instead, the priests treasured the remains as objects of worship. They were concealed in groves, in rural areas, as the Shrines of the first "Mysteries." Albert Pike, the theoretician of the Masonic movement, notes in his definitive work, "Morals and Dogma" that all Masonic rites originated in these Mysteries.

The priests became the Gnostics, the knowing ones, that is, those who knew where the body, or the relics of Nimrod, were hidden in the groves. Throughout history, these relies, or later copies, have persisted as the symbols of the Canaanite resolve to "hate your masters" and to destroy them in such orgies as the French Revolution and the Communist Revolution. Their final objective is to seize by force all the riches of the world and return them to the rebuilt Temple of King Solomon. Although perjury and abuse of the legal system remain crucial elements of the Masonic drive for control of the world, murder and assassination continue to be the final symbol of their operations.

Thus a citizen of the United States has no idea, when he enters an American court, that he is now entering an arena in which furtive conspiracy is the dominant factor, where perjury and assassination are considered to be routine methods of operation. If he could be informed of this reality, he would be able to cite numerous precedents denying the judge's qualifications on the grounds of bias. Equal protection to all is the basic principle on which rests justice under the law. Pierre v. State of In. 59 S.Ct 536, 306 U.S. 354, 83 L.Ed. 757.

"Prejudice of or bias on the part of the trial judge may constitute a denial of equal protection of the laws." Osborne v. Purdome, 250 s.w. 2d 159.

In a trial situation, the judge faces two imperatives; first, he must conceal the existence of his Masonic allegiance; second, he must impose by imperial decree his commands upon all who come before his court. There are many decisions which reflect these imperatives, such as U.S. Judge Thomas MacBride's decision in Case #9909, May 2, 1967, under Lord Coke's ruling of 1608 in Peter vs. The Crown, that "no Officer of the Crown could be charged with a crime, even if he were guilty.' Judge M.

L. Schwartz dismissed Case S 83-699 -MLS, April 11, 1984, under the Magna Carta of 215, that we had no right to file charges against public officials or members of the Bar because the Constitution of the United States did not apply in the jurisdiction of the federal courts. Judge R. A. Ramirez dismissed Case # 84-03 0503RRAR July 23, 1984, under Bell v. Hood, which was also based on Lord Coke's ruling of 1608, citing the Magna Carta's stand that persons of a lower caste cannot present charges against members of the titled peerage class.

These rulings in our federal courts ignore the first statute ever passed by the U.S. Congress in its first session, 1791. This statute concerned the punishment of judges and other public officials who failed to enforce the law. The statute commanded that the people be guaranteed the citizens' rights. The failure to do so was termed Insurrection.

Sydney Smith, in his "Fallacies of Anti-reformers," noted that "if the law be good, it will support itself; if bad, it should not be supported by irrevocable theory, which is never resorted to but as the veil of abuses. All living men must possess the supreme power over their own happiness at every particular period. When a law is considered immutable, instead of being repealed, it is clandestinely avoided, or openly violated; and thus the authority of the law is weakened."

Sir Francis Bacon noted in his "Judicature,"

> "Judges ought to remember that their office is *jus decere*, and not *jus dare*; to interpret law, and not to make law, or to give law. *Judicius officium est, ut res, ita tempora rerum.* A judge must have regard to the time as well as to the matter."

Ralph Waldo Emerson, in "Worship," states that

> "We owe to the Hindoo Scriptures a definition of Law which compares well with any in the Western books; Law it is, which is without name, or color, or bands, or feet; which is the smallest of the least, or largest of the large; all, and knowing all things; which hears without ears, sees without eyes, moves without feet, and seizes without bands."

Of Emerson's definition, the one most readily applicable in experiences with our court system is that it does indeed seize without bands. Seizure is always its prime moving force. Adam Smith notes in his "Wealth of Nations,"

> "Justice, however, was never in reality administered gratis in any country In order to increase their payment, the attorneys and clerks have contrived to multiply words beyond all necessity, and to corrupt the law with language."

Robert Ringer notes in his "Looking Out For Number One,"

> "The practical consequences of government are that it uses the threat of violence either to force you to stop doing something you want to do or to force you to do something you don't want to do, or to force you to give up something that is rightfully yours."

Daniel Webster stated on March 10, 1831 in New York City,

> "The judicial power comes home to every man. If the legislature passes incorrect or unjust general laws, its members bear the evil as well as others. But juridicature acts on individuals. It touches every private right, every private interest, and almost every private feeling. What we possess is hardly fit to be called our own, unless we feel secure in its possession, and this security, this perfect system, cannot exist under a wicked or even a weak and ignorant administration of the laws.' There is no happiness, there is no liberty, there is no enjoyment of life, unless a man can say when be arises in the morning, 'I shall be subject to the decision of no unjust judge today.'"

In retrospect, when Daniel Webster made this statement, the powers of the judiciary were almost nonexistent, compared to the powers which they exercise today. What would be say if he were now alive, and confronted with the dictatorial powers which the judicial system has assumed over every aspect of American life? We have seen the seizure of the schools, the decision as to how our earnings shall be spent, what sort of neighborhoods we are to live in, and a judicial system on which the government agencies depend to enforce their decrees.

A defense filed by Alan Stuart in Arkansas on July 3, 1978 noted that a Hearsay Substitute had filed the complaint against him, in violation of the United States Constitution, and that a Hearsay Substitute was his accuser, whereas he had the right to face his accuser. Stuart pointed out that the District Attorney served both as an "Officer of the Court" under the judiciary, and as a law enforcement official under the executive department, which placed him in flagrant violation of the doctrine of separation of .powers, and the system of checks and balances set up by the Constitution. Stuart also pointed out that the title, "Officer of the Court" is an unconstitutional title of nobility, that all lawyers are automatically a part of the Judicial Branch of the Government, whether elected, hired, or appointed. Article l, Sec. 9 and 10 forbid Titles of Nobility. With the Hearsay Substitute being a lawyer, and the judge also a lawyer, a Conflict of Interest exists by having lawyers, or Officers of the Court, representing both sides. Stuart deposed that all lawyer judges have to disqualify themselves because of conflict of interest, which prevents them from presiding over a fair trial. This would seem to provide a useful alternative to the present abuses committed by judges who claim to be operating under "due process of law."

Dr. Felix Cohen wrote in the Columbia Law Review, June, 1935,

> "due process of law' means nothing in the light of recent judicial decisions that it is a metaphysical coverup phrase (another ubiquitous justification of judicial tyranny is the much abused phrase 'having your day in court,' which means that merely by allowing you to set foot in his hallowed precincts, the judge is giving you access to more justice than you are due, and upon extending this gracious privilege, the judge is then free to render whatever horrendous decision be pleases. ED NOTE.)

Dr. Cohen continues,

> "Legal concepts (for example, corporations or property rights) are supernatural entities which do not have a verifiable existence except to the eyes of faith. Rules of Law, which refer to these legal concepts, are not descriptions of empirical social facts but are rather theorems in an individual system.

Jurisprudence is a special branch of the science of transcendental nonsense."

Thus Dr. Cohen, who has labored for many years in the field of jurisprudence, comes to the inescapable conclusion that his lengthy experience has really been in the realm of fantasyland. Few Americans realize that while they are sitting in court listening to their paid counsel "defend" them and their interests, the judges are bard put to keep from grinning at the nonsense they are paid to listen to. As Alan Stuart points out in his complaint, everyone and everything that is taking place in the court is Hearsay and Substitute, which is actually governed by abstruse concepts from the Kabbalah or from other mystical formulae which the citizen is never aware of. The present writer has heard much "transcendental nonsense" in our courts, precisely what Dr. Cohen describes, and was finally able to define its origin in "*The Curse of Canaan*" as the modern day presentation of the ancient Cult of Baal, as refined in the Kabbalah and the present statutes. It is not accidental that this "transcendental nonsense" is overseen by a judge who wears black robes. This itself in legal terminology is referred to the "cult of the Robe." since man's beginnings, the garb of justice has traditionally been white. We have never asked ourselves when or how the robes of justice suddenly became black, but at that moment, began. Instead of the color of unsullied purity, we now have the black robe as the sign of Babylonian justice, of the Canaanite precepts originated by Nimrod, presented against the backdrop of the sexual orgies and the madness of child sacrifice which were the hallmarks of the "religious rites of Baal and Ashtoreth. However, we must admit that there is no attempt to deceive anyone. The judge appears before us in his robe of Babylonian black, as the high priest of the rites of Nimrod. It is we who offer no objection, or ask the judge whatever became of his white robe. The dome of the courthouse itself is another symbol of Babylonian law, and is purposefully designed to confirm that we are now entering the jurisdiction of Babylonian justice, which is inflicted upon us by a Byzantine maze of secret intrigue and worldwide conspiracies.

The character of those who put on the black robe is amply documented by public records. Time magazine reported July 18,

1977 on the exploits of Associate Justice Yarbrough of the Texas Supreme Court. "Yarbrough was taped making a statement about a man who had testified against him, "I want Kemp wiped away... the best thing would be to do it myself if I had a gun and silencer.'" Yarbrough was referring to a 1974 fraud scheme, in which Kemp had testified against Yarbrough and his associate, John Rothkopf, after they had received a $30,000 payment for a collection of rare coins, which they never delivered. Yarbrough then used his judicial position to obtain forged papers and a new identity for Rothkopf, who hid out as a fugitive in Louisiana and Texas for several years. Yarbrough was subsequently indicted by an Austin Texas grand jury for soliciting murder, forgery, obstruction of justice, and perjury.

The Texas Supreme Court has been much in the news for the procedure by which its members are chosen. They campaign like any other politician for election to office, and must spend millions of dollars on their campaigns. Traditionally, most of their campaign funds are provided as donations from the Texas Trial Lawyers Association, with individual lawyers contributing as much as $25,000 to the campaign of a single candidate. Chief Justice Thomas Phillips, although running unopposed, managed to raise a $1.1 million campaign fund from some 4500 donors. The record-breaking $10.5 billion judgment which Pennzoil won against Texaco was followed by public consternation, when it was revealed that the lawyers who represented Pennzoil had contributed more than $355,000 to the nine Texas Supreme Court justices from 1984 to 1987, preceding the announcement by the court that it would refuse a hearing to review the $10.5 billion judgment against Texaco. Three of the justices then resigned from the court, although a present candidate for the court has also raised $1.1 million in campaign funds, nearly all of it donated by lawyers who will subsequently argue cases before this same judge, if he wins the election. If not, they will argue before another judge to whom they have also contributed substantial amounts in campaign funds.

Since the end of World War II, there has been increasing public criticism of judges, for abuse of power, corruption, and their arbitrary decisions, but little has occurred which improves the situation. The dirty secret of the judiciary is that their appointments always come from politicians, and that the moral or intellectual backgrounds of neither the judges nor the politicians is ever taken into consideration. Thus President Harry Truman was described by poet Ezra Pound in "*The Cantos,*" "Truman was loyal to his kind, the underworld." This was a direct quote from longtime Washington journalist Rex Lampman, whom I had taken to visit Pound. However, Pound was merely restating what most Americans already knew. Truman remained loyal throughout his career to Boss Pendergast, who was sent to prison for a multi-million dollar insurance scam. The New Republic noted March 10, 1952 that Truman's appointment of some one hundred and twenty-five federal judges "has weakened the federal judiciary and lowered its prestige. The political handshake gained its greatest triumph when Tom Clark was appointed to the Supreme Court of the United States." Clark was described in the New Republic as an oil lobbyist from the Texas State Legislature, and a protege of Senator Tom Connally. In retrospect, the cronies whom Truman appointed to the federal bench probably were no worse than the dreary procession of legal backs and lobbyists, ward heelers and bondsmen, who have been named to the bench by subsequent Presidents. President Carter probably sunk the prestige of the bench to a new low with his naming of some three hundred political activists from the ranks of feminists and minority class agitators, a club of lunatics which turned the federal courthouses into asylums.

In Harpers, Sept. 1934, Mitchell Dawson wrote, "Judging the Judges," "His Honor and his confreres on the bench have authority to rule upon the rights, duties, privileges, and immunities of everybody and everything within their respective bailiwicks. The aggregate power and responsibilities thus residing in the judiciary are appalling." Dawson went on to comment upon the moral attributes of such power. He noted that three judges were noted among the pallbearers of Big Jim Colosimo, "the first of the big shots in the liquor trade and bootlegging." Big Jim was the protege of Edward G. Robinson's characterization of the gangster, Rico, in his famous picture, "Little Caesar." Two judges and an ex-judge joined the cortege of city and state officials who followed the solid silver casket containing the body of Angelo Genna, the noted convict and killer. The Chicago Crime Commission said, 'A certain municipal judge was familiarly known to the criminal trade as 'cash register.' One magistrate was removed from office for accepting a 'loan' of $19,600 from Arnold Rothstein, the noted gambler. Evidence showed that the fixing of cases in the magistrates courts was an established business."

So much for the judicial situation in 1934. The American Law Journal noted in its issue of February, 1988 that a Wisconsin trial court judge and the senior partner of the state's largest law firm, the 278 lawyer firm of Foley and Larder, now faced sanctions for holding ex parte discussions in the fall of 1986. As we have pointed out, ex parte discussions, in which opposing lawyers and/or judges, hold secret conferences to discuss cases without the parties being present, constitute one of the gravest problems of a legal system which pits the lawyers against the rest of the citizens. In Texas, a judge was severely criticized because he had given a relatively light sentence to a criminal who shot two men. The judge responded with surprise, "But they were only queers." This brought a national protest from the powerful homosexual lobby. In Seattle, Judge Gary Little, judge of the King County Superior Court, shot himself after learning that a Seattle newspaper planned to run an expose of his twenty year sexual abuse of male defendants who came before his court. The local media had deliberately suppressed the story for decades. A reporter finally admitted that he had opened the door of Little's office in the state attorney general's offices, in 1968, and found Little kissing a blond, blue-eyed male student. Taped accounts had been available for years from juveniles who complained that little had molested them while their cases were being deliberated in his court. Some of them were invited to stay overnight in his Seattle home, or at his weekend cottage on an island.

In New York, a sensational trial of former Miss America Bess Myerson dragged on for weeks, before her acquittal. Myerson, who called herself "the Queen of the Jews" had faced sentences of up to thirty years on charges of obstruction of justice, mail fraud, bribery-related charges, and conspiracy. She and her lover, a contractor, had involved Judge Hortense Gabel in her lover's divorce proceedings. The chief witness against the judge was her own daughter, whom the press described as "eccentric" and suffering from depression.

The politically influential State Supreme Court of New York Justice Louis Fusco Jr., who was under investigation by U.S. Attorney Rudolph W. Giuliani on accusations that he had improperly directed business to an insurance company operated by a friend, announced that he would not seek renomination. The president of the insurance company in question was known as a longtime friend of the judge, whose nephew was named vice president of the company. Another prominent Bronx judge, former Surrogate Bertram Gelfand, was ousted last year for misconduct.

On Aug. 24, 1986, the Las Vegas Sun warned of "the ominous implication that federal judges - or any other citizen - will remain a subject to malicious prosecution for merely speaking out against injustice." The matter under discussion was the malignant persecution of Federal Judge Harry Claiborne, which finally wound up before Congress. Congress then voted for his impeachment. What was behind this case? The Nevada High Court had already rendered a decision, State Bar of Nevada v. Claiborne, 756 P2d 464 (1988) that Claiborne had been guilty of nothing more than "mere negligence." Judge Claiborne, the bearer of a proud Southern name, had served with distinction in the U.S. Air Force during World War II. He later became one of the most respected defense lawyers in the West, devoting more than thirty per cent of his time to pro bono (without payment) cases for the public good, probably a higher percentage then than any other lawyer in the United States. After being named to the judgeship, Claiborne continued to come down hard on the side of the public. He excoriated both FBI agents and IRS agents who brought cases before his court with fantastic, poorly prepared charges, which were usually based solely on information provided by their paid informants. In the paid informant business if you don't come up with something damaging against the subject, you don't get paid. This provides a constant stimulant to the imagination.

Department of Justice agents launched a concerted campaign to block Claiborne's nomination to the federal bench in September, 1978. Failing in their objective, they then began a campaign to destroy him. An editorial in the Reno Gazette Journal was quoted with approval by Justice Steffen, "The Justice Department and the FBI were so incensed at Judge Claiborne that the need for revenge blinded them to everything but one burning desire. The federal government could not rest after Claibome denounced its strike force lawyers as 'rotten bastards' and 'crooks and liars.' It could not bear Claibome's insinuations without retaliating."

The retaliation of the federal agents was balked when they could find no bases for bringing any charges against him. They were forced to dredge up one of the nation's sleaziest characters, Joe Conforte, the world's most famous brothel keeper. For thirty years, Conforte had operated the famous Mustang Ranch, which never had any mustangs. In May 1976, a well-known Argentine boxer was shot and killed outside of Conforte's Mustang Ranch. Three Reno Gazette Journal editorial writers won Pulitzer prizes for their stories exposing Conforte's operations. In 1977, both he and his wife were indicted for income tax evasion. He then fled the country to escape tax jeopardy assessments of more than twenty-six million dollars, as well as two lawsuits filed after the Argentina boxer's death. IRS agents realized that Joe Conforte would be the ideal vehicle to get Judge Claibome. They offered him a deal to testify about alleged "bribes" to Judge Claibome. In return, he would be allowed to return to the United States, all but three and a half million of the twenty-six million dollar assessment would be forgiven, he would be guaranteed that he serve no more than one year in a country club type of prison, and all other charges against him would be dismissed. It was an offer he could not refuse. The fact that IRS agents would be willing to forgive over twenty-two million dollars in overdue taxes proves that they are not serious about collecting taxes; it is much more important that they maintain the legal dictatorship over American citizens, invoking Lenin's 1917 rule, "confiscation of all assets as punishment for concealing income." In effect, federal agents were paying Conforte more than twenty million dollars in a conspiracy to commit perjury and to obstruct justice-standard procedure in our "legal system." In fact, Conforte's testimony against Judge Claibome was subsequently documented as being perjured. Nevertheless, Judge Claibome was indicted, convicted, and impeached by Congress. He served a short prison term, and is once again practicing law in the State of Nevada, despite threats from federal agents that they will "get" him again. The point had been made. The federal government had sent a message from the District of Columbia to judges in every state-cooperate with Washington, or else.

Establishment judges have been treated much more kindly in prosecution, notably Judge James M. Landis. A former law clerk to Supreme Court Justice Louis Brandeis, the leader of the Zionist movement, Landis later was named dean of the Harvard Law School, the private preserve of Viennese revolutionary Felix Frankfurter. Landis became one of the original Brain Trust in FDR's New Deal. He was named chairman of the Securities Exchange Commission, and became the eminence grise of President John F. Kennedy. Like many prominent Washington officials, he did not bother to pay income taxes. As a member of our "Nomenklatura," he saw no need to conform to the standards enforced against the peasants and the hoi polloi. It was revealed that he had paid no income taxes for the years from 1956 through 1960. The press hastened to defend him as "a longtime crusader for ethics in government. "While being charged with five years' delinquency in paying taxes, he was also named correspondent in a Washington divorce suit. Landis pleaded guilty to the tax charges, and paid back taxes on income of $410,000.

In the Chicago court system, which was still in the bands of the remnants of the Capone mob, a sting operation netted ten judges in a ring of some sixty officials, who were convicted of corruption. A Cook County judge, Earl Strayhom, was accused in 1974 of not filing federal income tax forms for 1966 through 1968, failing to declare $49,000 in income, and failing to pay $26,000 in taxes and penalties. He resolved the charges with a bargain payment of $11,000.

In Austin, Texas, an AP release dated Nov. 6, 1988 noted that a Texas judge had been reprimanded by the State Commission on Judicial Conduct for "allowing her child to run around her courtroom during proceedings." She also called litigants and others "pure trash," and threatened to shoot a lawyer. She finally left the bench, crying and shouting threats at attorneys. She told one lawyer that she had a gun, and that she could shoot two holes in his back before he could leave the courtroom. The Commission sternly noted that,

> "The comments of Judge Anthony are not consistent with the temperament required of a member of the judiciary."

During this same period, Mariposa County, Ca. District Attorney J. Bruce Eckerson was reported to have resigned under pressure of continued lawsuits and criminal allegations of corruption and misconduct; the chancery clerk in Rankin Cy., Ms. faced nine counts of embezzlement, and Middlebury Vt. county prosecutor Robert Andres was charged $400 for "kicking man in face." Meanwhile, Dr. Elizabeth Morgan piled up twenty-one months in jail after being jailed by District Court Superior Judge Herbert Dixon on contempt of court charges. Dixon is black; Dr. Morgan is white. Dixon had ordered her to turn over her six year old daughter Hilary to her ex-husband, whom Dr. Morgan claimed had been sexually abusing the child since she was two. Testimony from doctors and psychiatrists that the child had been abused had been ruled "inadmissible." Dr. Morgan has spent her time writing children's books, and becoming engaged to a Circuit Court Judge.

One avenue open to Dr. Morgan would be habeas corpus. Kent's Commentaries points out, I, 619, "Every restraint upon a man's liberty is, in the eyes of the law, an imprisonment, whatever may be the place or whatever may be the manner in which the restraint is effected." Kent hardly expected that a woman could be locked up for almost two years without conviction.

Corpus Juris Secundum 39A HC 159 states that a petitioner for habeas corpus has the right to represent himself in prosecuting the proceedings; the presence of the petitioner in court is not necessary to argue issues of law, but the presence of the petitioner is necessary where questions of fact are to be litigated. In the federal courts, habeas corpus provides a remedy for jurisdictional errors without limit of time. Dr. Morgan could cite CJS 39A, sec.

163, "A person whose detention is illegal, or a third person on his behalf, generally may present an application of habeas corpus; since it is intended for all who may be deprived of their liberty without sufficient cause and such person having stood to question their detention or deprivation of other rights." The writ must be brought against the proper person, generally whoever has actual custody of the prisoner. The title is Petition for Writ of Habeas Corpus.

The writ should state some reason for granting the writ, usually that

"Adequate relief is unavailable from other courts or in other forms; government intrusion upon petitioner's First Amendment rights to political expression, invalidating the prosecution and resultant confinement; that petitioners Fifth Amendment right to due process is denied by his confinement. WHEREFORE your petitioner prays that the Court issue an order that the respondents show cause why this Petition should not be granted and the petitioner discharged; that the Court set out in the order a return of three days. That the Court set the matter down for hearing within five days after the return; that the Court hear and determine this matter, and upon final hearing issue Writ of Habeas Corpus and an order directing the respondents to discharge the petitioner from their custody."

Because the law has established that any "restraint" is grounds for the issuance of a writ of habeas corpus, not merely physical restraint or imprisonment of the petitioner, but any governmental oppression or "restraint" is similarly grounds for a writ of habeas corpus, the respondent named being the government agents who are responsible for such restraint. Thus a writ of habeas corpus may be filed against any federal agent, whether IRS, FBI, BATF, CIA or UN, who is imposing stress upon any citizen of this nation, whether it be extortion, intimidation, or threats against one's occupation of family members. Section 171B, CJS 39A states that the writ must be made before the proper inferior court or judge; sec. 172B states the writ must be issued, or the court must show cause why it is not being issued. Sec. 179 states "The writ of habeas corpus is paramount authority over all other writs. Idaho; in re Dodd, 24I P 2d. Under a federal statute, state court proceedings pending proceedings in a federal court for a writ of habeas corpus will be null and void." Thus, a prisoner who applies for a writ of habeas corpus in federal court, in theory, can halt state court proceedings against him.

CJS 39A notes that habeas corpus is a prerogative common law writ of ancient origins directed to a person detaining another, commanding him to produce the body of the designated prisoner at a designated time and place, to do, submit to, and receive whatever the court shall consider in that behalf; it is called 'the great writ' and is a 'civil remedy.' The term derives from the Latin, "You have the body."

CJS 4I notes that

> "A person imprisoned for committing an act that does not constitute any offense may be released on habeas corpus. Hill v. Sanford, C.C.A. Ga. 13IF 2d 417. This also applies to a person detained under an unconstitutional or invalid statute or ordinance; this is grounds for a writ of habeas corpus."

Thus we find that any unconstitutional oppression or pressure against any American citizen is grounds for a writ of habeas corpus, that is, an order to relieve such pressure and to cease and desist. Habeas corpus is enshrined in the Constitution, Article 9, and cannot be suspended for any reason.

CJS 39A sec 37 states

> "Habeas corpus may be allowed where there has been a deprivation of fundamental or constitutional rights. It has been held that questions decided by court having jurisdiction thereof may not be considered in habeas corpus proceedings in another court, whether or not constitutional principles are involved. Craig v. U.S., C.A., C.C.A. Cal. 89 F 2d 980."

CJS 39A sec 39,

> "The writ of habeas corpus is designed to give a person whose liberty is restrained an immediate hearing to determine the legality of the detention." Walker v. Wainwright, Fla. 88, S.Ct 962, 390 US 335, L.Ed. 2d 1215.

Habeas corpus provides a prompt and speedy remedy or adjudication of a person's right to liberation from illegal restraint, or to be free of whatever society determines to be intolerable restraint." Bland v. Rodgers, D.C. 332 F.Supp. 989.

Thus the widespread impression that the writ of habeas corpus applies only to persons detained in prison is merely one application of the writ. It can and should be used to apply to every instance of illegal and unconstitutional oppression by any government agent against any American citizen, "whatever society determines to be intolerable restraint." Note that it does not say "whatever the court determines." The people have the final jurisdiction and determination in the matter of "intolerable restraint," and they must exercise their jurisdiction in determining that restraint. It applies not only to the forcible and illegal detention of a person's body, but it also offers an immediate legal remedy for any undue restraint upon any citizen of the United States in his pursuit of life, liberty and property. For the first time, our citizens now have a weapon which enables them to take action against any act of oppression by government agents, or power-crazed federal officials, many of whom are secretly in the pay of foreign powers. FREEDOM NOW! This is the message which the writ of habeas corpus brings to us. If any federal, state or local agent is acting to oppress you, now is the time to file a notice with the proper court, naming that person, the nature of the restraint, and requesting a writ of habeas corpus which will free you from that restraint. If the judge responds to your plea by dismissing it on the grounds that you are not actually being held in detention, you must refile the writ, stating the exact nature of the writ, and noting that the statutes do not require that you are being held in actual physical detention. The writ may be issued upon receipt of any governmental order which restrains you from any legal act or which attempts to deprive you of your personal property. The income tax functions as the primary restraint upon all citizens of this nation, because it sets up a primary lien upon all of our income and personal property, at the behest of the Federal Reserve System, which is the secondary lien upon all income and personal property in the United States. Thus the writ may be filed against the IRS or against the Federal Reserve System, or both; its ramifications may be extended to each and every restraint imposed upon us by King George and the Bank of England. The writ should state that, acting in his capacity of agent for, has willfully and intentionally sought to deprive you of your Constitutional liberties, and has thereby restrained you from exercising your privileges of citizenship in the United States (of the states)." The judge must then allow you to argue in his court the nature of your restraint; he must then decide if it is a restraint, which, in the light of the facts presented, would be difficult to deny. If so, he has no recourse but to grant you the writ of habeas corpus.

The Genocide Convention adopted by our Congress also offers opportunities for our citizens to seek relief under its provisions. For instance, the present writer was prevented from marrying or raising a family by the malicious acts of federal agents, who continuously had me discharged from gainful employment, thus effectively ending my line, and further sought to have me detained in an insane asylum, which they were unable to effect. This clearly constitutes an act of genocide under the terms of the Convention, because the actions taken against me by these federal agents were solely inspired by my presence by act of birth as one of a group of American citizens singled out for punitive action and eventual extermination by said federal agents, as part of the federal goal to commit genocide against my racial grouping. The Genocide Convention was actually drafted after World War II to protect Zionists and Zionists only; it has never been invoked for any other group. The Zionists sought to use it to punish, outlaw and exterminate all of their present and potential enemies, which encompassed all other groups in the world. However, the language of the Convention could not be written expressly to limit to the Zionist conspirators, thereby opening the door for anyone to invoke it in protection of other groups.

In Dec. 1948, the United Nations advised the convention on the Prevention and Punishment of the Crime of Genocide, the resultant legislation then being sent by President Truman to the Senate for ratification in the Senate, Senator Percy of Illinois led the fight to ratify the Genocide Convention. Hearings were held in 1950, 1970, 1971, 1977 and 1981. It was officially ratified by the American Bar Association in 1976. The British Parliament ratified it as the Genocide Act of 1969. Canada then followed suit.

Act II of the Act states that

> "In the present convention, genocide means any of the following acts committed with intent to destroy, in whole or in part, a national ethnic, racial or religious group, as such:
>
> a. killing members of the group;
>
> b. causing serious bodily or mental harm to members of the group;
>
> c. deliberately inflicting on the group conditions of life calculated to bring about its physical destruction in whole or in part;
>
> d. imposing measures intended to prevent births within the group.
>
> e. forcibly transferring children of the group to another group."

The last provision was designed solely to bring about the recovery of any Jewish children adopted by gentile families during World War II to save them, sec. 3 being intended to force these families to return the children to the Jewish group. However the other four provisions of the Act do apply to the present writer's experience, as documented in "A Writ for Martyrs," which reproduces 120 pages of my FBI file, and which establishes by official government documents that said acts of genocide were committed against my person. The Genocide Convention states unequivocally that intent to destroy any part of the group, that is, any single member of the group, is the same as the intent to destroy the entire group. Thus, sec. d is proven by government documents in my case, as are sec. a, b, and c.

The term "genocide" was coined by a Zionist propagandist named Rafael Lemkin, who intended, in his book, "Axis Rule in Occupied Europe," that genocide should be used solely as a term referring to the conditions of Jews under Nazi occupation during the Second World War. Thus it could have no application to any other racial group, and theoretically would no longer be valid at the conclusion of this war. It was a temporal designation for a specific historical situation, and was never intended to be applied for anyone else's benefit. Zionist collaborators encysted all over the world then conceived the idea of a worldwide prohibition against "genocide," which was intended to stifle any criticism of their subversive activities, and to enact dictatorial measures to eliminate any future criticism. Because no nation could possibly enact a measure which stated it was solely to protect Zionists, the wording had to be broadened to apply to all people. It now covers any group whose future existence is threatened by genocidal government measures, the most threatened target today being the middle class citizens of the United States, who have as yet undertaken no measures in their self-defense.

As it was ratified by the United States, the Genocide Convention states,

> "Whoever, being a national of the United States or otherwise under the jurisdiction of the United States, willfully without justifiable cause, commits within or without the territory of the United States in time of peace or in time of war, any of the following acts with the intent to destroy by means of the commission of that act, or with the intent to carry out a plot to destroy, the whole or a substantial part of a national ethnic, or racial or religious group, shall be guilty of genocide."

Note that the Act establishes jurisdiction throughout the world, "within or without the territory of the United States," thus extending the authority of the District of Columbia to the entire world. The American Journal of International Law notes that substantial questions are raised about implementing legislation. However, a complaint charging genocide can be charged in any federal court, and those questions of implementation can then be addressed.

In recent years, there have been increasing charges that the personal involvement of judges in the cases which they are hearing, the classic dilemma of "conflict of interest," are being ignored. The Wall Street Journal noted, Aug. 3, 1988, that "A federal judge refused to disqualify himself in an important patent case against Hewlett-Packard even though his son is employed by the computer giant." The suit, involving patent rights, had been brought by Apple Computer against Hewlett-Packard.

A case involving much greater stakes surfaced when the investment firm of Drexel, Burnham and Lambert requested that Judge Milton Pollack remove himself from the trial of securities fraud which originated with the SEC (Wail St Journal Oct 18, 1988). Drexel alleged that Judge Pollack would be unable to rule impartially because his wife, Moselle Pollack, stood to gain about $30 million from a leveraged buyout of her family firm, Palais Royal, which Drexel was financing. They claimed that Judge Pollack might be biased as a result of his family interests. Mrs. Pollack was selling her inherited interest to Bain & Co., with Drexel placing the securities.

A feature article in the American Lawyer, the trade publication, disclosed that Drexel dreaded an appearance before Judge Pollack because of his reputation as overwhelmingly "progovernment," as are practically all judges in the United States, with the exception of the ill-fated Judge Claiborne. American Lawyer quoted descriptions of Judge Pollack as "prosecutors' favorite judge," who conducts a "kangaroo court." The article went on to say,

> "he chooses sides early Pollack almost always chooses the government's side; once he does, evenhandedness all but vanishes." There were accounts of Pollack's calling in the U.S. attorneys and discussing pending cases with them ex parte (which is strictly forbidden by law) and "even advising them on how to handle the case." Does anyone consider this "impartiality"? The devastating American Lawyer critique continued, "Pollack is known as a judge who holds grudges. His wife Moselle will gain thirty million dollars if Bain Venture Capital of Boston buys Palais Royal from Mrs. Pollack, who, under the law of judicial conflicts, is considered to be the same person as her husband."

After Drexel filed a writ of mandamus requesting that Pollack disqualify himself, the Securities Exchange Commission launched a vicious smear attack against Drexel's lawyers, in which they strongly defended Judge Pollack. In so many words, this government agency stated, "We want this judge because he is our judge." Likewise Drexel wanted Pollack off the case because of his reputation as the government's judge. American

Lawyer concluded, "The system will have been disgraced by the charade played out in this case in which government lawyers have smeared other lawyers, misstated the facts, taken legal positions (on judicial conflicts) fallen all over themselves to bang onto a judge who promises to provide anything but the justice these lawyers are being paid for."

Realizing that their ship had been sunk at the dock, Drexel gave up any hope of an impartial trial under Pollack, and caved in, agreeing to pay some $650 million in fines and penalties, which probably had been the goal of the SEC all along, to force Drexel into payment without trial, knowing that they could not win before Judge Pollack.

The Wall Street Journal ran another front page story about another famous federal judge, Feb. 16, 1989, "hot-tempered 79 year old David Edelstein" who presided over the federal government's landmark case against IBM in the 1970s. IBM's lawyers were the aforementioned firm of Cravath, Swaine and Moore. The Journal took note of the "enmities among the judge, IBM, and Mr. Barr's pugnacious New York law firm, Cravath, Swaine and Moore. The enmities are deep. In the thirteen year anti-trust case, one of the most bureaucratic legal quagmires ever, Judge Edelstein became famous for raging against Cravath lawyers. Cravath twice sought to remove the judge from the antitrust case, a drastic step that rarely succeeds in any court." In fact, a request that a judge remove himself from a case for prejudice is a kamikaze move, because prejudiced judges are the norm in our courts, and is a suicidal move for both the lawyer and his client. Not only does the judge refuse to remove himself, as occurred in this case, but be now has even more reason for his deeply rooted prejudice. Cravath declared in its brief, "Judge Edelstein's mind is bent against IBM. No court has ever had before it such a long and consistent record of bias as that of Judge Edelstein's conduct." Cravath then backed its brief with two cartons of documents detailing its grievances, contending that Edelstein, among other things, "routinely abused" IBM witnesses, helped the government conduct its cross examinations, and secretly altered the trial transcript in the earlier antitrust case." Is this bias? Are government judges routinely prejudiced in favor of the government and against anyone who dares to question the tyrannical acts of government agencies and their agents? Is the sky blue? And more importantly, does justice exist in the United States? Famed lawyer Gerry Spence replies in his latest book, absolutely not! Early in this work, the present writer noted that lawyers and judges routinely conspire to obstruct justice by altering transcripts, deleting documents, and suborning perjury, as IBM has found, to its dismay.

The Journal notes that "Judge Edelstein, a wry New Yorker, has long been considered an irascible and impatient force in the courtroom. Appointed by Harry Truman, be is entering his thirty-eighth year on the federal bench." The Journal also notes that "Judges normally can only be removed for their conduct outside the courtroom."

Thus Judge Edelstein is one of those judges whom the New Republic pointed out March 10, 1952 had by Truman's appointment "weakened the federal judiciary and lowered its prestige." Yet there be is, some 38 years later, one of the Zionist judges whom Truman appointed as part of his re-election compact in 1948 to recognize and support the State of Israel. The Masonic B'nai B'rith nominated these judges, and Truman routinely appointed them as a burden which the entire nation must bear. Edelstein is merely one of the many choleric, acerbic and biased judges serving in New York and many other states because of their political and fraternal associations. The Zionist connection governs their choice because of the overriding Masonic connection. It has long been a truism on New York that the Anti-Defamation League of B'nai B'rith, the terrorist arm of this organization, nominates and passes on ALL CANDIDATES for judgeships in New York and all other metropolitan areas of the United States. So feared is the ADL that no American politician dares do anything which might be interpreted as offensive by its omnipresent and ever vigilant agents, who have fastened like leeches onto every aspect of American life. The fury exhibited by most judges in the United States when any citizen appears before them charged with being a "tax protester" or who is affiliated with any group suspected of patriotism, is aroused because the presence of any such American in his court is a direct affront to the Zionist and Masonic affiliations of the judge. In most cases, the American is unaware that he has offended the judge, or of the violent prejudice which will be shown against him. He is even more unaware that if he is a non-Mason, he is to be given as short shrift before the court as possible. No force in America dares to challenge the ADL domination of our process of judicial selection, which is then given even more routine approval by the selection committee of the ABA, after their assurance that the candidate meets with the approval of the ADL. The glittering career of the late Roy Cohn, whose meteoric rise was cut short by AIDS, contacted from one of his many $500 a night call-boys, was based solely on the fact that his father was a prime mover in the New York ADL, and was himself appointed a judge. With this family sponsorship, Roy Cohn could do no wrong, despite his many years of tax evasion, drug use and sexual promiscuity, none of which ever tainted the unabashed admiration which his friend, CIA propagandist William Buckley, exhibited for him in the pages of his organ, the National Review.

Because the secret bias and behind the scenes loyalties created by the furtive conspiratorial affiliations of the ADL and Freemasons has now poisoned the entire judicial system of America, we have become inured to the most despotic acts of our judges. Much of the pernicious influence exercised by the judiciary can be traced to the career of Oliver Wendell Holmes, a scion of the New England banking and Abolitionist One World conspirators. Holmes was responsible for the new direction in American jurisprudence, the growth of an iconoclastic liberal movement which challenged the traditional concept of judicial impartiality. Holmes' revolutionary doctrine was expressed when he wrote, "It appears to me that it has not always been sufficiently borne in mind that the same-thing may be a consideration or not, as it is dealt with by both parties." Note that this is a direct contradiction of the traditional concept that "law" is a fixed concept. Holmes is saying that there is no genuine basis for deciding whether anything in a legal matter is a consideration or not; this opens the door for all sorts of deviations, as well as making the way clear for the concepts of admiralty law, the law merchant, in which individual rights are no longer of concern. The damaging effect of Holmes' dictum may be seen in the erosion of the traditional sanctity of the law of contracts. Presser and Zwineldon's definitive work, "Law and American History" states that "the classical theory of contract has ended." Other authorities write of "the death of contract." But how is this possible, if the law merchant has been enshrined in our courts? Surely the law of contract is basic to the law merchant. Not at all; the law merchant ignores individual rights and responsibilities in favor of dedicated service to the greater influence and the greater power. Any contract can and will be overridden, if a party can bring enough money and influence to bear in his support.

Holmes also states, "The life of the law has not been logic; it has been experience." This opposes Lord Coke's definition of the law as reason, and justifies the constantly changing court decisions of our era, in which courts first rule in favor of something, and a short time later, deny its own precedent by ruling against it. In effect the rule of law has ended, because the concept of the law as a fixed force has been superseded by the Holmesian doctrine that there are no fixed principles or ethics in law; there is only "experience."

"Experience" has opened the door for the Pollacks and Edelsteins to seize control of our courts; for the principles of the American Revolution to be superseded by the blood-soaked aims of the French Revolution, in which the courts become kangaroo courts for a brief stop on the way to the guillotine; for Revolutionary Tribunals to try Americans, not for any legal offense, but because they have opposed the dictatorship of the Committee of Public Safety. Jacques Bainville has written that to write an exact history of the Third Republic of France, it would be necessary to know the official minutes of the Masonic assemblies. This necessity also applies to the history of such organizations as the League of Nations and its present day successor, the United Nations. M. Leon de Poncins published a full review of the Corps of Freemasons Congress of the allied and neutral countries which was held in Paris, June 28 through 30, 1917, which resulted in the League of Nations proposal being inserted *en blanc* into the conditions of peace agreed upon at the Versailles Peace Conference.

A director of a great New York bank was asked how it was possible for high finance to protect Bolshevism, a system hostile to that movable property whose existence is necessary to the banking industry, and also to those riches which are represented by land and buildings, not less a necessity for banks. The banker replied, "Those who are astonished at our alliance with the Soviets forget that the nation of Israel is the most nationalist of all peoples, for it is the most ancient, the most united, and the most exclusive. But its eyes are turned to the future rather than to the past, and its kingdom is not of this world. First comes this sentence; like the papacy, it is ecumenical and spiritual. But then, you will say that Marxism is the antithesis of capitalism, which is equally sacred to us. Itis precisely for this reason that they are direct opposites to one another, that this puts into our bands the two poles of the planet and allows us to be its axis. We are kings that the prophecies may be fulfilled, and we are prophets that we may not cease to be kings. They take us for birds of prey, but we are carrion birds. Israel is the microcosm and the germ of the City of the Future."

The arrogance of our judges stems from their assurance that they represent a higher power than the lawful government of the United States. No wonder they sneer at the Constitution and revile any citizen who comes before them citing the protection of the Constitution. The Masonic arrogance of these judges is epitomized by the name of Judge Irving Cooper. Time Magazine noted March 30, 1962 that Congressman Manny Celler, whose political career reeked with corruption and double dealing, had sent the name of his old friend and ally, Judge Irving Cooper, ADL approved, as federal judge for the prestigious South Side District of New York. Cooper had been born in London, the son of Max and Ruth Shimansky. Celler anticipated an easy confirmation of his friend, and was stunned when many witnesses came in to give page after page of damning testimony against him. One witness testified that when she used the word "we" in her testimony before Judge Cooper, he screamed "we! we! we!" about five times, meaning that "I had dared to put myself in his class. How dare you say we? Theo he started to rave. His eyes started popping. His face turned purple; he looked like a reincarnation of the devil, or something." Many other witnesses testified that Judge Cooper excoriated and publicly humiliated lawyers and others who appeared before him. "He turned his back on us and berated the group.' Many other potential witnesses feared to testify about his notorious behaviour, for good reason. Despite this overwhelming testimony against him, Cooper was unanimously confirmed as a federal judge. Twenty-five years later, Who's Who still lists him as the federal judge for the Southern District of New York.

The fact that a judge could win confirmation after such damaging testimony is proof that the Masonic influence overrides all other considerations in naming a judge to the bench. The press has carried hundreds of stories about apoplectic, cursing, and obscene judges who abuse anyone unfortunate enough to come into their court, but nothing is done. There is the constant fear engendered in their subjects by these tyrannical judges; there is the myth of "judicial immunity" which has no Constitutional basis; and most important of all, there is the terrible hidden Masonic power behind the bench.

The stranglehold which B'nai B'rith maintains over our courts leads to extreme financial abuses, a continual extending of bribes, favors, and undue influence, which the practitioners of the Will of Canaan exercise against all who come before them: The New York State Chamber of Commerce analyzed 3500 foreclosure cases, and found that 75% of the receivers who were paid fees of over $2500 were "either active political workers or personal friends or relatives of judges" Reader's Digest, Nov. 1948.

Of the courts which produce a steady stream of revenue for its intimates, none is more notorious than the probate court, of which the king is the notorious Surrogate Court of Suffolk, New York. The scene of many historic family battles, this court probates the wills of the nation's wealthiest families. The fees run into the hundreds of millions of dollars. This writer attended sessions in this court concerning a will which the lawyer prolonged over eight years, merely because he wished to maintain the case in his books. At these conferences, I was often supposed to be an attorney, and was taken aside by attorneys for some of the nation's largest firms, who delicately hinted they would "appreciate" any help I could offer in bringing the case to a conclusion. I could hardly admit that we maintained the case so that we would have an excuse for daily drives to the beach, a much less sinister reason than the determination of most lawyers to squeeze the last dollar from their clients.

When one enters a notorious court such as the Suffolk Probate, one can only smile at Plato's naïve statement, "Justice is the supreme virtue, which harmonizes with all other virtues." The administration of justice in America warns us that the most idealistic system can in a short time become a nightmare. Jeremy Bentham denounced "the most grinding of all grievances--the tyranny of judge-made law." The outcries of the people against legal abuses resounds throughout history. Magna Carta xiv promised that "We will not make any justiciaries, constables, sheriffs or bailiffs but from those who understand the law of the realm and are well disposed to observe it." Amos 5:7 criticizes those who abuse the process, "Ye who turn judgments into wormwood." One of the underlying causes of the French Revolution was a plethora of lawsuits, dragging on for generation after generation, and impoverishing everyone but the lawyers. Alas, the people exchanged these oppressive courts for the summary justice of the Revolutionary Tribunals. Charles Dickens was moved to write about the terrible ordeals endured by Englishmen embroiled in lawsuits for many generations in his famous case of Jarndyce v. Jarndyce, which was based on actual occurrences in English courts. Although Dickens' rendition of the behaviour of lawyers and judges was written as satire, it can be observed in any American court today.

Lord Campbell complained in his lives of the Chief Justices of the eighteenth century, that the bench was occupied by "legal monks, utterly ignorant of human nature and of the affairs of men." The decisions of these legal monks show not so much ignorance of human nature, as unalterable opposition to it, because their decisions are dictated by their secret allegiances and their hidden agenda.

A respected American judge, Judge Learned Hand, was never nominated for a seat on the Supreme Court, despite the general acknowledgement that he was our most distinguished jurist. In his memoir, "Fifty Years of Service" he says "I confess when I look at my service it seems to have been for the most part trivial As a litigant, I should dread a lawsuit beyond almost anything else short of sickness or death." speech Aug. 10, 1959, U.S. Court of Appeals.

Judge Samuel Rosenman, former adviser to President Franklin D. Roosevelt, told the Bar of the City of N.Y., Oct. 1964, "Let us face this sad fact; that in many-in far too many instances, the benches of our courts in the United States are occupied by mediocrities-men of small talent, undistinguished in performance, technically deficient and inept." Yet these are the men who continue to serve on the bench, because no one can remove them. Chief Justice Arthur Vanderbilt of New Jersey said, "In the eight centuries or more in which the judicial office has evolved in the Anglo American system of law, three essentials stand out in the definition of a true judge; these are impartiality, independence, and immunity."

The 1961 Handbook for Judges, (American Juridicative Society, Chicago), cites Jud. Canon 3, "It is the duty of all judges in the United States to support the federal constitution, and that of the state whose laws they administer; in so doing, they should fearlessly observe and apply fondamental limitations and guarantees." This canon contrasts sharply with the conduct of judges whose fury is aroused by a citizen pleading his constitutional rights.

Jud. Canon 4 states "A judge should not allow his name to be used for solicitation and charitable contributions." This is the most abused of judicial canons. Not only do judges constantly solicit (a synonym for prostitution), but they let it be known that a contribution to their favored charity might well affect their decision in some future litigation. The most obvious perversion of this canon is the practice of judges to sentence hardened criminals to "community service," to work free in a charity personally chosen by the judge. This is in itself both a solicitation and a contribution. A person who is judged guilty of a crime is expected to go to prison, not to become a social worker. Robert McFarlane, who was found guilty of a political offense, was sentenced to 200 hours of community service. Oliver North, also

THE RAPE OF JUSTICE

a political offender, was sentenced to 1500 hours of such service. The idiocy of this arrangement was lampooned by Ezra Pound more than fifty years ago, in his book, "A Guide to Kulchur," "The imbecility of America from 1900 onwards was loss of all sense of borderline between public and private affairs." The eradication of this line is a crucial goal of the Marxist State. An earlier editorial by Pound in his magazine, The Exile stated, "The republic, res publica, means, or ought to mean 'the public convenience': when it does not, it is an evil, to be ameliorated or amended out of, or into, decent existence." This definition of the republic should strike terror into the hearts of all bureaucrats. The thought of doing something for the public convenience would indeed amend them out of existence.

Samuel West's Election Sermon, 1776, notes,

"But though I would recommend to all Christians, as part of the duty that they owe to magistrates, to treat them with proper honor and respect, none can reasonably suppose that I mean that they ought to be flattered in their vices, or honored and caressed while they are seeking to undermine and ruin the state; for this would be wickedly betraying our just rights, and we should be guilty of our own destruction. We ought to persevere with firmness and fortitude in maintaining and contending for all that liberty that the Deity has granted us." An ancient legal adage says, "Blessed are the troublemakers." An even more ancient one claims that if there is only one lawyer in town, he will starve to death, but let a second one arrive, and both will become wealthy. A Spanish proverb says that "a peasant between two lawyers is like a fish between two cats."

De Tocqueville states that "In America there are no nobles or literary men, and the people are apt to mistrust the wealthy: lawyers consequently form the highest political class and the most cultivated portion of society. If I were asked where I place the American aristocracy, I should reply without hesitance that it is not among the rich, who are united by no common tie, but that it occupies the judicial bench and the bar." ("Democracy in America.")

One of the first precepts of an American judge is that he will exercise all of his power to harass and disqualify the bane of the legal profession, a citizen who refuses to hire a lawyer, and who chooses to represent himself in court, as is his Constitutional right. These mavericks, appearing as "attorney pro se," or more recently, as "In Propria Personae" cause consternation among lawyers and judges. A person who appears as his own lawyer threatens the entire financial operation of our legal system, "Let's Make a Deal." A lawyer cannot make a deal with a layman in litigation, because it would scuttle the system. In some forty years of representing myself, I have encountered every reaction from judges, ranging from supercilious tolerance to outright hostility. Early on, I was standing outside judge's chambers when I heard the judge raising his voice for my benefit, "You can be sure of one thing," he informed the opposing lawyer, "as long as I'm a judge, you will never see a favorable opinion from me for anyone who tries to represent himself in my court."

This judge, like his colleagues on the bench, remained true to his resolve. I never obtained equal treatment in his court. He seemed determined to teach me a lesson when I appeared, and always was disappointed when I came back for more. One lawyer actually tried to help me when I was still unaware of legal dodges. I had no idea what was going on when the judge asked me, "Are you going to file a motion, Mr. Mullins?" I didn't know what a motion was, and this lawyer nudged me, "Tell him you'll file the motion." I let the opportunity pass. This attorney, who was obviously not cut out for the conspiratorial world of legal practice, soon abandoned it for a political career. Philip stern quotes the edict of a professor at Harvard Law School when a student questioned the fairness of legal techniques, "If you believe in fairness and justice, you should be attending a divinity school." Law professors notify their students that once they have taken legal training, they will never be the same. Their outlook on everything, from morals to social life, undergoes a complete change, as they commit themselves for life to legal monkhood and the cult of the black robe. They have now joined the mystical world of Babylon, and have put aside the decencies of normal life and American citizenship for a stranger calling.

Both Philip stern and Professor Fred Rodell of Yale University agree that the person acting as Pro Per has little chance of ever having his case actually tried by a jury. Rule VIL, Sec. 2, U.S. Appellate Court states, "Briefs not signed by counsel who are members of the bar of this court and fully qualified under the provisions of this rule will not be considered by this court." When I filed an appeal with the U.S. Court of Appeals, the decision proved that it had not even been read by the judges; a law clerk had probably notified them that it didn't qualify, and they signed a pro forma denial of the appeal. In 1977, Chief Justice Berger issued an order that the U.S. Judiciary should not accept cases where the plaintiffs had no legal standing under the rules of court.

The judge has two effective weapons against persons appearing as attorney pro se; he can award attorney's fees against them, which can be ruinous, or he can invoke Rule 11, which sets up a number of conditions, that a pleading be "well-grounded in fact," "warranted by existing law" and other factors, which give the judge enormous leeway in invoking Rule 11 against persons representing themselves. U.S. District Judge Richard L. Williams invoked Rule 11 against a retired professor, J. Carl Poindexter, assessing him $11,202 for bringing a case against Virginia officials on a tax matter. Poindexter termed the sanctions "Soviet-style oppression," particularly when government defendants are granted attorneys' fees from citizens bringing a civil rights action. He stated, "Rule 11 violates the most essential of all civil rights - the right to enforce one's civil rights through free access to the courts. If lawyers are intimidated by this threat, they will not take any case from civil rights defendants if there is a chance of their being sanctioned."

The present writer sued a city and county for violation of jury selection rules, which was dismissed in federal court without argument, but not before the government attorney had leaped to his feet three times, shouting for "attorney's fees." In this case, they would have amounted to some $25,000, a sum which I did not have. The judge refused to grant attorneys' fees, because he had not adjudicated the case, and ran the risk of a reversal if I appealed, as I would be forced to do rather than pay $25,000 which I did not have. Charles Ashman's excellent work, "The Pinest Judges Money Can Buy," cites hundreds of pages of documented corruption among judges, beginning with Sir Francis Bacon's statement while Lord Chancellor of England, "I usually accept bribes from both sides so that tainted money can never influence my decision."

Deuteronomy states that "Thou shalt not respect persons, neither take a gift; for a gift doth blind the eyes of the wise, and pervert the words of the righteous."

On June 11, 1973, the California Judicial Qualification Commission recommended only censure of two Los Angeles judges who had issued numerous blank, presigned release forms to bondsmen friends. Judge Mitchell Schweitzer, who served twenty-six years on the Court of General Sessions with the support of both the Democratic and Liberal parties, was described in these words,

> "Some lawyers regarded Schweitzer's court as a circus. The judge shouts and he snorts and be huffs and puffs and he cajoles frightened lawyers and their clients to cop pleas to save time. But I must admit it's entertaining."

In Congress, fixer Nathan Voloshen used Speaker of the House John McCormack's office as his private headquarters to fix income tax cases. Dr. Irving Helpert, a Dayton urologist, gave him $300,000 to fix a case, and never heard from him again. Helpert was convicted and fined. Abe Portas graduated from Yale Law School and became the protege of FDR cabinet member Harold Ickes, who appointed Fortas Undersecretary of the Interior. Fortas later became the confidant of Lyndon B. Johnson, representing him in a Senatorial primary case where Johnson had been ordered off the ballot. Portas saved Johnson's political career by winning the case, making possible Johnson's later ascendancy to the Presidency. As President, Johnson named Portas to replace Arthur Goldberg on the traditional Jewish seat on the Supreme Court. Portas, who was to be named Chief Justice, accepted $15,000 from Troy Post to lecture at American University, and then became involved with wheeler dealer Louis Wolfson, who paid Portas $20,000, and put him on a life retainer

THE RAPE OF JUSTICE

of $20,000 a year. On May 14, 1969, Portas resigned from the Supreme Court.

Justice William Douglas of the Supreme Court married his fourth wife at the age of 66 after his third wife divorced him. Congressman Gross prepared articles of impeachment against Douglas, who was being paid $12,000 a year from the Parvin Foundation, a three million dollar foundation set up by Parvin when he sold the mob-connected Flamingo Hotel in Las Vegas; Parvin had been named as a co-conspirator with Louis Wolfson. Congressman Gerald Ford also called for Douglas' impeachment after he wrote an article for the Evergreen Review which appeared in an issue of the magazine replete with pornographic photos and articles. Unlike the earlier case of Sir Francis Bacon, Douglas was never impeached. Bacon was impeached after evidence that he had taken some 12,230 pounds in bribes, with twenty-eight charges against him. The judgment was that

"The Lord Chancellor bath given way to great exactions by his servants, both in respect of private seals, and otherwise for selling of injunctions."

The invoking of Rule 11 by federal judges is intended to seal off the courts from redress by private citizens, and to allow their secret aristocracy, with its hidden agenda, to continue its practices of bribery and other corruption. Lysander Spooner wrote in 1952,

"The legal effect of these constitutional recognitions of the rights of individuals to defend their property, liberties and lives, against the government, is to legalize resistance to all injustice and oppression, of every name and nature whatsoever, on the part of government. But for the right of resistance, on the part of the people, all governments would become tyrannical to a degree of which few people are aware. Constitutions are utterly worthless to restrain the tyranny of governments, unless it be understood that the people will, by force, compel the government to keep within the constitutional limits. Practically speaking, no government knows any limits to its power, except the endurance of the people Tyrants care nothing for discussions that are to end only in discussion. Discussions, which do not interfere with the enforcement of their laws, are but idle wind to them. Suffrage is equally powerless and unreliable."

CHAPTER 5

THE SUPREME COURT

"The Germ of dissolution of our federal government is in the constitution of the federal judiciary."
Thomas Jefferson.

Whether the case may be made that the federal government is in dissolution, or whether it has at last achieved supreme power over the citizens of the United States, is a matter which has not been resolved. Jefferson warned us,

"The great object of my fear is the federal judiciary. That body, like gravity, ever-active with noiseless foot and unalarming advance, gaining ground step by step and holding what it gains, is engulfing insidiously the (state) governments into the jaws of that which feeds them."
Writings of Thomas Jefferson, v.10:189.

Jefferson also stated,

"It has long been my opinion, and I have never shrunk from its expression (Although I do not choose to put it into a newspaper, nor like Priam in armour offer myself its champion) - That the germ of dissolution of our federal government is in the constitution of the federal judiciary: An irresponsible body (for impeachment is scarcely a scarecrow), working like gravity by night and by day, gaining a little today and a little tomorrow, and advancing its noiseless step like a thief over the field of our jurisdiction, until all shall be usurped from the states, and the government of all consolidated into one. To this I am opposed, because when all government, domestic and foreign, in little as in great things, shall be drawn to Washington as the center of all power, it will render powerless the checks provided of one government on another, and will become as venal and oppressive as the government from which we separated. It will be as in Europe, where every man must be either pike or gudgeon, hammer or anvil. Our functionaries and theirs are wares from the same workshop, made of the same materials and by the same band. If the states look with apathy on this silent descent of their government into the gulf which is to swallow all, we have only to weep over the human character formed uncontrollable but by a rod of iron, and the blasphemers of man, as incapable of self-government, become his true historians." *Writings* v.15:331.

Jefferson continued (v.15, p.341),

"Our government is now taking so steady a course as to show by what road it will pass to destruction, to wit, by consolidation first, and then corruption, its necessary consequence. The engine of consolidation will be the federal judiciary; the two other branches the corrupted instruments."

He went on to say,

"We already see the power, installed for life, the foundations are already deeply laid for the annihilation of constitutional state rights, and the removal of every check, every counterpoise to the engulfing power of which themselves are to make a sovereign part. If ever this vast country is brought under a single government, it will be one of the most extensive corruption, indifferent and incapable of a wholesome care over so wide a spread of surface. This will not be borne, and you will have to choose between reformation or revolution. If I know the spirit of this country, the one or the other is inevitable. Before the canker is become inveterate, before its venom has reached so much of the body politic as to get beyond control, remedy should be applied."

Jefferson was not alone among the Founding Fathers to warn us of the dangers represented by an unbridled judiciary. Now the Supreme Court has come to represent everything which they warned us against; excessive power, the destruction of the system of governmental checks and balances, and the annihilation of the principle of separation of powers. This development has come about because of the systematic "amending" of the Constitution, which was to guard the citizens from excesses of governmental power and its consequent abuses. To accomplish such amending, it was necessary to engage the states in a civil war, or, more properly, a Constitutional revolution, before this goal could be achieved. The subsequent 13th, 14th and 15th amendments effectively repealed the Constitutional guarantees which had been so painstakingly drawn up by the Founding Fathers. In place of the original intent of the Constitution, we were now saddled with the ruthless enforcement of the law merchant. The law merchant respects no individual rights, does not afford trial by jury, and renders useless the appellate process. The law merchant has converted the appellate courts, including the Supreme Court itself, into rubber stamps for the admiralty procedures and decisions of the inferior courts.

The legal profession has carefully concealed from the American people the fact that we no longer have an appellate court system, because the treadmill procedure of appeals continue to provide billions of dollars in fees. The legal profession continues to hold out the carrot on a stick, "We have excellent grounds for an appeal. The court has committed reversible error in numerous aspects of this case." Of course the court has committed reversible error, and every error will be upheld by the rubber stamp appellate court. Although American court procedure remains a game of Russian roulette for the litigant, an attorney knows exactly how much chance an appeal will have. If the client has enough money for an appeal, he will have an appeal.

Abraham Lincoln also expressed his concern about the judiciary, on March 4, 1861,·

> "If the policy of the government upon vital questions affecting the whole people is to be irrevocably fixed by decisions of the Supreme Court the people will have ceased to be their own rulers, having to that extent practically resigned their government into the hands of that eminent tribunal."

The Bill of Rights was affixed to the Constitution to assure the American people that their newly won freedoms, the result of a successful revolution, would not be abrogated by a later tyrannical government. For more than a century, the Supreme Court has been actively denying those rights. The present era of judicial activism began when Oliver Wendell Holmes inaugurated the era of "positivism" on the Supreme Court. Holmes abrogated the rule of written law by his personal view that the judge does not merely read and interpret the law - he also writes the law. Holmes argued that law is not based upon fundamental or universal truths (a denial of the definition of law as a 'fixed power'), but rather on the more psychological "felt necessities of the times."

During the 1920s, the Yale Law School continued Holmes' legal revolution with the rise of "legal realism." This doctrine claimed that the judge is the law. Meanwhile, Roscoe Pound was teaching his doctrine of "sociological jurisprudence" at the Harvard Law School, which demanded "a pragmatic, sociological legal science." In effect, this was merely a restatement of Karl Marx's theory of dialectical materialism. What was imposed upon the Russian people by armed force was to be fixed upon the American people by judicial fiat. When Franklin Delano Roosevelt appointed Felix Frankfurter to the Supreme Court, Frankfurter's initial gleeful aside to Justice William O. Douglas was "If we can keep Chief Justice Hughes on our side, there is no amount of rewriting of the Constitution that we cannot do." This was the same Felix Frankfurter, a Viennese immigrant and Socialist revolutionary, who was labelled by President Theodore Roosevelt as "the most dangerous man in America." Frankfurter saw his opportunity to use the Supreme Court as the vehicle to impose a Socialist tyranny upon all American citizens.

The Wall Street Journal has opened its editorial pages to views critical of the Frankfurter legal system. On Feb. 7, 1989, Prof. of Law Stephen L. Carter warned that "The decisions of the courts are the law of the land in the sense that the parties to them are legally obligated to obey them. They are not, however, the fundamental law of the land-not, at least, in the sense that the

Constitution itself is fundamental." In fact, the decisions of the post-Frankfurter court are binding upon the parties only through the law merchant, and not because of a Constitutional orientation. Carter concludes his argument with the admonition that "Obedience to the courts is obviously among the most fundamental of our traditions, but surely obedience to the Constitution is even more so." This flies in the face of the Holmes-Frankfurter brand of judicial activism and the imposition of admiralty procedure upon the American people. Its motto is "the Supreme Court decisions are the law of the land," even though these decisions regularly reverse themselves, to achieve the condition of national instability which the saboteurs have planned. Legal critic Wait Mann tells us that the seal of the Supreme Court is not the standard judicial seal of the blindfolded maiden and the scales of justice; instead, it is a copy of the Seal of Office of the President! Notes appearing in the U.S. Code, 28 USC 44 ad and 28 USC 88, appendix 1, indicate that the present Supreme Court is not the true Supreme Court, but an impostor. The original Supreme Court still exists in the District of Columbia, but its name was changed during Roosevelt's presidency in order to have a court which would support his National Recovery Act, legislation which was copied directly from the corporate state of Mussolini by Gerard Swope, the president of General Electric, and longtime vassal of Bernard Baruch.

The original Supreme Court is defined in the Constitution, Art III, and the 1789 U.S. Statutes at Large, the Judiciary Act. Since Roosevelt superseded it, U.S. courts have lacked all first instance trial prosecution and trial jurisdiction. Thus the U.S. Criminal Code does not contain specifications of crimes, but specifications of overt acts, that is, criminal contempt's of violations of previous injunctive orders. The courts rely on the injunctive process based on the violation of a court order, rather than providing a legal trial under Constitutional principles where evidence is argued and admitted or denied, with a jury making the final decision. Under this injonctive process, only the overt act of violation of the injonction itself need be proven to obtain a conviction. The "information" which has taken the place of indictments for violations of laws, has only to claim that a violation of the injonction has taken place. The crime itself will never be prosecuted. The U.S. Criminal Code itself was originally a civil code, because the Criminal Code, Title 18, was included in the Civil Judicial Code and the Aliens and Foreigners Control Code, Title 8. The 14th amendment was then written in order to provide the government authority to treat American citizens as aliens and foreigners, as decided by Frost v. RC, 27I US 583, 596-7, which defined us as mere aliens, and Lehigh RR. v. Russia, 2I F.2d 396, which ruled that the law enforcement powers in America apply only to foreigners, foreign relations, and international affairs.

The doctrine of federal judicial supremacy was fastened onto the necks of the American people as an irrevocable yoke because it was done insidiously, and under the cover of more striking and dramatic events, such as the Civil War. After the Second World War, the judicial activists, who had thoroughly cowed the leaders of our two political parties, imposed a series of stunning decisions which, in effect, placed the American people on notice that they now had no rights remaining to them. This situation was dramatized by Gov. Orval Faubus of Arkansas, in a speech to the Arkansas Legislature, Aug. 26, 1958, in which be quoted extensively from the resolutions passed by the Conference of Chief Justices of the State Supreme Courts earlier that month, concluding with their finding that,

> "The Supreme Court has been usurping the rights reserved to the states by the Constitution It is not merely the final arbiter of the law; it is the maker of policy in many major social and economic fields."

The activists' pretensions to judicial supremacy dates from the historic case of Marbury v. Madison, 1803. The decision was the work of Chief Justice John Marshall, who had been appointed to the court by President John Adams, the leader of the New England school of separatists. Marshall ruled that the judiciary has the power to strike down any law or act of Congress which violate the Constitution under Art. m, sec. 2 par. 1, or "the supreme law of the land" clause, Art. VI, sec. 2. However, Marbury v. Madison, rather than being a sweeping review which established the court as the final arbiter of government power, was actually a partisan political squabble over the spoils of election victory. Congress had passed a new Circuit Court bill Feb. 13, 1801, which authorized sixteen additional federal judges. Pres. Adams at once filled them with Federalists, who were confirmed by the Senate March 2, and their appointments signed by President Adams and sealed by Secretary of State John Madison on March 3. Marbury v. Madison arose from a comparable situation, the passing on Feb. 27, 1801 of the District of Columbia Organic Act, provided for the appointment by the President of justices of the peace for Washington and Alexandria within the District. On March 2, the President nominated twenty-three justices for Washington and nineteen for Alexandria and sealed by the secretary before midnight of March 3, the famous "midnight justices of the peace. The commissions were delivered that same night by Marshall's brother James. However, William Marbury of Washington did not have his commission delivered, which became the subject of litigation in December of 1801; the case was finally heard by the Supreme Court in Feb., 1803. John Marshall believed that the commissions were valid when the Seal of the United States was affixed, rather than when they were delivered. Today, the Supreme Court has no file on the case or any of the papers relevant to it. The only record is that made by reporter William Cranch. The Court ruled that Marbury had a right to the commission because of the power of the Court to adjudicate the validity of an Act of Congress. However, the Court refused to issue a writ of mandamus, thus deciding in favor of Madison (I Cranch at p. 70). The Court stated that the Constitution forbade the grant of power to issue the writ but that the Court did have the power of judicial review. The Court ruled that the Constitution was the superior and paramount law, unchangeable by ordinary means, and the supreme law of the land. Sec. 13 of the Judiciary Act of 1789 attempted to give the Supreme Court power to issue a writ of mandamus in an original proceeding against an officer of the United States, including the Secretary of State; the Court concluded that Art. ILI of the Constitution prohibited the grant of such power by Congress to the Supreme Court.

Thus the original dilemma, that Secretary of State James Madison had worked far into the night signing commissions of justices of the peace for the Federalist Party, including Marbury's commission, had had part of his work undone when the incoming Secretary of State, Thomas Jefferson, seeing the stack of signed commissions on the following morning, decided that he would not allow them, and threw them into the wastebasket. Marbury then sued to obtain the commission he had been promised for his dedicated party service. In deciding the case, Chief Justice Marshall, one of the leaders of the Federalist Party, cleverly avoided the main issue before the Court, that of partisan politics, and shifted the issue to one of governmental powers, by deciding that the final arbiter would henceforth be the Supreme Court.

Thomas Jefferson delivered his opinion on the Marbury v. Madison decision, stating, "Nothing in the Constitution has given them (the Supreme Court), a right to decide for the Executive, more than for the Executive to decide for them. The opinion would make the judiciary a despotic branch." Jefferson further warned about judicial supremacy in 1819, stating, "The Constitution, on this hypothesis, is a mere thing of wax in the bands of the judiciary, which they may twist and shape into any form they please." However, the court was careful not to flaunt its newly assumed power. Between 1803 and 1870, the Court declared as unconstitutional only six acts of Congress, three of those being decided in 1870. From 1871 to 1899, it overruled Congress sixteen times, a power which was increasingly used from 1900 to 1936, during the period of Holmesian judicial activism. During that period, the Court rendered fifty-one decisions against the Congress.

The battle over an American central bank also spawned landmark decisions by the Supreme Court. After the European Rothschilds had commissioned Alexander Hamilton to set up a central bank in the United States, immediately after the American Revolution, Thomas Jefferson led the fight against its adoption. In McCulloch v. Madison. 1819, the Supreme Court upheld the bank against the states. In Craig v. Missouri, 1830, the Supreme Court invoked the Constitutional ban on state-issued currency to invalidate loan certificates issued by a state, a decision which severely affected the growth of state banks, and encouraged the demand for a central bank. A longtime crusader against the central bank, Roger Taney. was rewarded for his opposition by President Andrew Jackson, who appointed him to the Supreme Court in 1836. In 1837, the Taney Court reversed Craig v. Missouri in the decision of Briscoe v. Bank of Kentucky, and upheld the state law authorizing the issuance of bank notes by a state institution. Lawrence Tribe comments on this decision,

> "The demise of the central banking system and consequent disruption of the nation's finances played a large part in triggering the devastating economic depression of 1837."

Although Tribe is a well-known legal scholar, be seems Jess aware of the facts about monetary history. Henry Clews stated, in his book, "Twenty-Eight Years in Wall Street," p. 157,

> "The Panic of 1837 was aggravated by the Bank of England when it in one day threw out all the paper connected with the United States."

As the present writer pointed out in *Secrets of the Federal Reserve*, the order to refuse any American securities, shares or loans came directly from Nathan Mayer Rothschild, who thereby deliberately precipitated the panic of 1837. The goal was to punish the United States for refusing Rothschild's central bank, and to drive down the prices of all shares in a financial panic, such shares then being available for purchase by the Rothschilds at a much lower price. Does Tribe known anything of these details? A Harvard law professor since the age of twenty-seven, be is described by Time magazine as one of the most powerful lawyers in the United States. He has long been in the five hundred dollar an hour fee range for consultation, and may be relied upon to present an acceptable justification for Establishment programs.

With the advent of Zionist power on the Supreme Court in 1916, the head of the World Zionist Organization, Louis Brandeis, being appointed to the Court by President Woodrow Wilson, the Court moved from its dedication to the enthronement of judicial supremacy, to a new program, the supremacy of Zionist interests around the globe. Because Supreme Court decisions are not binding upon other nations, this program first succeeded in placing Zionist interests firmly in control of the

federal offices in Washington, where they were then exported to
the rest of the world as "American" interests. President Wilson
appointed Louis D. Brandeis to the Supreme Court June 1, 1916;
he served on the Court twenty-two years. Another Zionist,
Benjamin Cardozo was appointed Feb. 1, 1917, serving twenty-
three years, until 1939; The Jewish seat was then given to Felix
Frankfurter by Roosevelt in 1939. Arthur Goldberg served on the
Court for three years; Abe Portas was appointed Oct. 4, 1968,
later resigning after charges of involvement with wealthy
Zionists who had matters before the Court.

Brandeis' appointment to the Supreme Court has been
explained as the result of a $50,000 contribution by Bernard
Baruch to Wilson's re-election campaign, and also as a
blackmailing effort by Zionist leaders who held Wilson hostage
for the Peck letters, a number of which purportedly established a
secret liaison between Wilson and a paramour. Brandeis'
appointment was affected by both elements. An indefatigable
social activist, he had aroused strong opposition for years
because of his controversial work, yet he was finally confirmed
by the Senate. He was known worldwide for his fanatical
leadership of the Zionist Organization of America; he fulfilled a
continuous round of Zionist meetings and policy sessions, stating
for the record that "Zionist affairs are the only important things
now," a curious allegiance for a Justice of the Supreme Court,
who was supposedly "impartial." Wilson later appointed
Brandeis' mentor, Bernard Baruch, as head of the War Industries
Board during World War I, and Baruch's partner, Eugene Meyer,
head of the War Finance Administration, in charge of Liberty
Loans. Baruch later boasted to Congress that as economic czar of
the United States, he daily exercised more power than any other
man in the nation. It was Baruch who, with Brandeis and Wilson
at the Versailles Peace Conference, wrote the impossibly
punitive reparations assessments against Germany, which made
a Second World War inevitable. A pivotal figure on the Supreme
Court during the 1940s and 1950s was Justice Hugo Black. Max
Lerner's biography of Black notes that he joined the Masons
before he reached the age of twenty-one. As the next step in his
political career, he then joined the Ku Klux Klan, even though
the Klan's charter expressly forbade the admitting of Jews,

Masons or Catholics. Black ran for the Senate with active Klan support, and won. Black then supported Roosevelt's court-packing plan in the Senate, and was himself appointed to the Court as a reward. After he was sworn in, the story was leaked in Washington that Black had been an active Ku Klux Klan member since 1927. Despite a firestorm of protest from the liberals and Communists who made up Roosevelt's entourage, Black refused to resign from the Court, and Roosevelt refused to request his resignation. A deal was made, and Black became known as one of the most liberal members of the Court. He worked actively to offset the votes of "the Four Horsemen" of the Hughes Court, the dedicated conservatives, Pierce Butler, Willis van Devanter, George Sutherland, and James McReynolds. As the "judicial activist" leader of the Court, Black led the writing of the decision against prayer in schools in 1954 as an absolutist doctrine. In a 1962 prayer case, Black claimed that by way of the 14th Amendment and the Bill of Rights, restraints upon the states were incorporated into the Constitution. This became the basis for the liberal wing of the Court in future argument, although other Supreme Court decisions refuted Black's claim. Justice Frankfurter ruled in Adamson v. Cal., 1947, that

> "the notion that the Fourteenth Amendment was a covert way of imposing upon the states all the rules which it seemed important to eighteenth century statesmen to write into the Federal Amendments was rejected by judges who were themselves witnesses to of the process by which the Fourteenth Amendment became part of the Constitution."

In Engel et al v. Vitale et al, Steven Engle and other parents of the New Hyde Park N.Y. v. Union Free District #8, plaintiffs objected to a nondenominational prayer from the State Board of Regents containing twenty-two words drawn from the state constitution, "Almighty God, we acknowledge our dependence upon Thee, and we beg thy blessings upon us, our parents, our teachers and our country." This innocuous prayer had been repeated at the beginning of each school day, with the Pledge of Allegiance; there was no compulsion of students to join in its recital. The Supreme Court itself opened each day's sessions with the prayer, "God Save the United States and This Honorable Court"; prayer was also used at the opening of both Houses of

Congress. However, Justice Black claimed that the school prayer served to set up a state religion, and thereby violated the establishment clause of the Constitution. "Congress shall make no law respecting an establishment of religion, or prohibiting the free exercise thereof. "Black's" argument that this clause forbade all religious expression actually perverted it into a prohibition against the free exercise of religion. The prayer issue continued to come repeatedly before the Supreme Court; in 1984, the Court's famous "reindeer rule" held that nativity scenes and menorahs could be permitted on public property only if they were accompanied by secular symbols such as reindeer, Santa Claus or his elves. This decision has been condemned as "tortured reasoning"; it is not reasoning at all, but rather, is a conscious attempt to inhibit and finally destroy the exercise of religion in the United States.

A succession of socialist activist decisions by the Court changed the quality of life for all Americans. The Shelby v. Kraemer decision, 433 USI 1984 1948, outlawed restrictive real estate contracts, and changed the capital city of the United States from a white middle class residential area to a largely black, crime-ridden city which is now known as "the crime capital of the world." Its mayor, Mayor Barry, is continually criticized for his close associations with known drug peddlers, some of whom have now been arrested. Barry formerly ran a black organization called "Pride" which collected payment from Jewish merchants on Seventh St. in Washington for assurances that their stores would not be vandalized or set on fire. After millions of dollars had vanished into Pride's coffers, Mayor Barry had his wife take the rap for the sum of $675,000, which had mysteriously vanished.

If an invading army had tried to destroy our nation's capital city, as the British did during the War of 1812, it would have met with armed resistance. However, when the Supreme Court decision launched a wave of "white flight," and handed the city over to blacks, not a protest was heard. Shelby v. Kraemer, did not, as was widely but erroneously believed, outlaw racial covenants in real estate contracts. It did take on the language which was widely used in such contracts, such as that quoted in

Ringgold v. Denhardt, "That the bouse on said lot now erected shall be used only as a dwelling bouse, and the same shall not be given, sold, rented or subleased to a negro or person of African or Mongolian descent." Many such racial covenants also excluded Jews or other groups, in an effort to continue the ethnic makeup of particular neighborhoods. The value of the real estate depended in large part upon such restrictions. Once those restrictions were abandoned, the value of the real estate would plunge.

Instead of outlawing such contracts, the Supreme Court did not face the issue squarely. To have done so would have violated the Constitutional provision against the impairment of contracts. The justices of the Supreme Court carried out a flanking attack on their objective; while their cowardice would not allow them to outlaw such contracts, they ruled that the courts would no longer enforce such contracts by legally upholding them. Their "rule of law" weaseled out of a necessary stance by establishing that the provisions of such a contract could not be enforced by the courts.

The famous interview with Philip Elman in the Harvard Law Review, vol. 1987, p. 817, revealed that the Department of Justice had intervened actively to secure the decision in Shelley v. Kraemer, filing a 150 page amicus curiae brief for the plaintiffs, which was later published as a book. Elman states, "I had friends working in the NAACP, the ACLU, the American Jewish Congress, the American Jewish Committee, and other organizations." Elman, as Felix Frankfurter's "law clerk for life," and closest confidante, was working for the plaintiffs as amicus curiae while his employer, Frankfurter, was hearing the case in preparation for handing down an "impartial" opinion. Elman states that the Solicitor General of the United States, Philip Perlman, had requested that he prepare the amicus curiae brief, again an improper procedure, because the clerk of a Justice cannot intervene on behalf of either the plaintiffs or the defense. The brief finally appeared with the names of five Jewish lawyers as its authors. Perlman was disturbed by this, and demanded of Elman, "Can't you find any gentiles to work on this thing?" Thus we find that the same organizations which orchestrated the complaint of Brown v. Board of Education also masterminded the Shelley v. Kraemer decision which destroyed our nation's capital. Their presence was illegal, conspiratorial, and constituted obstruction of justice.

The present writer was living in a pleasant home on Capitol Hill when the Supreme Court decision was announced. Within months, real estate speculators had begun the practice of bringing in one black family per block, the famous practice of "block-busting." At the sight of the black invasion, white owners would immediately sell their homes for as little as one-tenth of the amount they had invested in them. Fortunes were made overnight, as Washington became a black city. One Supreme Court decision changed a sleepy Southern white city with a minority black population into one of the largest black cities in the world, a crime-ridden, poverty-stricken enclave surrounded by well-to-do white suburbs in Maryland and Virginia.

Newspapers carried headlines such as "Fear Becomes Billion Dollar Industry," as sales of locks, alarm systems, security programs, and guns-yes, guns, soared. Many women found that if they chose to live in the District of Columbia, they must become proficient in the use of a handgun, the same handguns which Senator Teddy Kennedy and other bleeding hearts seek to deny to all Americans who are not criminals. As robberies and murders of cab-drivers soared in the District, many cab drivers stopped picking up black fares, and refused to deliver passengers to high-crime areas. A group of yuppy black lawyers recently sued several cab companies, because they had repeatedly been passed by when they tried to bail a cab. Mayor Barry had already forced a measure through City Council automatically fining cab drivers $100 for refusing a passenger. The *Washington Post*, in reporting on the yuppy lawyers litigation, mentioned that ninety-seven per cent of the cab drivers in the District of Columbia were black. The black lawyers were suing their racial colleagues! The Post also interviewed taxi driver Albert K. Acheampong, who said, "I discriminate a lot. I'll pay the $100 fine. I'm not going to put my life on the line." It is typical snobbery of black leaders such as Mayor Barry, who are surrounded by armed bodyguards and chauffeurs, that they wish to fine other blacks $100 because they are fearful of being murdered in what the press habitually refers to as "the crime capital of the world." In Western cities, fake gunfights are staged for tourists; in Washington, the gunfights taking place in Washington on Capitol Hill are real. Nevertheless, Mayor Barry was recently quoted in Newsweek as remarking that "The crime rate in the District of Columbia, if you don't count the killings, is lower than that in other major American cities."

In the case of Corn. of Pa. v. Board of Directors of City Trusts of Philadelphia, the Supreme Court ruled, in 353 US 230, 1957, that Stephen Girard, a patriot of the Revolutionary period, who died in 1831, erred in leaving his large fortune for "schools for poor white orphan boys." The funds, which were used to found Girard College in 1848, could no longer be spent for the purposes which Girard had devised, according to the Supreme Court. Despite a lengthy record of previous decisions which honored testamentary directives, the Court ruled that Girard's will, in the light of current sociological requirements, was now found to be discriminatory; his money could no longer be spent for the benefit of poor white orphan boys.

A farmer was sued for raising grain in excess of Department of Agriculture regulations and feeding the surplus to his cattle. A lower court ruled that some powers are granted to Congress by the Constitution, and others are later conferred by amendment; Congress had originally no power to enact an income tax or to prohibit the manufacture and sale of alcoholic beverages; but no amendment to the Constitution granted to Congress the power to regulate agriculture. The Supreme Court overturned this decision, ruling Per Curiam Feb. 24, 1949, "The judgment is reversed. Wickard v. Filburn, 317 US 111." The Court handed down no written decision, because its ruling for an order of reversal had violated both the Ninth and the Tenth Amendments.

Throughout our history, the qualifications for nomination to the Supreme Court have remained the same--solid political support. During the nineteenth century, nominees were frequently rejected by the Senate on partisan political grounds. In 1930, the Senate rejected an unusually distinguished nominee, Judge John J. Parker, because of his conservative views on race relations and labor law. A concerted propaganda drive by union political leaders persuaded the Senate to refuse him, in a preview of the famous Bork Hearings of our era.

Because of such political impasses as the shocking rejection of Judge Bork for the Supreme Court, Prof. Laurence Tribe suggested a compromise solution; that the Supreme Court should maintain a constant political balance of three liberals, three moderates, and three conservatives; when any Justice left the Court, he should be replaced by a successor chosen from the category to which he belonged. Tribe's suggestion was received with derision in Washington, because no one today can say for certain who is a liberal and who is a conservative, while moderates no longer exist. Judge Bork had been rejected by the Senate as too conservative, although during most of his life he had been considered extremely liberal; he had been married to a Jewish liberal, a socialist, and his closest friend for years had been the well-known leftwing Judge Abner Mikva, whose Congressional career had been marked by his extreme pro-Communist views. Prom the time of Brandeis, there had been a traditional Jewish seat on the Supreme Court, although no seat was ever reserved for anyone who might be considered even remotely anti-Jewish. When Frankfurter died, he was replaced by Artie Goldberg; when Goldberg was asked to resign to defend Zionist interests at the United Nations as the ambassador from the United States, he was replaced by Abe Portas. At that time, no one anticipated that Portas would have to resign because of his connections with Las Vegas mob figures and with wheeler dealer Louis Wolfson, who later went to prison. Portas had signed an agreement with Wolfson while on the Supreme Court that he would receive $25,000 a year from Wolfson's foundation for life. The public outrage over this arrangement forced Portas to resign. His firm, Arnold, Portas and Porter, had become the most powerful Washington lobbyist. While Portas was serving on the Supreme Court, his wife took his place with the firm, bringing in many large new accounts. The firm has since dropped the Portas name from its masthead.

As part of the growing federalization of the legal system, the Supreme Court ruled that all state courts must now follow

Federal rules of evidence, whether they were in conflict with state statutes or not. This placed much greater restrictions on the crime-fighting power of state and local police, as well as state courts. The Justices had reversed traditional police procedures. Henceforth, no evidence could be presented in court if anyone in the police department had erred in any way, no matter how trivial, in gathering the evidence, even if it meant that an obviously guilty and dangerous criminal would go free. A landmark reversal in the history of criminal justice in the United States, the notorious "exclusionary rule" was applied in the court's Mallory decision of 1957. Mallory's seven and a half hours of detention before his arraignment was held by the Supreme Court to have violated his Constitutional right to be brought before a magistrate without "undue delay."

In 1961, the Supreme Court invaded another realm of state law by limiting the ability of local police agencies to conduct searches in quest of incriminating evidence, a domain previously held to be within the domain of state law. In 1963, the court's Gideon decision released a convicted criminal, Gideon, on the grounds that every indigent such as Gideon should have a lawyer provided and paid for by the state. This decision, although doing nothing for the great majority of law-abiding Americans, who still had to pay for their own legal representation, proved to be a great boon for the legal profession. Only one task yet remains for the Supreme Court, to outlaw any citizen from representing himself in court, or to appear without a lawyer, to continue the Supreme Court's chosen role as the Santa Claus of the legal profession.

In 1964, the Supreme Court extended the exclusionary rule by barring evidence seized during the search and seizure operations involving an automobile. In 1964, the Escobedo decision freed a convicted murderer because he had not been allowed to see counsel at the station bouse before he made a full confession to the police. In 1966, the Supreme Court decided four cases comprising Miranda v. Arizona. The court ruled that the police could not question a suspect if he demurred, and the service of a lawyer must be energetically pressed on him and financed by the state if indigent. A further ruling declared that the presence of a uniformed policeman in the station bouse psychologically acted to coerce the defendant and violated his Fifth Amendment rights. The implication of this Supreme Court ruling was that whenever a criminal was being brought into a police station, those policemen present must either strip, or absent themselves.

Not only were these rulings ludicrous; they also reflected the dedication of the social activist justices to the wellbeing of the criminal. It also reflected their active dislike and distrust of the police and for members of the law abiding public. One might say that the Supreme Court no longer bothered to conceal its commitment to the criminal, and its distaste for the bourgeois property owners of society who had been caricatured by Karl Marx and other Communists in their writings. They ruled that the police must now be handcuffed, while criminals were being given carte blanche to carry on their profession. Because of these decisions, as well as the increasing concern of the Justices for Communists, public reaction quickly surfaced in national campaigns to impeach the more notorious liberal leaders of the Court, Chief Justice Earl Warren and Justice William O. Douglas. Earl Warren had not always been known as a liberal. As a young California politician, be had a brilliant career until a family problem threatened his reputation. His father, according to researches by famed classical scholar Dr. Revilo Oliver, had been sexually abusing a number of young women who were his tenants in a shantytown in California. Several rape charges had been filed against him, and Warren realized that he must act quickly. He went to talk to his father, who was then found with his head bashed in. Dr. Oliver states unequivocally that Warren murdered his own father in order to protect his political career. He was then elected Atty. Gen. of California, but made no effort to find the murderer of his own father. The case was closed.

As Atty. Gen. of California, Earl Warren showed few liberal tendencies. He led the Committee of 100, a nativist California group, in a campaign to have all Japanese small businessmen and farmers interned after Pearl Harbor. Despite the assurances of J. Edgar Hoover and other intelligence officials that these merchants had been investigated and presented no threat, Warren and his cohorts insisted that Roosevelt intern the Japanese. Their properties were then bought for a few cents on the dollar by Warren and the members of his Committee. Land which they obtained for a few cents an acre in 1942 is now worth millions. The fortunes from this campaign not only financed Warren's later career; it also provided the financial backing for the successful Presidential campaigns of Richard Nixon and Ronald Reagan. Later elected Governor of California, Warren went to the Republican convention in 1952 with a California delegation which had been pledged to the party's nominee, Robert Taft. At the convention, Warren was promised the post of Chief Justice if he would switch to Eisenhower. It was an offer he could not refuse.

When he arrived in Washington, Warren was told that the first case on the Court's docket was a very urgent one. It was Brown v. Board of Education, the school desegregation case. Hearings on this case had begun on Dec. 13, 1952. Chief Justice Fred Vinson soon let it be known that he was prepared to uphold the longstanding ruling of Plessy v. Ferguson, which had long ago established the "separate but equal" principle for American education. Few Washington insiders believed that the arguments in favor of Brown v. Board of Education would bring any surprises. It was but one of a series of cases which the National Association for the Advancement of Colored People had routinely been bringing to the Court. However, in this case, the NAACP had been given a special fund of many millions of dollars, donated by wealthy New York Jewish families such as the Spingarns, who had run the NAACP for many years. These funds enabled the NAACP to hire many "experts," more than two hundred such witnesses, at a cost of more than ten thousand dollars a day. Other funds donated to the NAACP came from such leftwing activist groups as the CIO Political Action Committee, the majority of whose dues-paying members were white; the Anti-Defamation League of B'nai B'rith; the American Jewish Committee and the American Jewish Congress; the American Civil Liberties Union, and allied interests. In all, the NAACP came to court for Brown v. Board of Education with a war chest of ten million dollars. In contrast, the southern states who argued against Brown had only a few thousand dollars of expense funds to present their case.

Despite their massive expenditures, the NAACP millions, after some months of argument, had made little impression on the Justices. The Court had originally allotted two weeks for the hearing of Brown v. Board of Education. As it dragged on during the 1952-53 term of the Court, it became obvious that the NAACP was desperately stalling for time. No one could then envision the denouement for which the NAACP had been told to wait. A plan had been put into effect which was to change the composition of the Court, and thereby to effect a favorable decision for Brown. The defending lawyer for the states, John W. Davis, a former Presidential candidate, sent a note to his associate, Robert Fig,

> "I have never read a drearier lot of testimony than that furnished by the so-called educational and psychological experts I think it is perfectly clear from interior evidence that the witness Clark drafted the appendix which is signed by the worthy social scientists, (typical). I can only say that if that sort of guff can move any court, God save the state."

Davis was referring to the well-advertised "psychologist," Dr. Kenneth Clark, whose professor at Columbia University, Dr. Henry Garrett, was the most respected psychologist in America. Garrett stated that Clark had been none too bright as a student. Now this student was testifying before the Supreme Court as the originator of the "doll tests." He had shown both black and white dolls to a few black children, and he claimed that they had picked the white dolls in preference to the black ones. From these "tests," Clark deduced that the Negro children were suffering from an inferiority complex, because they had picked the white dolls, and that this complex had been created in them because they could not go to school with white children. No evidence was ever presented to the Court which verified Clarks unsupported claims. However, later court cases revealed that he had deliberately falsified his testimony before the Court. He had conducted earlier tests in some northern states, where the public schools had long been integrated. It was in those integrated states that the black children had picked the white dolls! In the southern states which were not integrated, the black children had picked the black dolls. Nevertheless, Clark succeeded in placing his falsified findings before the Supreme Court.

This was not the most flagrant falsification presented to the Court in Brown v. Board of Education. The presence of the principal advocate for the plaintiff, the National Association for the Advancement of Colored People, never intimated in any way that this association was not a national association of colored people. It had been founded in 1910 by a small group of white people. Present at this meeting were John Dewey, who was to revolutionize American education on Socialist lines; Jane Adams, a lifelong Socialist; Mary White Ovington, only child of millionaire Theodore Ovington, from a well-known Abolitionist family; he owned Ovington's, the most fashionable store on New York's Fifth Avenue. Mary White Ovington was the epitome of the wealthy white liberal; although she listed herself as a Socialist in Who's Who, she resided for many years in a luxurious suite in Brooklyn's St. George Hotel. She spent her later years living on the fashionable Upper East Side of Manhattan. Also present at the founding of the NAACP were Rabbi Emil Hirschberg, Rabbi Stephen Wise, Dr. Henry Moskovitz, Lillian Wald, and Florence Kelly, who had changed her name from Weschnewetsky. Only one black was present at the founding of the NAACP, William E. B. DuBois, a lifelong Communist revolutionary who finally denounced the United States, gave up his American citizenship, and went to live in Ghana, Africa. For many years, no black was allowed to head the NAACP. Mary White Ovington was chairman of the board after its founding. Albert Spingam, of a wealthy Jewish family, was president from 1911 to 1940. He was succeeded by his brother, Joel Spingarn, a wealthy newspaper publisher who lived like royalty in a huge mansion. He also founded the publishing firm of Harcourt Brace. Joel became treasurer of the NAACP, his brother Arthur serving as president from 1940 until his death in 1971. The NAACP was the personal preserve of the Spingarn family from its inception until 1971. Even while the NAACP was arguing Brown v. Board of Education before the Supreme Court, the Justices never knew that no black person had ever served as president of the NAACP.

Walter White, secretary of the NAACP from 1931 to 1955, was described in Current Biography in 1942, "It is only through his own insistence on his negro blood (estimated by E. A. Hooten at about V64th) that anyone would ever take him for a negro. He has fair skin, blue eyes, and blond hair." The official report of the Communist Party's 4th national convention stated that the Party had "penetrated" the NAACP. Florence Kelly, or Weschnewetsky, a personal friend of Engels and Lenin, was on its board of directors, as was Felix Frankfurter. The field secretary, William Pickens, also a Socialist Party member, was active in Communist affairs.

The most interesting name among the founders of the NAACP in 1910 was that of Dr. Henry Moskovitz. His wife, Belle Moskovitz, was one of the most influential Democratic Party leaders in New York. She also had been a secret director of the Communist Party for years. "The Red Network" lists a Dr. Moshewitz as Communist Party central committee; this is believed to be another spelling for the name of Dr. Henry Moskowitz. Belle Moskovitz ran Gov. Al Smith's office for eight years, in alliance with Robert Moses and Judge Joseph Proskauer, the president of the American Jewish Committee.

Proskauer personally selected all judges in New York state for years. Louis Howe, Franklin D. Roosevelt's press aide, was envious of Proskauer; he said to him one day, "By God, Joe, you've gone too far; there's not a single gentile judge left in the state." Proskauer looked solemnly at him. "You know, Lou," he said, "I didn't expect to reach this goal for another five years."

Belle Moskovitz, born Belle Lindner, had married a Charles Israels; when he died, she married Dr. Henry Moskovitz. Nathan Miller's biography of Roosevelt notes that on p. 200, "Moskovitz and Proskauer felt that Roosevelt, as a cripple, would be unable to interfere in their direction of the campaign. Like Al Smith, they viewed the patrician in politics with contempt, regarding Roosevelt as little more than a handsome piece of window dressing." When Roosevelt succeeded Al Smith as Governor of New York, Smith said to him, "Now Franklin, you will want Mrs. Moskovitz, of course, and I think the best thing you can do is appoint her the Governor's secretary." Belle Moskovitz was a longtime social worker, Communist Party worker, labor leader, Jewish leader, head of the Council of Jewish Women, and the Communist who inducted atomic spy Julius Rosenberg into the Communist Party. It was she who put together the liberal coalition of Jews, Communists, Socialists, and labor leaders which became Roosevelt's unbeatable political base. As head of the Progressive Party, she had nominated Oscar Straus for Governor; she was introduced to Al Smith through Abram Elkus, law partner of Judge Proskauer, and became Smith's political alter ego. She became director of publicity for the Democratic National Committee, and was given credit for the political careers of Newton Baker, Herbert Lehman, and Al Smith, but her greatest achievement was making possible the election of FDR to the Presidency. She was denied her moment of glory when she fell down the stairs and was killed, a few days before Roosevelt's inauguration. Four thousand people came to her funeral at Temple Emanuel in New York. Al Smith described her as "his alter ego."

Neither then nor later did anyone ever challenge Felix Frankfurter, a sitting justice during all of the argument on Brown v. Board of Education before the Supreme Court, as to a possible conflict of interest, because he had been a director of the NAACP for eighteen years, and was now hearing a case brought before the Supreme Court by the NAACP.

The ruling which the plaintiffs of Brown v. Board of Education sought to overturn was a well-established precedent, Plessy v. Ferguson, which laid down a guideline observed since 1894.

> "Laws permitting, or even requiring, their (racial) separation
> in places where they are liable to be brought into contact do
> not necessarily imply the inferiority of either race to the other,
> and have been generally, if not universally, received as
> written within the competency of the state legislatures in the
> exercise of their state power."

Thus the overturning of Plessy v. Ferguson required testimony and evidence which would justify the nullification of the state power to control its education and its schools. No such evidence was ever presented before the Supreme Court. Instead, a furtive conspiracy between the plaintiffs and a Justice of the Supreme Court, involving murder, resulted in the unanimous decision in favor of Brown. This conspiracy is documented in the authoritative publication, the Harvard Law Review, 1987, pp.

817 et. seq. by Felix Frankfurter's longtime law clerk and confidante, Philip Elman. In an interview about Brown v. Board of Education, Elman stated,

> "There's no question that the grand strategist in all this inside the Court was Felix Frankfurter. To use the Yiddish word that Frankfurter used at the time, he was the Kochleffel, or cooking spoon, which kept things stirred up. Frankfurter was in touch with the lawyers who won Brown, Jack Greenberg, Thurgood Marshall, William Coleman. It was a victory that changed the whole course of race relations in the United States."

Elman showed no remorse at the fact that this "victory" was won by means of conspiracy, illicit contacts between a Justice of the Supreme Court and the attorneys for the plaintiff, in which Elman was the main go between. The interviewer asked him about the obvious impropriety of this situation, "Frankfurter was receiving a government briefing almost daily from you, to which Davis (lawyer for the defense) never had a chance to reply." ELMAN. "I regarded myself, in the literal sense, as amicus curiae."

Because of his complicity in illegally participating in the Brown decision, Frankfurter's later books, essays and articles mention neither the case nor his association with the NAACP. In an article on the Scottsboro boys, as well as in other civil rights articles, be makes no mention of the fact that he was legal counsel for the NAACP. His many biographies usually omit such reference, as does his Who's Who listing. "Justice Felix Frankfurter and Civil Liberties," by Clyde A. Jacobs, Univ. Cal. 1961, omits any mention of Frankfurter's position with the NAACP, or of Brown, Although one would suppose this would be central to the material from which the title was derived. Philip Kurland's book, "Felix Frankfurter" also "neglects" to mention the NAACP or Brown. Helen Shirley Thomas book, "Felix Frankfurter" confines the association to five words on p. 21, "Felix Frankfurter, legal adviser to NAACP." Liva Baker's biography, "Felix Frankfurter," p. 310, notes that Frankfurter was "legal counsel for the NAACP." Baker also makes the startling

THE RAPE OF JUSTICE

admission that "There was no doubt about where Felix Frankfurter stood; he had but one course to take on segregation."

Thus an "impartial" Justice hearing a case on segregation left no doubt about where he stood. And what about the arguments before the Court? How did they affect the decision? Elman leaves us in no doubt about that. In his interview, he states that the judges had already made up their mind. "Oral argument made no difference in their decision. In Brown, nothing that the lawyers said made a difference. Thurgood Marshall could have stood up and recited "Mary had a little lamb," and the result would have been exactly the same." However, the principal evidence impeaching both Frankfurter and the Court's decision in favor of Brown is the record of Frankfurter's eighteen year association with the NAACP, which both he and his biographers have tried to conceal. In "The Brandeis-Frankfurter Connection: the Secret Political Activities of Two Justices," Oxford 1982, B. A. Murphy notes p. 201, "In 1930, Felix Frankfurter organized a crack legal staff for the NAACP to litigate against segregation throughout society." Although Frankfurter publicly resigned all of his numerous political affiliations when he was appointed to the Supreme Court by FDR in 1939, including the NAACP, be continued to direct the legal staff of the NAACP from behind the scenes, as he had done for many years. During World War II, Frankfurter had one of his proteges, William D. Hastie, the dean of Howard Law School in Washington, appointed by Secretary of War Henry Stimson, a key member of the Brotherhood of Death, as a special assistant on Negro problems in the armed services. Frankfurter also had Stimson appoint as his two special assistants in the War Department two other Frankfurter proteges, Harvey Bundy and John J. McCloy. Murphy states that this was done "to provide Frankfurter with an indispensable means for influencing War Department policy." Why would a Supreme Court Justice need to influence War Dept. policy at the height of the Second World War? Because Frankfurter, a Viennese immigrant who had succeeded FDR's mentor, Bella Moscovitz, as commander of the secret Harold Ware cell of Soviet agents in the government in Washington, needed to direct our war strategy in favor of its principal goal, the rescue of the Soviet Union from attack by the German armies. Murphy states that Frankfurter served as a constant intermediary between Stimson and FDR throughout the war.

Throughout FDR's long regime, Frankfurter continuously placed his proteges in key government positions. Secretary of the Interior Ickes notes in his Diary, March 24, 1933 that he had appointed Margold as Assistant Secretary of the Interior "after advising with Dr. Felix Frankfurter." He explains that Margold had been serving as "special counsel for the NAACP."

It was necessary for Frankfurter to avoid any mention of his eighteen year association with the NAACP during the Court's hearing of Brown because he had personally organized, selected and trained the lawyers who were arguing the case. He had inaugurated the NAACP's campaign of litigation against segregation; each of the lawyers appearing before him was his personal protege; and another protege, Elman, was secretly serving as amicus curiae for Brown. This documented evidence proves that Brown was illegally decided through improper contact with attorneys, conspiracy to obstruct justice, and is invalid. As there is no statute of limitations on conspiracy, the Court's decision in Brown v. Board of Education, now stands invalid, returning the situation to the rule of Plessy v. Ferguson, maintaining "separate but equal" schools. Every racially integrated school in the United States, whether public or private, is now operating illegally.

Elman's Harvard Law Review interview also recounts the exact wording of Frankfurter when Elman met him at Union Station after the news of Vinson's heart attack. Elman says that Frankfurter stated "happily" and "sarcastically," "I'm in mourning. Phil, this is the first solid piece of evidence I've ever had that there really is a God." Elman also reveals that Frankfurter had code names for each of his fellow justices, which demonstrate his utter contempt and hatred for them; his private name for Justice Stanley Reed was Chamer, the Yiddish word for "fool."

Elman also expresses distaste for Dr. Kenneth Clark's testimony in Brown about his doll tests. "He trivialized the basic truth and opened himself and the NAACP to ridicule. John Davis was the lawyer for South Carolina. And he demolished the doll test. He cited an article by Clark, 'Racial identity and Preference in Negro Culture,' 1947, in which Clark stated they had given this test not only to black kids in southern states, but also to black kids in northern states, and the strange result was that the southern kids were significantly less likely to reject the white doll than the northern kids."

Elman also attributes Warren's use of the phrase, "with all deliberate speed" to integrate the schools in the Brown decision to Frankfurter. He states that it was originally quoted by Holmes from Francis Thompson's poem, "The Hound of Heaven," and that Frankfurter liked it so much that he quoted it in three of his decisions.

Thus we have a Supreme Court decision which changed the educational system throughout the United States, arrived at by the murder of one Chief Justice and his replacement by Earl Warren, who placed himself totally in Frankfurter's bands. We had an amicus curiae for Brown who was Frankfurter's law clerk, advising a staff of lawyers arguing for Brown who had been handpicked and trained by Frankfurter at the NAACP "to litigate against segregation." No other case ever heard by the Supreme Court so reeks of conspiracy, illegal activities, improper contamination of a Supreme Court Justice, and absolute nullification of the subsequent decision by these documented factors.

The academic argument for Brown and the NAACP was provided by a voluminous "scholarly" work, "The American Dilemma," by a Swedish Socialist, Gunnar Myrdal. Both Myrdal and his wife Alva were longtime Rockefeller Fellows. She served as a member of the Swedish Parliament, was a director of UNESCO, and a member of many United Nations organizations. She and her husband had toured the United States in 1929 and 1930 as Rockefeller Fellows, where they developed a deep-rooted contempt for native American workers. Gunnar Myrdal spent from 1938 to 1942 working on "An American Dilemma"; he was funded by the Carnegie Foundation, which was run by the Rockefeller interests as a subsidiary of the Rockefeller Foundation. The book, some 1483 pages, was published in 1944 by Harper Bros. New York. Carnegie had been headed for many years by Frederick Keppel, a director of Equitable Life and Guaranty Trust, the bank which had sought throughout the 1920sto increase American funding and recognition of the Soviet regime. Carnegie had also funded Lord Hailey's "An African Survey" and had given millions of dollars to Tuskegee and Hampton Institutes. Myrdal had also spent a year in the United States as a Fellow of the Laura Spelman Rockefeller Fund. With Keppel on the staff of Carnegie at this time were Ralph Bunche, named as a Communist Party member; M. F. Ashley Montague, a tireless Communist propagandist; Eugene Horowitz; Herbert Goldhamer; Melville Herskovitz; Edward Shils; and Benjamin Malzberg.

"An American Dilemma," which was never read by any of the Justices, reeked of Myrdal's contempt for native born Southern white citizens. On p. 563, we read,

> "The low level of education and general culture in the white South is another important background factor Another important background factor in the causation of lynching and other major forms of violence is the isolation, the dullness of everyday life, and the general boredom of rural and small town life in the South." Myrdal then excoriates the people as "narrowminded, intolerant, evangelistic." He writes with disapproval of their "evangelistic religion."

On p. 565, Myrdal writes approvingly of "the growing strength of Southern liberalism." On p. 582, be writes "there is a great class of Southern whites who are also poor, uneducated, coarse and dirty." One can envision the fastidious Myrdal recoiling in horror from the "dirty white Southerners." As an elitist and beneficiary of the Rockefeller billions, it must have been an ordeal for him to travel for four years in the South for his research on "the American Negro problem." The problem is not the Negro at all, but the coarse and dirty white Southerners. On p. 597, be writes of "the lower class whites in the South," but be never uses such terminology in writing of the Negroes. He also followed the Communist Party line by including several pages of vehement denunciations of police statistics on Negro crime. One wonders what Myrdal would make of the front page of the

Washington Post, which daily recounts the staggering incidence of Negro crime, which has made our a nation's capital the crime capital of the world. Had the Justices or the attorneys for the Southern school systems ever bothered to glance at the 1483 pages of "An American Dilemma," they would have been shocked at its rabid bias against the South and its white citizens. Yet this book was cited as a principal influence on the final decision of the Supreme Court in favor of the plaintiff in Brown v. Board of Education! This evidence, which was never argued before the Court, actually impeached its own goal. Why would black children be improved by being forced to attend school with "coarse and dirty Southern whites?" Perhaps it was a subtle ploy to aid Southern whites by giving them the opportunity to associate with immaculate, well-spoken and highly intelligent and motivated black children.

The 1952-53 session of the Supreme Court closed with no decision announced on Brown v. Board of Education. It was then scheduled to be carried over to the next session. However, the anticipated outcome was never in doubt. Justice Reed and others in the know stated that they expected Chief Justice Vinson to uphold Plessy v. Ferguson, ruling against any racial integration of the schools. John W. Davis, lawyer for the defending Southern states, announced that there would be a 6-3 decision against Brown v. Board of Education. The ruling was expected shortly after the opening of the fall term. On June 5, 1953, the five segregation cases before the Court were redocketed for Oct. 12, 1953 re-argument. Washington observers expected a short hearing, and that Vinson would then issue the 6-3 ruling against Brown. This had already been established by Internal memoranda of the Court.

This opinion was never issued; at 3:15 A.M. on Sept. 8, 1953, Chief Justice Vinson died suddenly of a heart attack in his suite at the exclusive Wardman Park Hotel. Only 63 years old, and enjoying robust health, Vinson had shown no sign of any health problems. It was but one more of those strange "government heart attacks" which have played such an important role in major policy decisions. Despite their shock at his sudden death, Washington insiders saw no reason to change their expectation that the NAACP would still lose the segregation cases, perhaps on a 5-4 ruling instead of the anticipated 6-3. Nevertheless, a few of the protagonists greeted the news of Vinson's death as "a day of liberation." Justice Frankfurter, on being informed of his longtime colleague's death, chortled gleefully, "This is the first indication I've ever had that there really is a God." He was referring to the Canaanite god, Baal, the agent of Lucifer, who apparently had been summoned to dispose of Chief Justice Vinson. Years passed before Frankfurter himself was revealed as the secret head of the influential, Harold Ware Communist cell in Washington. At the death of Bella Moscovitz, Frankfurter had inherited her leadership of the Communist agents in the Roosevelt Administration. At the same time that Frankfurter was serving on the Supreme Court, his brother, Otto Frankfurter, was serving a long sentence in the Anamosa State Prison of Iowa. On Oct. 5, 1953, President Eisenhower announced that he had named Earl Warren to replace Justice Vinson as Chief Justice. It was immediately noted that Warren, a newcomer to Washington, had placed himself in Frankfurter's bands. There was still no indication that the new appointment would change the expected ruling on Brown. Arguments in the case were desultorily resumed, but months went by, with the case still in limbo. Washington journalists still expected a brief announcement that a decision had been made against Brown. On May 17, 1954, at 12:52 P.M., with no prior notice, Chief Justice Warren began reading the Court's decision in Brown v. Board of Education. He first stated that all of the evidence presented by the NAACP had been "inconclusive," which seemed to verify the fact that Brown had lost. However, Warren then stated, AS A UNANIMOUS DECISION OF THE COURT,

> "We conclude that in the field of public education, the doctrine of 'separate but equal' has no place. Therefore, we hold that the plaintiffs and others similarly situated, for whom the actions have been brought, are, by reason of the segregation complained of, deprived of the equal protection of the laws guaranteed by the 14th Amendment In view of our decision that the Constitution prohibits the states from maintaining racially segregated schools, it would be

unthinkable that the same Constitution would impose a lesser
duty on the Federal Government."

Warren's statement that the Constitution prohibits "racially
segregated schools" went beyond the scope of the arguments of
the NAACP; the Constitution actually said nothing on the matter.
The decision unleashed chaos throughout public education in the
United States. The amazing ruling, even more amazing because
it was unanimous, instead of the long-anticipated 6 to 3 ruling
against Brown, was based on no legally acceptable evidence.
Clark's doll manipulations and Myrdal's vicious denunciations
of white Southerners were "evidence" which would have been
laughed out of most courts. Rumors immediately began to
circulate that Vinson had been "disposed or' in order to end his
opposition to a ruling in favor of Brown. His son, Fred Vinson (a
classmate of the present writer at Washington and Lee
University), also died suddenly while at the Department of
Justice.

Kenneth's Clark's "evidence," later revealed to have been
distorted, still threatened the validity of the Supreme Court
ruling. NAACP lawyer Jack Greenberg then took a desegregation
case before the Fifth Circuit Court of Appeals for a prearranged
decision, as follows,

> "We reiterate that no inferior federal court may refrain from
> acting as required by the Supreme Court in the (1954) Brown
> decision, even if such a court should conclude that the
> Supreme Court erred as to its facts or to the law."

This amazing ruling tried to dictate that Brown could never
be overturned, even if it were proved to be in error, as was the
case. However, in a later case, Evers v. Jackson Ms. Municipal
School District, 232 F. Supp. 241, 1964, Fed. Judge Sidney Mize
noted,

> "In this case, the evidence as to racial differences is of such
> significance as to reasonably require the separation of school
> children for educational purposes is overwhelming,
> undisputed and unchallenged. In the opinion of this court, the
> facts in this case point up a most serious situation, and indeed,
> cry out for a reappraisal and complete review of the findings

and conclusions of the U.S. Supreme Court in the 1954 Brown decision."

Washington insiders now concluded that Chief Justice Vinson had indeed been murdered as part of a sinister plot to force racially integrated schools on all Americans by the use of armed troops. Earl Warren became Governor of California through one murder, and Chief Justice of the United States through another.

Justice Felix Frankfurter was never criticized for the fact that he had been a director of the NAACP at the time he ruled in their favor. Nor did he reveal that he had personally selected the attorneys for the NAACP, Jack Greenberg, a longtime associate, and Thurgood Marshall. Marshall was then named to the Supreme Court himself, where he failed to disqualify himself in the long procession of racially sensitive cases before the Court. Loyal to the end, he always voted for his employers, the NAACP.

In 1987, the Harvard Law Review reported "a stunning fact" about the Supreme Court's milestone ruling in Brown vs. Board of Education "which declared racially segregated public schools to be unconstitutional; Justice Felix Frankfurter had secret, improper, and unethical contacts with a lawyer for the plaintiff, with a view to engineering a victory for that side. He succeeded." Detroit Free Press, Mar. 29, 1987. The editorial commented that had it been known, "Frankfurter would have been impeached, removed from the bench, and ruined." In fact, Frankfurter's association of many years with Jack Greenberg and Thurgood Marshall in the NAACP is proof that a legal conspiracy was effected, and that Brown v. Board of Education is thereby totally invalidated. All persons who claim injury as a result of the forcible integration of the schools can now bring action against the government, as can any school district which has been adversely affected by the ruling.·

It now seems evident that a further goal of the Brown v. Board of Education decision was to destroy the rapidly growing and independent black middle class throughout the United States. A black elite, composed primarily of ministers and educators, had succeeded in raising the standards of blacks in many areas, threatening the traditional plantation system by which Communist revolutionaries such as Frankfurter and wealthy white liberals as Mary White Ovington used black citizens for their own ulterior purposes. Thus blacks have as much reason to sue the government for damages resulting from the Brown v. Board of Education as whites, if not more so. Pleasant black residential neighborhoods are now drug tormented, crime-ridden areas in which no one is safe; neither stable family life nor an effective educational system is possible. The Brown ruling was recalled in the *Washington Post*, April 22, 1989, in an interview with Charles Lofton. Lofton had been principal of the black elite high school, Dunbar High School, which produced many black leaders in the Washington area. He commented that

> "I had more influence on my students in the segregated environment They used us as role models. I was at Dunbar when integration came in and-it knocked us out. We had been getting the cream of the crop, but with integration, students had to go to schools in their zones. I lost some of my finest teachers, because there was just not the same demand for subjects such as Latin or advanced calculus. Partly as a result of integration, our children do not have as positive a sense of self. We have lost a whole generation, the generation from sixteen to thirty-two, and we're never going to get it back."

The calculated destruction of the black elite has made possible the total government control of the black population. The dedicated black teachers and ministers have been pushed aside, replaced as role models by drug pushers and political demagogues. One black educator mourned that "We now realize that a terrible crime has been committed. An entire generation of black youth has been deliberately tossed onto the scrap heap by false leadership which has left the black community disorganized and without hope." Black leaders are also concerned about an apparent campaign to eliminate the entire black population in Africa through the deliberate inoculation of AIDS, and by famine and starvation. The Dark Continent can then be returned to the Rothschilds and to the tender ministrations of Global 2000, as a largely uninhabited area rich in natural resources, which can be plundered at leisure. After Brown, Chief Justice Earl Warren found that his most consistent supporter on the liberal Court was Justice William O. Douglas. In a later desegregation case, Douglas delivered the amazing opinion that "No one has a right to attend a segregated public school." Due to his continuous pursuit of young women, Douglas soon began to exhibit serious signs of mental and physical degeneration. He became increasingly paranoid, claiming that listening devices had been planted in his offices; he sometimes asked lawyers to step out into the hall to carry on conversations. He endured more criticism when he married again, in the well-advertised "case of the child bride." A *New York Times* story of Aug. 21, 1988 cited J. Edgar Hoover's opinion of Justice Douglas, as revealed in FBI files, "Of course, Douglas is crazy and is not in too good health." During years of senile degeneration, be continued to occupy his seat on the Supreme Court. His writings were a continuing puzzle to clerks and other officials of the Court. In "The Brethren," we are told, p. 243, "Former clerks were called regularly for dues to the meaning of Douglas' notes and his frequently incomplete references to old cases; his sentences were almost a private code, their meanings evident only to him." The book goes to discuss Douglas' continuing incontinence, which caused his family to ask him to resign. He indignantly replied, "No! There will be no one on the Court who cares for blacks, Chicanos, defendants, and the environment." Despite their increasing aggravation at Douglas' presence, protocol prevented the other Justices from filing complaints about him. He had long since lost control of his lower body functions, and the continuous noxious odors arising from his chair sometimes caused his fellow Justices to become physically ill.

At the time the segregation decision was announced, blacks occupied all of the low level service and maintenance jobs at the Supreme Court. There was not a single black secretary in the entire building. Court personnel were routinely ordered to do personal work on their own time for the Justices, such as taking oriental rugs to the cleaners, shopping, and going across the city on other errands. The Court was exempt from civil service laws, and employees could be fired immediately, with no appeal. Numerous work hazards existed throughout the building; the black service personnel worked on rickety scaffolds, sometimes resulting in serious injury. The great bronze doors were regularly cleaned and polished with hydrochloric acid, whose use had long been outlawed in American industry.

After Douglas' death, Justice Thurgood Marshall represented the most liberal bias of the Court. A protege of Zionist Justice Brandeis, be had been a member of the ACLU for many years, studied at the obligatory New York version of the Lenin School, the New School for Social Research, and served as special counsel for the NAACP from 1937, when he was personally approved by Felix Frankfurter, until 1961. He delivered a stinging denunciation of the Constitution in a recent speech. Rumor is rife in Washington that be suffers from Alzheimer's. An article by Dept. of Justice attorney Terry Eastland in the National Review, April 21, 1989, "While Justice Sleeps," notes that Marshall sleeps through oral arguments, and spends much of his time in the Court building watching television situation comedies; a favorite is "I Love Lucy." He lets clerks write his opinions, and told Life Magazine, anent petitions, 'I ain't giving no break to no drug dealer! Disgusting!' Although the Supreme Court renders 130 opinions each year, Marshall is only assigned fifteen. He refuses to retire, and vainly hoped that the Democrats would win in 1988, so that another liberal could be appointed in his stead.

In *The Brethren*, Marshall is described as being overweight, drinking too much, eating too much, and thoroughly soured on his work. He has had one heart attack, from which he has never fully recovered, but still refuses to retire until a Democratic President has been elected.

The history of the Supreme Court reveals a steady retreat from its assigned role of protecting the legal rights of all American citizens. In 1833, the Court ruled that the Bill of Rights provided only protection against federal authority, but not against state action. In Barron v. Baltimore, the city was sued because it had impaired the value of the plaintiff's property. Barron claimed this was taking his property without due compensation, and thereby violated the Fifth Amendment. Chief Justice Marshall ruled that the Bill of Rights only secured against "apprehended encroachment of the general government-not against those of the local governments." Marshall's ruling has never been reversed, although it was superseded by the three Civil War Amendments, the 13th, 14th and 15th. On restrictive covenants, the Court dismissed Corrigan v. Buckley in 1926, effectively upholding restrictive covenants. Twenty-two years later, the Court effectively nullified restrictive covenants by forbidding the state to enforce them. Chief Justice Vinson ruled in Shelley v. Kraemer and McGee v. Sepes, 1948, with three justices abstaining,

> "We hold that in granting judicial enforcement of the restrictive agreements in these cases, the States have denied petitioners the equal protection of the laws, and that, therefore, the action of the state courts cannot stand."

In 1989, the Court hesitated somewhat in its heretofore upholding of affirmative action cases, by stating that "a person cannot be deprived of his legal rights in a proceeding to which he is not a party." This seemed to end the era of class actions in which rulings affecting large groups of Americans had been routinely handed down, even though most of them had never been a party to the action.

In 1945, the Court vainly attempted to stem the rapidly growing monopolization of the media by ruling that "The First Amendment presupposes that the widest possible dissemination of information from diverse and antagonistic sources is essential to the welfare of the public." This decision was later used as the basis for a 1978 Court decision which prevented daily newspaper owners from buying radio and television stations in the same cities as their newspapers, and thereby establishing a media monopoly. The decision seems to have had little effect in preventing media moguls from expanding their empires. It was recently predicted that within the next decade, four giant corporations will control all of the world's communications.

The Supreme Court ruled in Totten v. U.S., 92 U.S., that "public policy forbids the maintenance of any suit in a court of justice, the trial of which would inevitably lead to the disclosure of matters which the law itself regards as confidential, or respecting which it will not allow the confidence to be violated." This would seem to guarantee personal privacy, but it has not restrained judges from routinely ordering all personal papers and records to be turned over to the opposing party in general lawsuits.

The considerable Masonic direction of the Supreme Court throughout its history was documented in 1988 by Paul A. Fisher's book, "Behind the Lodge Door." A veteran of the OSS and the Counter-Intelligence Corps, Fisher used his considerable talents for intelligence analysis to build an irrefutable case for the domination of the Court by Masons. He begins with Chief Justice Marshall, who was Grand Master of the Virginia Lodges, and documents the fact that the secret oath of the Masons has played a major role in Court decisions ever since. He notes that FDR's plan to pack the Court originated with four Masons, whom FDR subsequently appointed to the Court, Black, Byrnes, Minton and Jackson.

Another recent study shows that nine of sixteen members of the Congressional Committee on the Judiciary are Masons, showing that the continuing Masonic influence still permeates not only the Supreme Court, but the entire Judiciary. This influence extends not only to the Justices, but to their law clerks as well. In "The Brethren," we are told that the law clerks in the office of the Chief Justice exercised great power. "The way things worked in the Chief's chambers gave them tremendous influence. Warren told them how he wanted the cases to come out." so much for "impartiality." Woodward and Bernstein also quote Warren's successor, Chief Justice Burger, on Warren, "sloppy, politically motivated, interested more in results than in legal reasoning, a man without intellectual honesty."

Despite the fact that the RICO law, the Racketeer Influenced and Corrupt Organizations law enacted by Congress, has been perverted by the Department of Justice from its stated purpose of fighting organized crime to a weapon of terrorism against legitimate business, the Supreme Court recently refused to recognize this perversion. More than one thousand RICO suits are being filed each year; 93% of them have no connection with organized crime. The Wall Street Journal and other publications have repeatedly denounced this rape of justice. Nevertheless, on June 26, 1989, the Supreme Court refused to rein in the law. The Court ruled 9-0 to continue civil suits for triple damages, Although Justice Scalia admitted that the law is "so vague it violates the Constitution."

The Court now faces a challenge in its necessity of ruling whether the judiciary can impose direct taxes. U .S. District Judge Russell Clark had ordered Kansas City property taxes increased by 95% to pay the costs for forced desegregation, and ignored the will of the voters by authorizing the school district to issue $150 million of capital improvement bonds. The 8th U.S. Circuit Court of Appeals upheld the judge's arbitrary action, which clearly flouts the Constitution, and which totally abrogates Art. 1, sec. 8 by giving the courts power to tax. The Supreme Court is expected to issue a decision in the case by Oct. 1989.

Judge Clark's action is typical of the social activism in which the Supreme Court itself has taken the lead. A *Washington Post* story Dec. 28, 1988 declared "Many in Washington view it as judicial activism run wild; seven judges forcing this wealthy township, Bedminster, N.J., to build housing for the less fortunate, nearly tripling its population. Sen. Gerald Cardinale said of the justices, 'They think, like all social planners, that their view of society is superior to everyone else's. The court is destroying the democratic process.' For years, the N.J. Supreme Court has been headed by Chief Justice Robert Wilentz, heir to the political power wielded by his father, a Democratic ward heeler and B'nai B'rith activist. David Wilentz had prosecuted Bruno Hauptmann in the Lindbergh kidnapping case. As exposed by Anthony Scaduto in his ground-breaking book, "Scapegoat," Wilentz had never before tried a criminal case of any kind; he had been appointed Attorney General by Gov. Harry Moore as a political payoff for switching the support of the B'nai B'rith Masonic power to Moore's campaign.

Wilentz determined to convict Hauptmann, despite the lack of evidence. He rounded up a group of witnesses who were willing to commit perjury, bolstering their incredible testimony with crudely manufactured "evidence." Wilentz' principal witness was 87 year old Amandus Hochmuth, who testified that Hauptmann had driven up to him on the day of the kidnapping and inquired the way to the Lindbergh residence. Social Security records proved that Hochmuth was not only legally blind from cataracts, but was also hopelessly senile. Wilentz also withheld from the jury the Reliance Property Mgmt. paybook which proved that at the time of the kidnapping, Hauptmann was working in New York! When J. Edgar Hoover was informed of Wilentz' activities, he indignantly ordered all FBI agents to withdraw from the case. He refused to have the Bureau's work contaminated by such crude perjury; Hoover also expected the roof to fall in on Wilentz when his conspiracy was exposed. Hoover remarked to his associate, Clyde Tolson, "I don't know if Hauptmann will ever go to jail, but I'm damned sure Wilentz will." In fact, with the B'nai B'rith power behind him, Wilentz succeeded in having Hauptmann convicted and electrocuted. For years, his widow, Anna Hauptmann, worked to have the frameup exposed, but she was jeered at by the entrenched powers of the media and the legal system.

Wilentz typified the unbridled arrogance of the judiciary who daily wield their power in our courts. The Associated Press noted Dec. 29, 1988, that a Ft. Lauderdale judge, J. Leonard Fleet, routinely sentences lawyers who displease him or who are late coming to court, or even if their mode of dress offends him. He orders them to go to a supermarket and buy food for the poor. Again, this is social activism and has nothing to do with the administration of justice. However, it is typical of the rape of justice.

The Portland Me. Press Herald recently decried the practice of retired federal judges drawing full pay, even though they no longer hear any cases. It cited former Chief Justice Warren Burger, who receives $115,000 a year. The editorial noted that twenty per cent of all senior judges draw full pay, even though they do no work. However, in view of the omnipresent acts of judicial tyranny, it might be better if we retired all of them. The Yonkers case, which was headlined daily in the press throughout 1988, typified the judicial dictatorship which now terrifies our people. Federal Judge Leonard Sand personally decided that the city of Yonkers, the fourth largest city in New York, was not doing enough to "wipe out racial discrimination." He ordered the city to build one thousand new units for blacks in residential neighborhoods in which substantial racial integration had taken place. After residents opposed the order, he imposed $500 a day fines on three Yonkers city councilmen and a fine of one million dollars a day against the city itself. The judge resided in Chappaqua, a wealthy white suburb north of Yonkers. Columnist Pat Buchanan wrote,

> "What is happening in Yonkers is an outrage. A Harvard educated dictator in black robes, elected by no one, is ordering the fourth largest city in New York, against the will of its people and elected officials, to spend millions of tax dollars building public housing it doesn't want or need, in areas Sand alone will determine. If Yonkers refuses, the Judge will destroy the city financially, and jail its elected officials. Will someone explain to me what exactly George III did to our forefathers to compare to that?"

British troops who tried to enforce a decree as dictatorial as Judge Sand's would have been met with armed rebellion. The hidden explanation of Judge Sand's action, as the present writer explained in *The World Order*, is that every public official has a secret agenda to aggravate and increase racial tensions by every means possible, in order to provoke a raging conflict, and provide the excuse for active government repression against all groups. The minorities continue to be helpless pawns in this obvious but never openly stated program.

The Supreme Court again maddened the populace with its July Fourth approval of the desecration of the flag. One Joey Johnson, a New Yorker who echoes the staunchest tenets of Leninism, claimed that "the flag is a symbol of oppression, international murder and plunder of a sick and dying empire." He was then arrested in Texas for publicly burning the flag. The Supreme Court, in Texas v. Johnson, ruled 5-4 that burning the flag was a free speech exercise which was protected by the First Amendment as a political statement. The front page of the *Washington Post* headlined "Court Nullifies Flag Desecration Law." Just below it was another feature story, "Soviet U.S. Becoming Partners." The majority of the Justices ruled that conviction for flag-burning was not consistent with the First Amendment. Justice Stevens dissented, "The value of the flag as a symbol cannot be measured. The court is therefore quite wrong." Chief Justice Rehnquist noted,

"(The flag) has come to be the visible symbol embodying our nation. Millions of Americans regard it with an almost mystical reverence regardless of what sort of social, political or philosophical beliefs they may have."

Pat Buchanan wrote another stinging column about the flag burning decision. On July 6, 1989, he stated,

"For 30 years a despotic court has been writing into our Constitution, and law, its own arid ideology, its own prejudice, its own view of how a rational society should govern itself, casting aside as so much trash the deepest sentiments, traditions, beliefs of the American people, all of the accumulated wisdom of the race A predominantly Christian people has had yoked upon it an alien, secularist concept of the good society.

... America today is two countries, with values in conflict. Where they celebrate raucous dissent, we tolerate it. Where they believe the marketplace of ideas must remain open to all sentiments, no matter how pernicious, seditious, or disgusting, we believe there are limits to the toxicity of the moral pollution a democratic Republic can stand We have had enough judge-made law."

CHAPTER 6

THE COURT AS ARENA

Accoording to legend, the "court" originally referred to the courtyard of King Solomon's palace, where disputes were heard when the weather permitted. In mediaeval times, the "court" was the poultry yard, where chickens were allowed to run free and peck at worms. 1377 Lengl. P.P.O.B. vx 466 "Just as Capones in a court come to mannes whistlynge." Court also referred to the enclosures which surrounded the Jewish tabernacle. Later, it became known as the place where the sovereign or other high dignitary resided and held state, attended by his retinue. 1480 Caxton Descr. Eng. 17, "The messengers of Rome came to the grete Arthur's court."

The court is the arena where civil procedure takes its course. The basis of all civil procedure in the United States is the relentless application of the ancient legal maxim, "Fry the pig in his own fat." This means that the parties in a legal dispute are maneuvered by their lawyers and by orders from the judge to step into the pan and sizzle until they have been reduced to a passel of bones. The rendered fat is then divided up between the avaricious lawyers and the participating judicial authorities. If you are an American citizen worth some $300,000 in personalty, you may decide to enter into litigation to recover a debt, damages from an injury, or other payment to which you believe you are legally entitled. Until they step into the quicksand, most Americans look upon litigation as a comparatively simple matter. They engage an attorney for a reasonable fee, he presents the facts to a judge, perhaps before a jury; the opposing party recites his version of the facts, and a decision is rendered, with a judicial order for payment. The lawyer will then deduct his fees, and the litigant returns home with his collection.

The usual outcome is a far cry from these developments. Instead of collecting what is due him, the citizen with $300,000 in personalty may find that not only has his net worth vanished, but that he now owes his lawyer an additional $50,000, plus counterclaims advanced against him by the opposing party which have been allowed by the court, and that even now, officials are on his way to his home to evict him. Is this justice? Of course not. It is the law merchant in action, in which all legal realities are transformed into legal fictions. At any time during litigation, a plaintiff may be hit with minor fines, arbitrary jail sentences, and other misfortunes, while his original goal of collecting moneys due him now recedes into the distance, never to be realized.

The first ventures of the present writer into our halls of justice, some forty years ago, were marked by total ignorance of the details of the judicial process. Like most Americans, I naively supposed that if you had a grievance, you went to court, stated your grievance, and the opposing party stated some rebuttal. The impartial judge, having listened carefully to both sides, would then deliver a fair verdict. End of case. The reality turned out to be quite different, so different that I became a courthouse habitué for some four decades, not because I was seeking entertainment, but because I kept going back to see what new outrage would be perpetrated against me. My first judge, whom I was later told had never been known to deliver an impartial verdict in his entire career, frequently turned off his hearing aid and sat in blissful silence while the sweating lawyers (this was before the era of airconditioned courtrooms) strained over every word, hoping to make an impression upon His Honor. I also learned that there was really no need for the judge to listen to the testimony, because, in the great majority of cases, his decision had been reached long before the case actually came to trial. Thus he had no reason to burden himself with the dreary chore of listening to days and hours of contradictory, and often perjured, testimony.

I also learned in short order that lawyers in most instances had no intention of seeing my complaints come to trial. Their legal maneuvers were designed solely to get rid of me, a goal in which the judge heartily concurred. As a person representing himself, on Constitutional lines, I presented a threat to the economic base of all members of the legal profession. Ninety per cent of the cases heard in our courts could be presented without any lawyer being present. The attorney pro se virus is the AIDS of the legal profession, which could decimate its ranks.

In my initial case, whenever I appeared in court, a matter of some inconvenience, as I was then residing in another state, the opposing lawyers would first register surprise, and then disapproval that I had actually arrived. They would immediately ask for another postponement. After I left the state, they would hurriedly reschedule another hearing, hoping that I would not be able to return. This charade went on for several years, and was finally dismissed under the statute of limitations.

The mysteries of civil procedure, which at that time seemed to present an impenetrable code, were finally unveiled for me by one of the most able law firms in the state. I had sued a man who had attempted to kill me (see Chapt. The Strange case of the Schizophrenic Driver). Because he had been driving illegally, it was necessary to prevent me from bringing the case to trial. The firm's members expected to make short shrift of me, but because the offender was a prominent merchant, the firm's senior partner personally took charge of the case. He began his campaign with an inquisitorial fifty-nine questions, the First Set of Interrogatories, supposing that I would either refuse to answer them and throw them aside, thus defaulting out of the case, or I would trip myself up in my answers to the extent that he could have the case dismissed. In most cases, Interrogatories, which are answered under oath, are only answered in consultation with one's attorney. A layman could hardly be expected to answer them without digging a deep hole for his case. Refusal to answer means that the opposing lawyers appear in court and request dismissal on grounds of default. Judges always grant default dismissals as a quick method of getting rid of an obnoxious attorney pro se.

Being an indefatigable writer, I answered the Interrogatories with some eighty pages of answers, using the opportunity to interpolate many events of my career to illustrate the points I was making. This led to a further imbroglio in chambers. This case lasted for some three years, during which the highly paid lawyers tried every trick in their repertoire. The result was that I received an advanced course in civil procedure which no law school could have given me.

After forty years, I analyzed the process of civil procedure, reducing it to three items which must never be ignored; 1. Answer everything. 2. Deny everything. 3. Answer on time. Refusal to answer any pre-trial discovery, no matter how intrusive it may be, is seized upon by the opponent as grounds for dismissal, which the judge usually grants. Interrogatories, Requests for Admission, and Depositions are the three sacred cows of pre-trial discovery. Although I never failed to answer them, I always filed, upon receiving demands for these procedures, Motion to Quash Interrogatories, Motion to Deny Deposition, and Motion to Deny Requests for Admission. This forced the opposing attorneys (I always faced at least two, sometimes three or four, lawyers at every session) to go before the court and request a court order. The judge seemed mystified by these motions from me, because pre-trial discovery is the bread and butter of the legal profession. In every case, the judge issued a court order that I must answer pre-trial discovery. However, my motions usually postponed the sessions for several months, adding to the steadily running meter of opposing counsel, while my meter consisted solely of turning on my electric typewriter.

I repeatedly filed objections to pre-trial discovery, pointing out, accurately on my part, that it meant that opposing counsel simply tries the case himself, without judge or jury being present. Counsel conducts lengthy examinations under oath, in a procedure which is designed solely to harass the other party, put him to great expense, and hopefully, to break him down physically to the point that he no longer realizes what he is saying. He is then likely to make a statement which will destroy his entire case. These are the same principles of the Spanish Inquisition which are used by the Internal Revenue Service and by other government agencies. You are given the third degree until you finally confess, whether you are wrong or not. The abuse of this procedure proves that it is a flagrant violation of the

Constitutional prohibition against bills of attainder. The purpose of pre-trial discovery is to place you under a court-ordered bill of attainder, so that you must "taint" yourself, make some damaging admission, and testify against yourself in violation of the Fifth Amendment against self-incrimination. Ah, says the legal expert, but you are talking about civil procedure; the Fifth Amendment is only concerned with criminal procedure in which a citizen accused of a crime is protected against self-incrimination. However, if the Fifth Amendment protects one from testifying against oneself in a criminal charge, it is equally Constitutional that the same protection is extended to a citizen testifying in a civil case. The Fifth Amendment specifies that "nor shall be compelled in any criminal case to be a witness against himself." This amendment extends a specific protection against self-incrimination; it does not state that any citizen shall be compelled to testify against himself in a civil action, although its language in this instance mentions only criminal cases.

Art. I sec. 10 specifically states "No State shall pass any Bill of Attainder," yet state judges have repeatedly, over a period of forty years, issued orders compelling me to submit to inquisitorial pre-trial discovery for the sole purpose of attainting myself and my complaint, in a flagrant Bill of Attainder. The judges can do this because they are presiding over an Admiralty Court, and the law merchant does not prohibit bills of attainder. Under Admiralty procedure, an American citizen has no Constitutional safeguards, hence the judges freely granted Bills of Attainder against me. The Fourth Amendment guarantees "The right of the people to be secure in their persons, bouses, papers and effects, against unreasonable searches and seizures," yet I was repeatedly ordered to turn over all of my personal papers, photographs, financial records, tax forms for periods of from twenty to thirty-five years, to the opposing counsel so that they might turn up some damaging material to be used against me in the process of self-incrimination. Under the law merchant, the judges used admiralty procedure to order me to "stand and deliver," the time-honored phrase of the British highway robber, forcing me to turn over my property to the bandits.

The three principles which I developed as "Mullins' law," bear some elaboration. The first, "Answer everything," means just that. Refusal to answer means a dismissal of your case and sanctions, both financial and penitential, will be issued against you. However, in representing myself, I found that opposing parties almost universally refused to answer my interrogatories, or marked each question, "Not relevant"; their attorney had previously obtained guarantees from the judge that, because I was an attorney pro se, no sanctions would be ordered against his client. However, this is a flagrant dodge which you must never use in representing yourself, because sanctions will be ordered against you. If you don't like the question, such as "What is the color of your hair?", you may answer, "Even my hairdresser doesn't know for sure," and expound on this at some length, going into the reasons your grandfather left the old country, and why homesteading has lost its appeal in recent years. The answer should be held to less than 1500 words.

The second maxim, "Deny everything," is more crucial. Few Americans are aware that our court system functions on total duplicity. Everything in the judicial process is designed to trick the opponent. You may see no harm in answering a question with a straightforward answer which apparently does not imperil your case, but the attorney will eventually use it against you. Admit only your name.

The third principle, answer on time, is also part of the legal quagmire. A day late means that you are out of your case. Most Americans suppose that a judge will be lenient, and allow a day late in answering. This will never happen if you are representing yourself, although judges habitually extend all sorts of delays to their fellow attorneys. The least error by an attorney pro se will bring the judge down against him, dismissing his complaint. Despite the best efforts of their secretaries, lawyers frequently fail to answer on time, because they are by nature lazy and shiftless. In cities where a comfortable Masonic brotherhood creates a bond between the judge and the lawyer, such failures may result in a mild reprimand, or none at all. Lawyers are also frequently late in appearing to argue motions or for court appearances, and sometimes fail to appear at all. This too is usually met with mild amusement or a forgiving gesture from the judge. In like instances, attorneys pro se usually have their cases dismissed out of hand.

The problem of using the designation, attorney pro se, which the present writer has used for many years, is that it is defined in Black's Law Dictionary as "For Himself," which could mean that he is appearing as another person who appears "for himself." Black's also defines it as "in person," which seems adequate. Purists prefer the appellation "In Propria Personae," which according to Black's, is "In one's own proper person." In either case, you become the attorney of record. And whichever you use, your primary problem is not what you call yourself, but the fact that you are appearing in an admiralty court which denies you the protection of the Constitution.

The legal profession has set up generous protection standards for one who wishes to represent himself. The Standards Relating to Trial Courts, American Bar Assn Commission on Standards of Judicial Administration, 1976, sec. 2.23. Conduct of cases where litigant appeared without counsel.

> "When a litigant undertakes to represent himself, the court should take whatever measures may be reasonable and be necessary to insure a fair trial."

I have never met any judge or attorney who had read that particular recommendation.

On May 27, 1977, Chief Justice Warren Burger addressed the American Bar Association,

> "In the federal courts the right of self-representation has been protected by statute since the beginnings of our nation. Sec. 35 of the Judiciary Act of 1789, 1 Stat. 73, 92, enacted by the First Congress, and signed by President Washington, one day before the Fifth Amendment was proposed, provided that in all the courts of the United States, the parties may plead and manage their own causes, personally, or by the assistance of counsel. The right is currently codified in 28 USC Sec. 1654."

The decisions of the admiralty court frequently fly in the face of common sense, as well as law, because of the havoc created by illogical judicial pronunciamentos whose real purpose is part of the program of the hidden government. Thus Judge Charles Wohlstetter, chairman of Contel Corp., describes the judicial breakup of American Telephone and Telegraph as "Probably the most stupid and damaging decision that has ever been made in the history of business in any country." It has been suggested that Soviet prestige was constantly affected by its backward telephone system, while the United States had the best telephone system in the world. The judicial decision was that we must give up our smoothly functioning telephone system because it was a "monopoly," and break it up into inefficient smaller units, which would hopefully be as inefficient and backward as the Soviet telephone system. Many dissatisfied customers believe that objective has now been reached.

The Constitution plainly states, Art. 1, Sc. 10 that "No State shall pass Law impairing the Obligation of Contracts." Why was it necessary to place this prohibition in the Constitution? To "promote the general welfare" through business stability. However, the liberal Holmesian school now claims that contracts are "only words," which can mean whatever one wishes them to mean, and therefore cannot be upheld. In 1968, the California Supreme Court ruled in Pacific Gas & Electric vs. G. W. Thomas Drayage & Rigging that Although there was a clear indemnification provision in a contract, words didn't settle the matter. Chief Justice Traynor rejected the common law notion that parties must be free to negotiate among themselves, observing that individuals can use words that is, contracts-to allocate risks and rewards, is an old view which is "a remnant of a primitive faith in the inherent potency and inherent meaning of words. Words, however, do not have absolute and constant referents."

As a lifelong wordsmith, I use words to communicate certain facts. In a contract, words define the obligations of the parties. One would suppose that this would be sufficient even for an admiralty court, but the law merchant has now embarked on a wholly new tack, guided by Holmesian liberalism, that mere words do not define the provisions of a contract, because they are pathetic remnants of primitivism. Judge Traynor actually cited, in support of his opinion, semantic and anthropological evidence that only primitives ascribe binding meaning to words. "E.g. 'The elaborate system of taboo and verbal prohibitions in primitive groupstotemistic and protective names in mediaeval Turkish and Finno-Ugrian languages; the misplaced verbal samples of the Presieuses; the Swedish peasant custom of curing sick cattle smitten by witchcraft, by making them swallow a page tom out of the psalter and put in dough. "The Wall Street Journal terms this "moonbeam legal evidence." Perhaps the next step will be to make a defendant chew up and swallow his own confession, which, after all, is mere words. The Journal cites this decision as a dangerous development in contract law, noting that "The Pennzoil v. Texaco case put investors world-wide on notice that anything could happen in a Texas courtroom." The problem is not limited to Texas. The present writer has for years compared American civil procedure to Russian roulette. You go into the courtroom, the attorney bands you a loaded pistol after spinning the cylinder, and you put it to your head and pull the trigger. This is our legal system.

Lawyers have now come into court to obtain enormous awards for such legal discoveries as "Post-Traumatic Stress Disorder, which was defined in the American Psychiatric Assn Manual in 1980, and which spawned thousands of profitable lawsuits. It has been refined to encompass many more specific cases of stress-the Battered Woman Syndrome, the Rape Trauma Syndrome, the Child Abuse Syndrome, the Post Abortion Syndrome, Oppression Artifact Disorder, which was conjured up for blacks as a new version of legal voodoo, and Victimization Disorder. The American Psychiatric Assn was lobbied successfully by the homosexual community to remove homosexuality from its Diagnostic and Statistical Manual, where it had rested for many years as a profitable basis for recruiting clients from the gay community; it is now contained in an independent appendix. You may have overlooked the fact that you could be a victim of Paraphiliac Coercive Disorder-has anyone ever ordered you to do anything? See your lawyer. The real gold mine has been found in sexual discrimination lawsuits against businesses; if you can't prove sexual discrimination, you may have to fall back on a surefire complaint-sexual harassment. When your boss smiled at you this morning, he may actually have been laughing-that will cost at least $300,000, in the hands of a good lawyer. These stimuli to the legal imagination have come about through the liberalizing of the law school curricula. Goodbye to Kent's Commentaries and the Constitution. Coke and Blackstone have been gone these many years. The emphasis of the curricula now is on contract law and training in the law merchant. More esoteric offerings include "Feminist Legal Thought" at the highly touted University of Virginia Law School, which graduated Robert and Teddy Kennedy, as well as Race Relations Law, and Refugee Law. The University of Georgia Law School offers three hours of admiralty law; the law schools generally offer extensive courses on Federal estate taxes, trusts, and other developments of the Law Merchant State.

We may be forgetting the fact that the Republic of the United States of America was founded by refugees who were fleeing just this sort of legal dictatorship in Europe. North European individuals who had been born into the category of fit and able citizens were being persecuted and killed by the growing numbers of the unfit, who were unable to compete. They therefore gathered together in secret conspiracies and used their combined power to exterminate their fit competitors. That the extermination or expulsion of the fit caused havoc in the nation and brought ruin to the economy was less important than the goal of promoting the survival of the unfit.

Seeking no revenge against their enemies, the fit migrated to America, wishing only to escape, and, to some extent, to proscribe the unfit from pursuing them to these shores. The fit drew up a formula for self-government, which they called the Constitution. This remarkable document was not merely a prayer, in the legal sense, for protection, but a binding resolve in which they contracted to protect themselves and their descendants from the ferocity and the ruthlessness of the unfit. A system of republican self-government was devised, which carefully proscribed the machinations of the unfit, and demanded the protection of the fit from this dedicated enemy. To ensure that the unfit would never be able to use the powers of government against the fit, the Founders drew upon the greatest traditions of Western civilization, choosing the most admirable provisions of

Greek, Roman, and English law. They divided the government into three compartments, to prevent any department from establishing a dictatorial power. This constitutional republic was divided into the legislative, the executive and the judiciary. From the outset, the judiciary was considered the least powerful and the least involved in the processes of government. It existed as a potential referee if either the executive or the legislative branches tried to wield excessive power. Constitutionally, the judiciary was neither expected to make law nor to execute it. This tripartite system was designed, like the Titanic, to keep one or more compartments afloat, even if one was struck by disaster.

The Founders sought to protect themselves against a recurrence of their unfortunate experiences at the bands of the Black Nobility in Europe, which had become the champions of the unfit in the lists; they therefore tried to limit excessive power in the executive, making the President something of a figurehead, and relying upon the more representative legislative branch to exercise restraint in governing. The result is that we see an Imperial Congress conducting political show trials without objection from the judiciary, whose powers seemingly have been usurped. The judiciary does not object because it has reserved truly despotic powers for itself. Are you concerned about the crime, violence and dope in your child's school? The judiciary will not let you do anything about it. If citizens protest about conditions in their schools, the judiciary steps in and takes control of the schools. Do you favor public religious displays? The judiciary forbids such displays, even though you, as an American citizen, have a direct proprietary right in every public area.

However, the true despotism of the judiciary has been achieved by its continuous and furtive destruction of the Constitution, and replacing it with the dictatorial vehicle of the Black Nobility, the admiralty court, which was spawned by England's chartering of the Bank of England, its worldwide espionage empire, the Secret Intelligence Service, and by its enormous profits from the slave and drug trades. Because the judges no longer allow the Constitution to play a role in their decisions, their reaction to the introduction of Constitutional arguments in the courts range from derision to anger. Some judges allow Constitutional arguments to be introduced, knowing that they will not affect the decision. Other judges bridle at any citation of the Constitution, as a direct affront to the admiralty procedure of their court. The situation remains concealed from American citizens, because the media is forbidden to mention Constitutional issues. Instead, we get endless sob stories about a three-legged dog in Finland, or a paraplegic in New Zealand who has taken up ice skating. Wallowing in "compassion" and "caring" is now the substitute for responsible concern about the fate of our nation.

The tragic development of Americans who have been denied their Constitution was achieved because the Black Nobility, early on, noticed the Achilles Heel of our Constitutional system, the power of judicial review. The "original intent" of the Constitution was that no one branch of government could wield totalitarian power over the other two branches, or over the American people. This original intent was subverted by replacing Constitutional law with the law merchant. The Jeffersonian system of checks and balances enshrined in our Constitution does prohibit one branch of government from dominating the other branches. However, the law merchant allows the judiciary to issue imperial edicts that no one, even the President, is "above the law." The judiciary cleverly avoids mentioning that "the law" to which they are referring is the absolute decree of the law merchant, or that the federal agents who appear on your doorstep have been sent there in flagrant violation of the Constitution, but on direct commission by the admiralty court.

This charade can succeed only as long as you, the citizen, remain unaware of what is going on. For those who become informed, the door is opened for them to exercise their Constitutional rights as American citizens. Andrew Melechinsky has long been active in the lists with his Constitutional Revival Movement in Fairfield, Conn. When government goons filed a suit against him, Melechinsky responded by an Answer which be filed in the form of an Affidavit in the Enfield Land Records, v. 582, p. 1036, sending a copy to his accusers. He thus avoided giving the admiralty court jurisdiction by appearing and entering a plea. Melechinsky filed "Notice of Disclaimer of Unlawful Equity Jurisdiction: "The undersigned, Andrew Melechinsky, is not under the jurisdiction of the IRS. He has no connection with the IRS. No jury has ever found probable cause. No jury has ever declared liability." Melechinsky then cites his person, property, books and records which are private, protected and guaranteed under the Fourth through the Tenth Amendments. He states, "I demand a court of law (as opposed to equity), a neutral judge at law, and a probable cause jury to decide whether or not there is cause to bring an action against me Federal personnel in their official capacity can be sued for damages by a person damaged by an unlawful equity decree. This is a formal notice; govern yourselves accordingly." signed, Andrew Melechinsky; notarized.

In a case where he was assaulted by a deputy, Melechinsky filed a Jurisdictional Challenge; the judge then entered a plea over his objections. Melechinsky then filed a REPUDIATION OF USURPATION OF JURISDICTION AND ADDITIONAL COUNTER COMPLAINT AND CLAIM FOR DAMAGES.

The judge dismissed it. Another judge (Noren) killed himself after having locked Melechinsky up for exercising his right to remain silent. If more citizens could follow Melechinsky's example, we might see a wave of suicides among the corrupt officials of the judiciary. Their powers can only be exercised in the realm of darkness. Light will destroy them.

Andrew Melechinsky has drafted a simple change which should be included in every state code:

> "Whenever there is any variance between the rules of equity and the rules of the common law in reference to the same matter, the rules of the common law shall prevail."

Any citizen may legitimately object to granting jurisdiction over his person to a court, because the American courts have become the official endorsers and protectors of every type of deviation and perversion. The New York Court of Appeals recently ruled four to two that marriage is officially "a fictitious legal distinction," thus opening the door to the state sanction of homosexual couplings, animal associations and other odd combinations. This is the same court which a few years ago threw out the conviction of two homosexuals for sexual acts in a bookstore, on the grounds that because the acts occurred in a bookstore, this was an act of "free speech" which was protected by the Constitution!

Because of the Democratic majority in Congress, the committees are dominated by leftwing Democrats, not the least of which is the Judiciary Committee. Newsweek reported on the bias of this committee by quoting Rep. Chuck Douglas, April 10, 1989,

> "I don't know if you know who Barney Frank is, but he is one of the two members there who are only interested in members of their own sex. That gives you a little feel for the Committee."

The Congressman's reference to his colleague, Rep. Barney Frank, showed some irritation with Frank's personal background. Despite Frank's public revelling in stories about his homosexual "orientation," he was now in his fifth term in Congress, and had won 70% of the vote in the 1988 election in Massachusetts' 4th District. The Associated Press on August 26, 1989, carried revelations from the Washington Times that Frank's lover, whom he paid $80 for their first encounter, and then $20,000 a year for his "duties," had been operating a male prostitution ring from Frank's apartment on Capitol Hill. The lover, using the name of "Greg Davis," had been charged with oral sodomy, drug charges, and contributing to the delinquency of a minor. He was also charged with possession of cocaine, the "drug of choice" for our enlightened leaders.

Frank was astounded at the public interest in the revelations. As a longtime resident of Sodom-on-the-Potomac, a mecca for those of his persuasion because of the profusion of young sailors and Marines, be saw little merit in the story. He justified his conduct by maintaining, during an hourlong press conference, that he "has been in a monogamous homosexual relationship for about two years with a very sensible person and a steadying influence." (without issue, of course).

His fellow Democratic Party member, Speaker Tom Foley, who recently replaced Speaker Jim Wright of Texas, leaped to Frank's defense by praising Frank's "outstanding service to his constituency and the nation." He prudently refrained from explaining that Frank's service may have gone beyond the call of duty.

The extreme leftwing bias of the .Judiciary Committee has an inevitable effect upon the types of decisions rendered by the judges, who take their lead from the political stance of the Committee. The citizen also should be aware of the differing Constitutional origin of the courts before which they appear. Many present day "courts" are actually administrative law courts set up by Congress. These are known as "Article I courts" because they were originally territorial courts established by Congress in the territories before they gained statehood. The most typical of these administrative law courts is the Tax Court, whose judges, although acting with the powers of a federal judge, are not and cannot be federal judges, because they are appointed for fifteen year periods, whereas federal judges, under Art. III, sec. I of the Constitution, hold their offices for life, unless impeached. A legitimate court in the United States is an Article III court. An Article I territorial court authorized by Congress depends entirely upon admiralty procedure for its rulings, which means that it functions as a branch of the Bank of England through the London Connection (see *Secrets of the Federal Reserve*, by Eustace Mullins). There is also a serious question as to whether Article III judges are now legitimate. Several people have caused consternation in judicial ranks by requesting that an Article III judge preside at their trial, that is, a judge who functions under the Constitution, meaning that he is a judge who qualifies under Art. III, Sec. 1, which requires that "the Judges receive a Compensation, which shall not be diminished during their continuance in Office." Because all judges today have payments withheld from their salaries for social security, insurance, tax charges and other deductions, there is no question that these deductions "diminish the Compensation" of the judges while they are in office. Consequently, said judges can no longer qualify as judges under the provision of Article III of the

Constitution. Those who request a true Article III judge at their trial are raising a problem which is difficult to resolve.

Because Congress is not granted any power in Article I to establish courts of any kind in the United States, the Tax Court, as an Article I court, has no jurisdiction over any American who is a citizen of a State. To prevent this and other questions from being raised before Tax Court, the court refuses to allow anyone to practice before it who has ever challenged the basic premise of the income tax law. The present writer appeared before Tax Court as attorney pro se, and the "deficiency" was hastily resolved by a court judgment that I had no tax deficiency. At that time, I had not been researching the Article I dilemma, but should I have occasion to appear before Tax Court again, the question will be raised.

During my time in Tax Court, I saw that the persons appearing there were the most obvious victims of a tyrannical and insanely greedy federal authority. There was a pathetic elderly couple, shabbily dressed, with many grocery bags filled with cash register receipts; a mentally retarded youth dressed in castoff clothing, who had little concept of what was happening to him; and a contractor who had accepted enormous bribes in a state paving contract, not realizing that although bribery is an omnipresent fact of life and is accepted by the government, the government also requires that all bribes, without exception, must be reported as income. The Criminal Investigation Division of the IRS now had him on a greased slide to the penitentiary.

A territorial court such as the Tax Court, which is illegally situated in any State of the United States, illustrates the boldness of the admiralty court in replacing our Constitutional courts throughout the nation. For the past five hundred years, Anglo-American jurisprudence has required proof of an intent to break the law-the principle of mens rea-before a criminal conviction can be obtained. As Judge James Buckley pointed out on the Washington Court of Appeals, in reversing the criminal conviction of President Reagan's aide, Lynn Nofziger, on vague charges of "lobbying," prosecutors must prove both a criminal act (actus reus) and a guilty mind (mens rea). Despite his acquittal, Nofziger's legal battle cost him one and a half million dollars. Just as our Constitutional law has been supplanted in its "original intent" by the bold tyranny of the admiralty courts, so the necessity of proving mens rea has also been tossed aside as excess baggage by the law merchant. Supreme Court Justice Robert Jackson previously called the intent requirement "as universal and persistent in mature systems of law as belief in freedom of the human will and a consequent ability and duty of the normal individual to choose between good and evil."

Political show trials of Republican White House aides in Washington, who are routinely convicted by black Democratic juries, cannot establish intent, but the victims are hurriedly legally keelhauled by admiralty procedure before they or their attorneys realize what is happening to them. In most of these cases, their attorneys are charging from one to three million dollars to defend them; for that kind of money, you have to go along with the Establishment. However, these same political show trials have exposed aspects of the jury system as totally unqualified to make a just decision; in any case, these trials never had any such goal. They were conceived to make a political point, and "justice" or its rape, was a side issue. Dean Griswold of Harvard Law School stated, "Jury trial at best, is an apotheosis for the amateur. Why should anyone think that twelve persons brought in from the street, selected in various ways for their lack of general ability, should have any special capacity to decide controversies between persons?" David Peck calls jury trial "geared to the assimilation of the unfamiliar by the inexpert." Prof. Prosser ridicules "the twelve housewives, bakers helpers, and unemployed individuals we get today in the United States." In Washington's political show trials, North, Nofziger, Deaver et al, both the judge and the jury are expressly selected to obtain a conviction of a political opponent. The ballot box has been transferred to the jury room.

The magical number of twelve used for the jury is taken from Kabbalistic numerology; twelve is known as a number of completeness, as is seven. Of the twenty-two letters of the Hebrew alphabet, twelve are definitely connected with the twelve signs of the Zodiac. Eleven or thirteen jurors would be more practical, as it would lessen the chance of a deadlock. However, twelve satisfies the need to identify the judicial process with the cult of Babylon, as well as conforming with the importance of the number twelve in many aspects of our existence; the twelve hour day, twelve months, twelve disciples of Jesus, twelve Labors of Hercules, and many other usages. Revelation states that God's mark was placed on 12,000 from each of the twelve tribes for the number of 144,000, who will survive to stand on Mt. Zion with the Lamb. Revelation also describes the New Jerusalem as walled with twelve gates, on which stand twelve angels; the wall has twelve foundation stones with the names of the Twelve Apostles and adorned with twelve jewels; the tree of life within the city bears twelve kinds of fruit; the dimensions of the city are multiples of twelve.

Bushell's Case, which was tried over three hundred years ago in London, was a landmark jury case, in which the jurors held that every person has a right to worship according to his own conscience. It marks the birth of the modern jury system. The importance of the jury in nullifying an arbitrary judge has been perverted by the judge's "instructions" to the jury. These instructions change the ancient concept of the jury as "trial per pais," that is, trial by the country, meaning "by the people," as distinguished from our present system of the law merchant, which is trial by the government. No one should ever be tried by "the government," that is, by an arbitrary power, but only by one's peers, those of the same origins, goals and ambitions as oneself. As Lysander Spooner points out, "An Essay on the Trial by Jury,"

> "The object of this trial 'by the country' or by the people, in preference to a trial by the government, is to guard against every species of oppression by the government. In order to effect this end, it is indispensable that the people, or 'the country,' judge of and determine their own liberties against the government; instead of the government's judging of and determining its own powers over the people."

The judge's arbitrarily extended power to "instruct" the jury is part of the same law merchant process which was used to extend Article I legislative courts based in the District of Columbia, and created by Congress' exclusive legislative power

over the District of Columbia, Art. 1, Sec. 8, Cl 17, by a secret
interpretation of the commerce clause of the Constitution. These
legislative courts had no power to punish, but this power was
later "assumed" through admiralty procedure. The result is that
the federal courts throughout the United States are extended
District of Columbia legislative courts which have no legal or
judicial power to "punish" any American citizen, or to pronounce
punitive sentences upon us. Further, they are illegally seated in
the States, because the Constitution, Art I Sec 8 Cl 17, limits
them to the Seat of Government, the District of Columbia. This
problem has been "resolved" by extending the District of
Columbia to encompass the entire United States!

The courts have become the preserves of a small section of
the American legal profession, that ten per cent which comprises
the members of the American Association of Trial Lawyers,
which has 63,000 members of the 707,000 licensed members of
the American legal profession. These trial lawyers, in their quest
to obtain multi-million dollar fees, have created the $300 billion
a year tax on American business which Peter Huber defines as
the harvest of current tort liability, an amount greater than our
trade deficit; which allows the average worker who wins a sex
harassment or sex discrimination suit to receive an award of
$602,000, and even greater awards in wrongful termination suits,
an average award of $732,000, according to the Wall Street
Journal, Feb. 3, 1989. After ten years of litigation, according to
the *Washington Post*, May 9, 1989, of suits brought by the
Vietnam Veterans of America, resulted in two million dollars in
payments to veterans who charged they were victims of dioxin
poisoning, and in twenty million dollars being paid to their
lawyers! But that's impossible, we might observe. Contingency
fees are one-third of the award. Two-thirds should go to the
victim. As proposed by the lawyer, a case taken on contingency
fee does allow one third to the lawyer, and two-thirds to the
victim. However, legal expenses, fees for appeals etc., often
mean that the lawyer winds up with ninety per cent of the award.
The victim, instead of being awarded 66% of the damages, often
winds up with no more than five or ten per cent.

An even more flagrant action of trial lawyers occurs when they persuade their clients to be "magnanimous," and to lower their expectations. Such an appeal to a client's generosity usually occurs after the lawyer is approached by opposing counsel, who says, "Look, we haven't got a prayer of winning this one. You're going to wipe us out. Go back and tell your client he should be satisfied with a moral victory, and forget any monetary awards." No lawyer would agree to such an outrageous procedure unless some private allowance has been made to spur his generosity. A stunning example of this appeal of "magnanimity" occurred when the American Medical Association faced disaster, after being convicted of criminal conspiracy in an effort to maintain its illegal Medical Monopoly throughout the United States, by trying to destroy the competing skill of chiropractic. On Aug. 27, 1987, after eleven years of desperate legal maneuvers, Federal Judge Susan Getzendammer of U.S. District Court found the AMA guilty of conspiring to destroy the profession of chiropractic. The AMA faced damages of hundreds of millions of dollars, which, after conviction, could have been tripled as punitive damages. Their lawyers persuaded the chiropractors to accept "a moral victory," with the result that the members of this profession are still being assessed payments of millions of dollars to their lawyers for the lawsuit which they "won"! Magnanimity, anyone?

In Maryland, a new court ruling is a first strike against the "litigation lottery," stating that in the future, suits against professionals will have to prove "actual malice" to collect punitive damages. The ruling has no effect on actual compensatory damages, but Richard P. Gilbert, chief judge of the Maryland Court of Special Appeals, overturned a $750,000 award against an ophthalmologist, as a new departure in the field of medical malpractice. The court defined "actual malice" as "the performance of an act without legal justification or excuse, but with an evil or rancorous motive influenced by hate, the purpose being to deliberately or willfully injure the plaintiff." This is an accurate description of the FBI thirty-three year campaign against the present writer, ("A Writ for Martyrs," by Eustace Mullins), which resulted in a fifty million dollar judgment against the government.

U.S. government responsibility in another case surfaced in the Shimoda Case (American Journal of International Law. v. 59, 1965): An individual sued the Japanese Government for damages sustained in the atomic bombing of Hiroshima and Nagasaki in a suit filed Dec. 7, 1963. The District Court of Tokyo ruled that the United States violated international law by dropping atomic bombs on Hiroshima and Nagasaki, and that the plaintiff had no grounds to recover from the Japanese government. Article 19 of the Peace Treaty with Japan waives all claims of Japan and its nationals against the Allied Powers and other nations arising out of the war or out of actions taken because of the existence of the war. The Japanese Government also cited its diplomatic protest to the United States in a formal note presented through the Swiss Government August 10, 1945, in which the attacks were ruled "a new offense against the civilization of mankind." It described the aerial bombardment of the cities of Hiroshima and Nagasaki as an illegal act of hostilities and the indiscriminate bombing of undefended cities, further citing the prohibition against poison gas as outlawing such attacks Art. 23, Hague Regulations Respecting Land Warfare 1899, and General Protocol 1925. Recovery by any Japanese citizen was unlikely under the principle of fait accompli; it happened. Despite the fact that the atomic bombing of Hiroshima and Nagasaki actually happened, it was a lawful reality which after the fact could only be treated as a legal fiction, history being essentially fantasy, as contrasted to the real present and the unimaginable future.

Because of the emphasis on the court as a Roman arena for political show trials, the court as a place where criminals are brought to the bar of justice to atone for their crimes has faded into insignificance. On Jan. 5, 1986, the *New York Times* reprinted an editorial from 1983 on the New York Criminal Court, headlined "The Crime of the Criminal Court." "Rarely has any public institution been held in such open contempt by those who work in it and those who pass through it. Judges call it a sham and a fraud. Lawyers say that justice is unpredictable. Only one in one hundred cases are tried." This ratio does not apply to the number of political offenders who are tried, convicted and sentenced. This ratio is one hundred of one hundred. The process is mercilessly pilloried in a recent book, "RAILROAD: U.S.A.

Vs. LYNDON LAROUCHE ET AL." LaRouche's crime was that he sought the presidency of the United States four times as an independent political candidate, in a "bipartisan" nation which allows only two political parties, each with the same program of Marxist oppression and worldwide revolution. LaRouche was brought before Chief Judge Albert Bryan Jr. U.S. District Court for the Eastern District, whose treatment of political offenders earned his court the nickname of "the Rocket Docket." The *Washington Post* headlined on Nov. 20, 1988, "LaRouche Trial Expected to be Speedy; Alexandria's Rocket Docket Federal Court." LaRouche called the court, "the only railroad in the United States which runs on time." At a secret meeting in his Alexandria office, in the autumn of 1988, U.S. prosecutor Henry Hudson described the Bryan court as "our window of opportunity," and "our last chance to get LaRouche." It is gospel that it takes from three to five years to get a case through our over-burdened court system, yet LaRouche was indicted Oct. 14, 1988, and pronounced guilty Dec. 16, 1988! The case originated with a letter from Henry Kissinger to FBI director William Webster (the defendant in the present writer's suit against the FBI) Aug. 19, 1982, "suggesting" it was time to do something about LaRouche. Kissinger controlled the President's Foreign Intelligence Advisory Board, which gave the LaRouche strike force official White House backing. Senator Robert Dole remarked of the "conspiracy" charge which the secret task force brought against LaRouche. "Conspiracy? That's what they do when they can't get you on anything else."

LaRouche responded to the indictment by listing the federal and state agencies which had sworn to get him: the FBI; the U.S. Secret Service; the IRS; U.S. Attorney for the Eastern Dist. of Va.; U.S. Postal Service; BATF; Va. Atty Gen. office; State Police of Va.; Va State Corp. Commission; the Virginia-Israel Commission. Anyone who has all those agencies against him couldn't be all bad. William Weld and Henry Kissinger had set up a special government task force, The General Litigation and Legal Advisory Section of the Criminal Division, Justice Dept. to finish off LaRouche. He was quickly tried and sentenced, Judge Bryan virtuously noting at his sentencing, "this idea that this is a politically inspired, politically motivated prosecution, that is errant nonsense."

One could only admire Judge Bryan's ability to say this with a straight face. LaRouche has never been anything but a political figure; he has never been a tobacconist or a social worker. During the proceedings, Jan. 19, 1989, Judge Bryan stated that any information asked of jurors by the defense would be "badgering." Mr. Webster, defense attorney, replied, "I would prefer a different term, Your Honor." BRYAN. I know. That's my term. It's not yours or the governments." The idea that any defense attorney would "badger" a prospective juror who would later rule on the innocence or guilt of his client itself was ridiculous. Judge Bryan had a long record of anti-LaRouche activity, having previously participated in the shutdown and seizure of LaRouche publications, and later denying a motion which appealed a secret ex parte proceeding and the fact that the U.S. government (read Kissinger) had exercised prior restraint against a publishing company in violation of the First Amendment. Bryan denied the motion.

LaRouche appealed Judge Bryan's sentence in Case No. 89-5518 to the U.S. Court of Appeals for the 4th Circuit, citing numerous violations of constitutional rights, interference with the process of jury selection, and many other violations. The appeal cited the principle of law, "*Difficilem oportet aurem habere ad crimina*; In a court of law, one must not descend to listen to slander." This is a fundamental Principle of Legality. The appeals cited LaRouche's conviction on charges of failure to repay loans, "a fact which occurred and which no parties in this case try to deny, is not a criminal act in itself." The loans were political loans, which legally are different from business loans, loans for educational purposes etc. In any case, the federal agents made it impossible for LaRouche to keep track of or repay the loans because they seized millions of documents in a raid on his headquarters in Leesburg, Va., Oct. 6, 1986.

Because of his geographic location, LaRouche was forced to appeal to the notorious 4th Circuit Court of Appeals (which denied an appeal from the present writer on grounds so incredible it was obvious that no member of the court had even glanced at the pleadings). LaRouche faced an additional problem with the 4th Circuit; Judge Bryan's father, Albert V. Bryan Sr. was himself a judge on the 4th Circuit Court from 1961 until his death in 1984, and the court had maintained a record of rarely overturning any rulings of the present Judge Bryan. "The Circuit Court is known to be extremely protective of Albert Jr. and 'the rocket docket.'"

Representing oneself in court, as this writer has now done for some four decades, is a heady experience. It allows one to choose at will from the entire repertoire of legal strategy, without fear or favor. Strangely enough, strategy is a word rarely used in the legal profession, because its members prefer the devious techniques of conspiracy and treachery. I once asked a former "richest man in the world" who was embroiled in a legal battle, "What is your strategy?" He was puzzled by the question. Could anyone believe that Napoleon had no strategy in his succession of lightning like victories throughout Europe? He began to lose when he tempered his military genius with political considerations. Waterloo was not far off.

Once a litigant has dredged his way through the quagmire of pretrial discovery, there are a number of strategies available. If a defendant, you file "Motion to Dismiss." If a plaintiff, you file a Motion for Summary Judgment. These motions are pro forma, and rarely succeed, but they give you another turn at bat. Counter-claims are always good, as well as a lawsuit filed against opposing counsel. These suits need little preparation. One need only look over the file of the case and note all the illegal acts which the counsel has perpetrated against you. Some of my consultants advise filing suits against the judge; it is noteworthy that all persons known to me who regularly urge me to do this have themselves never filed a suit against a judge. There is no risk of turning him against you; he is already against you. The problem is that such a suit opens the door for punitive actions of contempt, remanding to jail or whatever he may trump up to get you out of his courtroom and into confinement.

Court demeanour is important, Although it will not win you any friends there; nothing can do that. You should be well-spoken, well-dressed, and unflappable. Almost every judge I have appeared before has done his best to goad me into some outburst, by actions so flagrantly prejudiced that most plaintiffs would have to react. Because you are surrounded by armed men, any gesture which might be interpreted as "violent" would bring an inevitable response. On one occasion, 1 wore a large Masonic ring, which I had picked up at an auction in a madhouse, and flaunted it before the judge at every opportunity. It made not the slightest difference; they know who is a Mason and who is not.

In an address to the American Bar Association in 1940, John W. Davis, a distinguished jurist, stated the ten principles for court argument:

1. Change places in your mind with the court.

2. State the nature of the case, and a brief history.

3. State the facts.

4. State next the applicable rules of law on which you rely.

5. Always go "for the jugular vein."

6. Rejoice when the court asks a question.

7. Read sparingly and only from necessity.

8. Avoid personalities.

9. Know your record from cover to cover.

10.   Sit down.

Lawyers rarely lose an opportunity to create chaos in international affairs-the career of the late John Foster Dulles is ample witness to that. The Nation noted on Feb. 6, 1989 a new development, "revolution by litigation," as evidenced by the action of a Washington wheeler dealer, William Rogers, of Arnold and Porter (formerly Arnold, Fortas and Porter). In ongoing efforts of Washington insiders to unseat Noriega in Panama, who had somehow been transformed from a partner in government drug operations to a competitor, Rogers gave Noriega's political opponent, and apparent President of Panama, Eric Delvalle, control of some fifty million dollars of Panamanian assets in the U.S. The Justice Office of Foreign Registration notes that Arnold and Porter received $450,517 in fees for ten weeks of work for Delvalle's shadow government, and could receive millions more. The Nation noted that this could make Rogers the highest paid revolutionary in history.

As part of a supposed campaign against organized crime, Congress passed the RICO statute in 1970. The bill was intended to "wipe out" organized crime by charging it under the sweeping provisions of the new Racketeer Influenced and Corrupt Organization, or RICO law. In some unexplained manner, the enforcement of the statute somehow overlooked organized crime altogether. Those charged under the RICO statute were legitimate businessmen, who quite often had neglected to make the right political contributions. In short, RICO, instead of punishing the Mafia for its extortion racket, went after businessmen who had refused to yield to extortion from Congress. Chief Justice William Rehnquist spoke to the Brookings Institution April 7, 1989, noting that RICO was the basis for nearly one thousand cases a year.

"Civil RICO is now being used in ways that Congress never intended when it enacted the statute. The time has arrived for Congress to enact amendments to civil RICO to limit its scope."

However, the Supreme Court, when a RICO case was recently appealed there, refused in its ruling to limit RICO in any way. Its punitive measures, such as triple damages and fines, have been used to put many American businesses into bankruptcy. No relief is in sight.

Another lucrative field before the courts is libel action. Yet the Wall Street Journal noted in an op-ed piece, July 13, 1989, that what most litigants in libel actions wanted was not monetary payment, but public vindication. A three year study by the University of Iowa, begun in 1982, found that only one-fourth of libel litigants were after monetary awards. Three-fourths said they would have been satisfied if the allegedly false story had been corrected. Two factors intervened; first, the unbridled arrogance and wealth of the media so sue me; and second, the fact that most libel plaintiffs are represented by attorneys on contingency fee. A retraction or public apology would net these lawyers nothing. Consequently, they refuse to arbitrate, or to offer the offending publication a chance to settle by an apology.

The Journal commented on "the influence of lawyers, whose interests may not be congruent with those of their clients." This is such a basic fact of our legal system that it is amazing that anyone should have to mention it. Of course the interests of the lawyer are not congruent with those of his client. The American public's refusal to acknowledge this inescapable fact of life lies at the bottom of most of our problems with the legal profession.

CHAPTER 7

THE DEPARTMENT OF JUSTICE

Most Americans believe that they have in Washington a superior bulwark of their liberties, not above the Constitution, but existing to bring the Constitution to life in prosecuting violations of their freedoms. This bulwark is known as the Department of Justice. Unfortunately for our comfortable supposition, the Department of Justice exists, and was created, not as a bulwark of justice for the citizens of America, but as an instrumentality by which political crimes could be committed against us.

Congress created the Department of Justice in 1870, almost a century after the signing of the Declaration of Independence. The century prior to the creation of the Department of Justice was a period of unparalleled growth and prosperity for the American nation. The century since its creation has been a period of steady decline. How did this happen? America inaugurated its existence as the land of opportunity, the land of freedom, and the land of justice. Of the three, justice was always the most unattainable, but it existed, in however warped or inadequate a fashion. After 1870, the activities of the Department of Justice served to remove the possibility of obtaining justice in the courts permanently beyond the reach of most Americans. This does not mean that justice could not be had. It was always there for the fortunate few, for those who had created the Department of Justice and who subsequently benefited from its creation.

The Department of Justice, by its very nature, has no permanent bias or prejudice in its mode of operation. It exists solely to serve its creators and directors, the PIPs, or Party in Power, which is also known as the Perverts in Power, because of their propensity for perverting every aspect of American existence. Although all government departments in Washington are permanently tainted by political opportunism, the Department of Justice is the most reprehensible, because it is advertised as the final arbiter of our problems. Of all the departments, the Department of Justice is the most flagrant prostitute, boldly advertising that she will do anything for her pimps.

The present writer has advised the Department of Justice routinely over the past thirty years of serious criminal acts committed and which fall directly within the purlieu of this department. Because these letters are sent Registered with Return Receipt required, the department has regularly answered these notifications, and as regularly has refused to take any action. Reported violations of civil rights are met with the identical Department of Justice response, usually in a sneering tone, that I should hire myself a private attorney, if I really think that my rights have been violated. Notifications of routine theft, using the mails to defraud, and conspiracy to defraud, all amply documented, have been met with the same response, that I should hire a private lawyer. This is the same Department of Justice which recently spent some forty million dollars to determine how Col. Oliver North paid for a couple of tires!

When I wrote to Mr. Oliver (Buck) Revell in 1986 (the current acting director of the FBI) complaining of continuous violations of my copyright on my book, *Secrets of the Federal Reserve*, I received a response dated May 28, 1986 that "the FBI pursues criminal investigations and prosecutions of copyright matters generally in the areas of sound recordings, motion pictures and audiovisual works) the FBI will not institute a criminal investigation relative to this matter." Few people know that the vast resources of the FBI for years have been diverted to protecting the profits of a few Hollywood film moguls, who are also among the largest donors of political funds to national campaigns. FBI resources are confined to stopping unauthorized copies of these moguls' films and records. Faced with the refusal of the FBI to act in this matter, I went into state court, and later into federal court, with several lawsuits against violators of my copyrights. In each instance, the judge intervened actively on behalf of the defendant, and my complaints were consigned to the waste-basket.

The overt activity of the Department of Justice on behalf of the political powers that be is proof that the five thousand lawyers there do work to earn their salaries. When not carrying out humiliating errands for party bosses, they may be found conspiring with the dread KGB to commit atrocities against American citizens, or indulging in their favorite pastime, volunteering to carry out hatchet jobs against critics of the State of Israel.

From one point of view, the Department of Justice may be acting to protect the public. One shudders to think what the effect might be if its five thousand lawyers were suddenly discharged and unleashed upon an unsuspecting public. The consequences would be calamitous, and could bring on the total collapse of the nation. A visitor to these hallowed halls complained that the marijuana smoke was so thick in one office that he couldn't see to read his brief. For some decades, the Department of Justice has been the first stop out of law school for arrogant young graduates from Harvard, Columbia and Yale. Typical was the revelation, at the height of the Watergate imbroglio, that one young Department of Justice lawyer had become quite popular at parties in Washington and New York. In return for supplies of Acapulco gold, he was playing the super-secret Watergate tapes at liberal yuppy parties, and was the hit of the circuit. The episode was a one day source of gossip, and was quickly forgotten.

Since the advent of Franklin D. Roosevelt in 1933, the Department of Justice has been unrelentingly "liberal" in its bias. The long parade of Republican White House advisers convicted and sent to prison reflects not only the power of the Democratic Congress, but the overwhelming prejudice of the Department's attorneys. Like the Supreme Court, the Department of Justice can be said to have read the election returns, but its interpretations of them occurs on a much lower and more petty level. The dedication of department officials to statism, more aptly known as Marxism, has never been a secret in Washington. However, in recent years, there have been rumors of two conflicting philosophies of government in the Department of Justice. In fact, the most active rivalry and longtime opposition of two fanatical sects has now come to roost in the halls of Justice. In 1933, with the sudden dominance of the Stalinist wing of the Communist Party, assuming absolute direction of the Democratic Party, government officials vied with each other in exhibiting their newfound loyalty. Large posters of Lenin and Stalin were placed in offices and homes of prominent officials; the Internationale was routinely sung at weekend parties hosted by these officials, and earnest students could be seen poring over the latest edition of Stalin's speeches from International Publishers. However, these were mere tokens of a fanatical loyalty. These officials were not token Communists; they were actively engaged in espionage activities in our halls of government. Members of the notorious Harold Ware cell, presided over by Felix Frankfurter and his ubiquitous proteges, who were known as his "Happy Hot Dogs," were named to key roles in the departments of government. Longtime government employees, who had served ably and well at very low salaries, were now shunted to the background, irreversibly tainted as "good Americans." Few of these unlucky ones could even boast a foreign accent.

The Stalinists remained firmly in control of the Democratic Party for many decades. Meanwhile, a rival group had been headquartered in the United States, the followers of Leon Trotsky, who were committed to "world revolution now." They bitterly opposed the Stalinists, who echoed Stalin's dictum of "Socialism in one country," that is, Russia, although a purer form of Communism had now been established on the banks of the Potomac, perhaps the only genuine Communist government which has ever existed anywhere. In 1940, Stalin, fearing Trotsky's divisive influence on the brink of world war, had him hacked to death in Mexico City. The Trotskyites now had a martyr, and a cause worthy of continuing financial support by the various Rockefeller tax exempt foundations. The Trotskyites finally came to rest under the aegis of the League for Industrial Democracy, a shadow name for the old Socialist Workers Party, the Trotskyite movement in America.

Firmly committed to the principles of Marxism and Trotsky's doctrine of world revolution now, the League for Industrial

Democracy began to infiltrate conservative American groups. After 1948, the LID became the nesting place for the most fervent Israeli propagandists in the United States. First advertising themselves as "neo-conservatives," they gradually became more militant and virulently anti-Stalinist. In 1980, with the election of Ronald Reagan as President, the LID, masquerading behind its vocal contacts in the Hoover Institute at Stanford University, seized control of the Reagan Administration. Reagan unwittingly found himself playing the Hollywood role of General Coster, completely surrounded by the Indians at the Little Big Horn, while his few remaining genuinely conservative supporters were chopped down. The Trotskyites now had total power in the White House. They wrote virulent speeches for Reagan to deliver, denouncing the Moscow regime as the Evil Empire, and threatening to avenge the death of Trotsky by an all-out war against the Soviets.

The realities of international politics forced them to tone down these toxins, but they continued to develop "anti-Communist" regimes in Latin America. After the Goldwater election fiasco, the "neocons," the Trotskyites who now considered Tel Aviv as their Kremlin, moved into control of the Republican Party by default, as the Eastern control, the traditional Wall Street direction of the Republicans, floundered under the uncertain leadership of Nelson Aldrich Rockefeller. In Nicaragua, the "neocons" found their golden opportunity. For decades, Nicaragua had been the playground of such banking bouses as J & W Seligman Co., and Brown Bros. (now Brown Bros. Harriman, the family firm of President George Bush). The Nicaraguan dictator, Gen. Alberto Somoza, invited some Israeli entrepreneurs into his country, in the hopes of quick profits. They made millions for him, but abused the people so mercilessly that a reaction took place. The Sandinistas, a Stalinist Communist group, seized power, exiled Somoza, whom they subsequently murdered, and seized the Israeli enterprises. The Israelis began to finance an opposition movement, called the "contras."

When Reagan came into the White House in 1980, the "neocons" sought U.S. financing for the contra movement, in the hopes of recapturing the Israeli businesses in Nicaragua.

However, the Democratic Congress, still firmly committed to the support of Stalinist Communism throughout the world, refused to allow U.S. support of the contras. An impasse developed which has paralyzed the American government for almost a decade. The Kissinger "neocons," led by his personal proteges, John Poindexter and Oliver North, and supervised by Elliott Abrams of the Dept. of State, (son-in-law of the Israeli powers, Midge Decter and Norm Podhoretz of Commentary, the agitprop publication of the American Jewish Committee, sought to finance the contras through tax-exempt donations. Congress then forbade contra support by the Boland Amendments.

To punish those who supported the contras, Congress sought to take over the executive branch of government. The traditional system of checks and balances was thrown overboard, as Congress appointed "Special Prosecutors" to crucify North and other scapegoats of the "neocons." Even trials, the traditional purlieu of the executive department, were taken over, as Congress staged spectacular televised Moscow show trials of its victims, such as North, in the grand tradition of Josef Stalin. The American public, totally bemused by the spectacle of two wings of the Communist Party battling to the death in Washington like insane pit bulls, was never informed by the servile press, which was now largely under alien domination, about the true nature of the struggle. Meanwhile, the economy, the national borders, the environment, the military, and other responsibilities of the national government, were abandoned, leaving the nation to flounder and then to sink into total disarray.

Another expensive and well publicized Department of Justice operation has been its mad pursuit of "Nazi war criminals," almost a half century after the event, a campaign whose equivalent would be the indictment of Soviet officials of the present regime for mass murders committed during the purges of the 1930s by Stalin. Although these alleged "crimes" took place outside of American jurisdiction, the law merchant principles of our legal system allowed the U.S. government to take action against persons who later became American citizens. Justice set up the Office of Special Investigations, which acted as the U.S. office of the KGB, and also worked closely with Mossad, Israeli

Intelligence, to manufacture "evidence" against several elderly American citizens who were claimed to have been "guards" in German concentration camps nearly fifty years ago. Many millions of dollars was expended by OSI to have these elderly victims deported and executed. One of the principals of OSI was Nate Lewine, who mysteriously became the compulsory lawyer of choice for Republican White House executives accused of "influence peddling" and other offenses.

Nate Lewine began his lucrative career at the Department of Justice as a top operative of the "Get Hoffa" squad at the Department (this may have been the cause of John F. Kennedy's assassination). He is a former roommate of Philip Heymann, President Carter's director of the Criminal Division at the Department of Justice, and now at Harvard Law School. Walter Sheridan, chief of the "Get Hoffa" squad, was the dirty tricks mentor of the operation. This group leaped to the defense of Stephen Bryen after he was accused of passing vital defense secrets to Mossad. Bryen is now on the staff his longtime associate, Asst. Secretary of Defense Richard Perle. The vicious assault on John Tower when he was nominated as Secretary of Defense was masterminded by the Mossad group at Defense; they feared that he might balk at their continued espionage on behalf of Israel. The notorious Office of Special Investigations had been organized at the behest of Congresswoman Elizabeth Holtzman, abetted by Heymann and Lewine. It was set up specifically as a dirty tricks unit of Mossad and the KGB, operating in deep cover at the Department of Justice. Lewine's clients usually went to jail after paying him millions of dollars. He first defended Congressman George Hansen, who was charged with failure to properly fill out ethics reporting forms. His real offense was that he had gone to Iran to try to free American hostages, thus invading the sacred preserves of the Middle East, which had long been the property of Mossad and Israeli politicians. Hansen paid Lewin one million dollars to be sent to federal prison, where his treatment was so brutal that 258 Congressmen petitioned the Bureau of Prisons to alleviate his suffering. Millions of Americans deluged Reagan with demands that Hansen be paroled; all of their requests were thrown into the wastebasket at the White House by the sneering "neocons" who held Reagan captive.

Michael Deaver, Reagan's closest confidant, was the next victim. Lewine charged him three million dollars. Deaver was convicted. Americans have shown little reaction to the procession of Moscow show trials which have been held in Washington since the Watergate episode, "the scandal of the century," in which a Democratic office was burglarized by Republican henchmen. White Republican White House executives have been tried by black Democratic juries, and convicted in every instance, the latest being Oliver North. This is not racism on the part of the juries, as much as it is the "Moscow process," in which Democratic Stalinists are sworn to convict Republican Trotskyite neocons, no matter what the charges or the evidence against them. This mockery of the judicial process is typical of the "law merchant" court system, which functions solely on power and money. No legal standards need apply.

The Office of Special Investigations evolved into a small conspiratorial group of fanatics who assumed control of all Department of Justice operations. This group was known as "Nesher," the Hebrew word for "eagle." Its origins may be found in a book by John J. Dziak, historian of the Defense Intelligence Agency, "Chekisty: A History of the KGB." Dziak exposes a worldwide espionage and assassination bureau run by the KGB through Dr. Max Eitington, a close personal associate of Sigmund Freud. It was Eitington who brought the use of psychiatry and drugs into international espionage. He also prepared the documents for the 1937 secret trial, which resulted in the nine top generals of the Soviet Army being executed. These documents were later revealed to have been prepared by Hitler's Gestapo. Eitington had cooperated fully with Reinhard Heydrich to prepare this "evidence," with the same techniques which were later employed by the U.S. Department of Justice to use fake evidence from the KGB to have American citizens deported and executed by OSI.

Among the many murders arranged by Max Eitington was the murder of Trotsky's son, Leon Sedov, in a Paris hospital; Rudolf Kleist, a German Trotskyite whose decapitated body was found in the Seine; and Walter Krivitsky, a KGB defector who was murdered in a Washington hotel only a few feet from the halls of Congress. Eitington's brother ran the foreign espionage operations of the KGB, the expenses being paid by the income from the Soviet Fur Trust. Max Eitington set up the Berlin Psychiatric Institute, whose graduates later came to the U.S. to establish branches of the Tavistock Institute (the British Army Dept. of Psychological Warfare operation), which has systematically brainwashed officials of the major U.S. foundations and educational institutions.

The Eitington group, known as the Killerati, pioneered in the use of drugs and psychiatry in espionage coups. Its techniques became the basis of the British Secret Intelligence Service and its subsidiary, the Central Intelligence Agency. The Department of Justice takeover by Nesher, the spawn of this unholy group, provided a happy meeting ground for the ostensibly hostile forces of the KGB and Mossad. Provided with unlimited funds by the American taxpayer, they were enabled to carry out their sinister worldwide campaigns of systematic murder and destruction in every nation of the world. Nesber financed bit teams to assassinate Palestinians who were cooperating with the U.S. government, thereby ensuring the continuance of chaos, on which Israel feeds, throughout the Middle East, and resulted in the taking of U.S. hostages, not as retaliation against the U.S., but as protection against further assassination attempts by Mossad. Nesher ousted Duvalier in Haiti, creating widespread chaos and suffering in that nation. Meanwhile, Nesher's principle operative in the U.S. government, Jonathan Pollard, was busily securing thousands of pages of vital U.S. documents for his Israeli employers, in order to assure further economic chaos and foreign diplomatic catastrophes for our nation. Pollard operated under the aegis of Under Secretary of Defense Fred Ikle, whose Swiss connection is now involved in a vast scandal. Ikle's two principal aides were also prominent in Nesher operations, Richard Perle and Stephen Bryen. They set up another front group, JINSA, the Jewish Institute for National Security Affairs, as a cover for their furtive operations, working closely with Moscow Procurator and Soviet Attorney Natalya Kaleznikova, and the mastermind of the Irangate affair, David Kimche, the director of Mossad, who was

Pollard's controller. The Pollard coverup was led by Dep. Atty Gen. Arnold Burns and Nate Lewin of Nesher. Burns's law firm handled the books for the Lansky Syndicate operation through Sterling National Bank. Burns set up fifteen illegal tax shelters through Israeli connections, which criminally evaded some forty million dollars in taxes. An investigation into Burns' operations was stopped by DJ's head of the Criminal Division, William Weld, of the Wall Street banking family whose control of the Bank of Boston funneled payments to Pollard for his espionage operations. The background of the Nesher group was found to originate in the Swiss espionage and banking interests, one of whose proctors, Tibor Rosenbaum, had financed the Israeli conquest of Palestine. Swiss law enforcement was headed by Elizabeth Ikle Kopp, cousin of Assistant Secretary of Defense Fred Ikle. She was married to Hans Kopp, who headed a billion dollar holding company for espionage groups operating worldwide, the Shakarchi Trading Co. Shakarchi handles enormous sums for CIA, Mossad and other espionage operations. Ten million dollars of Iran Contra proceeds from the illegal sale of Arms to Iran was first deposited in the Chase Manhattan Bank in New York by Arab wheeler dealer Adnan Khashoggi; the money was then transferred to credit Suisse, and later laundered by Shakarchi executives. This money paid for the delivery of 1000 TOW missiles to the CIA, for clandestine delivery to Iranian terrorists. As a result of investigations into the Iran Contra dealings, both Kopp and his wife are now under investigation, while Khashoggi languishes in a Swiss prison. The case is expected to uncover interesting corollaries between the international drug cartel, international espionage, and Israeli intelligence.

The Department of Justice was formerly headed by Ronald Reagan's friend, Edwin Meese III, who publicly denounced the American Civil Liberties Union. Meese was hounded from office, and forced to hire Nate Lewin as his personal attorney to defend him against a host of charges, none of which were ever proved. Meese was then replaced by a Republican from the Eastern Liberal Establishment, Dick Thornburgh, former Governor of Pennsylvania. Thornburgh had formerly been a director of the ACLU! He now heads some 77,000 employees at the Department of Justice, and has announced his intention to dismantle fourteen regional strike forces against organized crime. Under Meese, the personnel of the Department of Justice had grown by 34%, while its achievements dwindled to the point of invisibility. Thornburgh had developed a cozy relationship with the Merrill Lynch stockbroking firm while Governor of Pennsylvania; his largest expenditure was the authorization of an $807 million bond issue to improve the rapidly decaying Pennsylvania Turnpike. He later became a director of Merrill Lynch at a salary of $35,000 a year. Merrill Lynch's former chairman, Donald Regan, was President Reagan's chief of staff in the White House.

The Department of Justice continues to offer a spiritual home to personages who could be most generously described as "kooks." The *Washington Post* of March 11, 1989 recounted the strange tale of federal prosecutor Judy Russell, who had been widely hailed as "one of the most promising young attorneys in the United States." she faked death threats against herself, and was diagnosed as schizophrenic, "with four distinct personalities." She was found not guilty of obstructing justice "by reason of insanity."

The FBI continued to offer money to a host of odd personalities. A well-known member of Richmond, Virginia's City Council, Henry Richardson, had pleaded guilty in February 1988 to the possession of dangerous drugs and drug paraphernalia. He was fined fifty dollars, and received a contract from the FBI to finger other drug users in the city government. His attorney, Michael Morchower, reported in an AP release, April 29, 1989, that

> "Richardson may have flimflammed the FBI out of six thousand dollars Mr. Richardson sent the FBI on a wild goose chase that with information that had no value."

Richardson later admitted his heroin addiction, and was being dunned for ten thousand dollars for his "cure" in a local institution.

Attorney General Dick Thornburgh, who had been chosen for this cabinet post by President George Bush, promises to take the

Department of Justice on a new, and even more liberal, tack. When we remember that George Bush campaigned actively against the ACLU (his opponent, Michael Dukkakis, boasted that he had long been a member of the ACLU) throughout his presidential campaign, it becomes more puzzling that as soon as he ascended to the White House, Bush immediately chose for his most sensitive Cabinet Post a director of the ACLU.

Thornburgh then announced his most crucial appointment, the selection of his Deputy Attorney General. He named Robert Fiske Jr., a choice which caused cries of rage to emanate from most Republican conservatives. Fiske had long been notorious as the liberal agent of the American Bar Association from 1984 to 1987. As the dominant member of the ABA "screening committee," Fiske had passed on to the most vociferous liberal activist organizations the names of prospective judicial nominees during his years of "screening." These activists then dug up the entire history of each nominee, carefully scrutinizing it for any sign of pro-Americanism. Those who had failed to make ritual obeisance to the nation's most powerful behind the scenes liberal forces had their names tossed into the wastebasket. Only those with tried and true liberal records were given the ABA's recommendation for nomination. The result was that the nation's judicial system became loaded with judges whose personal history embraced drugs, sexual "liberation," and who openly espoused the most violent principles of virulent leftwing organizations.

The ABA screening process was not as important during the administration of Democratic Presidents. Jimmy Carter was notorious for the liberal activists, some three hundred judges, whom he stacked in the nation's courts. However, during Republican Administrations, the ABA screening process was crucial to the Stalinist Democrats as the means to subvert and stall Republican programs. Judges who were suspected of being "conservative" encountered a phalanx of opposition in the ABA screening committee.

In 1985, Fiske was forced to admit that he had indeed sent the names of Reagan's prospective nominees for conservative judicial posts to such well-known liberal activists as the Alliance for Justice Judicial Selection Project, to determine if the nominees had any provable record of "bias" towards women or minorities. The result was that Reagan's nominees encountered months of stalling, open animosity, and in many cases, denial of their nomination for judgeships. When Thornburgh nominated Fiske as his Deputy Attorney General, it was seen by Washington insiders as a payoff to a saboteur for his career as a notorious wrecker, destroying Reagan's chances of nominating a more conservative judicial bench. Fiske, whose mother was a Seymour, of a prominent Wall Street family, had become a partner in the prestigious Wall Street firm of Davis Polk and Wardwell. One of Washington's most respected legal observers, Paul Kamenar of the Washington Legal Foundation, described Fiske as "basically a liberal type milieu, Wall Street lawyer, country club type Republican."

Although the previous Attorney General, Edwin Meese ILI, had left office under a cloud, having become involved in the notorious Wedtech scandal with the State of Israel, he may be vindicated when one looks at the record of his successor, Dick Thornburgh. A Yale graduate and longtime personal friend of President George Bush, Thornburgh is also a protege of Don Regan, President Reagan's former White House Chief of Staff and head of the giant stockbroking firm, Merrill Lynch. Thornburgh not only became a director of Merrill Lynch; he also is a director of the giant scandal ridden drug store chain, Rite Aid Corporation. The scion of the Rite Aid family, Martin Grass, was arrested in Room 158 at Cleveland's Sheraton Airport Hotel. Prosecutors had seized him as he was in the act of handing a $33,000 check to Melvin Wilcyznski, a voting member of the state pharmacy board. In return, Mr. Wilczysnki had signed an undated letter of resignation from the pharmacy board. The entire incident was videotaped by prosecutors, who had also recorded four prior telephone conversations between Grass, former executive vice president of Rite Aid, who had been recently named president of the firm, and Wilczynski. The news of the arrest caused Rite Aid stock to tumble $1.875 per share, down to $34.75. Rite Aid is the nation's largest drug store chain, with 2270 stores and 28,000 employees. It owns 65 auto parts stores, ADAP, and a 40 store chain of retail bookstores, Encore. It also owns a dry cleaning chain, Begley Corp., of which Martin Grass is director.

Rite Aid's overweening interest in the Ohio State Board of Pharmacy was due to its acquisition of 162 Gray Drug Fair stores in 1987. Rite Aid has 349 stores in Ohio. Members of the State Board of Pharmacy had fined Rite Aid fifty thousand dollars on January 1989, for allowing nonpharmacy employees access to prescription drugs. The board had previously refused to allow Rite Aid a grace period to correct the many drug security problems which were endemic in its stores. The Wall Street Journal account of the affair, an extensive one, stated that Martin Grass had planned to submit Mr. Wilczynski's resignation to Governor Richard J. Celeste, who, as Grass told Wilczynski, had agreed to appoint pharmacists chosen by Rite Aid to fill future vacancies on the state pharmacy board. Prosecutors alleged that Rite Aid was attempting to stop the pharmacy board from proceeding with enforcement actions against it. Investigators had learned that the Grass plan, to which Celeste was claimed to be a party, was to replace three members of the pharmacy board with Rite Aid supporters, and to oust the board's executive director. Ninety of the Gray Drug Fair stores acquired by Rite Aid had been raided in a two day period and charged with not having proper security alarm systems, as well as other violations.

In New York state, Rite Aid had become involved in another imbroglio when the firm's vice president for governmental affairs and trade relations threatened to boycott the New York State Employees Prescription Plan, when new rates were proposed in 1986. The Federal Trade Commission then charged Rite Aid with illegally forcing an increased reimbursement rate on prescriptions, a move which subsequently cost New York State an added seven million dollars in charges.

A well-known Wall Street drug chain analyst noted that "Marty wanted to show his father that he could handle anything which came up during his presidency. At this rate, he will never be named president of the Federation of Jewish Philanthropies (a position carrying great personal prestige in the community)." The analyst was referring to the record of Marty Grass's father, Alex Grass, a Miami lawyer who had married into the hierarchy of Rite

Aid stores. He married Lois Lehrman (the Lehrman family are the chief stockholders in Rite Aid). Grass later became chief operating officer of the giant drug firm, leading to his zooming to a prominent role in community philanthropies. He is currently listed as chairman of the United Jewish Appeal, the Israel Endowment Fund, the Jewish Federation, the Jewish Agency for Israel, and the Israel Center for Social and Economic Studies. He is the brother-in-law of the well-known neoconservative, Lewis Lehrman, who led in the purchase of the Republican Party by wealthy neoconservatives in 1980. While he was still president of Rite Aid stores, Lehrman ran for Governor of New York, breaking all spending records in his campaign, which was unsuccessful. Although his campaign of loyalists assured him that "A Jewish candidate can't lose in New York," he insisted on spending seven million dollars for TV ads, while his successful opponent, Cuomo, spent only one and a half million. Cuomo's campaign workers bad also assured him that he could not lose, telling him that "A Roman Catholic Italian can't lose in New York." When the votes were counted, they were right.

Lehrman then promoted himself as an arch conservative, endowing his own "rightwing think-tank," which be modestly named "the Lewis Lehrman Institute." Lehrman is also a chief financial backer of such well-known "conservative" groups as the Heritage Foundation, which is led by a British Fabian Socialist, and the American Enterprise Institute, both of which are Rockefeller sponsored agitprop operations masquerading as "rightwing political groups."

Lehrman bad already won some recognition (principally through his favorite magazine, the National Review), as the ideological genius behind President Reagan's famous "supply side revolution." Lehrman was also an ardent advocate of the "goldbug" principles of the French economist, Jacques Rueff. Lehrman then became the mentor of a former liberal, David Stockman, who had switched sides when the Republicans gained the ascendancy. When Stockman and his cohort, Jack Kemp (now Bush's cabinet choice as bead of the giant Health Education and Welfare boondoggle in Washington) published a controversial report early in the Reagan administration warning of "an approaching economic Dunkirk," it was common knowledge in Washington that they had merely plagiarized an earlier Lehrman Report reaching the same conclusion.

In 1977, Lewis Lehrman placed three million dollars of his rapidly burgeoning personal fortune into the Lehrman Institute, which be installed in a luxurious Manhattan townhouse. When Lehrman announced his intention of running for the Governorship of New York, the Lehrman family stock in Rite Aid was worth $92 million, of which Lewis Lehrman's share was $60 million. During his campaign, the stock increased in value by ten points, reaching a high of 40 on the exchange. Wall Street analysts apparently believed that the Rite Aid firm would benefit financially by having its principal stockholder in the Governor's seat. In fact, Lehrman spent some ten million during his campaign, while his stock holdings in Rite Aid increased by $15 million, meaning that he had realized a tidy increase of $5 million in his personal fortune by seeking public office. This was a unique twist to the usual pattern of events in the United States political domain, whereby poor farm boys dedicate themselves to a life of public service and wind up with fifty million dollars' worth of corporate stock, as did the late Lyndon Baines Johnson.

Lewis Lehrman had long been one of a very small group of gods in William Buckley's pantheon, routinely eulogized in the pages of the CIA agitprop sheet, the National Review; Lehrman's companions in this strange pantheon were Sir James Goldsmith, a relative and partner of the Rothschilds of Europe; Bill Casey, director of the CIA; Jeane Kirkpatrick, known as "Miss Israel" of the Washington set; and Milton Friedman, the tireless spokesman of the Rothschilds' Viennese School of Economies. These gods were known collectively as the "neocons," intellectual slang for "neoconservatives," who were well represented on the board of directors of the Trotskyite priesthood in the United States, the Rockefeller financed League for Industrial Democracy, the old Socialist Workers Party (Valhalla of the martyred Leon Trotsky, a victim of Stalin's insatiable urge to kill). The Rockefeller fascination with Trotsky dated back to the heady days of 1917, when old John D. himself saw Trotsky off to spark the Bolshevik Revolution in Russia. John D. charitably stuffed ten thousand dollars into Trotsky's pocket as he embarked on his career of world revolution, a startling departure from Rockefeller's standard gift of one dime to those of whom he approved.

Despite Lehrman's image as a loser, which was compounded by his aura of great wealth, and his habit of buying those whom he wished to impress, the pages of the National Review sparkled with tributes to Lehrman's great deeds in peddling aspirin to the public. William Buckley also has a daily newspaper column, in which he rolled out his big guns to support Lehrman's candidacy (Oct. 26, 1982), praising Lehrman as "a brilliant public servant" who was also "prominent in Jewish affairs." Lehrman later discovered that hardly anyone in New York read Buckley's outpourings, which may explain why he lost.

Frustrated in his drive for the governorship of New York, which would bring the coveted White House into view, as witness the strange career of Franklin Delano Roosevelt, Lehrman threw his money and influence behind the political career of Jack Kemp, who proved as difficult to sell to the American public as Lehrman himself. National Review described Kemp as "the political fugleman of the Lew Lehrman economic school." Despite Lehrman's influential backing, Jack Kemps' quest for the Presidency, along with Lehrman's other political ambitions, sank without a trace.

Lehrman's fortune originated with his grandfather, an itinerant peddler whose principal stock, as his grandson was fond of recalling, consisted of shoelaces and sugar. The grandfather finally accumulated enough cash to open a small grocery store, which, as so often happens in our climate of creating wealth, became a large wholesale grocery chain. When the accountants' reports showed that the profits from drugs far exceeded the much smaller returns on meat and potatoes, the eider Lehrman went into the retail drug business. After the millions had piled up, his grandson, Lew, was able to marry a Protestant, Louise Stillman, a member of New York's most prestigious banking family, and the historic bankers (National City Bank, now Citibank) of Rockefeller's billions of income from Standard Oil, the world's most successful monopoly. Two of the Stillman daughters had married into the Rockefeller family, which brought Lew

Lehrman into the family's golden aura. As a student at Harvard, Lew Lehrman was awarded a Carnegie teaching fellowship and a Woodrow Wilson fellowship. It has long been a truism in the more august Ivy League establishments that great family wealth should not be considered a deterrent to a student receiving fellowships, even though the donors may have originally intended them for needy scholars.

Alex Grass, the Miami lawyer who married Lew's sister, was also prospering with Rite Aid. The political campaign which increased Lew's fortune by some twenty per cent had a corresponding effect on Alex and his wife Lois' holdings. However, Alex Grass became oppressed by growing envy and dislike of his more famous brother-in-law, a situation which was deftly profiled by writer Michael Kramer in New York Magazine. Grass promptly filed a $24 million defamation suit against New York, of which nothing has been heard in recent years. Kramer noted in New York's issue of April 5, 1982, from lengthy discussions with Rite Aid executives, that "Alex has always been jealous of Lew." There had been considerable infighting within the firm for years, as Alex and Lew each battled to support his claims that he and he alone had been responsible for the phenomenal growth of Rite Aid and its burgeoning profits. No mean publicist himself, Alex Grass had chosen to promote himself through immersion in Jewish affairs, finally achieving the most desired position in Jewish philanthropy, when he was named national chairman of the United Jewish Appeal. Lehrman continued to devote himself to "public affairs," hiring Robert F. Kennedy's dynamic speechwriter, Adam Walinsky, to draft his pronunciamientoes. The rivalry between the relatives finally subsided when Lehrman withdrew from active participation in the firm, and Alex was able to name his son as president. Insiders believe that it was the Grasses' frantic determination to "show up" Lew which led to Marty's involvement in the Ohio bribery scandal. As previously noted, the deep involvement of the new Attorney General with the scandals of Rite Aid raises serious questions as to the motives of President Bush's drive for a "kindler and gentler America," but not necessarily a more honest one.

In addition to Thomburgh, other directors of the Rite Aid firm are Richard Kogan, president of the drug firm Schering Plough, a three billion dollar operation. Kogan also has the requisite London connection, being a director of one of England's Big Five banks, National Westminster, which provided the most recent choice to head the Bank of England. Kogan's fellow directors at Schering Plough include William A. Schreyer, chairman of Merrill Lynch; Harold McGraw, chairman of the business publishing giant, McGraw Hill; Virginia Dwyer, director of the Federal Reserve Bank of New York, Baton Corp., Georgia Power, and the Southern Company, which has been much in the news recently; and James Wood, chairman of A&P Co.

Federal agencies have shown no curiosity as to whether Kogan's position as head of one of the nation's largest drug manufacturers poses a conflict of interest with his position as director of the nation's largest retail drug operation. Other directors of Rite Aid are Leonard Stem, Philip Neivert, Henry Taub and Gerald Tsai Jr. Formerly known as the Boy Wonder of Wall Street, Tsai is now chairman of the holding company, Primerica, which owns the Wall Street investment firm, Smith Barney Co., and Continental Life, as well as Fingerhut, a textile firm grossing $800 million a year. Directors of Primerica include Washington's most famous wheeler dealer, Joseph Califano Jr., known as the highest priced lawyer-lobbyist in Washington, and former Secretary of Health, Education and Welfare, the world's largest boondoggle. Charles Hugel is also director of Primerica; he is chairman of Combustion Engineering Co., one of the nation's most fervent proponents of "trade with Soviet Russia" and USTEC, the secretive "businessman's organization" which is desperately trying to salvage the collapsing economy of the Soviet Union, all expenses to be paid by the American taxpayer, and to rescue the Leninist Marxist philosophy of government from well-deserved oblivion. Califano serves with Hugel on the board of Combustion Engineering. Hugel is also chairman of RJR Nahisco, director of Pitney Bowes, and director of the Baton Corp., the creation of the late Cyrus Baton, a protege of John D. Rockefeller who became famous for his connections to the Soviet KGB through his sponsorship of the mysterious "Pugwash

EUSTACE MULLINS

Conferences," and who was advertised for years in the American press as "the nation's most pro-Communist financier."

The final director of the present Rite Aid Corp. to attract our attention is Henry Taub, chairman of the giant Automatic Data Processing Corp. ($1.38 billion a year). The firm's finances are handled by Manufacturers Hanover Bank in New York, the Rothschild Bank, according to little-known Congressional hearings. Its directors include Alan Greenspan, a director of J. P. Morgan Co., who is now in charge of the nation's monetary system as chairman of the Federal Reserve Board of Governors; Joseph Califano, previously mentioned; Laurence Tisch, the tycoon who swallowed the CBS media giant; and Frederick Malek, known as one of the pillars of the fallen Nixon Administration.

Although Rite Aid's officers and directors have many historic connections with the fate of the embattled Middle East country, Israel, none are more prominent than Henry Taub. He is a director of American Technion, which provides funds for Israel's burgeoning science industry; the Bank Leumi Trust, which financed the takeover of Palestine from the Arabs through Tibor Rosenbaum of Switzerland and points west, and other Jewish agencies. A former director of Rite Aid, and protege of the Lehrman political drive, is Maxwell Rabb, the grey eminence of the Eisenhower Administration, who for many years has represented "American" interests as the United States Ambassador to Italy. Another prominent Washington wheeler dealer who interlocks with Rite Aid is H. Guyford Stever, director of Schering-Plough, who has held many important government posts in such agencies as NASA, the National Science Foundation, president of Carnegie-Mellon University, chairman of the U.S.-U.S.S.R. Joint Committee for Science and Technology, board of governors of the Israel Science Foundation, and director of the giant defense contractor, TRW Corp. Stever is a member of the exclusive Cosmos Club of Washington, and the famed Bohemian Club of California, where the elite meet to plan their personal goals for the great American future.

The sinister combination of banking and legal interests exposed in these connections has been itemized in great detail in this writer's book, *The World Order*. Confirmation of its conclusions are to be found in the dramatic show trials held in Washington in recent years, in which persons suspected of "conservativism" were deliberately pilloried by the devotees of One World, the historic liberal political movement. To protect themselves in the courts, these special interests have gone to great lengths to ensure that the cases would be heard by judges who were proven to be sympathetic to their hidden goals. The instrumentality has been an agency of which few Americans have ever heard, the American Bar Association's Standing Committee on the Federal Judiciary. This relatively unknown group, elected by no one, has exercised a virtual veto power over judicial nominees for many years, confining its approval to those prospective judges with an extensive record of service to its largely unpronounced but well-known and well understood goals. An editorial in the Wall Street Journal of March 22, 1989 noted that "Politics disguised as objective evaluation characterized the ABA's quasi-official role in judicial selection during the Reagan years." The Washington Legal Foundation, a public interest group, is now suing the ABA, because the Standing Committee refused to give this conservative foundation information on nominees which it had willingly shared with leftwing groups. The standing committee has maintained its principles of closed deliberations and secretive voting, much like its preceptor, the secretive Federal Board Reserve Board of Governors. The WLF lawsuit was based on the ABA's well established record of sending information on prospective judicial nominees to the NAACP, People for the American Way, the ACLU, and other prominent liberal operations, while steadfastly denying this information to conservative groups such as the WLF. The ABA process ensured the nomination of liberal activist judges which now plague the American bench, and which represent for most Americans who do not fall into that category. The Washington Legal Foundation maintained that "the investigations have been conducted and are continuing to be conducted in such a way as to penalize or discredit candidates who hold or profess conservative principles or ideology, and to delay or prevent their nomination by the President."

In response, the ABA maintains that it only investigates "the judicial temperament" of nominees, but fails to explain why it only sends the names of prospective judicial candidates to leftwing organizations. ABA committee member Stewart Dunnings has testified that they wanted to confine judicial selection to candidates who had an affirmative action commitment. Susan Liss, director of the People for the American Way, revealed that it was routine for the ABA to give the names of potential candidates to the Alliance for Justice, an umbrella group of civil rights organizations such as the NAACP and ACLU. This practice allowed these groups to mount an offensive against prospective candidates long before their names had reached the President, or before conservative groups could defend them. Sen. Orrin Hatch described this process as follows: "It exercises a virtual veto over our judicial nominees." Sen. Gordon Humphrey also has forcefully objected to the sinister behind the scenes operation of the ABA, stating to the Senate Judiciary Committee that "the system is a mouldering, corrupt, malodorous old relic which should be given a quick burial for the sake of public health." Sen. Humphrey then wrote a letter to President Bush complaining that during Robert Fiske's tenure as chairman of the ABA Standing Committee, "there is evidence that committee evaluations were tainted with ideological bias against conservative nominees selected by President Reagan." He stated that Fiske had leaked the names of prospective nominees to activist liberal groups which could target them for reprisal even before their names had been announced to the public. Despite these protests, Atty. Gen. Thomburgh announced on June 2, 1989 that his choice of Fiske as his Deputy Atty. Gen. still stood, and that he intended to continue to send the names of prospective judicial nominees to the ABA Standing Committee. Thomburgh claimed that the committee had promised to change its liberal bias, whereupon the committee members promptly retorted that they had not changed and had no intention of changing their methods of approving judicial candidates. They continued to deny that religious or philosophical stands of candidates affected their conditions of approval, despite the fact that the Wall Street Journal editorial page gave considerable space to the protest of Arthur Schwab on April 11, 1989, that the ABA had blocked his judicial appointment for religious and political reasons, mainly because he was a practicing Christian. He submitted a 20 page recitation of his complaint concerning a three year "investigation" of his candidacy by the ABA. His nomination to the Third Circuit Court of Appeals in Pennsylvania was withdrawn by President Reagan, because he could not win approval by the ABA. The committee member assigned to question him, Jerome Shestack, is known as one of the most liberal of the 15 man Standing Committee. He pointedly asked Schwab why his children went to a Christian school, even though the ABA claims they do not take religious affiliation into account in approving prospective nominees. Shestack was also a director of the far-left Lawyers Committee for Civil Rights Under Law, and served on a Joe Biden for President Committee, even while the ABA was masterminding the Biden Judiciary Committee assault on Robert Bork.

The determination of the World Order to prevent the selection of any judicial appointee who was not committed to their sinister international program has not only been a rape of justice; it has been the handmaiden of the rape of the entire American people. The consequences of this campaign are now raging in Washington, in what is being called "a feeding frenzy," as conservatives take their revenge for the outrages committed against their candidates during the past thirty years by the ABA Standing Committee on the Federal Judiciary. The liberal conspiracy against conservative candidates reached its apogee in the Moscow show hearings on the candidacy of Judge Robert Bork for the Supreme Court, followed by the widely leaked ABA report on his nominal successor, Judge Douglas Ginsberg, who was said to have smoked a marijuana cigarette some years earlier. The greatly over-extended Bork Hearings caused a breakdown of Americans' confidence in the processes of government, which was reflected in the 500 point drop in the stock market in the October 1987 Crash. This was followed by the prosecution of Congressman George Hansen on charges of "ethics violations," charges which were based on the fact that he had not entered some items on the proper line, at a time when most Congressmen admitted they did not know how to properly fill out the newly required forms. Hansen, a Republican, and a Mormon from a Western State, Idaho, was pilloried because he had long been an outspoken critic of brutal abuses by agents of the Internal Revenue Service against American citizens, and because he had interfered in the politics of the Middle East. Because Hansen had flown to Iran to try to secure the release of American hostages, and thereby imperiled a billion dollar operation of the Chase Manhattan Bank, he was chosen for crucifixion. None other than Nate Lewin, of the Department of Justice infamous Office of Special Investigations was hired to defend Hansen. Lewin charged Hansen a million dollars to defend him; Hansen was duly convicted on orders of Mossad for having dared to barge into the sewer of Middle Eastern political conspiracy, where he was not wanted. He served every day of his sentence, in the most brutal of the federal prisons, at Petersburg, Va., despite pleas from 258 Congressmen that he be released on parole. He was judged "too dangerous" to the minions of the World Order to be allowed early parole, despite the fact that the court records showed he had not profited from the alleged "violations."

The brutal treatment meted out to Congressman Hansen alerted some Congressmen to the fact that they had to fight back or be destroyed. They now went after the most notorious of the wheeler dealers in Washington, the Democratic Speaker of the House, James Wright. Wright was one of the most dedicated left-wingers in Congress, and had upheld the Stalinist war against the Trotskyite Republican effort to aid the Contra movement in Nicaragua. A list of 69 ethical violations was drawn up against Wright, although the Wall Street Journal stated that the original list had numbered 116, but had been cut almost in half by those who wished to protect Wright from the consequences of his own actions. At the height of the investigation, Wright was further compromised by a family matter. His personal protege, John Mack, whose brother had married Wright's daughter, was found to have received extremely favorable treatment after committing one of the Washington area's most shocking crimes. In 1973, Mack had lured a twenty year old girl into the back room of a discount store where he was employed. He seized a hammer and smashed in her skull with repeated blows, exposing her brain in five areas. He then stabbed her five times in the breast near her heart, leaving part of her heart exposed, and then slashed her repeatedly across the throat. He then carried the body of his victim, Pamela Small, to her car, and drove her to a remote area, where he left her for dead. Amazingly enough, she revived some eight hours later, and drove to an Exxon station, where she persuaded the attendant to get her to a hospital. She then underwent seven hours of surgery; her left lung had collapsed and her heart required extensive repair. Mack was subsequently arrested, and powerful influences swung into effect to defend him. He was merely charged with "malicious wounding," and received a 15 year sentence. Instead of being sent to state prison, he served his time in the county jail, where he worked as a cook. Congressman Wright had written to the judge, offering Mack a job even before he was sentenced. With this opportunity awaiting him, Mack was released after 27 months. Wright obtained a job for him in the Congressional mail room at $9000 a year (the present writer earned a mere $1500 a year as a deck attendant at the Library of Congress, but had no Congressional patron). As Wright's influence grew, so did that of his protege. John Mack became the executive director of the Democratic Steering and Policy Committee, and was described by reporters as the most influential Congressional staff administrator on Capitol Hill. However, Mack's victim continued to live and work in the Washington area. Several years ago in 1987, Wright's office summoned the leading newspapermen in Washington, the Capitol Hill reporters for the *Washington Post*, the *New York Times*, and the Wall Street Journal, for a consultation on the Mack affair. The goal was to prevent an approaching firestorm about the Small assault. These reporters, including the CBS representative, agreed that it was "an old story," and that it had no foreseeable interest. The reporters now admit that "they blew it." What seems more likely is that they had the opportunity to curry favor with the most powerful politician on Capitol Hill, Jim Wright, who was third in line for the presidency of the United States, and that they did it the Washington way.

When the story broke in the *Washington Post* on May 4, 1989, the usual efforts at "damage control" were taken. Wright issued a statement to the press that he was not "told the details of the crime," apparently giving the impression that he thought Mack had been charged with jaywalking. Wright's statement praised Mack as "an exemplary and truly inspiring person outstanding remarkable capacity for intellectual growth." Other Democratic leaders joined Wright in effusive praise for Mack's accomplishments. His wife was serving as executive assistant to Congressman Mavroules, a leading Democrat. In fact, Mack had exhibited the highest qualities for political activity, an instinct for the jugular, blood lust, and capacity for direct action such as cold blooded attempted murder. This writer has repeatedly lectured on the element of criminality in those who seek political office; Mack now verified the strongest statements on the matter. In the face of the Democratic chorus of praise for this remarkable human being, stories of other acts committed by Mack surfaced. The Democratic phalanx of defenders was shaken by the defection of several radical feminists, who were alarmed by the fact that Mack had never apologized for his acts, or sought to make any restitution to his victim-she had taken care of her own hospital expenses. Congresswoman Pat Schroeder and other women on Capitol Hill expressed their unease at having to deal with Mack in their political lives, and because Mack's defense of his actions had been that he had been under "stress" (Washington traffic is indeed very stressful), Schroeder publicly showed concern that he might again be overtaken by "stress" while she was in his office discussing Democratic Party policies of which he was the final arbiter. In the face of these protests, Wright suggested to Mack that he had better resign, a decision which was motivated by the fact that Wright was now battling for his own political survival. Mack's departure did little to help him, and Wright finally announced his own resignation. The Associated Press noted that he received a standing ovation from his colleagues in the House.

Another leading Democratic liberal, Congressman Tony Coelho, then announced that he was resigning as Democratic Party whip, and leaving politics. He found it difficult to explain his association with the junk bond king, Michael Milken, who earned $500 million last year, and who apparently tried to share the wealth by cutting Coelho in on a deal or two. The Post revealed that Congressman Tommy Robinson had a 22 year old model on his staff, who was being paid $60,000 a year. He owed her father $100,000, (Jerry Jones, a wealthy oilman who owns the Dallas Cowboys).

The Republican National Committee, in commenting on Coelho's imminent departure, responded to Coelho's spirited defense of John Mack, who happened to be his business partner, that it was the second time that Coelho had come to the defense of a man convicted of an attack on a woman. This was followed by an apology from the Committee, after being informed that the first time Coelho had defended a man convicted of an attack, it had been on a boy, not on a woman. Such are the pitfalls of describing the public sewers of Washington.

Although the press delicately refrained from dwelling upon the details of Coelho's intervention on behalf of a convicted felon, the New Republic, in its issue of June 12, 1989, noted that the Congressman had not only intervened on behalf of his business partner and personal political confidante, John Paul Mack, but also on behalf of David Weichert. Weichert was the son of John Weichert, a 1982 Coelho campaign contributor who had donated several thousand dollars to the cause of Coelho. He now asked Coelho to intervene on behalf of his son, who was about to be sentenced for the crime of first degree murder. This crime was brutal enough to be compared to the Mack assault. Weichert had kidnapped, tortured and killed a retarded youth because he feared the youth might testify against him in a burglary case. Weichert choked the youth, then stabbed him, beat him furiously with a baseball bat, and forced him to dig his own grave. According to the account of his accomplice, he threw the youth into the grave while he was still alive, seized the shovel and threw in the earth, burying his victim alive. Coelho immediately went to bat for the murderer, contacting the judge, and giving him to understand that as an influential Washington politician, he had a deep concern over this case. The judge apologetically informed Coelho that he could do very little about the sentence, as conviction for this crime now carried a mandatory sentence of life in prison.

In the wake of Wright's resignation, columnist R. Emmett Tyrell Jr. noted that one of Wright's aides had been imprisoned for tax evasion, while Wright's press aide and righthand man in dealing with the media, George Mair, had written a titillating work in 1982, titled "The Sex Book Digest: A Peek Between the Covers of 113 of the most Erotic, Exotic and Edifying Sex Books."

The Democratic Party had maintained control of the House of Representatives with the coalition welded by Franklin Delano Roosevelt in the early 1930s with the able assistance of Bella Moscowitz, a leading New York Communist organizer. This was a consensus of Communists, blacks, the Mafia, and various other special interest groups, which exercised iron control over the corrupt political machines of the nation's largest cities. Although this weird coalition could control the House, it could not deliver a Presidential majority, resulting in a Republican Administration held at bay by an activist and fanatical Communist and Zionist Democratic alliance. Paralyzed by this impasse, the nation sank into deeper disarray, its assets being stripped by a horde of eager aliens, while the infrastructure built at such cost and effort by previous generations rotted into oblivion, seemingly beyond repair.

Alarmed Democratic leaders, with the blood of Robert Bork, John Tower and other Presidential appointees on their bands, now shrieked that the "feeding frenzy" must end, that the departure of Wright, Mack and Coelho should have satisfied those who mourned the ritual slaughter of George Hansen, Robert Bork and John Tower at the bands of a fanatical Stalinist Democratic Congressional bit team. However, Republican leaders noted that they still had long lists of other Democratic stalwarts with even longer lists of ethical and financial violations. Despite, the struggle goes on.

CHAPTER 8

DURANCE VILE

Our present custom of confining criminals in expensive prisons is a costly relic of humanist thought. It can be traced back to the Renaissance period in Italy. In the classical world of Greece and Rome, society protected itself by killing or exiling criminals, or persons who presented a clear and present danger to society. The purpose was to remove a threat to the common weal. With the rebirth of humanist influence on society, a Phoenix-like revival of a cult which had been feared and hated by society since the blood thirsty rites of Baal and Ashtoreth, some five thousand years earlier (see *The Curse Of Canaan*[7] by Eustace Mullins), came the "compassionate" pretext of preserving and coddling the criminal element. The thought of maintaining such a threat in perpetuity would have seemed the height of insanity to classical thinkers, who evolved the cultural basis of our civilization. During the Middle Ages, wielders of power built huge castles, fortresses where they could defend themselves against their enemies. Deep within the bowels of these castles, dungeons were built for the incarceration of enemies whose sudden death might have unleashed dangerous forces; claimants to power or religious martyrs who, for various reasons, might be allowed to live for many years, but whose imprisonment itself constituted a living death.

With the growing infiltration of the Black Nobility into the European monarchy, the aristocracy was persuaded that the

---

[7] Published by Omnia Veritas Ltd. www.omnia-veritas.com.

imprisonment of criminals could serve as a deterrent and a warning to others who posed a threat to society. The most famous prisons resulting from this concept were the Tower of London, and the Bastille in Paris. The Tower of London became the home of many prominent political offenders, including Sir Edward Coke. In France, the Bastille held a curious mix of hardened criminals and political offenders. The liberation of a total of seven prisoners in the Bastille on July 14, 1789, which is now the French national holiday corresponding to our Fourth of July, resulted in the freeing of four professional forgers, one libertine who had been imprisoned at the insistence of his exasperated family, and two lunatics. One of the lunatics was then carried through the streets by a cheering crowd. He believed that he was Julius Caesar, and that Rome had once again become the center of the world. The only casualty of the liberation was the warden, who was dragged out into the street and torn to pieces by the mob. Four days earlier, the warden had insisted upon the release of the Bastille's most famous prisoner, the Marquis de Sade, who had continuously floated notes from the window to the street below demanding that he be freed. "Bastille Day" not only celebrates the triumph of lunacy and sadism, but also the triumph of the Masonic conspiracy over the French monarchy. Some sixty years earlier, the rise of the House of Hanover in London had installed Freemasonry in England under the royal patronage.

Early nineteenth century reformers such as Jeremy Bentham, the protege of the East India Company, and William Godwin, whose daughter wrote "Frankenstein," invented the intellectual foundation of a fantasy structure which was called a "correctional" system. The term "prison" was deemed too calumniating; henceforth, "prisoners" would be known as "victims of society" who must be "corrected" and imbued with "correct" social attitudes. Instead of society being protected from criminals, it was now the criminals who were to be cosseted and cared for while they prepared for the day of their revenge upon society. The heirs to the cult of Baal, the humanists, claimed that "bad environment" created the criminal class. The removal of the criminal from this unfortunate situation, to a prison where he could be cared for, would "correct" his criminal tendencies. The humanists then developed a new social science, penology, which like all the misconceptions spawned by this new wave, psychology, civics, and social welfare, gradually merged to form a huge modern combine or trust, nurtured by the tax-exempt humanist foundations. Penology began with the praise-worthy efforts of a few conscientious persons to alleviate the harsh conditions of prisoners in the early 1800s. Remember that life was harsh for most Americans at that time, and it was unlikely that prisons would be maintained with better living conditions than those enjoyed by the average pioneer. Conditions were slowly improved, but by the turn of the century, prisons had become part of the overall bureaucracy, which meant that they were part of the spoils system, graft, and political influence. Like insane asylums and other government institutions, prisons were turned into gold mines of graft for those fortunate enough to wield political power, most of the funds appropriated for the feeding and care of prisoners being pocketed by those who had mastered the democratic process. Faced with the difficulties of influencing the bureaucracy, the humanists began to develop new methodologies in their campaign for prison reform. Their first discovery was that no human being should ever be incarcerated. This was hardly a revolutionary thought-it had been the precept of the founders of classical civilization. The humanists began to implement their goal of emptying the prisons by formulas for work release, early parole, and family furloughs for prisoners. The problem was that these techniques resulted in a dramatic increase in crime, and caused the prisons to become more overcrowded than ever. The humanists also developed programs of intensive psychotherapy for those prisoners who were not yet eligible for the release program. The released prisoners, most of whom were recidivists, or habitual criminal psychopaths, committed horrendous crimes, which caused public outrage, and the demand that more millions be spent for police protection, and for the building of more prisons. Faced with the prospect of vast increases in their funding, the bureaucrats of the crime industry realized that the humanist procedures were indeed evidence of the gratifying results of the new science of penology. Burdened with the task of spending more millions than they had ever envisioned, the prison bureaucracy became enthusiastic converts to the obvious advantages of social activist penology.

The "science" of penology came into its own after World War II, when a horde of rapacious humanists, who had been indoctrinated by the professional social scientists of the Tavistock Institute and its numerous American satellites, obtained lucrative employment throughout the prison system. The Tavistock Institute had been set up after the First World War, as a branch of the British Army Department of Psychological Warfare, to study the methods of controlling shell-shocked soldiers. Their purpose was to use these unfortunate victims of the war as guinea pigs, testing them to see how much strain was necessary before the average human would break under stress. The technique of Communist brainwashing was one of the more successful offshoot of these studies. It spawned a host of refinements, such as "motivational technology" and "stress management," which educational and government leaders, and business executives, are now required to undergo at one of the Tavistock Institute spinoffs throughout the United States. The purpose of these brainwashing techniques is to trick the subject into admitting some sexual misconduct, a hidden fear, or other weakness exposing an Achilles heel by which he can then be "manipulated" for the rest of his career. The goal is people control. It originated in the Jesuitical techniques of the Inquisition during the Middle Ages, and is now the basis for the entire operation of the United States government, especially those departments engaged in "intelligence" work, such as the CIA, the IRS, and other conspiratorial areas.

The purpose of the Jesuitical confession is always control. For this reason, the American judicial system insists not only upon confession, but, upon conviction, an expression of remorse. Many Americans who have been convicted of some political offense in our courts self-righteously refuse to express remorse, which justifies the gleeful judge in giving them a much harsher sentence than he could have pronounced if they had groveled and spouted emotional recriminations. This was graphically demonstrated at the end of the political show trials called the Watergate trials. Republican political offenders were sentenced to long terms by a Democratically controlled court, the longest sentence being handed down to Nixon's former aide, G. Gordon Liddy, because he refused to recant. This religious error resulted in his spending many years in prison, which he might have avoided by the required cringing and apostasy. Even so, the process was more humane than that of the Middle Ages, where the prisoner was tortured until he recanted, and was then burned.

The purpose of our criminal justice system is not to remove the criminal from society, but to find the lever by which he can be manipulated by the conspirators. His "handler" does not care whether it is sex, drugs, an irrational fear, or whatever weakness; the goal of the Tavistock method is to find that lever. Another key point in manipulating the subject is to convince him that everything that is being done to him is being done "for his own good." He cannot make any progress until he relieves his mind through the technique of "confession." The appalling cynicism of these manipulators is beyond most moral individuals' capacity of understanding. They cannot comprehend the Satanic origin of these techniques, unless they are familiar with the five-thousand-year-old cult of Baal and the worldwide Canaanite conspiracy.

Even after conviction and sentencing, the prisoner is still expected to offer continuous acts of contrition, which will result in an early release through parole or furlough. The result is that many prisoners "find Christ" the moment the prison doors clang shut behind them, the most notorious being one of the Watergate victims, Charles Colson, who was so successful in charming his way out of prison that he opted for prison religious work, rather than returning to his lucrative law practice.

Although the prison parole system remains firmly grounded in bribery and political influence, the members of the parole boards still place great stock in Jesuitical expressions of contrition from those who seek release. Such expressions also offer a convenient screen for the hidden reasons behind the sudden parole of a notorious criminal.

Because penology is based upon humanism, the modern version of the cult of Baal, prisoners who have been accused of anti-humanist activities, such as religious belief, patriotism, or belief in the Constitution, are never granted parole. They always serve out their entire sentences. Such offenders include those Americans suspected of anti-Communism, tax resisters (who are often referred to by the servile media as tax "protesters" — it has never been a crime in the United States to protest against any tax imposition), and members of the white ethnic minority who have been indicted for "racism." In our legal terminology, a racist is anyone who publicly refers to white racial ethnicity. It is obligatory for blacks, Jews and Hispanics to constantly parade their racial loyalties, and to beat or kill anyone who criticizes them, actions which find instant approval in the media and in our courts. Should one of these activists accuse a white citizen of "racism," the white citizen is promptly arrested and convicted. The Department of Justice has publicized for years its policy that only whites can be charged and convicted of the crime of "racism." The present writer has letters from high ranking officials of the Department of Justice that the white citizens of the United States have no civil rights and cannot claim any redress for violations of civil rights. The Department of Justice apparently bases its stance upon the 14th Amendment that special rights and privileges were conferred upon blacks and other minorities, while apparently stripping white citizens of these same rights and privileges. The Oxford English Dictionary defines "privilege" as "the grant of a right," and also as "a grant of immunity" which the Department of Justice interprets as being conferred upon racial minorities by the 14th Amendment (passed under martial law, therefore invalid), but which is denied members of white ethnic groups in this nation.

During the 1950s, the already outmoded and discredited nineteenth century humanistic claims of penology were expanded into increasingly vaporous and unrealistic programs. Prison guards were forced to endure extensive "human rights" and "sensitivity" sessions by the Tavistock manipulators as part of a nationwide brainwashing diktat. Guards were told that they must address prisoners as "Sir"; they must never raise their voices to them, no matter what the provocation, and they must deliver printed menus to the cells before the prisoners were marched to the mess halls. A new California prison has developed an even more costly program, in which the meals are delivered by hot carts to each cell! States dominated by the more humanistic conspiracies, notably in Massachusetts and Maryland, eagerly adopted the most extreme "advances" of the new penology. The

Massachusetts program was so exhaustive that it caused a taxpayer revolt. It also cost its Governor, Michael Dukakis, the 1988 presidential election. A notorious murderer, Willie Horton, had been released on one of the numerous furlough programs of the new penology; he promptly killed again. The liberal colleges of Massachusetts had previously indoctrinated a horde of practitioners of humanistic penology, the most notorious being Dr. Norma Gluckstem. A leading radical at the University of Massachusetts during the 1960s, Gluckstem initiated a program at the university which gave students academic credit for spending time in jail cells with extremely dangerous prisoners. The University of Massachusetts also promoted one of the most pernicious doctrines of Maoist Communism, that professors and business leaders should spend six months of each year in working at some form of manual labor.

It was hardly surprising that Dr. Gluckstem would be appointed head of the nation's most troublesome prison, the notorious Patuxent Institute in Maryland. Patuxent originated after some Maryland politicians went on a paid junket to Denmark. After the obligatory visits to brothels and pornography shops, the politicians realized that they had to justify their pleasant vacation at the taxpayers' expense. They decided to "study" some innovative prison techniques at a new institution outside of Copenhagen, which treated dangerous offenders by psychiatric techniques. The politicians were immediately convinced that this program offered them considerable political benefits in a caring and compassionate nation. They returned to Maryland as converts to the "new wave" of prison treatment. The result was that in 1955, the state of Maryland established what has now become the nation's most criticized and talked about prison. Salem A. Sarh, a scholar at the National Institute of Mental Health, who has studied the relationship of law and psychiatry for thirty years, notes that "it was the heyday of the mental health movement. The feeling was that to just lock people up was not effective. You had to treat them."

The "treatment" consisted of interviews of the prisoners by well-paid mental health experts, who asked them, "Do you think you are dangerous? Do you think you would ever rape again?"

These interviews allowed those prisoners who were professional criminals to play the favorite indoor sport of our prisons, "Schmoozing" or conning the liberals. The prisoners immediately embraced the Tavistock and Jesuitical techniques of confessing what the interviewer wanted to hear. "I'm in jail because I couldn't control my greed," because of "my insensitivity," or "my self-destructive tendencies." "The only person I have ever really harmed is myself." Such "Stroking" convinced the penologists that the criminal had experienced a genuine reform; he was now a model prisoner who was ready to be returned to society. One of the prisoners who was thus returned to society was Robert Angell, who had murdered two policemen in cold blood during the commission of other crimes. It was disclosed in November of 1988 that this triple murderer had left Patuxent eleven times on unsupervised furloughs. He had killed a teenager in 1975, choosing him at random, and then murdering him, and he killed two policemen in Potomac a year later during a bank robbery. Dr. Gluckstem justified her decision to release Angell by her conviction that Angell was "a completely different person," who "deeply regrets" murdering three people. The Gluckstem program of sending the most dangerous criminals from Patuxent inaugurated a reign of terror and fear among residents of the area. Some people sold their homes and moved away, certain that they would never be safe while Patuxent remained a fertile breeding ground for crime. One prisoner, while on an unsupervised furlough, raped and killed an 11 year-old boy. Another prisoner, Charles Wantland, was paroled after serving five years of a thirty year sentence; he raped and killed a twelve-year-old boy in Clinton, Maryland. A few weeks later, convicted rapist James Stavarakis, whose earlier parole had been revoked, fled while on work release from Patuxent and allegedly raped another woman. Patuxent records proved that its inmates served substantially shorter sentences for violent crimes than inmates at other Maryland institutions. Fernando F. Stewart was paroled by Patuxent in 1981, seven years after he had been convicted of the murder of a county police officer, and sentenced to life in prison. When questioned about Stewart's release, Dr. Gluckstem replied, "People can change." The Gluckstem program of daily work release, unsupervised furloughs, and early parole was compounded by intensive psychotherapy and peer counselling sessions. These programs were made to order for hardened criminals, many of whom had spent years in their cells boning up on psychological studies and psychiatric treatises on the criminal mind. They eagerly embraced the Jesuitical techniques of confession and recrimination as the golden keys which would unlock the doors of the prison. Because the Gluckstem method was tailor-made for the most ruthless classes of criminals, the murderers and the rapists, its benefits were never offered to the political prisoners, the protesters and constitutionalists, who were forced to serve out their entire sentences. The Patuxent board was composed of Dr. Gluckstern, other Patuxent administrators, and law professors. Coming under fire for her policies, Dr. Gluckstern protested, "This place had a mission, whether you believe in that mission or not. I sort of was the caretaker of a historic institution. And when you see it being wiped out, there's a certain sadness." She was referring to the rising tide of public outrage at her methods of managing Patuxent Institute. Russell E. Hamill, vice chairman of the Montgomery Criminal Justice Commission, said, "Public safety is too important to be left to psychiatry." He derided Patuxent as "nothing but a psychiatric sandbox." State Senate President Mike Miller Jr. said, "Dr. Gluckstern was a disaster." Refusing to express any concern for the victims of her pampered inmates, Dr. Gluckstern vanished from the scene. The *Washington Post* later found her in the liberal encampment of Telluride, Colorado, operating a bed and breakfast inn!

After the unsupervised furlough and work release programs at Patuxent were ended in Dec., 1988, Jerald A. Vaughn, former director of the International Assn. of Police Chiefs, wrote an op ed piece for the *Washington Post*, Dec. 13, 1988, in which he pointed out,

> "The Willie Horton and Robert Angell cases are not all that unique Last year alone, more than 200,000 weekend or multiday furloughs were granted to prisoners in our federal and state institutions. About 5% commit a violent act while on furlough, nearly 1,000 violent crimes each year. Prisoners only serve 45% of their total sentence, on average. Prison furloughs in their current form undermine the integrity of our

criminal justice system and make a mockery of meaningful sanctions against criminal behaviour. Government does have a moral obligation to protect the public from criminals adjudicated guilty of heinous crimes."

Increasing public apprehension about criminals walking the streets after being sent to prison was reflected in the presidential campaign of 1988, in which George Bush, a pleasant but uninspiring candidate, faced a long uphill struggle to overcome the vast lead amassed by the Democratic candidate, Michael Dukakis. Dukakis had the media, the entire academic community, the bureaucracy, the unions, and the minorities, allied in the rebirth of the old Roosevelt coalition which had been put together by Communist leader Bella Moskovitz in 1932. This phalanx of political power seemed destined to crush the Bush appeal. A Bush adviser, Lee Atwater, finally became aware of the most widespread emotion in America, fear. He advised the public of the Massachusetts penological machine which had unleashed a horde of vicious criminals on the nation, the most notorious being one Willie Horton. The people responded by marching to the pools, and voting against the criminal psychology program of Dukakis and his Massachusetts leftwing demagogues.

Nevertheless, penology continues to be a growth industry in the United States, with a number of private firms entering the field. The Corrections Corp. of America is the industry leader; its directors interlock with gambling interests and the Bronfman liquor empire. RCA operates the Weaversville prison unit in Pennsylvania; The Eckerd Foundation operates the Okeechobee prison in Florida. The prison bureaucracy has also developed its own version of the Soviet slave labor camps, called UNICOR. It produces 192 different products in our federal prisons, paying the inmates an average of sixty cents an hour. UNICOR states that it is a government corporation, wholly owned, despite the fact that on Dec. 6, 1945, Congress passed 31USCA866, "No corporation shall be created, organized, or acquired by the federal government. No wholly owned government corporation shall continue after June 30, 1948. The private corporate authority of every such corporation shall take the necessary steps to institute dissolution or liquidation proceedings before that date."

UNICOR bureaucrats are now demanding that the government double its prison capacity to fulfill its burgeoning slave labor contracts. The federal government is now kidnapping many persons and holding them for years in prisons.

UNICOR also has many contracts with government departments. At the Lexington Federal Prison, HUD, the Department of Housing and Development, contracted with Federal Prison Industries, UNICOR, to process some 60,000 credit applications for mortgages. Prisoners operating 35 computer terminals processed forms containing credit card numbers and other vital bank and credit information from the 60,000 applicants. One prisoner, Beverly Hirsch, was horrified to find that such personal information was being made available to prisoners, who could pass the numbers along to accomplices outside the prison. She talked to a reporter from the Lexington Herald Leader; the result was that she was immediately placed in solitary confinement. Her security status was changed to a derogatory one, and she was soon transferred to California, far from her children and her recently-widowed mother. Prisoners who run afoul of the penology bureaucracy receive the full treatment; Joss of rights, "diesel therapy," that is, repeated transfer further and further away from their loved ones, often with months passing in which relatives do not know where they are; and "loss of rights while in transit." The U.S. Marshals Service uses more than 800 county jails as "stopovers" for the victims of "diesel therapy." As a "snitch" on prison corruption, Beverly Hirsch will remain "in transit" for many months.

Another well-known prisoner, Rudy Stanko, has also been the victim of "diesel therapy," for blowing the whistle on UNICOR's slave labor practices in our federal prisons. Stanko has been the victim of "diesel therapy" eighteen times, sometimes being moved from one prison to another three or four times in a period of two or three weeks. In less than two years of imprisonment he has been in solitary confinement 472 days. The story of this "criminal" illustrates the depths to which our criminal justice system has sunk. Stanko was one of the fastest-growing meatpackers in the United States. A rival meatpacking group tried to force him out of business; when that failed, they offered to buy him out. He refused. He was then subjected to public pillorying by several national television programs, where ex-employees, who had been bribed by his competitors, claimed he had sold spoiled meat to school luncheon programs. He was then indicted and convicted on the perjured testimony; his rivals took over his plant for ten cents on the dollar. Stanko wrote a book about his experience, "THE SCORE," for which the present writer wrote foreword. He identified his persecutors as a Zionist cartel, which enraged the manipulators of the secret government. Stanko was sentenced to a long prison term. There would be no psychotherapeutic coddling for him. His captors were told to give him the full treatment; continuous "diesel therapy," solitary confinement, and brutal mistreatment which, after some months, has caused the deaths of many political prisoners. Never having committed any crime, Stanko is at a great disadvantage in our prison system, which is run by and for criminals. To this day, not one ounce of "tainted meat" has ever been identified with his meatpacking operation. It was a classic example of bribed witnesses, professional perjurers, and dedicated opposition obtaining their goals.

Federal Prison Industries is listed at 320 1st St. HOLC Bg, Washington D.C. 20534. In the Reader's Guide, prison labor is listed under "convict labor." UNICOR, as well as the privatization of "corrections" industries, is but one of numerous spinoffs from our crime problem. We have had enormous growth in police forces, as well as other parts of the bureaucracy. However, the greatest single beneficiary of the growing crime problem is the insurance industry. It has long been a truism that the insurance industry is almost totally dependent upon a consistently high rate of crime; otherwise, burglary, liability, and other profitable insurance lines would shrivel up. The media cooperates by dramatizing the daily perils of life in the United States, particularly in our larger cities. On Feb. 16, 1989, the Atlanta Journal headlined,

> "METRO CRIME UP 14% in 88. DOUBLING 87 INCREASE. Law enforcement officials blamed most of it on escalating drug use and prisoners released too soon."

On Jan. 27, 1989, the *Washington Post* headlined,

"A LETTER FROM A FRIGHTENED METROPOLIS. Violent Crime Wave Rattles Even Hardened New Yorkers. Fear Stalks Subways." The story noted that there were 1840 homicides in New York City in 1988, a figure greater than that in most major countries of the world. Fear stalks the city so routinely that reporters are bard put to find more clichés to describe the situation.

The Daily News headlined,

"A City Under Siege," "Three Long Island women, all of whom had obtained protective court orders, were shot and killed in a nine day period by their estranged husbands, who then committed suicide." The women were actually killed by government psychiatrists, who, under their new designation of "socially cured" had routinely diagnosed homicidal lunatics as presenting no further threat to society, even though these men had declared their intention of murdering their wives as soon as they were released. The story continues, "A pregnant doctor was raped and killed at Bellevue Hospital, and police arrested and charged a vagrant secretly living on the 22nd floor massive publicity focused on the trial of Joel Steinberg, the Greenwich Village lawyer accused in the beating death of his illegally adopted daughter. Two other small children died in the custody of parents whose cases were botched by the city's welfare agencies."

More than fifty women have been murdered in recent years after their criminally insane husbands were treated and diagnosed as "cured" by government staff psychiatrists. Hundreds of children have been killed after welfare agencies and supposedly well trained social workers demanded that judges order them returned to brutal family situations, where they were beaten and tortured until they died. The women who notified authorities that their husbands intended to kill them were also routinely judged by social workers and psychiatrists to be suffering from delusions, and, most serious of all, they were guilty of "paranoia." Paranoia is one of the most serious charges a psychiatrist can make against you. It means that you suspect someone may try to harm you, an obvious delusion in this-perfect world. In the *New York Times* magazine, Mar. 19, 1989, W. H.

Wash, editor of Psychology Today, offers an authoritative definition of paranoia, as "an elaborate and rigid system of delusional beliefs," complicated by "an elaborate and rigid belief-system." He states that a paranoid streak characterized such populist politicians as Huey Long, with their grand conspiracy theories. He informs us that a paranoid person has a rigid and judgmental thought process. (Rigid) is a favorite word of liberal psychoanalysts; it means that they must find a client who will hold still while they pick his pockets. He also tells us that the paranoid person characteristically exhibits grandiosity and hostility, and that paranoid delusions originate in one's self-dislike.

Since Max Eitington, the colleague of Sigmund Freud, introduced psychiatry as a key element in the world Communist conspiracy, those who oppose Communism have always been diagnosed as suffering from delusions and paranoia. The greatest paranoid personality of all time, of course, was Adolf Hitler, who nearly toppled the Communist empire, proving that Eitington and his fellow KGB agents were correct in fearing the paranoid enemy. In the United States, any citizen who reports the Communist activities of government employees finds himself facing a quick ride to the insane asylum. When a senior State Department official, Felix Bloch, was recently photographed handing over a briefcase to a KGB agent, only a paranoid suffering from anti-Communist delusions would claim that he was doing anything more dangerous than exchanging family pictures of a vacation on the beach. We mention paranoia in such detail because of the psychiatric insistence that it is always delusional, and that it originates in "self-hatred," a mental problem which exists only in the world of psychiatry. The fifty women who were slain by their lunatic husbands after repeated boasts that they intended to do just that, were one and all dismissed by psychiatric experts as suffering from paranoia. Apparently it is a fatal illness, because they died of it.

The crime problem forces American citizens to live in a constant state of warfare. The *Washington Post* headlined Jan. 29, 1989 that "Fear Leads D.C. Cab Drivers to Defy Law." Mayor Barry's scandal-ridden District of Columbia government had passed a law fining any cab driver $100 if be passed by or refused a "dangerous" fare. For "dangerous," read "black." The fact that D.C. Cab drivers now number 97% black, and that they know what they are doing when they refuse a fare, did not prevent the Barry regime from labelling them as criminals. On Jan. 18, 1989, the murder of a 73 year old cab driver in one of the city's most crime ridden areas, at 3rd and Underwood NW, in the shadow of the nation's capitol building, forced the drivers to become more choosy in accepting their fares.

In recent months, worldwide TV news coverage, particularly in Europe, which sends many tourists to Washington, has caused the city to win the title, "crime capital of the world." No other city comes close to Washington's capture of the label, "the murder capital of the U.S." With 372 murders in 1988, and 120 more in the first few months of 1989, Mayor Barry moved quickly to staunch the flow of blood. He announced that 25 police would be detailed to arrest jaywalkers! An estimated 10,000 jaywalking tickets will be issued by the alert Barry police force this year. Meanwhile, Sen. Mark Hatfield witnessed a shootout in the street near his office, but didn't bother to report it. He says it is so commonplace that there is no point in filling out a police report, which will promptly be buried. Barry will do nothing about the city's murder rampage, but jaywalkers have been placed on notice.

Because of academic inability to see cause and result, no one has analyzed the capture of the title "crime capital of the world" as the inevitable result of a previous crime, the illegal decision of the Supreme Court in Shelley v. Kraemer in 1948. Because the decision was arrived at through the efforts of Justice Frankfurter's law clerk as amicus curiae, and his close connections with the organizations which had brought the suit, the American Jewish Congress and the American Jewish Committee, the decision must be stricken from the record as invalid. The Court ruling which brought about the white flight from Washington, and the resulting crime wave, must be corrected.

Although the Federal Prison Bureau has a good thing going with its convict slave labor program, there is no congruent resultant reduction in the crime wave. *Time* noted May 12, 1986 that the going rate for prison work in New York State prisons was from 32c to 65c an hour. The paperwork for the Dept. of Motor Vehicles was being handled by the women's prison, the Bayview Correctional Facility. Time noted Aug. 29, 1988 that an inmate at California's Lompoc prison had authored an article for the San Francisco Chronicle, "The Gulag Mentality" which exposed the slave labor operation. Indignant prison officials immediately ordered a dose of "diesel therapy" for him. Martin was shipped to San Diego, and then to Phoenix. He sued for restraint of freedom of speech, but the judge refused to lift the orders of transfer, noting that it was "for the good of the correctional system."

A recent study by the Rand Corp. shows that each criminal costs society $430,000 a year in loot. It costs $25,000 a year to keep him in prison, indicating that society saves $405,000 a year for each criminal kept in prison. It now costs $16 billion a year for the states to bouse inmates; about $1 billion per year goes for their health care. AIDS has presented a new and even more expensive medical dilemma for prison authorities, as has the rapidly aging prison population. In 1987, there were 40,000 federal prisoners, a total of 533,000 prisoners held in all U.S. prison facilities. There are constant calls for the building of thousands of additional cells. Construction costs for federal prisons run from fifty to one hundred thousand dollars per cell, depending on how many Congressional relatives are contracted for the job. Offenders average 187 crimes each, or one every couple of days, Although some energetic offenders exceed this number. To fulfill the demands of corrections officials would cost $130 billion in new prison construction, with annual budgets for prison operation rocketing to from $36 billion to $60 billion per year. Although this is still a reasonable figure as compared to the $249 billion a year we spend for defense, without defending anything, it would probably result in the United States becoming even more of a police state than it is at present, with the real crackdown wielded, not against criminals, but against "political dissidents."

The direction in which government officials are likely to move was graphically demonstrated in the strange case of Congressman George Hansen. Hansen had violated the secret code of Washington, that no one interferes in Middle East politics without the permission of Henry Kissinger. Hansen tried to have some American hostages freed, and promptly became the only Congressman ever tried under the new "ethics" laws, which required Congressmen to report their financial dealings. He incurred one million dollars in legal fees, lost his home and all his possessions, and was locked up for six months in Petersburg, Va. which is considered the most brutal of the federal prisons. In contrast, Speaker of the House Jim Wright, accused of 116 ethics violations, which were later shaved to 69, was allowed to depart Sodom on the Potomac with not even a wrist slap. After serving his sentence, Hansen was then arrested for speaking at a religious gathering in Omaha, and flown back to Washington with his bands cruelly handcuffed behind his back. He was then held under a false name so that persons interested in his fate could not locate him. The *Washington Post* wryly commented, June 6, 1987, "If you believe the Justice Department, American streets are safer these days because George Hansen is back in prison." The Post pointed out that Hansen "was punished well in excess of his offense." In fact, he had never committed any offense, excepting his unauthorized hegira to Teheran. His brutal treatment was protested by 239 Congressmen in a petition to President Reagan, and by 300,000 telephone and telegram pleas on his behalf. All were tossed into wastebaskets by the arrogant Kissinger-controlled Reagan officials.

The dedication of the Department of Justice, the Federal Bureau of Investigation, and the Federal Bureau of Prisons to strictly political law enforcement makes it inevitable that these agencies must and will be disbanded, the sooner, the better. We cannot suffer the Department of Justice to continue as the private operation of the fanatical Zionist agents, Nesher; we cannot allow the FBI to continue to serve the Perverts in Power as a private political police, and we cannot allow the crime wave to continue unabated while the Federal Bureau of Prisons serves as a convenient place to stash critics of our criminals in government.

CHAPTER 9

THE CASE OF THE STRANGE DIRECTOR

On April 25, 1973, the present writer filed at the U.S. District Court in Washington, D.C. a three million dollar lawsuit for damages against the Estate of J. Edgar Hoover, the late director of the FBI. Within hours after the report of this lawsuit went out over the national wire services, L. Patrick Gray m, Acting Director for the FBI, who had aspired to become Hoover's successor in power, hastily withdrew his name as a candidate. Already under fire for having burned stacks of documents from FBI files, Gray feared that he would be summoned to testify during the Mullins suit. He decamped from the Washington scene.

I had initially filed the suit in Superior Court in Washington, D.C., but the Court informed me that they had a limit of fifty thousand dollars on damage suits. I had to file a Praecipe dismissing my own case, and refile it in the U.S. District Court. Although I was suing the private estate of a U.S. citizen, the case was defended by Harold H. Titus, the famed U.S. prosecutor of the Watergate trials. Presiding over my suit was Judge Sirica, also of Watergate fame. I protested the involvement of the Department of Justice, filing a Memorandum to Cease and Desist, on the grounds that one party should not hire the counsel for the opposing party. I was paying for my prosecution of this action as the plaintiff and as attorney of record, but the Estate of J. Edgar Hoover, which consisted of the person of Hoover's consort, Clyde Toison, was defended by the Department of Justice, the world's largest law firm, employing five thousand lawyers, and with 72,000 employees to back up the lawyers. The problem was that as a taxpayer, 1 was paying taxes to support the operations of the Department of Justice, and the Department of Justice was supplying the lawyer for my opponent.

The five thousand lawyers at the Department of Justice have a long history of incompetence when handling cases, because they are generally dominated by a small band of traitors known as "Nesher," the Hebrew word for "eagle." When Nesher called for the prosecution of some American for an alleged offense against the international Zionist movement, the Department of Justice was marvelously efficient, totally relentless, and avid in the pursuit of a conviction. However, on other cases, they have a long record of bungling, muffs and general ineptitude. This is shown by the files of my case; Counsellor Titus filed a Memorandum to the Court, noting that on November 6, 1973, defendant's counsel discovered that a motion to dismiss had never been filed, although one was prepared for filing on July 26, 1973! Counsel then requested that the motion to dismiss be considered timely filed.

UNITED STATES DISTRICT COURT
FOR THE DISTRICT OF COLUMBIA

EUSTACE C. MULLINS,

Plaintiff,

V. Civil Action

No. 779-73

ESTATE OF J. EDGAR HOOVER,

Defendant.

MEMORANDUM TO THE COURT

On November 6, 1973, defendant's counsel principally assigned to defend this action checked the Clerk's Office docket entries, as well as the Court file, to ascertain whether the Court had taken any action with respect to the defendant's motion to dismiss. Upon checking the official records, it appears that a motion to dismiss had never been officially filed, although one was prepared for filing on July 26, 1973. Defendant's counsel believed the motion was filed in the regular course of business on that date, and no further action was taken by counsel pending a response and/or a disposition by the Court. Attached is a copy of defendant's motion which has been a part of defendant's file since July 26, 1973.

Defendant respectfully requests that the attached copy of the motion to dismiss be considered timely filed.

HAROLD H. TITUS, JR.

United States Attorney

Titus then retired from the Department of Justice, on grounds of nausea. Other members of the five thousand Department of Justice lawyers arrayed against me continued their defense of the case. The result was, that without any court argument or any court appearance of the defendant, U.S. District Judge Joseph Waddy dismissed the case on Dec. 10, 1973. There had been no adjudication, no hearing of any evidence in the case, and no consideration of my Constitutional rights. The decision was rendered according to the law merchant as an equity decision by a United States Judge, on behalf of the United States, as Judge Waddy mentions in his dismissal, "the opposition filed by the United States"... I had not brought suit against the United States; as a citizen of the United States I would be suing myself. The prejudice shown by Judge Waddy against me was not because he was black and I was white, although this may have played a role. The prejudice was based on the grounds that I was a middle of the road American citizen, and Judge Waddy had gone on record that he favored liberal or leftwing activists. When a number of rioters had been taken off the streets of Washington to protect American citizens and their lives and property, Judge Waddy had awarded them enormous sums of money as gifts from the government of the United States, for the inconvenience they claimed to have suffered by being detained. Judge Waddy did not wish to hear the evidence of the harassment and surveillance I and members of my family had suffered at the bands of government agents for some thirty-three years, harassment which was documented by official government reports, and which would have been submitted to the court, had I been allowed to present any evidence in this case. Prejudice prevented me from prosecuting this claim for damages, although damages were freely bestowed by this same judge on rioters who presented a clear and present danger to the people of the United States.

The stage was set for the actions which precipitated this lawsuit, when Congress created the "Department of Justice" on June 22, 1870, providing for a national justice system and a federal Attorney General. In 1908, in answer to inaudible demands from the American people for a team of "national investigators," Congress included in the Sundry Civil Appropriations Bill for 1909 the funds to establish a "Bureau of Investigation." The force behind this "demand" was a small band of Jacobins, or Masonic Canaanites, who wished to establish a national political police based upon European models. These political police were intended to implement programs designed and enacted by insidious international conspirators to enslave and rob the people of the United States. These political police were intended to punish opponents of these sinister programs.

The then Attorney General, Charles Joseph Bonaparte, a member of the family of Napoleon, warned Congress during the deliberations and testimony on this appropriation that it presented a very real danger of setting up "agents provocateurs" in the investigative branch of the Department of Justice. Bonaparte showed remarkable foresight in 1908. The Bureau of Investigation (renamed the Federal Bureau of Investigation in 1935) became a nest of agents provocateurs under the leadership of J. Edgar Hoover, whose philosophy of "fighting crime" was to ignore it, as political goals were all that mattered. His agents soon realized that they were expected to find something to investigate on the political realm, and if there was nothing in this vein, it was their mission to create it, to plan it, finance it and instigate it. The FBI became the B.A.P., the Bureau of Agents Provocateurs.

In March, 1909, the new Bureau of Investigation began its operations under Bonaparte's successor as Attorney General, George Wickersham, a wealthy Wall Street lawyer and law partner of President William Howard Taft. The Bureau was still a modest operation, with only a few agents, when a young deck attendant from the Library of Congress joined it in 1917, apparently to dodge the draft. J. Edgar Hoover had worked on the decks at the Library of Congress for some years, attending the

Georgetown Law School at night. After he had completed his studies, and qualified for the bar, he had the requisite qualifications to become an agent for the Bureau. In this position, he was also classified as a "vital government employee," and was removed from the lists of young men who were being drafted into the armed forces of the United States.

At the conclusion of the First World War, J. Edgar Hoover became a flunky in the national anti-Communist crusade inspired by Attorney General Harry Daugherty, and implemented by the Chief of the Bureau of Investigation, William J. Burns, who served as Director from 1917 until 1924. Burns was the most able and the most famous detective in the United States. He came from a family which had long been distinguished in the profession of law enforcement. His father had been Police Commissioner of a scandal ridden city, Columbus, Ohio, where he finally sent many prominent officials to prison. William Burns himself, at the age of twenty-four, had exposed the election frauds of 1883. He made his national reputation by cleaning up graft in San Francisco, where he sent many corrupt officials to jail. He solved the Times building bombing in 1910, an act of terrorism which killed twenty people. It was Burns' brilliant detective work which sent the McNamara brothers to prison for this act of wanton terrorism. Burns then joined the U.S. Secret Service, where he uncovered a national counterfeiting ring which had been operating unmolested for some twenty-five years. In New York City, Burns made headlines again when he solved the murder of the notorious gambier, Herman Rosenthal, which culminated in a police lieutenant and four gunmen being sent to the electric chair. As the conclusion of the First World War, Burns was enlisted by Attorney General Daugherty to lead the battle against revolution in the United States. The Communists, exulting in their heady victory over the Czar in Russia, and the bloody massacre of his entire family, saw the United States as ripe for a Bolshevik takeover. Their goal was to break down the orderly processes of government on every level, and to take advantage of the resulting confusion and demoralization of the people by instigating a national Bolshevik takeover. On June 2, 1919, during this battle, the home of Attorney General Mitchell Palmer, at 2132 R St NW in Washington D.C., a peaceful neighborhood of government officials, was blown up. Assistant Secretary of the Navy Franklin D. Roosevelt, who lived across the street, found bits of the bomber's body on his doorstep. This bombing was intended as an act of retaliation for the famous "Palmer raids," in which hundreds of wild-eyed Communist revolutionaries, most of whom were illegal aliens, had been arrested. Congress, even as today, was pronounced in its sympathy for the revolutionaries. In a concerted counterattack against the campaign of the Attorney General, the House Rules Committee summoned Palmer to a formal hearing, where hostile members of Congress denounced him for his actions against the revolutionaries. They demanded that the "rights" of the aliens be protected. Those who believe that Congress is only concerned with the problems of Communists saw the demonstrable proof of their beliefs in the Moscow show trial which Congress recently staged featuring Oliver North. However, they have no knowledge of the fact that Congress has been relentless in defense of Bolshevism since 1920.

As a junior assistant to Director Burns, J. Edgar Hoover participated in the Palmer raids. This activity enabled him to pose for the rest of his life as a militant anti-Communist. In fact, Hoover proved to be the Trojan horse in Bums's Bureau of Investigation. He had become the well-known "protege" of a prominent liberal in a Wall Street plot to destroy not only the anti-Communist campaign, but President Harding's entire administration. This campaign culminated in the strange death of President Harding, the "suicide" of prominent figures in his administration, and conviction of others, including Attorney General Harry Daugherty, on various charges, sending them to prison. It was a classic demonstration of a Democratic Congress impeaching a Republican Administration and trying its officials on Congressional charges. Thomas Jefferson's principle of checks and balances, the three departments of government having equal power, was thrown into the wastebasket. Again and again we have seen this same technique, which resulted in the removal of a Republican president, Richard Nixon, from office, and the imprisonment of his principal advisers, and the conviction and imprisonment of most of Ronald Reagan's closest advisers. All of these convictions were obtained by the spectacle of typical Moscow "show trials" which were made world famous by the blood-thirsty dictator, Josef Stalin in Moscow in 1938. Congress learned the technique well.

After Daugherty had been charged, he was replaced by a well-known liberal, Harlan Stone, who also happened to be the mentor of J. Edgar Hoover. The two had been the subject of ribald discussion for some months by the omnipresent Washington gossips. As an astute detective, Burns was aware that Stone might be subject to blackmail, but he resolved to ignore the situation. He was stunned when Stone, as his first official act as Attorney General, notified him that the entire anti-Communist campaign of the government was now abolished. Stone disbanded the GID, the General Intelligence Division, which had been the backbone of the national drive against the Communist revolutionaries. When Burns requested that he be given several weeks to wind up the work of the GID, Stone called him into his office. This was the provocation he had been writing for. He informed Burns that he was fired as Director of the Bureau, as of that moment. The audacity of this action, in summarily discharging the nation's most able detective, was typical of the arrogance of the leftwing bureaucrat.

Stone replaced Burns with J. Edgar Hoover. At one stroke, a dewey-eyed young man of twenty-four, wistful and demure, had become one of the most powerful bureaucrats in Washington, a position he was to hold for the rest of his life. Burns went to some of his powerful friends in Washington, complaining that Hoover had come in "by the back door" but be discovered that as a former officeholder, he no longer had any clout. He never again worked for the government, founding his own very successful private detective agency, which endures to this day.

With Burns out of the way, Stone proceeded to enlist the entire Department of Justice in a massive frontal attack against members of the Harding Administration. This campaign was not only intended to punish the Harding officials for their prosecution of the national anti-Communist campaign; it also had a deeper and perhaps more vital purpose in staging a massive coverup of a number of billion dollar swindles which had been perpetrated as "national emergencies" during the First World

War. The principal benefactor of this coverup was the Standard Oil interests; Rockefeller had double billed the military forces for billions of dollars in oil and other vital military supplies throughout the war. An investigation of U.S. Food Administrator Herbert Hoover was also under way, to trace the black market activities of his officials in sugar and other foodstuffs. The second in charge of his administration of the Food Administration had been Lewis Lichtenstein Strauss, who then became a partner of the Wall Street banking house of Kuhn, Loeb Co., the American representative of the Rothschild interests. Hoover himself had been a Rothschild agent for years, serving as a director of Rio Tinto Zinc, one of the three firms on which the Rothschild fortunes were based. There were also impending inquiries into the disposition of fonds raised by the Belgian Relief Commission, which Hoover had headed for several years, and whose improprieties later became the subject of a number of books, among them "The Strange Life and Career of Herbert Hoover." An investigation was scheduled of the activities of Eugene Meyer, a partner of Bernard Baruch, and head of the War Finance Corporation, whose administration had printed billions of dollars worth of Liberty Bonds in duplicate, one duplicate being sold to the public and the other as asset to the Meyer fortune, which later enabled him to purchase the *Washington Post*, today the most influential political newspaper in the United States. There were also calls for investigating the activities of Bernard Baruch, who had served as head of the War Industries Board, and whose stock speculations in U.S. Steel and other munitions firms had made him one of the wealthiest men in the United States.

All of these investigations vanished into oblivion, as the nation's press indulged in an unequalled orgy of media hype about a "real scandal," the Teapot Dome oil operations. Today, many Americans exhibit a kneejerk reaction when asked about Teapot Dome, but they show no reaction to inquiries about the Rockefeller scandals, the Hoover scandals, the Meyer scandals, or the Baruch scandals. These were all shoved under the rug, while the attention of the nation was focused for the next eight years on the "Teapot Dome" scandal. During all of this hype, the real story was completely submerged. Two competitors of the

Rockefeller oil interests, Harry Sinclair and Edward L. Doheny, had been persuaded by Washington bureaucrats to engage in an act of "public service." They were asked, as a patriotic effort, to pump out a national oil reservoir at Teapot Dome, because geologists had warned that the oil was slowly sinking into a sandy substratum, and would soon be lost forever. Although Sinclair and Doheny were skeptical that they could afford such a gesture of public service, they were finally persuaded to proceed. They formed the Mammoth Oil Corporation, and leased Teapot Dome from the Secretary of the Interior, Albert Fall, whose name, as a result of this episode, entered the language as a "fall guy," or patsy, also inspiring the colloquial phrase, "to take a fall." On the advice of his departmental oil experts, Fall routinely approved the lease. At the time, Fall owned the largest ranch in the United States, Tres Rios in New Mexico, some 750,000 acres, an area 55 miles long and· 24 miles wide. Acting on secret instructions from Washington, New Mexico tax officials suddenly doubled the taxes on his ranch, an amount he was unable to pay. Faced with the loss of his holdings, Fall requested Sinclair for a temporary loan to pay the taxes, which Sinclair agreed to do. The Rockefellers then sent one of their more unsavory henchmen, John Leo Stack, on a secret mission to the nation's most unsavory newspaper publisher, Frederic Bonfils, owner of the Denver Post. Bonfils had become a newspaper publisher by a circuitous route. He had operated a lottery in Kansas City, where the ticket purchasers learned that there would be no winning ticket. Bonfils hurriedly left town ahead of a lynch mob. With his profits, Bonfils arrived in Denver, where he found that the local newspaper, the Post, could be had for cash. He bought it as an ideal investment for a new and even more profitable operation than his fake lottery. The Post became his personal vehicle for a lucrative blackmail operation. He would make up a dummy front page involving some local luminary in a scandal (the scandals were always real, even though the page was a fake), and send it to the victim, noting that a suitable donation, usually five or ten thousand dollars, would "stop the presses." The victim always paid up.

Stack brought Bonfils an even more attractive offer. He promised Bonfils a cash payment of $200,000 to print the story of Teapot Dome. The account, as a Rockefeller operation, presented it as a terrible national scandal, the looting of the nation's oil reserves by unscrupulous profiteers. Other editors had already turned down Stack, despite the lucrative offer, because the story was obviously phony, and could result in expensive libel suits. Bonfils accepted the bribe without a second thought, and broke the story of the "scandal." Once he had printed it, other editors were willing to take their chances. At any rate, Sinclair and Doheney had no opportunity to sue anybody, because they were soon victims of the entire legal staff of the Department of Justice.

Bonfils later complained that Stack had withheld $40,000 of the bribe money; Stack claimed that this was his commission for acting as a bagman for the Rockefellers. Bonfils finally dropped his complaint, perhaps on the commitment from the Rockefellers to bring him even more lucrative deals in the future. The Dictionary of National Biography provides further insight into the swindles perpetrated by Bonfils and his longtime partner, Harry Tammen. They are memorialized by the historian F. L. Mott, in his "American Journalism; A History of Newspapers in the U.S. through 250 Years," as "paternalistic pirates of journalism." Frederic Bonfils was the grandson of Salvatore Buonfiglio, a Corsican immigrant who married into the patrician New England family of Aiden, direct descendants of John Aiden. His grandson changed the spelling to the more French "Bonfils," and became an insurance agent in the Midwest. He made a small fortune in the Oklahoma land boom, and with this stake, he launched his own business venture, the Little Louisiana Lottery in Kansas City. The purchasers of tickets were outraged to find that the lottery paid no prizes. William Rockhill Nelson, founder of the Kansas City Star, ran a series of articles exposing Bonfils. The result was that Bonfils was arrested. Judicious payments to law enforcement officials enabled him to escape with most of his funds.

Bonfils then went to Denver, where he teamed up with Harry Tammen, a bartender at the Windsor Hotel. Tammen had a profitable sideline, selling fake scalps of Sitting Bull and Geronimo to Eastern tenderfeet who wandered into the bar. He also ran dog and pony shows, which he later built into the renowned Sells-Floto Circus. The Sells family was at that time the most famous name in the circus business; the fact that none of the family was connected with Tammen's operation deterred him not at all. Under threat of lawsuits, he finally made an agreement with a distant relative of the Sells family to use the name.

After his success with the lottery, Bonfils was looking for something more profitable than Tammen's swindles. Tammen informed him that he could buy the Evening Post in Denver for $12,500. Bonfils bought it, taking Tammen in as his partner. They changed the name to the Denver Post, and began a free wheeling blackmail operation, which brought them a handsome return. Strangely enough, none of their victims ever attacked them, although they were both shot and seriously wounded in the Post's office. The disgruntled gunman was a lawyer whom they had hired to sue Governor Charles Thomas over a pardon which Thomas had failed to grant, presumably after having accepted the required investment customary in these matters.

The Dictionary of National Biography notes that "the journalistic operations of the pair became a national issue as the result of the Post's part in the Teapot Dome scandal." The DNB relates that after accepting Stack's bribe, Bonfils sought even greater rewards, by approaching Harry Sinclair with a proposition that the Denver Post would drop any further developments in the story. Sinclair paid Bonfils $250,000, with the promise of $750,000 more if the Post refrained from any further Teapot Dome articles. Bonfils was not without his detractors among his fellow editors, some of whom saw fit to lay the full details of this arrangement before the convention of the American Society of Newspaper Editors. The ASNE carefully considered the evidence, which was overwhelming; they then declined to act, claiming that the bribe had been paid just before the national code of ethics had been installed by the association!

The Teapot Dome story is still enshrined in our history books as "the greatest scandal in history," Although it has become routine for contemporary journalists to award that title to another Moscow show trial, the Watergate scandals. A Democratic

Congress luxuriated in the opportunity to drag former Republican officials in for the next eight years, and to hammer away at their "terrible crimes," while the real villains, Rockefeller, Hoover, Meyer and Baruch, snickered in the background. Fall was not sent to prison until 1931, some seven years after the event. He was convicted of having accepted a bribe from Edward L. Doheny, although, in a later trial, Doheny was acquitted of having given him the bribe! Fall lost both his ranch and his reputation. He died, a broken man, in 1944.

The Great Depression, which followed these Moscow show trials in Washington, was the logical outcome of the deliberate manipulation of the national government, both the Congress and the federal agencies, by the sinister international speculators. These political show trials provided the ideal smoke screen behind which the manipulators could execute their longtime program of systematically looting and destroying the nation. During these Golden Years of the conspirators, J. Edgar Hoover flourished in Washington. He was the only bureaucrat who could provide a corps of political police for any purpose, providing that the customer had sufficient money and political clout. Hoover had come into office as the personal protege of a dedicated liberal activist who had singlehandedly eliminated the government's counterattack against Communists in America. Hoover always remained loyal to his mentor. He found an able accomplice in his strange desires when he hired an up and coming young Washingtonian, Clyde Toison, as his assistant. Like Hoover, Toison had also been the protege of a powerful Washington official, former Secretary of War Newton D. Baker. As the "confidential secretary" to Baker, Tolson's duties had never been obvious but the association was a satisfying one. After Baker's departure from Washington, Toison followed Hoover's advice and went to night school, obtaining his law degree as Hoover had done. Like Hoover, Toison was also a dedicated Mason, active in the Washington lodge. In his entire career, Hoover accepted only one business directorship, as director of the influential and wealthy Masonic insurance company, Acacia Mutual Insurance.

Hoover's rise to power in the Bureau of Investigation was preceded by his becoming much more active in Masonic endeavours. On Nov. 9, 1920, he was raised to the Sublime Degree of Master Mason in Federal Lodge No. 1. In April of 1921, he attained various degrees in the Royal Arch Masons. In July of 1921, he joined Washington Commandery No. 1. He was then named Assistant Director of the Bureau of Investigation, August 22, 1921. On March 1, 1922, J. Edgar Hoover joined the Aimas Shrine Temple, and a few weeks later, he was given a commission as Captain in U.S. Army Intelligence. In "The Royal Masonic Encyclopaedia," Kenneth Mackenzie defines the Acacia as "the symbolic plant of Freemasonry. The Acacia, known as Jebbeck in Egypt, flourishes in the Levantine countries. It was the sacred wood of the Jews, called Shittah. "The acacia was used to indicate the place where dead bodies had been interred among the Jews."

William Sullivan later stated in his revealing book about the FBI, "The Bureau,"

"But for reasons that were never entirely clear, Toison rose quickly, and was soon working at the Director's side." Sullivan also commented that Toison's sole duty at the FBI seemed to be to agree with whatever Hoover proposed. If Sullivan had intended in later writings to make the reasons for Tolson's rise to power in the FBI, "more clear," he was not to have the opportunity. He was shot in a "hunting accident."

While steadily building important political alliances in Washington, J. Edgar Hoover cultivated close relationships with the nation's leading gangsters. He ignored ordinary criminals, while consorting with the family heads of the national crime syndicate. In a revealing work, *Secret File*, Henry Messick states, (p. 197),

"Reinfeld had headed the Reinfeld Syndicate during the great days of the Big Seven, in partnership with the Bronfman brothers in Canada, and Longie Zwillman, 'the Al Capone of New Jersey.' Much of the liquor brought to the East Coast was transported there by the Reinfeld Syndicate."

On p. 277, Messick says,

"The Reinfeld Syndicate was divided into two parts; the Canadian end was headed by the four Bronfman brothers, Samuel, Abe, Harry and Allen. They began as owners of a small hotel and ended as the richest men in Canada and head of Distillers-Seagram. It was the Bronfmans' duty to buy Canadian booze and ship it around the East Coast to the Rum Rows of Boston and New York."

What was J. Edgar Hoover's part in all this? He began to receive substantial donations from the mobsters, and set up a private holding operation, the J. Edgar Hoover Foundation, as conduit for the moneys. He detailed his personal publicity agent at the FBI, Louis Nichols, (who later named his son after J. Edgar) to head the foundation. Nichols became the confidential assistant to the notorious Lew Rosenstiel, a bootlegger who became head of the Schenley Corporation. In this capacity, Lou Nichols was installed in Washington as the highly paid lobbyists for the ex-bootleggers who were now respectable liquor distillers, thanks to FDR's successful "repeal" program. Nichols used his Capitol Hill contacts, which he had developed during his years as J. Edgar Hoover's righthand man at the FBI, to save the liquor moguls many millions of dollars in taxes. He acquired large estates in Virginia and New Jersey, as the result of his loyalty to the liquor kings. In 1958, Nichols was successful in lobbying an excise tax bill through Congress which saved Schenley Corporation fifty million dollars in taxes. He sponsored the Forand Bill, which extended the storage period for whiskey from eight to twenty years. As soon as this bill was passed, the value of Schenley stock increased sixty-seven per cent in value.

Drew Pearson, the Washington scandalmonger who had become one of the incorporators of the J. Edgar Hoover Foundation, recorded many items in his diaries which he never published in his daily columns. He made an observation dated July 18, 1949, about a Syndicate operator, Bill Relis, who had purchased the Tanforan racetrack from Joe Reinfeld, the head of the Syndicate. "Now I understand why Bill Relis contributed three thousand dollars to the J. Edgar Hoover Foundation. He was a front for Reinfeld."

On June 17, 1948, Pearson made an entry as follows: "Truman (President), complained about J. Edgar Hoover collecting gossip; he was particularly sore about a FBI report on David Niles about a love affair." The "love affair" concerned Niles' perverted activities; he was a notorious homosexual, an alcoholic, and a Communist agent. One of Niles' sisters worked at KGB headquarters in Moscow; another of his sisters worked in the headquarters of the Israeli Intelligence Agency, Mossad, in Tel Aviv. Niles boasted that be had all bases covered.

To punish J. Edgar Hoover for having kept Niles under surveillance, Truman demanded that he furnish two FBI agents to accompany Niles each evening on his homosexual forays around Washington. While Niles lured a burly truck driver into an alley, the agents bad to crouch behind garbage cans, remaining concealed until Niles bad completed his work. If the truck driver threatened to rob him or beat him up, the FBI agents then rushed forward to protect him.

Unbeknownst to Truman, his closest crony, Gen. Harry Vaughn, was actually J. Edgar Hoover's personal agent in the White House. Not only did Gen. Vaughn report personally to Hoover each day on what was being said and done in the White House; be also lobbied to advance Hoover's power, working with great fervor to persuade Truman to place the OSS, and later the CIA, under Hoover's control. Despite his great influence with the President, Vaughn was unable to persuade Truman to grant Hoover these concessions. In return for this valuable assistance, Hoover funneled expensive gifts to Gen. Vaughn from his wealthy contacts in the Syndicate.

On Nov. 23, 1949, Pearson noted in his Diary that he had a phone call from J. Edgar Hoover demanding that he kill a story about a White House employee or go to jail. "I told Edgar be was nuts; Hoover said Steve Early made him do it."

With Clyde Toison at his side, J. Edgar Hoover had long been a regular visitor to the more lavish Syndicate vacation spas. The couple were a winter regular at the notorious Florida headquarters of the Syndicate, J. Meyer Schine's Roney Plaza Hotel in Miami. On the West Coast, they were wined and dined at the Del Mar racetrack because of its Syndicate connections. In return for these favors, J. Edgar Hoover held national press conferences each year, during which he routinely denied that there was such an entity as a national crime syndicate. In response to an inquiry from Assistant Attorney General Theron Caudle (who later attained national fame as "mink coat Caudle" for his role in a payoff scheme), J. Edgar Hoover wrote Caudle a personal memorandum, dated Oct. 13, 1948, "Please be advised that a search of the records of this Bureau fails to reflect that Zwillman has ever been the subject of an investigation conducted by the FBI." As that time, Zwillman was reputed to be the No. 2 man in the national crime syndicate! In the fall of 1958, according to Victor Navasky in his book, "Kennedy Justice," fifty-two numbered copies of an FBI report on the Mafia, apparently prepared without J. Edgar Hoover's knowledge or consent, were distributed to the twenty-five top officials in the government who were directly concerned with law enforcement. This was the first time that the FBI had officially recognized the existence of a national crime syndicate. When he learned of the report, the day after it had been distributed, J. Edgar Hoover was furious. He immediately had each copy of the report recalled and destroyed.

He denounced the report as "baloney." It was never mentioned again.

In the mid-1930s, J. Edgar Hoover embarked upon a massive public relations campaign, portraying himself as a fearless crime fighter wielding a machine gun as he mowed down the criminals. In fact, be had never fired a gun at anyone during his career, nor did he do so at any later time until his death. Pressure from opponents on Capitol Hill at that time, he had not yet attained his later ascendancy over Congress-forced him to become more involved in criminal matters. Longtime friends of Senator Burton Wheeler and Tom Walsh had vowed to get Hoover because of his illegal use of FBI agents in a frenetic campaign to have these Senators indicted on charges of taking bribes. Their friends made impassioned speeches on the floor of the Senate, not only denying the charges against them, but also making pointed comments about Hoover's lack of personal experience in the field of law enforcement. Although they avoided direct charges that Hoover was operating a political police force in the United States, one critic noted that it was a matter of record that. Hoover had never participated in an arrest during his entire career! Stung by this criticism, and facing a possible widespread demand on Capitol Hill for his removal, Hoover notified his agents that they should delay the arrest of any prominent criminal, his famous "Public Enemy" category, until he was summoned to arrive on the scene. A few weeks later, he received a wire from New Orleans that FBI agents there had trapped Alvin Karpis, Public Enemy No. 1. Hoover flew to New Orleans, where his agents assured him that Karpis had indeed been secured. Hoover rushed up the back stairs and burst into the room. Karpis was already surrounded by FBI agents, who had disarmed him. Hoover tried to put the handcuffs on him, and was informed that no one had remembered to bring them. One agent whipped off his necktie, and the most dangerous man in America was hustled out to the car, his hands secured by an ordinary necktie!

Hoover realized that Karpis could make the story of his arrest a matter of public record, if he was ever released from prison. The Director notified the Bureau of Prisons that under no circumstances was Karpis ever to be given parole. The result was that an embittered Karpis spent much of the rest of his life in prison. When he was finally released, he did write a book, in which be referred to the Director in unprintable terms, describing both his reputed racial origins and his sexual habits.

President Franklin D. Roosevelt considered Hoover's personal life a matter of great amusement. Roosevelt himself, despite his crippled condition, was an inveterate heterosexual. He often regaled his dinner guests with comments on Hoover's personal life. After one of these dinners, the British Ambassador noted in a memorandum to the Home Office in 1938,

> "FOR fancies himself the reincarnation of a Byzantine Emperor; in keeping with this image, he has placed a eunuch in charge of his household, as Hoover's FBI is principally concerned with keeping the government employees in rein."

Some of the more daring Congressmen on Capitol Hill were no less scathing in their references to the Director. Representative

THE RAPE OF JUSTICE

John Rankin of Mississippi, who was well-known for his iconoclastic remarks both on and off the record, incurred Hoover's wrath by a pointed reference to requests for huge increases in the annual FBI appropriations bill. Speaking on the floor of the House, Rankin quipped, "A lot of these statistics sound like fairy tales to me."

As administration after administration came and went in Washington, Hoover remained imperturbably fixed in his seat of power, seemingly impregnable to the changing moods of the voters. At the beginning of each new administration, there were loud demands for his removal from office. One of the more vociferous of President Truman's leftwing aides, Max Lowenthal, rushed into Truman's office shortly after the demise of FOR. "Whatever priorities you may have lined up, Mr7 President," he said, "you must realize that at the earliest possible moment, you should remove J. Edgar Hoover from the FBI, replacing him with someone more amenable to our Democratic program. And you certainly must be aware of his ah, proclivities." Truman listened without comment. Weeks went by, and he took no action. Lowenthal had failed to realize that Hoover's impregnable position rested not only on the famed Black Cabinet, a file of photos and telephone tape recordings of Congressional sexual peccadilloes and financial maneuvers, but also on the fact that J. Edgar Hoover was one of the nation's most powerful Masons. Truman himself owed his entire political career to the years he had put in as chief Masonic organizer for the state of Missouri. Hoover's companion, Clyde Toison, was also a high ranking Mason. Truman ignored Lowenthal's demand.

Lowenthal then wrote a book denouncing Hoover and the FBI, primarily because of his supposed anti-Communist activity. Like most liberals in the United States, Lowenthal had accepted without question the public relations campaign which portrayed J. Edgar Hoover not only as the greatest crime fighter in the nation, but also as its most active anti-Communist. This was the first of a succession of books on the FBI by Washington's professional liberals. Ali of them ignored the true basis of his power, his Masonic affiliation. Lowenthal would never have believed that it was Hoover and his mentor, Harlan Stone, who had successfully sabotaged the national campaign against the Communists in 1924. This movement lay moribund until Senator Joe McCarthy revived it briefly in the 1950s. Like his forerunners in this movement, McCarthy was hounded until he died in disgrace, having been officially reprimanded by the Senate of the United States for having dared to oppose the Communist Party in this country.

Although President Truman officially ignored Lowenthal's book, his personal assistant, David Niles, wrote him a glowing letter, "You are doing a wonderful service to the country by writing a book of this sort."

Even if he had been sincere in his opposition to Communism, J. Edgar Hoover would have had to accept the fact that the new administration in 1933 consisted of a Democratic Party which had been captured by the fanatical Stalinist wing of the world Communist movement. Not only did Roosevelt come into office with a prepared agreement to officially recognize the Soviet government of Russia; be also surrounded himself with dedicated Communist espionage agents. His three closest confidants were Alger Hiss, later sent to prison for lying about his activities on behalf of the Communists; Lauchlin Currie, who was named by Elizabeth Bentley and other ex-Communists in testimony before Congress as a Communist agent, and Harry Dexter White, personal assistant to Secretary of the Treasury Henry Morgenthau in the Roosevelt administration, who shipped the U.S. plates for printing American occupation currency in Germany to the Soviet Union. The Soviets ran off some $35 billion in U.S. occupation marks, which enabled them to pay the costs of their occupation of Germany. All of these marks were later paid for by American taxpayers. Hoover's files bulged with documented information about the Communist activities of many leading members of the Roosevelt administration, most of which be prudently kept under wraps. Roosevelt understood the situation, and knew that Hoover, as an accomplished bureaucrat, would do nothing as long as the Democrats were in power. During the Second World War, General Wild Bill Donovan, anxious to please Roosevelt, staffed the new Office of Strategic

Services, (now the CIA) with many known Communist agents. To needle his rival, Hoover sent to Donovan some of the more damaging dossiers about his closest lieutenants in the OSS. Donovan reported the ploy to Roosevelt, with the wry comment, "Of course I knew they were Communists; that's why I hired them!"

As a sop to the Stalinists who controlled Washington, J. Edgar Hoover hired none other than the founder of the Communist Party of the United States, Jay Liebstein, or Lovestone, as the ghostwriter for his projected book on Communism. The resulting book was artfully titled "Masters of Deceit." Perhaps as a joke on Hoover, Lovestone had included in the book a complete Communist manual for organizing local chapters of the Communist Party throughout the United States. Hoover apparently remained unaware of the deception, probably because he never read it. He was content to collect the considerable sums which the book, an immediate best seller, brought into his bank account all of the expenses, including Lovestone's fee, had been paid from the FBI's special informant funds.

J. Edgar Hoover's famed state of chronic paranoia was not due to the fact that he suspected people around him of being Communists or Nazis; he was always suspicious that they might use their position to amass information which would help his enemies to get rid of him. His Maginot Line of protection against this much wished for event was his Black Cabinet of incriminating information on the leading political figures in Washington. Only his longtime personal secretary, Helen Gandy, had access to it. Jack Anderson and other Washington journalists might boast that they could gain access to any FBI file in Hoover's headquarters by offering favors or a discreet payment, but none of them could get to the material in the Black Cabinet. When a new President came into office, J. Edgar Hoover always made a point of sending him over some of the choicest tidbits about his political rivals. The President would be made aware that if Hoover had such information on others, he probably had equally damaging information on the present incumbent. The ploy served both as an offer of ingratiation, and as a warning. Of postwar Presidents, Lyndon Johnson probably appreciated these tidbits more than anyone. Known to his political intimates in Texas as "Dry Gulch Lyndon" because of the fate of those who threatened his political rise, his personality was closely related to that of the Director himself, totally dedicated to greed, lust and power.

Having secured the White House and Capitol Hill, J. Edgar Hoover was now free to indulge his inordinate appetite for luxury. He and Clyde Toison continued to be wined and dined by the nation's crime leaders. A 1957 cover story on Hoover by Time magazine noted that when he and Toison went to New York, they were usually met at their reserved table at the Stork Club by none other than Frank Costello, the acknowledged head of the national crime syndicate. While Hoover was in Washington, the columnist Walter Winchell served as the official courier between Hoover and the Mafia. If a particular "family" was causing law enforcement problems anywhere in the United States, Winchell would arrange for a family member to meet with Hoover at the Stork Club. With the gregarious Costello sitting in as referee, the problem would be ironed out in a convivial manner.

J. Edgar Hoover developed a small circle of multi-millionaire patrons, who cemented the friendship by showering him with expensive gifts. Hoover expected nothing less than solid gold cufflinks, sterling silver candelabra, and rare Oriental carvings of precious jade. At Christmas, the unofficial president of the J. Edgar Hoover fan club, Louis Marx, would deliver to Hoover expensive train sets and other high priced items from the Marx Toy Co., which Hoover, as Santa Claus would then pass out to the children of FBI employees. Marx had profited greatly from the looting of conquered Germany. His firm took many intricate toy patents from German manufacturers, and reproduced them profitably in the United States.

FBI agents also were expected to favor Hoover with expensive gifts. One agent borrowed money to have a Persian rug custom made for "the Boss" with the initials "JEH" woven into the center. This agent later enjoyed a meteoric career with the FBI. Hoover launched the practice of an annual birthday party at his office, at which the agents, who received modest salaries, were expected to present him with solid gold or sterling silver gifts. No one was compelled to do so, but those agents who ignored the festivities were sometimes transferred to Boise, Idaho, the legendary Siberia of the FBI.

Although no one ever dared to fire a shot at Hoover during his legendary career, he maintained at government expense, ($30,000 each), a fleet of five heavily armor plated limousines. Two were kept in Washington, one in Miami, one in New York, and one in Los Angeles. Hoover frequently circulated photos of himself brandishing a machine gun, although he had never been known to fire it except on the firing range.

J. Edgar Hoover's gilded existence ended suddenly, when he was found dead in bed by his longtime housekeeper, Annie Fields. This unexpected event (he had had no previous health problems) was linked by Washington insiders to the Watergate scandal, which was then at its height. An FBI agent in Mexico City had come up with some photos which directly linked top officials in Washington with the inner operations of CREEP, President Nixon's confidential reelection team. Someone apparently decided that Hoover could only be prevented from using these photos for his own advantage (that is, by offering them to the highest bidder) by bringing a halt to his long career. This was done.

J. Edgar Hoover's last will and testament did little to dispel the Capitol Hill rumors and ribald comments at the National Press Club about his personal life. He seemed to confirm longtime conjectures by resolutely cutting off his relatives in his will, and leaving his entire estate, with the exception of a few bequests to other associates, to his consort, Clyde Tolson. Tolson was also named executor of the will. Five thousand dollars was left to his secretary, Helen Gandy; three thousand to his housekeeper, Annie Fields, and two thousand to his chauffeur, James Crawford. The millions of dollars worth of gifts which Hoover had received over the years were appraised at a fraction of their value. His important collection of Oriental jade, said to be worth more than a million dollars, was listed at a few thousand dollars. In the published list of the appraisals of hundreds of items from his estate, we find Hoover's personal gold FBI shield listed at five dollars. A collector would probably pay $1500 for it. Hoover's leather bill fold with the Department of Justice seal set with thirteen diamonds was listed at $50.00. This would probably bring three thousand dollars at auction. A jade Phoenix bird on stand was listed at $35. This would be a thousand dollar item. The appraisal, which was duly notarized by Clyde Tolson as "a true and perfect inventory" listed a collection of one thousand books, most of which had been autographed by the authors to J. Edgar Hoover, at one dollar each. The collection included books by a number of Presidents, from Herbert Hoover to Richard Nixon, and from many other prominent figures. At autograph value alone, these would be worth hundreds of dollars each. Dozens of sterling silver items were listed at $5 or $10 each. Two sterling silver candelabra were listed at $16 for the pair; these would probably bring $350. Fifty-two pieces of Masonic flatware, the "Royal Arch Mason" pattern in heavy sterling silver, were listed at $166 for the lot. Four yellow gold Masonic rings, one with diamond, were listed at $80 for the lot. Even at these deflated prices, Tolson inherited more than half a million dollars from J. Edgar Hoover.

Hoover's successor at the FBI, Acting Director L. Patrick Gray ILI, an Annapolis graduate, admitted burning many FBI documents. Hoover's secretary, Helen Gandy, appeared before a special Congressional Committee to testify that she had shredded Hoover's secret files, the contents of the dreaded Black Cabinet. Instead of having her tried on criminal charges, as was later done with Col. Oliver North, the Congressmen, greatly relieved, all but commended her for a job well done. The *Washington Post*, on Jan. 19, 1975, carried a lengthy story that she had given twelve file cabinet drawers of "particularly sensitive files" to Assistant Director of the FBI W. Mark Felt, who was rumored to be the Deep Throat informant of the Watergate massacre. Despite this documented testimony, the *New York Times* carried a story from its huge Washington bureau on Feb. 9, 1975 that "Unconfirmed reports claim that Mr. Hoover's friends removed or destroyed the files in the hours before Mr. Gray took office." Apparently the Times Washington bureau never read the *Washington Post*.

Basking in the heartfelt approval of the Congressional investigators, Helen Gandy retired to Florida. She died of cancer in an Orange City nursing home on July 7, 1988, at the age of 91, leaving no survivors.

Clyde Toison died April 14, 1975. The *Washington Post* printed a photo with his obituary, which turned out to be a photo of Louis Nichols. The error was corrected on April 16. Like his friend, J. Edgar Hoover, Clyde Toison also disinherited all of his relatives. The *Washington Post* commented that Tolson's will, disposing of some $540,520 (June 22, 1975), represented the Hoover bequest. Toison left $200,000 to other Hoover cronies; another $4,000 to Helen Gandy; Tolson's secretary, Dorothy Stillman, received $27,000. The No. 3 man in the FBI, John Mohr, was named executor; he received $26,000. Hoover's former employees, Annie Fields and James Crawford, received $32,000 each. One might conjecture that these bequests, which deliberately cut off Tolson's relatives in favor of Hoover's cronies, could be considered a tribute to the late Director's memory; they might also be considered a reward for continued discretion.

A further imbroglio developed when Mohr attempted to carry out Tolson's bequest of J. Edgar Hoover memorabilia to "the J. Edgar Hoover room in the new FBI building." The problem was that there was no J. Edgar Hoover room in the new FBI building, nor was there likely to be, due to spirited opposition on Capitol Hill. A few Hoover mementos were on display in one area of the guided tour, but officials were wary of setting up a special room in J. Edgar Hoover's memory. Disturbing rumors about his personal life were still circulating throughout the city, and considerable opposition had been voiced by Congressmen, media personalities and other spokesmen. They feared that at any moment, a national news story might break, which would document the rumors about Hoover's personal life. This might necessitate renaming the building, and declaring J. Edgar Hoover a "nonperson," in the accepted Stalinist style. The present writer had already filed a lawsuit against the estate of J. Edgar Hoover, and the possibility of a court hearing, and the presentation of witnesses and documented evidence, caused some Congressmen to demand that the new FBI building should not bear J. Edgar Hoover's name. The media cooperated in banning all further mention of my lawsuit, while the United States court system closed ranks to prevent any trial of the action. It was quietly dismissed, with no evidence, no witnesses, nor this writer ever being permitted to enter the courtroom. Justice (the Department of Justice, that is) had been served.

The only living person who had dared to oppose J. Edgar Hoover at the FBI had been given the bum's rush by Hoover when Sullivan, who had long been the No. 2 man at the FBI, finally summoned up the courage to ask Hoover just when he planned to retire and relinquish his position to Sullivan. For eight consecutive years, Hoover had made a solemn pledge to Sullivan at the beginning of each new year, that this would be his last year at the FBI, and that his only desire was to retire and live quietly at home with his pet dogs. The morning after Sullivan delivered what amounted to an ultimatum to Hoover, he arrived at the FBI headquarters to find that the locks had been changed on his door. His parking space and secretary were gone, and his personal effects were later delivered to him by a flunky.

Sullivan later wrote a revealing book about the Boss, which was published under the title, "The Bureau." It skirted many important issues, which Sullivan had planned to treat in a later and more startling book. Sullivan had been Hoover's personal choice for the director of the controversial COINTELPRO program, a campaign of unparalleled hatred and vindictiveness against targets chosen by Hoover himself, including the present writer. In 1977, Sullivan was to be subpoenaed about COINTELPRO's operations, which included many illegal acts, including political conspiracy, black bag jobs or burglaries, the manufacture of phony evidence, and stories planted to harass innocent victims, illegal wiretaps, seizure of mail, and many other crimes which had led to great suffering and often death of the victims. Many details of the COINTELPRO operations were contained in some 52,000 pages of FBI files which had been obtained by the Citizens Investigation Bureau of Ohio through the Freedom of Information Act. Shortly before he was due to testify about COINTELPRO, Sullivan was shot and killed in a mysterious "hunting accident." He was shot in an open field, in broad daylight, ostensibly by the son of a law enforcement official, while wearing bright red safety hunting clothes. The "accident" occurred when a shot was fired from a high powered rifle, using a telescopic sight. It had all the manifestations of a professional bit job, but the FBI resolutely resisted all demands for an official investigation into the death of its former No. 2 official, claiming that it was "a local matter."

Hoover's successor, L. Patrick Gray ILI, hurriedly decamped when the present writer filed suit against Hoover's estate. He was replaced by a former FBI agent, Clarence Kelley, who was then serving as the police chief of Kansas City.

Kansas City was a notorious Mafia controlled city, yet Kelley's wife refused to move to Washington, claiming that the city had too high a crime rate. (It was only a fraction of the present rate, which has won Washington the title of "murder capital of the world.") Kelley had to go home to Kansas City every weekend, leaving the running of the FBI to Hoover's longtime cronies.

The Bureau was then presented to a federal judge with liberal credentials, William Webster, whom the present writer also sued for thirty-three years of harassment and surveillance. Webster was moved to the CIA, and replaced by another judge, a Texas protege of Senator John Tower, William Sessions. He also became known as an absentee director, spending most of his time travelling around the United States and visiting the field offices. The FBI was run in his absence by one of the old crowd, Assistant Director Buck Revell. Oliver (Buck) Revell, one of the FBI's Old Guard, had been in line for the position of director when Webster left for the CIA. He had developed a close relationship with Col. Oliver North; when the Iran-Contra story broke in Washington, Revell was deemed to be too compromised by this relationship, and was passed over in favor of Sessions. After repeated criticism of Sessions as an absentee director, and newspaper stories that Revell was actually running the FBI, Sessions hurriedly named a new Assistant Director, and suggested that Revell should retire.

CHAPTER 10

THE STRANGE CASE OF THE SCHIZOPHRENIC DRIVER

I n 1979, the war of attrition against me was intensified by furtive officials lurking on my home front. I was arrested and charged with driving 50 mph in a 35 mph zone. At the time, 1was driving about 4 mph, trying to locate a side street on which I wished to turn. I was convicted and fined in a local court, as the scene was described in a letter to the local newspaper under the heading "Shades of the Old West."

"Admirers of the code of the Old West and the rough and-ready six-gun justice administered by such courts as Judge Roy Bean's might not realize that this era has not yet vanished from American life. I had a taste of it when I answered a speeding charge in a local court. Although my case was posted as first on the docket, I sat on the bench for three hours, while every other case was heard. The court was then cleared of 'civilians,' that is, anyone who might later corroborate my version of events. Apparently I am reputed to be very dangerous, as I gave my testimony in an otherwise empty courtroom, surrounded by heavily armed bailiffs. The nearest 35 mph sign is 1.1 miles away, but a 55 mph sign is clearly visible where I was stopped. The officer falsely testified that this 55 mph sign was 'out of sight on the other side of the bill.' Judge Roy Bean, where are you?"

I sued the Mayor and the Chief of Police, who then answered under oath that they had no responsibility for the actions of any policeman in the city. They requested a Bill of Particulars, which I filed, stating in part,

"I As a chief instigator and prosecutor of government officials in the Nuremberg Trials in Nuremberg, Germany, the Federal Government of the United States firmly established as legal precedent the precept that officials such as city mayors and police are wholly responsible, actionable and liable under a law for acts committed by their agents and underlings whether said officials have specifically commissioned and required such acts from said underlings or not, and the Federal Government of the United States convicted said officials and exacted the death penalty Although none of the said officials had personally participated in the acts of which they were accused. The indicated defendants, while not personally present at the scene of the acts of assault against plaintiff, did commission, instruct, uniform and send forth yon arresting officer to commit said acts against plaintiff and defendants, by the precedents established as law at the Nuremberg Trials, and by numerous other legal precedents, are wholly and fully liable for acts committed against plaintiff by their official, commissioned, assigned and instructed uniformed agents. According to the Precepts of the Nuremberg Trials, defendants are wholly and legally able and answerable for impeding plaintiff's progress on a public street, and defendants have no evidence and cannot exhibit any evidence that plaintiff was in violation of any law when his progress was impeded by an armed agent of defendants on a public street."

This case also dragged on for some three years; much of plaintiff's complaint was printed verbatim in the local press. An interesting development occurred when the judge refused to grant a demurrer, (a dismissal as insufficient cause of action) for the city. He was exiled to a remote village where, presumably, be remains today. A "ringer" was brought in on the day of the trial, as a more malleable substitute. He allowed me to testify, and then granted a motion to dismiss by the city attorney. He benignly announced that I now "had had my day in court," a half hour having elapsed since the trial began. I filed a Motion to Vacate Judgment, which was routinely denied.

MOTION TO VACATE JUDGMENT

Now comes plaintiff, Eustace C. Mullins, as attorney pro se, and respectfully moves the Court to Vacate the judgment of February 11, 1982 in this action, on the following grounds:

1. 49 Corpus Juris Secundum 265. "Courts of record or of general jurisdiction have inherent power to vacate or set aside their own judgments." Pavelka v. Overton, Civ. App. 47 S.W.2d 369.

2. 88 Corpus Juris Secundum 139. "A motion to strike evidence is premature if addressed to evidence, the competency or relevancy of which may thereafter be made to appear." Keber v. American Stores Co. 184 A.795, 116 N.J. Law 437. And plaintiff deposes that the competency and relevancy of his testimony would have been corroborated by the testimony and subsequent cross-examination of the defendants in this action, and that the premature motion of the defendant to strike plaintiff's evidence and dismiss this action prevented plaintiff from curing any defects in his evidence. 30 A Corpus Juris Secundum, 262. Equity. "Defects cured by subsequent pleadings, proof or proceedings. Aided by the evidence." Kemp v. Kemp, 63 So. 2d 702, 703, 258 Ala. 570.

3. 88 Corpus Juris Secundum 143. "A motion to strike evidence is too broad where a part thereof is admissible and the motion does not point out specifically the particular part objected to." Paparazzo v. Perpel, 84 A.2d 11, 16 N.J. Super 128. And plaintiff deposes that defendant's motion to strike was too broad, and flawed in that it did not specifically cite any part or parts of plaintiff's evidence as grounds for said motion.

4. 88 Corpus Juris Secundum 144. "Unless the right to have the evidence stricken clearly appears, the court is not bound to strike it." Scarlett v. Young, 183 A.129, 170 Md. 358. And plaintiff deposes that defendant's motion to strike, being flawed, the Court was not bound to grant it.

5. 88 Corpus Juris Secundum 134. "As a general rule, evidence competent for any purpose and relevant to any issue should not be stricken." Lewes Sand Co. v. Craves, 8 A.2d, 2I I Terry 189. "The fact that evidence does not come up to the offer of proof, provided it is material, does not constitute ground for striking it." smith v. Martin, 106 A. 666, 93 Vt. 111. And plaintiff avers that his evidence was competent and relevant to the issues in this action, and that it was material, and that it should not have been stricken.

6. 88 Corpus Juris Secundum 237. "A motion to strike or exclude all the evidence, sanctioned under the practice of some states, is in the nature of a demurrer to the evidence and had the effect of such a demurrer in so far as it tests the sufficiency of the evidence." McCaull-Dinsmore Co. v. Stevens. 194 P.243. 59 Mont. 206, 64 C.J.P. 390 note 62. "It must be tested by the same rules as a demurrer to the evidence." Hawley v. Dawson, 18 P. 592, 16 Or. 344. "A motion to strike all evidence of the plaintiff from the record on the ground that the petition has failed to show a cause of action is not the equivalent of a motion to dismiss, with a statute providing for such a motion after plaintiff has completed presenting of his evidence." Munday v. Austin, 218 S.W. 2d 624, 358 Mo. 959. And plaintiff deposes that defendant had previously submitted a Demurrer on the same grounds and that the Court had on September 14, 1981 denied defendant's Demurrer. 88 Corpus Juris Secundum 235. "A demurrer is properly overruled where the petition is sustained by competent evidence." Cargill Commission Co. v. Mowery, 16I P.634, 162 P. 313, 99 Kan. 389. Thus we have a situation where plaintiff's evidence is ruled competent on September 14, 1981, and the same evidence is ruled incompetent in the same Court on February 11, 1982.

7. "Demurrers are no favorites of courts of equity." Harlan v. Lee, 9 A. 2d 839, 177 Md. 437. Plaintiff, after defendant's motion to strike his evidence, pointed out to the Court that defendant's motion was in the nature of a demurrer, as cited above in par. 6, and that said demurrer had already been denied by the Court, but the Court took the position that defendant's motion to strike was not in the nature of a demurrer, and plaintiff prays the Court whether its decision of September 14, 1981 denying the demurrer should not take procedure over its decision of February 11, 1982 to grant a motion to strike plaintiff's evidence, said motion being in the nature of a demurrer.

8. 88 Corpus Juris Secundum 237. "A motion by defendant to strike plaintiff's evidence should be reserved until plaintiff has rested his case." Burke v. Gale, 67 S.E. 2d 917, 193 Va. 130. And plaintiff did not state that he had rested his case, as plaintiff was expecting to make more of his evidence explicated to the jury during the cross-examination by defendant, which cross-examination was not forthcoming, and by plaintiff's cross-examination of the defendants, and said motion by defendant to strike plaintiff's evidence, which was not complete, constituted denial of due process. 16A Corpus Juris Secundum 591. "Suppression of evidence may be a denial of due process where it is vital evidence, material to the issue of guilt or penalty." Thompson v. People, 102 N .E.2d 315, 410 III. 256.

9. Defendant's motion to strike plaintiff's evidence, and to dismiss this cause, constituted irregular judicial proceedings because plaintiff had no prior notice of defendant's motion or any opportunity to prepare to argue it. Although said motion does not in itself constitute "surprise" in its judicial definition, in this instance it definitely qualified as surprise because plaintiff, having already seen defendant's demurrer denied by this Court, had no occasion to expect or to prepare for a motion to strike plaintiff's evidence which was "in the nature of a demurrer."

10. "The declaration, complaint, or petition, or a count thereof, will be sustained if it is good on any theory." City of Madison v. Drew, 265 N.W. 683, 220 Wis. 511, 104 A.L.R. 1387. And plaintiff avers that he was and is prepared to sustain all counts of his petition before a jury. In his opening statement to the jury, plaintiff stated that the jury would be asked to decide fundamental features of our civil law, including the question of agency, violations of civil rights, involuntary servitude, the right to due process, the right to equal protection of the laws, and a consideration of whether radar, admittedly hearsay, could be accepted as valid evidence. Yet the jury was not allowed to consider or decide any of these questions.

11. Defendant's motion to strike plaintiff's evidence and to dismiss this cause was based on the claim that defendants had no connection with this cause, which in effect denied the entire body of civil law which enunciates the doctrine of agency. "The master made the pledge of his servants. *Omnes qui servientes habent.*" Edward the Confessor, Bract. fol.124 b. "If I make a deputy, I am always officer, and he performs the office in my right and as my servant." Y.B. 11 Edward IV. 1, pl.1. "The driving of the servant is the driving of the master." smith v. Shepherd, Cro. Eliz. 710; M. 41 & 42 Eliz. B. R. "Under Charles II it was laid down that the high sheriff and the under sheriff are one officer." Cremer v. Humberston, 2 Keble, 352 (H.19 & 20 Car. II). "For all civil purposes the act of the sheriff's bailiff is the act of the sheriff." Lord Mansfield. Ackworth v. Kempe, Douglas 40, 42 (M.19 G. III, 1778). 2A Corpus Juris Secundum 1. "The law of agency is based on the Latin Maxim, *'Qui facit per allum, facit per se.'*, which may be translated 'One acting by another is acting for himself.'" Gustavson v. Rajkovich, 263 P.2d 540, 96 Aris. 280. 27A Corpus Juris Secundum 4. Agency. "In its broadest sense, it includes every relation in which one person acts for or represents another by his authority." state Comp. Ins. Fund v. Industrial Accident Commission, 14 P.2d, 306, 310, 216 Cal. 351. Yet defendant has this action dismissed on the claim that the Chief of Police of Waynesboro has nothing to do with any activity of the Waynesboro Police Department!

12. 88 Corpus Juris Secundum 136. Trial. "As a general rule, where a party consents to the introduction of evidence or where no objection is made to evidence when offered, or to a question when asked, or no proper or timely objection (Lewis v. Shiffers, Mun. App. 67 A.2d 269) or no proper or timely objection, specifying the grounds thereof, is made (Berry v. Adams, App. 7I S.W. 2d 126, a motion made, after the evidence is admitted or the question answered, to strike may properly be denied." Terwilliger v. Long Island R.R. Co. 136 N.Y.S. 733, 152 App. Div. 168, affirmed 106 N.E. 1114, 209 N.Y. 522. And plaintiff deposes that at no time during plaintiff's opening statement to the jury or his subsequent testimony did the defense offer any proper or timely objection to any of plaintiff's testimony, yet the defense then moved to strike all of plaintiff's testimony in toto, no prior objection having been made to any of it, and to obtain a dismissal of this cause thereby.

13. The decision of the Court to dismiss this action was also partially based on the cited refusal of the plaintiff to appeal his conviction in Waynesboro District Court on July 16, 1979, but at that time plaintiff had already filed his Motion for Judgment with the Circuit Court of the City of Waynesboro, which would have heard said appeal, and said Motion for Judgment dealt with the question of plaintiff's guilt or innocence of the speeding charge, and said question was subjudice in the Waynesboro Circuit Court during the entire period when plaintiff supposedly had refused to refer said action to the Waynesboro Circuit Court, thus the Waynesboro Circuit Court dismisses an action for failure to appeal it to the Waynesboro Circuit Court, when the question was before the Waynesboro Circuit Court during the entire period.

14. The decision of the Court to dismiss this action on the grounds that plaintiff had refused to appeal his conviction in Waynesboro District Court to the Waynesboro Circuit Court bases a decision in a civil action on a step in criminal procedure. The Oxford English Dictionary, under "civil," states, 16. Law. Distinguished from criminal. 1611 COTGR. Civilizer v. criminal. to change his Indictment into an Action; to turn a criminal into a civille cause. 1764. BURN Poor Laws 289. Civil, implies an offence of a private nature between party and party, and not where the king is party. 1844 H. H. Wilson British India II 395. In the administration of civil law, Panchayats were had recourse to, while criminal cases were investigated by the British functionaries in person. Thus the question is raised whether a civil action can properly be decided by the rules of criminal procedure.

15. Although he was appearing as attorney pro se, plaintiff was not properly instructed by the Court at the conclusion of this action of his right to request that the decision be set aside.

16. Corpus Juris Secundum 16. 178. "Statute conferring the police power on municipalities, however, should be construed as not to authorize an unreasonable exercise thereof." Father Basil's Lodge v. City of Chicago, 65 N.E. 2d 805, 393 Ill. 246. And plaintiff avers that his arrest was a violation which prevented him from engaging in his lawful occupation. 16 Corpus Juris Secundum 224. "One has to carry on his business free from all unlawful interference." Wallace v. Ford, D.C. Tex. 2I F. Supp. 624.

17. Corpus Juris Secundum 199. "The police power must at all times be exercised with scrupulous regard for private rights guaranteed by the Constitution and even then only in the public interest." Okla. Natural Gas Co. v. Choctaw Gas Co. 236 P.2d 970, 205 Okla. 255. And plaintiff avers that the police power exercised in his arrest was not in the public interest and violated his private rights.

18. Plaintiff was threatened with imprisonment for debt, in violation of his Constitutional rights. 16 Corpus Juris Secundum 204. "Ordinarily, a debt owed to a governmental unit is no exception to the Constitutional provision." Clark v. City of Cincinnati, Corn. Pl. 12I N.E. 2d 834.

19. 53 Am. Jur 435. "The courts are generally agreed that an employer may be held accountable for the wrongful act his employee committed while acting in his employer's business and within the scope of his employment, Although he had no knowledge." Palmer v. St. Albans, 60 Vt. 427, 13 A 569.

WHEREFORE, plaintiff respectfully moves the Court to grant his Motion to Vacate Judgment on the grounds that it is contrary to law and the evidence.

Meanwhile, at a meeting of Freemasons at a local synagogue, other matters were shelved while an agitated discussion took place as to what "could be done about Eustace Mullins." One member stood up and bravely offered that he would "do something." A few days later, while I was driving down a side street, a huge Lincoln came roaring out of a business lot, and crashed into the side of my car. As my complaint later stated,

> "3. On Sept. 19, 1979, at about 1 P.M. defendant did feloniously and with great force crash his automobile into the side of the vehicle owned and operated by plaintiff, and did strike plaintiff's vehicle on the right hand front and rear doors, crushing them in, and plaintiff did suffer great bodily harm and property damage thereby."

"7. Plaintiff's vehicle, an Oldsmobile 98 sedan, which was severely damaged, is a rare surviving example of a collector's vehicle known as the Chappaquiddick Special, a model in which a girl met her death during an association with a prominent upstanding figure, and this vehicle could be worth a large sum during a forthcoming political campaign and must be fully restored.

"Defendant stated to plaintiff that defendant was at fault and would assume full responsibility for all damages, but when police were called, defendant stated he did not wish to talk to the police, and as police drove up, defendant fled the scene of the accident."

"Plaintiff remained at the scene of the accident, and gave police full details of the circumstances of the accident, whereupon the investigating officer stated that defendant should be charged with hit and run and leaving the scene of an accident before an investigation was completed."

"Plaintiff was overcome by intense chest pain, nausea, vomiting, dizziness, fainting spells and intense back pain, whereupon plaintiff went directly to the Emergency Room." Powerful fraternal influences immediately went to work for the defendant, who was never subsequently charged with any offense. There were interesting ramifications which I did not learn for several years. First, the driver had been suffering from advanced schizophrenia for years, and under state law, he should have turned in his license. He had avoided this by going to private mental institutions, as state institutions would have required that he turn in his driving license.

Second, at the time of the accident, the defendant had for years been taking a number of powerful drugs, according to his physician, among them Dilantin, Phenobarbital, Tolinase, Dyzazide, and Haldol. His physician later stated in a sworn deposition that "Mr. S. has diabetes mellitus type two, he has a seizure disorder, he has an organic brain syndrome, he has hypertension essential, and he has manic depressive illness and a complication of medication called tardive dyskinesia, resulting in uncontrollable movements."

In short, the defendant's insurance was inapplicable because of these problems. City officials and attorneys now embarked on a weird three year campaign to keep the case from being heard. The result was one of the most amazing legal three ring circuses ever recorded in this nation. The attorneys first sent me a 54 question set of Written Interrogatories, supposing that, as an attorney pro se, I would refuse to answer them, and the case would be dismissed. I answered with eighty pages of single spaced legal size forms, which more than answered their questions. Their next step was to "discover" a witness to the accident. They "found" an elderly black alcoholic and mental patient, who claimed to have been drinking in an alley near the scene of the accident with some of his buddies. This good citizen was brought in for deposition. The attorney asked him, "Is this Mr. Mullins here beside you?" Answer. "I don't believe it is. I think he was a taller man. In my opinion, it looked like he was a taller man." Question. "Do you remember what kind of car it was?" Answer. "Now that, I would not know. It was just an automobile, in my opinion."

Although this witness could neither identify me nor my automobile, he was still listed as the defendant's principal witness. I had the court order his police and mental hospital records, which disclosed that he had been arrested for carrying a concealed weapon, that be bad been arrested numerous times for being drunk in public, and that he had been sent to the mental institution "on detention order from wife for threatening behaviour and abuse of her. Threatened with axe. Drinks cheap wine or whiskey all day. Was convicted of shooting and maiming a woman. Has been on probation since that time."

This pillar of the community remained the defendant's chief witness, until fraternal ties brought in another one. This relative and notorious black sheep of our family came in on deposition to give hearsay testimony that I had told him I ran into's car, and that it was my fault. I had not spoken to him for months. On cross-examination, I asked him what drugs he was on. He refused to answer. I asked him what drugs be had taken that day. He still refused to answer.

By this time, I had filed suit against the attorneys.

"As and for his complaint, plaintiff respectfully alleges that, for the promise of large money, defendants did conspire and act in concert to attack, injure and destroy plaintiff, by speaking, writing and filing false statements and false accusations against plaintiff which are false, defamatory and prejudicial against plaintiff, as follows:

(a)   At a Pretrial Conference, defendant did state to the Court that plaintiff, in his pleadings, bad repeatedly referred to defendant's client as being "of the Hebrew race" and as "being of the Hebrew religion," and as "that Hebrew," and defendant wished to inform the Court that he resented the references to his client. This allegation, made before six persons, was immediately denied by plaintiff, who truthfully stated that nowhere in his pleadings bad be made such statements defendant persisted, stating to the Court, "I know it's in there somewhere," although those present, searching through the file of plaintiff's pleadings, could not find said allegations."

This was typical of the vicious tactics of this outstanding law firm. They immediately filed Demurrer, whereupon plaintiff cited the statute, "Liability for words used in proceedings concerning conduct. No lawyer, or association or corporation composed of lawyers, shall be held liable in any civil action for words written or spoken in any proceeding unless it be proved by plaintiff that such words were used with actual malice, were false, or were used without any possible or probable cause."

I further stated, "Defendants err in their presumption that a license to practice law is a license to gratuitously attack and injure other persons without cause."

The friendly judge nevertheless granted dismissal to his close associates, whereupon I refiled and forced him to dismiss it again.

Although the judge repeatedly tried to alight his colleagues in their blatant attempts to prevent the case from coming to trial, I forced the motion through. At the trial, the attorneys came up with another miracle witness. They claimed that defendant, who had been alone in the car with his wife, had her sister sitting in the back seat! I later learned she had been in a Hadassah meeting in Norfolk on the day of the accident. The judge had warned me that the strange statutes forbade the mention of "insurance" in an accident trial. The attorneys then announced that their star witness, the black alcoholic, had conveniently been recommitted to the mental institution hours before the trial. I insisted that he be brought in. After a delay of a half hour, he was brought in under heavy armed guard. I then took the stand, where the attorneys tricked me into mentioning the word "insurance." The senior attorney leaped to his feet, screaming, "Mistrial!"

I filed Motion to Vacate Order of Mistrial, which went the way of all of my motions.

MOTION TO VACATE ORDER OF MISTRIAL

Plaintiff, Eustace C. Mullins, respectfully moves the Court to vacate the Order of Mistrial issued on July 29, 1981 in this action, for the following reasons:

1. The Order of Mistrial requested by the defendant, because of the inadvertent mention of the word "insurance" in the presence of the jury, and apparently in violation of statutes prohibiting same, and which was subsequently granted by the Court on July 29, 1981, bas, in effect, added a new party to these proceedings, the entity of insurance, and a party whose interests must be safeguarded by casting over them an impenetrable armor of silence. This insurance entity, whose presence, Although known to the parties, and being known to the Court, was not to be made known to the jury, Although Virginia statutes, which require compulsory motor vehicle insurance for all residents of the State of Virginia, which the members of the jury qualified to be by reason of their being called to service on this jury, was therefore already known to the members of this jury before plaintiff's inadvertent mention of the compound noun "insurance agent" presumably revealed to the jury a hitherto unknown and unacknowledged presence in the courtroom. Statutes thus prohibited the mention of an entity which was already known to the Court, to the parties, and to the jurors, a peculiar presence, like Banquo at the feast, haunting the proceedings in the manner described by Paul Valery, in the Cimitiere Marin, as quoted by William Butler Yeats in "A Vision" as "a seaside cemetery, a recollection, some commentator explains, of a spot known in childhood. The midday light is the changeless absolute and its reflection in the sea 'les oeuvres pures d'une cause éternelle.' The sea breaks into the ephemeral foam of life; the monuments of the dead take sides as it were with the light and would with their inscriptions and their sculptured angels persuade the poet that he is the light, but he is not persuaded. The worm devours not only the dead, but as self-love, self-hate, or whatever one calls it, devours the living also." Thus plaintiff's cause is devoured by the all-conquering worm of an unseen entity, the entity conjoured up by the defense, the entity of insurance.

2. By requesting a mistrial because plaintiff inadvertently used in his giving of evidence the compound noun "insurance agent," the defendant effected a transfer of liability, and was no longer liable because an entity had been conjoured who simultaneously relieved defendant of further defense of his liability at this trial, and transferred it to an entity who was not liable at this trial.

3. A statute denying plaintiff the opportunity to give evidence in which the compound noun "insurance agent" is mentioned thus enthrones insurance corporations and their private stockholders and insulates them against paying due awards from their profits, thus granting them a title of nobility and creating a nobility class. The Constitution of the United States, Art. 1. Sec. 10, expressly forbids the establishment of such a nobility class, as follows: "No state shall grant any title of nobility." The establishment of insurance companies as immune from legal mention not only violates the Constitution, but renders plaintiff out of law, or dead in law.

4. A state statute denying plaintiff the opportunity to give evidence in which the compound noun "insurance agent" is mentioned, violates the Constitution of the United States in these several particulars: That it creates an involuntary servitude forbidden by the Thirteenth Amendment; That it abridges the privileges and immunities of citizens of the United States; That it denies to the plaintiff the equal protection of the laws; That it denies plaintiff due process of the law. The Fourteenth Amendment says, "No State shall make or enforce any law which shall abridge the privileges or immunities of citizens of the United States. Nor shall any State deny to any person within its jurisdiction the equal protection of the laws." In 16 Wall. 36, 2I L.Ed.394, Mr. Justice Field stated, "It is nothing less than the question whether the recent amendments to the Federal constitution protect the citizens of the United States against the deprivation of their common rights by State legislation. In my judgment the 14th amendment does afford such protection, and was so intended by the Congress which framed and the States which adopted it."

5. If such state statutes prevent plaintiff from presenting evidence before a jury, the question is raised as to whether plaintiff should transfer his case to a federal court in which such statute would not apply.

6. It is a well-established precept of trial procedure that if the defendant sees that he is losing the case, any opportunity for a mistrial must be seized upon, as occurred on July 29, 1981. It was defendant's lack of a viable defense which caused plaintiff to file a Motion for Summary Judgment on June 9, 1980.

7. In plaintiff's Reply to Grounds of Defense filed by defendant, plaintiff stated on Nov. 7, 1979, "Defendant had promptly given the name of his insurance agent and the telephone number of said agent to plaintiff but defendant did not request plaintiff's insurance agent as defendant had assumed full responsibility and had no intention of seeking any payment from plaintiff's coverage." It was this evidence, which is crucial to plaintiff's case, which plaintiff attempted to inform the jury as to the issues of fact which were to be determined by them, but plaintiff was prevented from doing so by defendant's motion for mistrial. In future hearings of this action, if statute still prevents plaintiff from informing the jury of the facts of the case, due process will not occur, plaintiff will be out of law, or dead in law, and by not giving said evidence, plaintiff will be guilty of withholding evidence from the jury, and of obstructing justice, even if in so doing, plaintiff is following the express instructions of the Court and is in accordance with statutes prohibiting the mention of insurance in the presence of the jury. 71 Corpus Juris Secundum 4: "What Constitutes Pleadings. It covers all proceedings taken during the progress of the trial. Snelling v. Darrell, 17 Ga. 141.

(a). 46 Corpus Juris Secundum 1308. "Plaintiff must prove every material allegation or fact in issue. Christ v. Pacific Mut. Life Ios. Co. 231 II., app. 439, affirmed 144 N.E. 161, 312 III. 525, 35 A.L.R. 730. Plaintiff alleges that he is prevented from proving the facts in issue.

(b). 71 Corpus Juris Secundum 525 C. "Matters eliminated from case or admitted. The pleadings on which trial is had are determination of whether evidence is admissible. Pecos R.R. Co. v. Crews. civ. app. 139 S.W. 1049." Plaintiff alleges that said evidence had already been included in his pleadings without objection.

(c). 71 Corpus Juris Secundum 528. "Generally, any evidence is admissible under the general issue which contradicts, or tends directly to contradict, the allegations which the adverse party must establish to sustain his claim. Sylvis v. Hays, 6 P.2d 1098, 1100, 138 Or. 418. Plaintiff alleges his evidence is thus admissible.

(d). 71 Corpus Juris Secundum 2. Statutory Provisions. "Codes of civil procedure and rules promulgated thereunder are designed to simplify pleading and to eliminate some of the technicalities of pleading at common law; but generally, except as modified by such provisions, the common law rules of pleading are deemed to remain in force. Stinson v. Edgemoor Iron Wks, D.C. Del. 53 F.Supp. 864." Plaintiff alleges that his evidence is admissible under common law pleading, and that common law precedent overrides any statute designed to protect insurance entities from legitimate awards.

8. Although plaintiff had filed a Motion to Bar Inadmissible Testimony before the trial was heard, defendant did not file such a motion and thereby indicated no inadmissible testimony was expected from plaintiff.

WHEREFORE, Plaintiff's Motion to Vacate Order of Mistrial should be granted.

The judge then intimated to me that the attorneys wished to negotiate a settlement, but they did not wish to negotiate with me because I was not an attorney. He promised that if I hired an attorney, they would settle. I was still naïve enough to believe this judge. I inquired around, and hired a young attorney who would frequently break out into strange equine giggles. When we met to negotiate with the defendant's stellar attorneys, be promptly jumped up and ran to the men's room. "What's wrong with him?" I asked a friend who was sitting in with us. "Oh, he just went to throw up," he replied. "It's his first negotiation." When he returned, he promptly agreed that I should pay witness' fees to the sister-in-law, some $400. No other negotiations were concluded. I fired him that afternoon, and sent the following notice to the defendant.

NOTICE

Plaintiff, Eustace C. Mullins, as attorney pro se, hereby serves notice to the defendant that your position at the pretrial conference of April 11, 1983 was openly and positively and definitely reaffirmed, that you have refused and continue to refuse to negotiate any pretrial agreement or settlement with the plaintiff, a position you have steadfastly maintained for the past three and a half years. You are hereby placed on notice that the mounting legal costs of this action are and have been and continue to be solely due to your refusal to enter into any pretrial negotiations with plaintiff, and that, on recovery of these costs, plaintiff will demand that said legal costs in this action be deemed punitive in assignment and arrogation to defendant, and thus doubled by decree of this Court, because the large costs of this action are and have been and continue to be solely consequent to defendant's refusal to negotiate any pretrial agreement or settlement with plaintiff, and plaintiff reiterates that he has been and continues to be willing to negotiate a pretrial settlement at any time since this action was filed on October 1, 1979, and that any and all legal costs since that date should be attributed, assigned and arrogated to defendant as his liability because of his refusal to enter into any pretrial negotiations with plaintiff.

After months of further deliberations, I succeeded in having the case brought to trial again. The attorneys introduced the deposition from the defendant's physician, stating that defendant was now in a psychiatric hospital and would not be appearing at the trial. The judge then ruled that I could not make any reference to the drugs or schizophrenic and many depressive condition of the defendant, ruling the entire physician's report "inadmissible."

Two days before the trial, the policeman who was my sole witness died suddenly in a local hospital, of medical treatment. I was warned by my automobile mechanic, a black man well versed in the vagaries of small town existence, that the jury would be stacked. "They got this same list," he said. "Nobody else ever gets on that list."

Without my only witness, and denied any opportunity to present to the jury the evidence that the defendant had been driving illegally, while under the influence of seizure-causing drugs, and suffering from schizophrenia, my case did not take long to present. The judge suggested that I bring my car up so that the jury could examine it. The jury filed out, made a lengthy examination of the two smashed-in side doors, and returned to the jury room to deliberate. Eight minutes later, they returned to find for the defendant. In effect, they had ruled that I had indeed backed my car into the front fender of defendant's car, which, in some manner, defying the laws of physics, crushed in the two side doors!

CHAPTER 11

THE STRANGE CASE OF THE SENILE MILLIONAIRE

In 1982, the present writer received a telephone call regarding his book on the Federal Reserve System. An elderly gentleman suggested, in a quavering voice, that he would be interested in financing a new edition. I promptly informed him that all previous arrangements regarding this book had been a personal disaster for me, and that I was not interested. He gave me his name, one that I had never heard of. A few evenings later, he called again. He was very persistent, and he informed me that he had resolved to finance the book, with all proceeds to go to me, because of the unfortunate experiences I had had with previous publications. I had researched his name, and found that he was one of the wealthiest men in America. I agreed to meet with him.

I found that he was indeed a very elderly man, and that he had been donating money to some conservative causes for years, although he had never donated to anyone I was acquainted with. One of the recipients of his largesse was a Lebanese lawyer with the improbable name of Dr. Peter Beter. It was Dr. Beter's thesis that all of the prominent personalities in the world had been shot through the forehead with one bullet, including President Jimmy Carter, and that they had been replaced by robots. Because they had always been robots for the World Order, no one but Dr. Beter had noticed that anything was amiss. It should have been a warning to me that the old gentleman was impressed by this type of fertile imagination, but by that time, I had sold myself on the idea that I was now a writer who had at last found his patron. The fact that the patron was a little loose in the upper story did not concern me. I would write the book, he would have it printed, and turn over all the proceeds to me.

I began work on the book with my usual energy and enthusiasm. Within a few weeks, I had made considerable progress, renewing my trips to the Library of Congress, where I had done my original research almost four decades earlier. It was then that I received a sign, one which should have alerted me to later developments. The old gentleman's chief assistant, a man much younger than myself, suddenly died of a heart attack. I had already seen that my benefactor was extremely demanding on all those who worked for him; this did not bother me, because I always worked at top speed, seven days a week. I ignored a very obvious warning, and plunged ahead with the book. We had made no formal agreement, but he was advancing small sums for my expenses. I completed the manuscript, and at that time, he informed me that his lawyers had drawn up a Joint Venture Agreement. Although I never saw or talked with his lawyers, who were in another state, the agreement contained a very attractive paragraph:

> "The publisher (as my partner was referred to throughout the agreement) shall receive five per cent of the gross receipts from the sale of the book and the author shall receive all of the net profits from the sale of the book."

I had been doing my own legal work for years, and the agreement seemed very straightforward. He informed me, rather apologetically, that his lawyers had told him the agreement would not be legal unless he would receive something, hence the five per cent of the gross receipts which he had opted for. He also assured me that he would never try to collect it.

There was another clause in the agreement, which struck me as somewhat odd; "Upon the death of either party, this agreement shall terminate and all interests herein shall belong to the survivor."

Because he was almost two decades beyond the Biblical limit, and born long before my father, it seemed odd that he would include this clause, but I privately supposed that it would assure my receiving all interests in the book if he should die before me. Here again, I was given another warning, which I failed to heed.

After the book had gone to press, he became even more demanding upon me, setting up meetings with people he thought I should meet, trips I should take, and frequently calling me at home in the evenings and on weekends. His secretary informed me that he constantly did the same with her; she then reminded me of the sudden death of his manager. We began to call each other when we wished to discuss things in the book which he had challenged. She suggested we use the code name, Fagin, to refer to him, which we did henceforth. The book was published, and because the new edition had been awaited for many years, it began to sell very fast. I banked all of the receipts, without drawing on them, because, according to our agreement, they were all mine anyway. Suddenly he began to demand considerable sums, for "expenses." By this time, I was totally dominated by him, and I wrote the checks and handed them to him. Over several months, I gave him $25,000, most of what had come in, because of his insistence. He seemed to exercise a hypnotic influence over me, and I never balked at anything he demanded. When I arrived at his home, he would now rush into the kitchen and prepare me a cup of coffee, not allowing his housekeeper to do it, as she had done on prior visits. On one occasion, after leaving his home, I passed out at the wheel. I thought it was exhaustion. Other drivers had begun honking wildly, and I came to and regained control of the car. On my next visit, this happened again. I drank the coffee, and on the way home I lost consciousness, and slumped over the wheel, at seventy miles an hour. I came to find that I was almost touching the side of a car on my left, as I veered towards him. I avoided the accident, but, after I got home, I recalled the strange clause in our agreement that the survivor would receive all interests in the book.

I then received an alarming letter from England, from a financier named Alex Herbage.

"Dear Mr. Mullins:

I have just read a review in the National Educator of your new book, "*The World Order*." I assume this is an update of 'The Federal Reserve' and would be most grateful if you would forward me a copy. I have recently had some correspondence with E.D. (my partner, ED.) who led me to believe he controlled the rights over your books, as I could be interested in re-publishing these over here, for distribution in Europe."

Alex Herbage.

The entire picture was now revealed to me. Not only was Fagin determined to finish me off, in order to have sole rights to my Federal Reserve book, but, in anticipation of my early demise, he was already making arrangements to republish all of my books, both in the United States and Europe. Once I was out of the way, who would challenge him?

Shortly thereafter, Alex Herbage was much in the news. The *Washington Post* headlined "High Society Financier Indicted."

"A British financier with ties to some of the country's top Conservative politicians was indicted yesterday on charges of defrauding 3,000 Americans of $46 million through a mail order investment scheme. Alex Hermage, a 450-pound figure who has entertained the cream of British society at his million dollar estate, was charged with falsely promising to invest the Americans' money in gold bullion, commodities and European currencies. Instead, according to an indictment returned. in Orlando, Fla., Hermage spent the funds on a 'lavish life style' that included chartered jets, Rolls Royce and Mercedes Benz automobiles, an expensive art collection, the 44 acre estate in England and villas in Scotland, France and the Netherlands."

Herbage, which the Post insisted on spelling "Hermage," (which is pretty close, as critics of the Post will allow), was later sent to prison. Herbage was typical of the swindlers and criminals with whom Fagin was involved. I called his secretary and informed her that I would have to file suit against Fagin, unless be withdrew from our agreement. She said that she had repeatedly told him that I should have some of the proceeds from the book, whereupon be retorted, "There ain't gonna BE any profits!"

I sent Fagin a copy of a standard Termination Agreement, which he refused to sign. I was left with no alternative but to file suit against him. He responded by employing, not one, but two, of the state's most influential and expensive counsels. Obviously he intended that I would have to pay for all this. Both firms were well connected with such agencies as the FBI and the CIA, and could count on these alliances to obtain as much damaging information about me as possible. This did not bother me. I was already planning to publish some 120 pages of my FBI file in my next book.

I charged Fagin with intent to defraud, embezzlement, conspiracy to defraud, violation of copyright, making false statements, and misrepresentation, for starters. Much more would come later. All of my charges were documented. His lawyers responded with the standard tactics intended to trip up and get rid of an attorney pro se. They filed a Decree with the Court, but did not send me a copy. I checked the court file at least once a week, and discovered it. I immediately filed a Motion stating I had not been sent a copy of pleadings. There was never an apology from this highly-esteemed firm, but undoubtedly chagrin that their obvious tactic had failed. I then filed a Motion to Amend Complaint.

MOTION TO AMEND COMPLAINT

Now comes the Plaintiff, Eustace C. Mullins, appearing for himself, and respectfully moves the Court for permission to amend his Complaint, for the following reasons:

1. Plaintiff has uncovered numerous further violations by said defendant of the statutes which should be heard by the jury in this action.

2. Defendant, as chairman of _____ Co., continues to wage a war of attrition against plaintiff.

WHEREFORE, plaintiff respectfully moves the Court for permission to Amend his Complaint.

The courts will always grant at least one request for amendment of complaint, and sometimes more than one. It is all part of the legal hopper, and keeps the wheels turning.

I filed an amended complaint, and, to protect my life's work, my writings, I filed a Motion for Injunction.

"Now comes plaintiff, Eustace C. Mullins, as attorney pro se, and moves the Court for an injunction against the defendant,_____, ordering defendant to refrain from assigning or conferring re-publishing rights of any or all of plaintiff's published works, on the following grounds:

1.   Defendant, according to correspondence with one Alex Herbage (Exhibit A attached) is claiming the rights to plaintiff's published books, and making arrangements to lease, sell or otherwise convey said rights to others.

2.   Defendant, in awarding said rights, is once again dealing with the confidence men, tricksters, and double agents with whom he prefers to deal, and whom plaintiff has repeatedly tried to avoid, despite ,defendant's repeated orders that plaintiff shall meet with and work with persons of this type."

When Fagin had corresponded with Herbage, he had assumed that by that time I would have been disposed of, by special treats of coffee, or by other means. It was hardly his fault that his plan had gone awry, or that his confidante was now facing a long prison term for embezzlement. Despite my documentation of my motion with copies of Herbage's letter, and the Post article detailing his criminal career, the judge refused to grant my Motion for Injunction, on the incredible excuse that "He hasn't yet actually re-published any of your books, and his attorneys assure me that he will not." This was in the accepted tradition of never granting a motion from an attorney pro se. I was to see it again and again throughout the next three years of this proceeding. An injunction against the defendant would be damaging in the record of the case, and would be prejudicial against him with a jury.

One of the most sadistic actions of Fagin against me occurred shortly after I met him; he persuaded me that rare early editions of my books were unsafe in my home, and that they would be "protected" in his safe deposit box. He was right; they are still there today. Although the books were worth thousands of dollars, I was never able to recover them. One of them was a first edition of "Mullins on the Federal Reserve," which I had inscribed to my father. It was my only memento of him. I pleaded with Fagin to return it, but he ignored me.

Fagin had noted one payment of $12,500 to his personal lawyer for drawing up the Joint Venture Agreement, a standard four page agreement. This was included in some $90,000 which he claimed to have invested in the book; he had actually spent about four thousand dollars in its production, and I had repaid him almost $25,000. He was eventually to cost me more than three hundred thousand dollars on this book alone. During my legal researches, I found that his lawyers had neglected to consult the state statutes, which gave the following requirement under "Partnership Certificates: No two or more persons shall carry on business as partners unless they sign and acknowledge a certificate setting forth the full names of each and every person composing the partnership, with their respective post office and residence addresses, the name and style of the firm, the length of time for which it is to continue, and the locality of their place of business, and file the same in the office of the clerk of the court in which deeds are recorded in the county or corporation wherein the business is to be conducted."

No such certificate had ever been drawn up, signed, or recorded. I thereupon filed a Motion for Summary Judgment. "Plaintiff, appearing for himself, moves the Court to grant the Plaintiff Summary Judgment against the Defendant, on the grounds that defendant had failed to answer or deny the documentary evidence which Plaintiff submitted with his Complaint."

I had filed photostats of the statutes requiring the signing and filing of the Partnership Certificate, a requirement of which Fagin's attorneys were not aware. This should have been a routine judgment in my favor, but the judge denied my motion without comment. At no time did Fagin's attorneys ever try to explain why he had never executed the requisite Partnership Certificate, which rendered the Joint Agreement invalid, and gave me full reason for judgment in my favor.

Fagin's attorneys were now in full cry after me with the usual pre-trial discovery demands for depositions and production of documents. I had countered with my usual Motions for Protective Orders. As always, my motions were denied by the court, and I was ordered to proceed with the depositions and production of documents. I realized that I was trapped in a court in which every decision would be against me, and that this was primarily due to the pernicious Masonic influence which guided the court. It was imperative that I move out of this court. I filed a Motion to Remand to Federal Court, citing the number of federal questions involved in the case, copyright law, interstate fraud, etc. The judge replied to my motion with a personal letter that he would not hear the motion! This was astounding, because the United States Code cites many pages of precedents for remanding to federal court when federal questions are involved. I debated bringing an action against the judge for refusing to hear my motion, but I realized this would be useless, given the state of our legal system. I then filed a Motion for Voluntary Nonsuit; if I could obtain nonsuit, that is, drop my suit in the state court, I could then refile it in federal court. However, I had little hope that this would happen; the court had routinely denied all of my motions.

My dilemma was solved by one of those miraculous events which take place just when it seems that I have nowhere to turn. The day before the hearing on my Motion for Voluntary Nonsuit, a friend called on a radio talk show, mentioning that she knew someone who was due to appear in court the following day, and that he had no chance, because the lawyers and the judge were all Masons. The next morning, when we appeared in chambers, I noticed that the judge's eyes looked like boiled liver. I sat down and waited for the usual decree, Motion Denied. Incredibly, the judge began by saying, "I am inclined to grant Mr. Mullins' motion." Fagin's lawyers were amazed. "But, Your Honor" one of them exclaimed, "it's too late in the case for that. We have these other matters pending (referring to Discovery)." I thought his point was well-taken, but the judge seized a volume of statutes from the shelf, opened it at random, and pretended to consult it. "No," he said, "it's right here. It's all right. I am granting the Motion for Nonsuit."

I left chambers, jubilant that at last I had had something decided in my favor. My friend, to whom I owed this development, was also smiling. Fagin's lawyers were so angry that they refused to get in the elevator with us. Instead, they stomped down the stairs.

I promptly filed my complaint against Fagin in federal court. More than a year had gone by, with my suit bogged down in a court where I had no chance. Now I could argue the federal questions in my suit. Fagin's lawyers answered the complaint with their usual Motion to Dismiss. I then filed a Motion to Amend Complaint, which was granted. In my amended complaint, I upped my request for damages to $25 million, with an additional $25 million in punitive damages. My complaint documented every item. Fagin's description of his $12,500 payment to his private lawyer stated "Professional services-Tax planning for publishing venture, opinion on joint venture, and drafting joint venture with Eustace C. Mullins." I pointed out that this read as though I had been in consultation with Fagin's lawyer, when in fact I had never met or talked with him. Fagin had also diverted considerable funds from receipts of the Federal Reserve book to publish one of his personal pamphlets; large sums paid for his personal phone bills, payments to his secretaries, and to his other employees and acquaintances for private work having nothing to do with the joint venture. Fagin also sold one thousand of the books to his personal financial counselor below cost, in order to curry favor with him, despite my strong objections to the transaction. He opened a private bank account with proceeds from his sale of the book. None of this money was ever accounted for.

During hearings in state court, I had filed several Motions for Censure against Fagin's attorneys for their improper actions. We now engaged in more than a year of federal court maneuvers, during which I again repeatedly filed Motions for Censure. One of Fagin's attorneys frequently called me at my home, trying to trap me into agreeing to some procedure or to make a damaging admission. I complained of this in one Motion to Censure, which put a stop to the telephone calls. In each instance, however, the judge would deny my Motion to Censure, trying to laugh it off as a whimsy, instead of a flagrant violation of ethical procedure.

I then came down with a painful kidney stone attack, probably due to the daily stress of fighting this action. The day after I came out of the hospital, I was due for deposition. I appeared, but informed Fagin's attorney that I was still too ill to answer extended questions. The attorney promptly demanded sanctions against me from the judge, which he refused. I then filed a Petition for Public Trial, as follows:

PETITION FOR PUBLIC TRIAL

Now comes plaintiff, Eustace C. Mullins, as attorney pro se, and petitions the Court for a public trial of this action. Plaintiff prays said petition as a citizen of the United States of America and the domiciled voter of the State of Virginia, under Article 4. Sec. 4, CONSTITUTION OF THE UNITED STATES, and under Article 1, Sect. 11, CONSTITUTION OF VIRGINIA.

1. The object of said public trial would be to determine the validity of plaintiff's claims against defendant by a jury of his peers, and 'to determine the innocence of said defendant by said jury if defendant is able to prove said innocence.

2. Plaintiff prays said petition as a necessary step in maintaining the public order, in maintaining the courts as an essential part of the public order, so as to avoid anarchy and a general breakdown of law and order.

3. The public must remain sovereign, and the public cannot have sovereignty without public trial.

4. Plaintiff paid substantial court fees for a request for jury trial, and neither wishes to be defrauded of said payments, nor does be wish his fees to pay for a closed trial in which the plaintiff is not only the defendant, but in which the plaintiff had previously paid the court fees for the defendant to attack him.

5. Said closed trial would be a Bill of Attainder against plaintiff, which would violate the Constitution of the United States, Art. I Sec. 9.

6. Said closed trial would violate Article L, Sec. 11, Constitution of Virginia.

7. Said closed trial would violate the 13th Amendment to the United States Constitution.

8. Said closed trial would violate the 14th Amendment to the United States Constitution.

WHEREFORE, plaintiff respectfully moves the Court to remand this action for jury trial as provided by the Constitution of Virginia, with plaintiff as the plaintiff and with defendant as the defendant.

Respectfully submitted,

Eustace C. Mullins

This Motion was also denied, and Fagin's lawyers pressed on with their demands for discovery. Despite my health problems, I was very confident of the suit, looking forward to a jury trial where I could present the documentation of my complaint for damages. Fagin's lawyers were equally determined that the case would never go to trial. As I suspected, Fagin was now hopelessly senile, and would never be able to appear on the witness stand. I no longer had any contact with his secretary. Our telephone conversations ended when she made an obvious attempt to trap me into making a misstatement. I realized that the conversation was monitored, and never called her again.

We had now entered the third year of proceedings. At no time did Fagin ever make a personal appearance in the action. Time was on my side, and I was not pushing for a trial date. In any case, I could not have obtained it without complying with the pre-trial discovery procedures. However, I realized that I needed to get on with my other books (I now had twenty-two projected volumes which I must write over the next twenty years), and it seemed time to speed up the legal process. I did this by filing a Motion for Joinder of Additional Parties. This is a very technical motion which must be phrased just so, or the court will deny it. I did what any paralegal or legal secretary would do; I copied it verbatim from West's book of legal forms. Fagin's lawyers were amazed that I could have produced this motion. They informed the judge that I must have obtained legal counsel without having informed the court, as I was still attorney of record. As the hearing on the motion, the judge sternly asked me, "Mr. Mullins, do you now have a lawyer?" I was surprised by the question, but answered, "No, Your Honor." He then had no choice but to grant the motion. I had named Fagin's son, his accountant, and the treasurer of his firm as co-defendants although they were deeply involved in Fagin's swindle, I knew that they would not wish to appear and be questioned about their activities. It seemed that at last I was on the verge of forcing Fagin into a settlement. However, 1 reckoned without the depths to which the attorneys would sink. They immediately devised a plan of counter attack which proved successful.

The judge had ruled as follows:

1. Defendant's motion to dismiss the amended complaint shall be, and it hereby is, denied.

2. Plaintiff's motion for summary judgment shall be, and it hereby is, denied.

3. Plaintiff's motion to censure shall be, and it hereby is, denied.

4. Plaintiff's motion for a protective order with respect to production of documents shall be, and it hereby is, denied.

5. Plaintiff's motion for a protective order with respect to depositions shall be, and it hereby is, denied.

6. Defendant's motion to compel discovery shall be, and it hereby is, granted. Plaintiff shall respond to defendant's request to produce documents on or before Oct. 14, 1986. Plaintiff shall present himself for deposition on Oct. 15, 1986, at 9:30 A.M., at a location mutually convenient to the parties. Defendant's motion for attorney's fees in connection with this motion shall be, and it hereby is, denied.

7. Ruling is deferred on the motion for an accounting made in defendant's counterclaim.

8. Plaintiff's motion to join _____, _____, and _____, as defendants in this action shall be, and it hereby is, granted."

My Motion for Protective Order Against Deposition noted that

"**2.** Said defendant used the same tactic against plaintiff in a previous action, aided and abetted by counsel in a vicious campaign of attrition against plaintiff, forced plaintiff to cancel all his speaking engagements for the months of April and May by continuing demands for appearances at depositions in order to force plaintiff to drop proceedings against defendant, and cost plaintiff many thousands of dollars in lost income, in the great tradition of the practice of law as laid down by Roy Cohn when he appeared on Sixty Minutes, 'I make it so damned expensive for the S.O.B.s that they have to drop out.'

3. Defendant has scheduled said deposition so that his hired man can act as judge and jury, and conduct a private trial of this action, thus denying plaintiff the jury trial which he has requested. In a previous action, defendant managed to have plaintiff's complaint moved into chancery for private trial, Although plaintiff had requested jury trial.

4. Corpus Juris Secundum 26A 1. 'As a word of legal terminology it (deposition) is usually limited to the testimony of a witness, taken in writing, under oath or affirmation, before some judicial officer At common law, the right to take depositions in law actions was unknown in the absence of consent.' The plaintiff deposes that be objects to said private trial without jury before counsel for defense as a proceeding in chancery.

5. CJS 26 A9: Grounds for Taking. The statutes limit the power to take testimony out of court to clearly marked emergencies and situations. Thus an application to take depositions may and shall be granted only where one or more of the established grounds therefore exist, where there is some reasonable ground for believing that actual necessity requires it." And plaintiff deposes that defendant's demand to take deposition cites no emergency or necessity for said demand.

6. CJS 26A cites as basis for demanding deposition the non-residence or distant residence, disability, or that it is unlikely that the person will appear at the trial, yet defendant cites none of these bases as none are applicable.

7. Defendant has a proven record of seeking deposition from plaintiff solely for the purpose of harassing and embarrassing him, oppressing plaintiff with undue burden and expense and as a threat to plaintiff's health. Defendant has deliberately set the stage for such oppression by calling for the deposition to be held in the office of one_____, with whom plaintiff has been in litigation since 1979, and plaintiff as personally sued _____ and is considering further action against said _____, thus forcing plaintiff into a hostile atmosphere, in which the hired hand of defendant can freely oppress him. Since defendant persuaded plaintiff to begin association with him in 1982, plaintiff subsequently became gray-haired and developed a heart condition and high blood pressure solely due to said association and defendant's manager dropped dead of a heart attack during this same period.

8. Defendant has not established jurisdiction over the person of plaintiff.

9. Defendant Command to take deposition is an integral part of defendant's ongoing campaign to ruin, impoverish and destroy plaintiff, the many details of which plaintiff will duly present before a jury as a revelation of the incredible malice and malevolence of said defendant."

It had long been obvious to me that I had fallen into the clutches of a truly demonic being, who for a time exercised total control over me, and who had provably attempted to murder me and seize control of all of my life's work. I had filed Written Interrogatories and Requests for Admission to Fagin, which he had refused to answer, with no sanctions being levelled against him by the court. He had responded, but without direct answers. During the three years of this action, I had been saving the revelations of the true nature of this demonic being for the jury, and had been holding back the most shocking evidence of his behaviour.

The judge had now placed me under Federal Court Order to take Deposition, and for Production of Documents. Although I still had no inkling of danger, the plan of Fagin's attorneys had now begun. The first strike was a completely new request for Production of Documents, which demanded that I produce "1. Originals or, if not available, copies thereof, of all Federal and State Income Tax Returns filed for the years 1952 and through, 1985. 2. All documents, writings and records of every kind and description which in anyway relate to income received, and any expenses related thereto, from 1952 through the date hereof in relation to the publication of the book "Mullins and the Federal Reserve."

Fagin's attorneys could not even get the title of the book accurately, it was "*Mullins on the Federal Reserve.*"

I immediately filed Motion to Censure-Abuse of Process. There was no question that the judge would see that the request was impossible. I had already submitted testimony that during many of those years, I was homeless. The FBI agents had had me fired from job after job. I slept by the side of the road, or in empty buildings, or stayed with friends. I had no doubt that the judge would throw out the substituted request. "The Plaintiff, Eustace C. Mullins, appearing for himself, moves the Court to Censure Counsel for Defense for violating the integrity of this Court (a bit of sarcasm on my part. ED)., open defiance of a Court Order, and malicious abuse of process, as follows:

1.   On June 2, 1986, counsel for defense filed a Request for Production of Documents. Plaintiff then filed a Motion for Protective Order on same, which was duly argued in open court on Sept. 16, 1986. The Court denied Plaintiff's Motion for Protective Order, but deferred defendant's motion for an accounting.

2.   Counsel for defense later substituted a different Request for Production of Documents from the one which had been argued on Sept. 16, 1986, serving this new request on Plaintiff on Sept. 26, 1986.

3.   Counsel for defense switched Request for Production of Documents commanded plaintiff to bring all his Federal and

State income tax returns for the years 1952 to and including 1985, to counsel for defense's associate counsel's office on Oct. 14, 1986, and all of plaintiff's expense accounts connected with the book which is the subject of this action for the years 1952 to the present date. Counsel for defense had not argued this request before the Court in response to plaintiff's Motion for Protective Order. Counsel for defense had no legal basis for this illegal request, because the earliest date mentioned in Plaintiff's Amended Complaint is October 15, 1982, which counsel for defense apparently misread as 1952 and called for records from 1952. By demanding an accounting from plaintiff of tax returns and accounting of expenses connected with said book from 1952 through 1985, counsel for defense openly and flagrantly and contemptuously defied the decision of this Court on Sept. 16, 1986 and the Order of this Court that 'Ruling is deferred on the motion for an accounting.'

4. Counsel for defense's demand that plaintiff produce said accounting records for the past thirty-four years is malicious abuse of process with a two-fold purpose: First, to invent conditions impossible for plaintiff to meet, as it is unlikely that any individual can produce Federal and State tax returns and detailed expense accounts for the past thirty-four years, during much of which time plaintiff slept in empty buildings and by the side of the road, and cannot return to said empty buildings and retrieve detailed expense accounts therefrom, and counsel for defense filed such demand with the Court in expectation that plaintiff would drop this proceedings because of inability to meet said demands. In over two years of litigation, counsel for defense has not been able to answer plaintiff's documented charges against defendant, who continues to avoid any physical appearance in Court, remaining secluded on his vast estates like a latter day Howard Hughes while daily ordering out his paid hirelings to attack and destroy anyone who dares to oppose his malignant operations; and second, counsel for defense's associate counsel, with whom plaintiff has been in litigation for ten years, and whom plaintiff has sued for improper conduct, desires plaintiff's income tax returns so as to involve plaintiff in a second vendetta with the Internal Revenue Service, as said associate counsel succeeded in doing when plaintiff sued said associate counsel's client for damages, and said associate counsel boasted, 'Don't worry about Mullins now; I've seen to it that the IRS will handle him,' and shortly thereafter, plaintiff was summoned by the IRS for an audit, whereupon plaintiff was forced to file suit against the IRS, litigation continuing for many months, and dismissed without trial by jury against plaintiff 's wishes.

5. Malicious abuse of process is designed solely to force plaintiff to drop this action against said defendants, as evidenced by the *Washington Post*, May 19, 1980, "Discovery Cases Abuse Due Process" :U.S. District Judge John F. Grady on April 17, 1980 said much of discovery in the ATT case was irrelevant and immaterial. U.S. District Judge Harold H. Green said the discovery process had become a trial by combat,' in which the litigant most able to afford the necessary expense or willing to spend funds will eventually prevail by hiring a law firm willing to engage in endless and needless rounds of discovery maneuvers Useless discovery must be curtailed if justice is to be done.' The Post commented, "Abuse of discovery clogs up the courts and unnecessarily inflates attorney's fees." 17 CJS 10. "Abuse of legal processes or proceedings is a contempt." in re Toepel, 102 N.W. 369, 139 Mich. 85.

WHEREFORE, plaintiff respectfully moves the Court to censure counsel for defense for the above detailed violations and to award plaintiff full summary judgment against the defendants because of these abuses of process."

I never doubted that the judge would order the defendant to withdraw the demand for Production of Documents as excessive and unreal. I was stunned when he upheld the demand that I produce thirty-four years of state and federal income tax forms. During most of those years, the state had not even had a state income tax!

On the appointed day, I and a friend hauled two huge boxes of documents to associate counsel's office. I obtained a receipt from them for delivery of 10,000 documents. To this day, there is no record that any of those documents was ever returned. Included in the boxes were some, but obviously not all, of the tax

returns and expense receipts which I had been placed under
Federal Court order to produce. The setup, with cooperation on
the highest levels, was now in place. I then appeared for the
Deposition. I was expecting an interrogation of from a half hour
to an hour. Instead, I was subjected to a ruthless assault of some
nine hours of the most intensive grilling I have ever undergone.
I was recovering from another kidney stone attack, and had gone
on record in my pleadings as having developed high blood
pressure and heart trouble due to Fagin's persecution. The
attorney, a vigorous man in his thirties, expected that I would
collapse and perhaps die from the stress of such a prolonged third
degree. After some hours, he began to subject me to pointed
questioning about my sex life, hoping to develop something
damaging about a relationship with a married friend. She was
present at the deposition, and had faithfully supported me
throughout the proceedings. I objected, but he pressed harder
than ever, as he questioned me about my sex life over the past
thirty years. I anticipated filing suit against him on this line of
questioning, but when I paid an enormous sum for the transcript,
all of these questions had carefully been edited out, as had my
responses to them.

Few laymen realize that the supposedly sacrosanct
depositions, which are given under oath, are frequently edited by
the attorneys before being typed in their final form. There are
numerous deletions and alterations, all of which are illegal, and
all of which are done with the full cooperation of the court
reporter, who depends upon the lawyers for all income. It is but
one more development in the total corruption of the legal process.

In previous depositions, the attorneys had usually found me
unshakeable, and had given up after a half hour or so. I had had
one equally intensive deposition some years earlier, when I sued
the *Washington Post* for a million dollars for criminal libel. Their
columnist, George Sokolsky, had pilloried me as a "subversive."
Sokolsky died of a heart attack shortly after I brought suit against
him. The Post remained as a defendant. Their attorneys,
Covington and Buding, which employed Alger Hiss' brother
Donald, and a host of other pillars of Washington's liberal
Establishment, were the corporate counsel for the Post, one of the

properties owned by the international bankers, Famille Meyer, who bought the paper with the proceeds from printing and selling Liberty Bonds in duplicate during World War I, through the War Finance Corporation. At that deposition, I had an attorney, who sat by and said nothing while the Post's attorneys mercilessly threatened and hounded me for several days. Your attorney is supposed to object when the questioning becomes obvious harassment, but this dummy refused to do anything to help me. I fired him the next day.

As the afternoon wore on, Fagin's attorney began to wilt. He became increasingly red-faced, and excused himself several times to go out into the hall. It was apparent that he was on some sort of drug, as he became back refreshed and full of vigor. However, this only lasted a half hour or so, and he would have to go out again. I sat in my uncomfortable chair, totally at ease, making certain my answers contained as much damaging information as possible about the incredible malevolence of the demonic Fagin, who of course was not present. The fact that this material was going into the record infuriated his attorney, who began to scream and shout at me. As the sun sank over the horizon, he suddenly collapsed, and halted the deposition. As we were leaving the building, he came up to me, and with considerable respect, for he had been soundly beaten at his own game, he said, "I think it is time we got together and settled this thing, don't you?" I agreed, and we set a date for the following week. I was jubilant, because I expected a reasonable settlement. I was asking for fifty million dollars, and a tenth of that was now a good prospect.

When I arrived at the attorney's office, I noticed that be seemed calm, rather than downcast, as I had expected. We sat down, and he immediately said, "You haven't produced the tax returns or the expense accounts, have you?" I replied, "No." He said, "You know you are under Federal Court order." I said, "You know, and I know, and the judge knows that I don't have those records for thirty-four years." He said, "In that case, we have to go to the judge for sanctions. That means you will be remanded to custody until you comply with the order."

I understood why the judge had refused to grant my Motion for Abuse of Process, and had upheld the demand that I produce thirty-four years of records. Fagin's associates were desperate, after I brought them in as co-defendants, and their only chance was to have me put in a box. I was now to be committed indefinitely to prison. Since I could not produce the records, I would be in for life. The attorney now offered an alternative. "I mentioned the other day that we should settle this," he said. "I've prepared this quit-claim."

The quit claim stipulated that I drop all claims against Fagin, allow him to keep $16,000 that he had illegally banked from the sale of my book, and that I turn over the entire $23,500 I had kept in the bank without drawing upon a cent of it. He was confiscating all of the proceeds from my book.

I realized that this was extortion and blackmail obtained under duress. I signed the quit claim. This same judge had already dismissed two suits with prejudice which I had brought before him; I knew that he would agree, and had probably already agreed, ex parte, to carry out the indeterminate jail sentence until I produced the nonexistent records. I believed that I now had sufficient evidence to have the entire crew prosecuted under criminal statutes. However, after leaving the office, I reconsidered, and decided not to give the attorney the check after all. I went to Charlottesville to consult pertinent statutes in the law library, and returned to my home late in the evening. After I sat down, my front door suddenly was flung open (I had neglected to lock it), and Fagin's attorney came rushing in. He was red-faced, breathless, and extremely distraught. It seemed obvious that he was going to attack me, and my gun was upstairs. He was standing between me and the stairs.

"What do you want?" I asked.

"You've got to give me the check, right now!" he exclaimed. There were only the two of us in the room, but I suspected he might have U.S. Marshals waiting outside to take me to prison. I decided the check would be the final evidence I would need to institute criminal charges, and I wrote it out. He insisted it be made out to his firm, not to Fagin. This again was evidence which I wanted. I wrote him the check.

I then wrote to two United States Attorneys in the states we had been operating in, and to the Department of Justice, as follows:

> "The statutes governing misprision of a crime require me as a citizen of the United States to report to you the following offenses: interstate conspiracy to defraud and injure; violations of use 17; violations of use 18245, unlawful coercion, blackmail and extortion. (documents attached) showing Racketeer Influenced Corrupt Organization."

I included documentation, including Fagin's lawyers' assurances that they would obtain rights to all my published books and articles, the receipt for 10,000 documents from the attorneys, the check and its endorsement by Fagin's attorneys, as well as a number of other documents from the file of the case.

I reckoned without Fagin's widespread political influence. Like most very wealthy men, he made regular campaign donations to prominent officials. One U.S. attorney replied to my letter, "You have settled your case, and there is nothing we can do." The registered complaint of extortion, blackmail and undue duress was ignored. I had seen the American legal system in action.

CHAPTER 12

FREEDOM OF SPEECH, ANYONE?

I was uniquely qualified to found the American Council of Freedom of Speech Organizations, because I not only was the only person ever fired from the staff of the Library of Congress for political reasons; I also was the only writer who had had a book burned in Europe since 1945. The announcement that my history of the Federal Reserve was to appear in a German edition was greeted with horror by U.S. High Commissioner James B. Conant. I have repeatedly memorialized James B. Conant as the most notorious war criminal of the Second World War, a title which no one has sought to wrest from him. As a chemist, he developed an anthrax bomb on request from Winston Churchill, which would have killed every human being and every animal in Germany. The war ended before the bomb, (which Conant succeeded in perfecting) could be used. He then returned to Washington, where be advised President Truman to drop the atom bomb upon Japanese women and children. After the war, he became the ruthless Gauleiter of the conquered German people. I made legal objection to his wanton act of book-burning by filing the following complaint:

IN THE UNITED STATES COURT OF CLAIMS

EUSTACE C. MULLINS,

Plaintiff V.)

THE UNITED STATES,

Defendant

No.

PETITION FOR DAMAGES

As and for his Petition, the plaintiff, Eustace C. Mullins, seeks redress from the defendant for the following acts committed by defendant:

1. On or about July 10, 1955, defendant, acting through its duly appointed agents and respondent subsidiaries, did cause and order to be confiscated and seized and destroyed the property of defendant, the entire German edition of a book, "DER BANKIER VERSCHWORUNG VON JEKYL ISLAND", by Eustace C. Mullins, Plaintiff. The only recorded instance of a book being burned in Europe since 1945, defendant's act has been termed "one of the most barbarous acts of the twentieth century. The said seizure and destruction was duly reported by Reuters News Agency, the *Washington Post*, and other international news agencies.

2. From July 10, 1955 to the present date, defendant has continuously, consecutively and concurrently acted to cover up said crime of burning or destroying plaintiff's books, and has continuously conspired to obstruct justice by refusing plaintiff any compensation for said act of burning plaintiff's books, and has conspired to deny that said book burning took place, said conspiracy having been in effect from July 10, 1955 to the present date.

3. Said act by defendant of burning plaintiff's books took place as part of defendant's military occupation of a defeated nation, West Germany, and constitutes a WAR CRIME as defined by the Nuremberg Trials of which defendant was a participant and signatory.

4. Said order to burn plaintiff's books issued from the office of James Bryant Conant, in his capacity as United States High Commissioner of West Germany, and said order by defendant's principal agent to officials of a defeated and occupied nation constitutes a WAR CRIME.

5. Defendant, through its duly appointed agents and respondent subsidiaries, did further cause the said book to be continuously banned in West Germany from July 10, 1955 to November 1980, thereby causing the death of the publisher, Guido Roeder, Widar Verlag, in Oberammergau, Germany, from shock, harassment and impoverishment. Plaintiff's book has been published in Oberammergau, the home of the Passion Play of Jesus Christ, as an act of Christian piety.

6. Said agent of defendant, one James Bryant Conant, did act and seize plaintiff's book from hidden motives in his capacity as the second ranking Communist agent in the United States, to forestall any resurgence of anti-Communist feeling in Germany, because plaintiff's book exposed the financial origins of the Communist rise to power.

7. Said agent of defendant acted illegally because plaintiff's book had been widely circulated in the United States for three years, in two editions, with no legal action from any United States official, and had been publicly praised by such great Americans as Congressman Wright Patman of the House Banking and Currency Committee (letter of Nov. 23, 1953).

8. In November, 1980, Roland Bohlinger, Wobbenbull Husum, West Germany, did defy the illegal ban instituted by defendant, and did publish and circulate plaintiff's book in West Germany, with the approval of the present government of West Germany, solely because defendant, its agents and respondent subsidiaries, no longer have the power to demand obedience from West German officials or to bum plaintiff's books in West Germany. Said sequence of events proves sole guilt of defendant in the seizing and burning of plaintiff's books in West Germany on or about July 10, 1955, and in the subsequent conspiracy to injure plaintiff by the continued ban to November, 1980, and the conspiracy to obstruct justice in covering up this crime, and defendant is solely liable for all damages resulting from said act.

WHEREFORE, plaintiff seeks damages from defendant for losses from sales of this book in West Germany from 1955 to 1980 of deprived royalties of six million dollars ($6,000,000.00), plus an additional six million dollars ($6,000,000.00) which plaintiff would have earned from the sale of plaintiff's other books and articles in the market in West Germany and Europe which would have been created by the circulation of the destroyed book, plus punitive damages in an amount to be determined by the Court.

In further pleadings, I referred to this action as follows:

Nature of the Case

"Plaintiff's petition is the oldest and most historic civil rights case now in litigation. Plaintiff came to the U.S. Court of Claims because plaintiff has been consistently denied a hearing of this case and legal redress. Plaintiff had not exhausted legal remedies but had been denied legal remedies.

The Dept. of Justice has repeatedly and illegally refused to act on plaintiff's complaints of violations of his civil rights, as evidenced by attached copy of letter from Jerris Leonard, Asst Atty Gen, Civil Rights Division, dated March 5, 1970, which concludes,

> "If you believe your rights have been violated, you may wish to retain a private attorney to determine what remedies, if any, are available to you."

This case was dismissed without a hearing.

I had also sought vainly for reinstatement to the staff of the Library of Congress since I was discharged in 1952. I had been discharged by the pathetic drunkard, Luther Evans, on charges that I had used the letterhead "Aryan League of America," and that I had been the American correspondent for "The Social Creditor," a small English newspaper. The American Library Association had risen in anger at the spectacle of numerous plays, movies, and television productions which showed courageous Bette Davises battling prejudice as leftwing small town librarians. The ALA Council announced that it had formed two new committees to deal with the clear and present danger. "The Office for Intellectual Freedom (OIF) and the Intellectual Freedom Committee (IFC) will announce that they are ready, willing and able to take action on complaints of violations of the Library Bill of Rights whether from ALA members directly through the State Intellectual Freedom Committees, or indeed, from anyone else."

Unfortunately for the ALA, the OIF and the IFC, I was the only person who had been fired from a library for political reasons, and I was a known anti-Communist! They dashed for the exits each time that I contacted them, and have been running ever since. As I wrote to the redoubtable head of the American Library Association OIF, Judith Krug,

Judith F. Krug,

Office for Intellectual Freedom American Library Association 50 E Huron St Chicago III

Dear Mrs. Krug;

Thank you for your letter of January 8, 1970, which contains the statement that I did not exhaust the administrative remedies available. After receiving Mr. Mason's letter, I requested the hearing before the Librarian of Congress, Dr. Luther Evans, and was granted this hearing. Dr. Evans stated that he had no choice but to discharge me. This exhausted the administrative remedies available. The following week, Dr. Evans made a speech before the American Library Association defending the principle of freedom of speech, and displaying a remarkable moral agility after his action in my case. I do not know how you obtained information that I did not exhaust the administrative remedies.

As for being a probationary employee, I have heard this for seventeen years, but no one has ever explained to me why a probationary employee can be denied his civil rights, as I know of no other probationary employee who was denied them. A probationary employee means one who is allowed to work a certain length of time while his qualifications are evaluated in order to reach a decision as to his fitness to hold the job. My competence and my moral background, as well as my relationships with customers and fellow employees, was never questioned. The exercise of totalitarian Fascism in this instance by Dr. Evans and Mr. Mason is an outrage that will be remedied, although from your response I am beginning to wonder if the Office for Intellectual Freedom is seriously interested in this case. For the record, I believe your office will stand or fall by its decision in this case, as it is a historic case which will be pressed in every possible manner as an exposure of totalitarian Fascistic activity by Dr. Evans and Mr. Mason, who reached a personal decision to deny me my civil rights and in so doing violated Section 241 Title 18 of the United States Code in a criminal violation.

Sincerely,

Eustace Mullins

In my thirty year campaign for reinstatement to the Library of Congress, I wrote to Luther Evans'successor, L. Quincy Mumford, L. Quincy Mumford, Librarian of Congress, Washington, D.C.

Dear Mr. Mumford;

7-31-69

Your letter of July 16, 1969 to Senator William B. Spong Jr. carefully avoids discussing the facts of the case in my discharge from the staff of the Library of Congress. You do not mention that no public expression of prejudice was made to any staff member or customer of the Library of Congress, or that said "prejudice" had not prevented me from carrying out my duties and maintaining satisfactory working relationships in a racially integrated group for six months prior to my discharge.

Nor do you mention that the complaint, coming from outside the Library by persons who had never seen or spoken to me, was drawn up by J. Epstein, an active member of the Communist Party then serving on the staff of Senator Herbert Lehman, D.N.Y., and sent to the Library over Senator Lehman's signature. These persons did not appear in person to make a complaint.

Is it not a fact that no member of the Communist Party has ever been discharged from the staff of the Library of Congress?

Is it not a fact that if I had expressed pro-Communist views, instead of the anti-Communist ones in the article in dispute, I would have received no disciplinary action?

Your letter to Senator Spong shows a total amorality and complete disregard of my rights as an American citizen and as a human being. Although the great majority of Federal employees are loyal, decent, hard-working American citizens, it is regrettable that the department heads are still being drawn from the sinister cabal organized during the 1930s by Harry Dexter White and Lauchlin Currie, and that employees not in sympathy with their amoral, foreign allegiances are discharged, in the same ruthless manner as I was discharged from the Library of Congress.

I have been informed that persons ordering any of my eight titles from the Library stacks invariably have the slips returned marked, "Not on Shelf." Is this not the accepted practice of book-burning? The next step will probably be to deny me access to Library facilities, which I frequently use in research for my books on Christian themes.

I seek justice, not only for myself, but for the vast majority of disenfranchised American citizens.

Sincerely,

Eustace Mullins

I then filed suit against Mumford, as follows:

"Defendant has willfully, maliciously and capriciously refused to reinstate plaintiff as a member of the staff of the Library of Congress because of personal pique and prejudice even after being informed of the distorted and false claims advanced in plaintiff's letter of dismissal, and said claims were initiated by agents of the Federal Bureau of Investigation in open and flagrant violations of plaintiff's civil rights."

The following press release, sent to all major news media, was never printed anywhere.

CIVIL RIGHTS SCANDAL

A historic civil rights scandal surfaced here with the filing of a suit asking two and one half million dollars in damages.

E. Mullins, 51, has sued L. Quincy Mumford, Librarian of Congress, charging that Mumford, in refusing to reinstate Mullins on the staff of the Library of Congress, has shown, "pique, prejudice and violation of his civil rights."

The only person ever fired from the Library for political reasons, Mullins was given a letter of dismissal stating that he bad used a letterhead named The Aryan League of America, and that he had written an article on foreign aid for The Social

Creditor of England, a now defunct monetary journal which had a circulation of eight hundred, and which was not circulated in the United States.

Mullins had earlier received two promotions during six months on the Library staff, and had been personally hired by the Librarian, who had heard him give a reading of his poetry.

Since his dismissal, Mullins has repeatedly requested reinstatement, but Mumford has ignored these requests, taking the position that, as a "probationary" employee, Mullins had no civil rights.

"This legal confrontation is of vital importance to every Federal employee," says Mullins. "The courts must decide whether the bureaucrat is answerable to the law."

Judge June L. Green, famous for her capricious decisions, dismissed my suit with prejudice Jan. 14, 1975.

CHAPTER 13

TAXATION WITHOUT HOPE

During much of my adult life, the years spent in research and study, I had no contact with the Internal Revenue Service, because I had nothing to report. My first taste of the financial rewards of a writing career came when I received a $1500 advance for my biography of poet Ezra Pound, in 1961. In exchange for my room and board, I was teaching at a small Christian school in the mountains, when I received a summons to travel to the city. I was called into an IRS office, where the agents indignantly demanded a reason why I had not paid $500 of this sum as income tax. I contacted my brother, who was an excellent tax adviser. He informed me that I need only file a revised return, proving that I had spent more than $1500 in researching the book. I did so, and the IRS was satisfied.

Some fifteen years passed before I heard from them again. I had been embroiled in several lawsuits, during the course of which I was forced to file suit against an attorney for the defense. He had persisted in repeating outrageous and malicious lies about my pleadings to the judge, in order to justify the judge's one hundred per cent denial of all of my motions. I sued under the statutes, which provide legal redress when an attorney makes false statements. This not only caused consternation (apparently no one had ever sued a lawyer in my town before), but also doubled his malpractice insurance. He seemed anxious to convince me that my effrontery had not gone unnoticed, and one morning when I was passing by his office, he was trudging towards the door. "Mr. Mullins," he said. "Oh, good morning," I replied, without halting stride. For those who persist in claiming that there is no God, this attorney, at the very moment he was uttering vicious lies against me, was stricken, and his face began to rot away from a malignant and rapidly spreading growth. I had little desire to come closer to this apparition, a head of Medusa, and a reminder to all that God is not mocked, when he said, "Just a minute," "Yes?" I asked.

> "You may think you are getting somewhere by filing these lawsuits," he said, "but you won't be a problem much longer."

> "How is that?" I asked.

> "The IRS will be taking care of you," he said. "I have no problem with the IRS," I told him.

> "You do now," he said. He tried to smile, with the result that his decaying features contorted into a grin which would have done credit to a corpse.

The next day, I received a summons from the IRS to appear for an audit. I appeared at the office with a tape recorder, which I did not know how to turn on, and two truculent friends. After a brief encounter, we left the office. I had already filed suit against the IRS agent for damages, asking $300,000 for terrorism. The government promptly remanded my suit to federal court. I then filed a petition for remand to state court.

PETITION FOR REMAND TO STATE COURT

Comes now plaintiff, as Attorney pro Se in this action, and moves the Court to remand this action to State Court for the following reasons:

1. Plaintiff filed this Motion for Judgment against an individual in a State Court.

2. Plaintiff filed a Motion of Opposition to defendant's Petition for Removal to federal court.

3. Defendant has admitted in Motion for Summary Judgment dated March 10, 1980 that federal court lacks jurisdiction over the subject matter of this action.

4. Plaintiff denies that the United States District Court has jurisdiction pursuant to Title 28, U.S. Code Section 1346 (a) As plaintiff denies that this is a claim against the United States.

5. Plaintiff denies that defendant was "acting within the scope of his office or employment. N.C.St Hwy Comsn v. U.S. D.C. N.C. 1968 288 F. supp. 757 affirmed 406 F 2d 1330.

6. Plaintiff denies that the United States of America can be substituted as defendant in place of C. L. Wright Jr. pursuant to Title 28, United States Code, Section 2679 (d) and plaintiff cites Title 28, United States Code, Section 2680. "Exceptions. (c) Any claim arising in respect of the assessment or collection of any tax or customs duty or the detention of any goods or merchandise by any officer of customs or excise or any other law enforcement officer. (h) Any claim arising out of assault, battery, false imprisonment, false arrest, malicious prosecution, abuse of process, libel, slander, misrepresentation, deceit, or interference with contract rights. (1). Any claim for damages caused by the fiscal operations of the Treasury or by the regulation of the monetary system."

7. Plaintiff cites Title 28, Section 1446-2, United States Code. "Construction. Grounds and procedure of removal will be strictly construed in effort to preserve jurisdiction and comity of state and federal courts. Wood v. DeWeese D.C. Ky 1969 305 F Supp. 939. This section should be strictly construed in favor of state court jurisdiction. Vilas v. Sharp D.C. Mo. 1965 248 F.Supp. 1019. Higson v. North River Ins Co. C.C.N.C. 1911 184 F.165. Daugherty v. West Un Tel Co C.C. Ind 1894 6. F. 138. Proteus Fds & Industries Inc v. Nippon Reizu Kabushiki Kaisha D.C.N.Y. 1967 279 F Supp 836 Ziegler. V. Hunt D.C.La. 1941 38 F Supp 68 Soldifar v. Heiland Res Corp D.C.Tex. 1940 32 F. Supp 248."

8. Plaintiff further cites Title 28, United States Code, Section 2680, note 67. "Test of whether government officer is immune from tort suit depends on whether individual defendant was exercising a discretionary function. Garner v. Rathbum D.C.Colo. 1964 232 F Supp 508. affirmed 346 F. 2d 55. Note 14. Abuse of discretion. Abuse of discretion does not impose liability on the United States under this chapter and section 1346 (b) of this title. U.S. v. Morrell C.A. Utah 1964 331 F 2d 498 certiorari denied 85 S Ct 146 379 U.S. 879 13 L Ed. 2d 86.

9. Plaintiff denies that this proceeding is a tort action brought against the United States as defined by Title 28, United States Code, Section 2671 et seq.

10. Plaintiff cites Title 26, United States Code, Section 7214 (a). "Unlawful acts of revenue officers or agents. Any officer or employee of the United States acting in connection with any revenue law of the United States (1) who is guilty of any extortion or willful oppression under color of law. 4. whoever conspires or colludes with any other person to defraud the United States shall be dismissed from office, fined not more than ten thousand dollars, or imprisoned not more than five years, or both."

11. In "MY LIFE IN CHRIST," Faith and Service Books 1968, by Eustace Mullins, plaintiff has written, on p. 87, "The secret of Christ Power lies in the nature of human potential." Defendant's action in singling out plaintiff's poverty level tax return for "special attention" is due solely to plaintiff's Christian work, to plaintiff's work as officer of a taxpayer organization, and to plaintiff's authorship of numerous articles such as "WITHHOLDING TAX IS ILLEGAL," Christian Vanguard, Issue #86, Feb., 1979, and reprinted by popular demand in the March 1980 issue of the Christian Vanguard, and thereby defendant's prejudicial actions against plaintiff were outside the scope of his office and employment.

12. On Feb. 24, 1980, on the program "60 Minutes" Paul Strassels, former Internal Revenue Service official and nationally-recognized authority on the operations of the Internal Revenue Service, stated that any citizen reporting an income of below $15,000 had little chance of being audited, and that any citizen reporting an income of less than $10,000 had NO chance of being audited, yet defendant bypassed the established procedures of the Internal Revenue Service to order an audit of plaintiff's poverty-level income.

13. Plaintiff has requested a jury trial of this action, and remand to state court would preserve plaintiff's constitutional right to jury trial.

14. Defendant acted beyond the scope of his official duties in singling out plaintiff's poverty-level income for "special attention" because plaintiff is listed as No. 2 on a list of American patriots who have publicly opposed the subversion of the legal government of the United States by the State of Israel, and said list was compiled by Mossad, the Israeli Intelligence Service, and turned over to the Internal Revenue Service by said alien saboteurs with the demand that the Internal Revenue Service take immediate action against plaintiff and other patriots.

WHEREFORE, plaintiff prays the Court to remand this action to state court as originally filed by plaintiff.

JURY TRIAL DEMANDED

I then filed a request for my IRS file.

MOTION FOR PRODUCTION OF ESSENTIAL DOCUMENTS

Comes now plaintiff, Eustace C. Mullins, a citizen of the assembled States of the Republic of the United States of America, with all rights and privileges attendant, and moves the Court to order defendant to produce for plaintiff all pertinent records of the Intelligence Division of the Internal Revenue Service concerning plaintiff in any way, for plaintiff's due perusal and study as an essential part of plaintiff's prosecution of this action.

In almost two years of litigation, the IRS never produced any documents. I also filed Written Interrogatories to the Commissioner of Internal Revenue. I never received any answer to these Interrogatories.

I then filed a motion for injunction to prevent the government from sending the fraudulent 1040 form through the mail.

MOTION FOR INJUNCTION TO DENY DEFENDANT USE OF MAILS FOR FRAUDULENT DOCUMENTS

Comes now plaintiff, Eustace C. Mullins, as attorney pro se in this action, and moves the Court to issue an Injunction against Defendant To Deny Use of Mails for Fraudulent Documents (1040 Forms), for the following reasons:

1. The 1040 Form which is mailed to citizens of the United States by the Internal Revenue Service, Department of the Treasury, is a fraudulent document because it is a legal summons, but nowhere on this form is the recipient notified that this is a service of a legal summons, thereby creating a fraudulent act by sending said document through the mail improperly and illegally lacking any identification as to its true nature, nor does it warn the recipient of the penalties for disobeying said summons: United States Code Title 26-7210. Fail to obey summons will result in fine of not more than $1000.00 and imprisonment of not more than one year, or both.

(a). Corpus Juris Secundum, v.83, p.795. A Summons is defined as "A call to attend, or to act, as at a particular place or time." The 1040 form is a call to attend, or to act, as at a given place or time, and is a legal summons.

(b). 1672 Rec. Proc. Justin. crt Edinb. (S.H.S.) II 77 A Messenger executing a Summonds must shew his warrand.

(c). 1578 Lindsaye, (Pitscottie) Chron. Scot. (S.T.S.) 1.150 Than was send ane summondes of foirfaltour.

2. The 1040 form is a legal warrant, but nowhere on this form is the recipient informed that this is the service of a warrant, and it thereby becomes a fraudulent act to send said document through the mails improperly and illegally lacking identification as to its true nature. United States Code 265557 authorizes Internal revenue agents to issue search warrants but said warrants must be properly identified. United States Code 26-7608 (b) also authorizes Internal revenue agents to execute and serve search warrants, but does not authorize the service of same without proper identification. United States Code 18-2234, Authority exceeded in executing warrant. "Whoever, in executing a search warrant, willfully exceeds his authority or exercises it with undue severity, shall be fined not more than $1000 or imprisoned not more than one year." Je 25 48, C645 62 Stat. 803. The action of defendant in sending the 1040 search warrant through the mail without proper preliminaries is a violation of United States Code 182234, because it exceeds statutory authority for sending a search warrant without proper legal preliminaries. United States

Code 18-2235. Search warrant procured maliciously. Whoever maliciously and without probable cause procures a search warrant to be issued and executed should be fined not more than $1000 or imprisoned not more than one year. Code of Virginia 19.2-52. When search warrant may be issued: 19.2-55 issuing general search warrant without affidavit deemed malfeasance. 19.2-59 Search without warrant is a misdemeanor. Plaintiff, a citizen of the sovereign State of Virginia, is protected against said violations.

(a) Corpus Juris Secundum, sec. 932. "The guaranty of the Fourth Amendment to the federal Constitution against unreasonable searches and seizures includes searches and seizures under, or in connection with, Internal revenue laws. Amos v. U.S. S.C.4I S.Ct.266, 255 U.S.313, 65 L.Ed. 654. U.S. v. Costner, C.C.A.Tenn. 157 F. 2d 23 U.S. v. Swan 1D.C.Cal. 15 F.2d 598 U.S. v. One Kemper Radio, D.C.Cal. I 8 F.Supp.304." The burden of these decisions is that the 16th Amendment to the Constitution authorizing the income tax does not confer upon defendant any authority to violate other provisions of the Constitution.

(b) Corpus Juris Secundum, sec. 933. "An affidavit on which a warrant is issued must conform to the statutes and to the Fourth Amendment In view of the provisions of the Fourth Amendment, a showing of probable cause is necessary to justify the issuance of a warrant."

(c) Corpus Juris Secundum, Sec. 934. "A search without a warrant contravenes the Fourth Amendment."

3. The 1040 form is a legal contract between the party of the first part, the citizen who makes out and signs the form as a statement of debt and promise of payment, and the party of the second part, the defendant who receives payment but does not sign the contract, and said contract is therefore invalid. O.E.D. A contract is defined as "to enter into mutual obligations." L. *contractus,* an agreement enforceable by law, an agreement which effects a transfer of property, a conveyance."

a) 1588 A. King tr. Canisius Catech. 39. AU unlawful usurping of their mens geir be thift usurie, injust winning, decept, and other contractis." The 1040 form effects a transfer of property from the party of the first part to the party of the second part, even though the party of the second part does not fulfil its obligations, and is therefore a fraudulent document, and cannot legally be sent through the mail.

4. The 1040 form of defendant, demanding monies with the tacit and implicit use of force, is legally an extortion note, and is in violation of United States Code 18-875, 876, 872, 606, 607, 597 and 602. Because the 1040 form attempts to extort monies from citizens of the United States by force in order to give or pay tribute to foreign potentates and princes with said monies, said extortion is in violation of United States Code Chapter 11, Section 18-201.

5. The 1040 form of defendant contains a section for the Presidential Election Campaign Fund, "Do you want $1 to go to this fund?" This violates United States Code 18.606. Intimidation to secure political contributions, 607, Making political contributions, 597, Expenditures to influence voting, and 602, Solicitation of political contributions. This also violates the fundamental Constitutional principle of secrecy of the ballot, a basic principle of our Republic, because the citizen who refuses to offer $1 to this fund publicly indicates his political preference as a political dissident who does not support either of the government financed and controlled political parties, and the citizen thereby becomes subject to audit by the Internal Revenue Service, as plaintiff was selected for audit solely for said reason. Thus the 1040 form, which is in violation of the principle of secrecy of the ballot, cannot legally be sent through the mail.

In further support of said Injunction, plaintiff cites Title 26, United States Code, Section 7426 (b) (1) and Title 26, Section 2613, Note 28.

WHEREFORE, plaintiff's Motion for Injunction should be granted.

Included in some 38 motions filed during this lawsuit were five Motions for Injunction to halt the collection of income true, one of which is as follows:

MOTION FOR INJUNCTION AGAINST DEPARTMENT OF THE TREASURY/INTERNAL REVENUE SERVICE COMMISSIONER OF REVENUE TO HAIT FORCIBLE COLLECTION OF MONIES TO BE PAID AS TRIBUTE TO ALIEN PRINCES

Comes now plaintiff, as attorney pro se in this action, and moves the Court to issue an Injunction against Department of the Treasury/Internal Revenue Service Commissioner of Internal Revenue, to halt collection of monies by force and/ or intimidation from citizens of the assembled States of the Republic of the United States of America if any portion of such monies are designated to be paid as tribute to foreign princes and alien potentates, for the reason that plaintiff cites in paragraphs 5 and 13 of his Motion for Judgment, the subversion of the Internal Revenue Service by aliens and collaborators and the ensuing harassment of plaintiff and other American patriots and patriotic organizations who have publicly opposed the subversion of the legal government of the United States by said collaborators who are in violation of Chapter Eleven of the United States Code, and that cited activities of defendants are in violation of Chapter 105 of the United States Code, "Sabotage," and that defendants may be held under the Emergency Detention Act of 1950, Sections 811, 813 and 825, and that this injunction shall remain in effect until such times as the defendants are no longer in violation of said Sections of the United States Code and said violations are corrected. In support of this Injunction, plaintiff cites Title 26, United States Code, Section 7426 (b) (1). "Injunction. If a levy or sale would irreparably injure rights in property which the court determines to be superior to the rights of the United States in such property, the court may grant an injunction to prohibit the enforcement of such levy or to prohibit such sale."

Plaintiff further cites Title 26, United States Code, Section 2613, Note 28. "Apart from this motion permitting injunction restraining making of assessment or levy where taxpayer has not received proper notice, suits to restrain assessment or collection of tax may be maintained despite Section 7421 of this title prohibiting maintenance of suit to restrain assessment or collection of a tax."

Thus, plaintiff's Motion for Injunction should be granted. I also filed a Petition for Remand for Jury Trial:

PETITION FOR REMAND FOR JURY TRIAL

Eustace Clarence Mullins, Defendant, as attorney pro se, respectfully petitions the Court to remand this cause for a jury hearing, for the following reasons:

1. The Virginia Bill of Rights provides (8) "... jury of his vicinage"

2. The English Act of 1309, restraining chancery jurisdiction without jury. 3 Ed II.

3. An impartial jury, being fundamental to a fair hearing in a fair tribunal, is a basic requirement of constitutional due process. Durham v. Cox, 328 F. Supp. 1157 (W.D.Va. 1971).

4. Magna Carta (1215) Cap 35, "the writ called praecipe shall not in future be issued so as to cause a freeman to lose his court."

5. Magna Carta (1215) Cap 39. "No free man shall be taken or imprisoned or diseased, or outlawed, or exiled, or anyways destroyed; nor will we go upon him, nor will we send upon him, unless by the lawful judgment of his peers, or by the law of the land."

6. "THE LAW OF THE FEDERAL AND STATE CONSTITUTIONS OF THE UNITED STATES," by Frederic Jesup Stimson, The Boston Book Co., Boston, Mass. 1908, p. 11. "The Right to Law. The law required by this general right, furthermore, must be the Common Law of the English people. That is to say, in origin, the body of their free customs and usage, made by themselves, not by a king, and also, in earliest days, enforced by themselves; and furthermore, it must be the Common Law, not the Roman or Civil Law, nor the Canon or Church Law, nor any supposed Administrative Law, or orders of decrees of the king, or king in Council. Even chancery jurisdiction, which rests originally on the royal power as wielded by the king's chancellor (whence the writs of injunction, mandamus, prohibition etc. are called Prerogative writs) is hardly an exception. For many

centuries we find statutes restraining or limiting chancery jurisdiction. p. 12. In early English trials, therefore, what was tried was rarely whether the man did the deed (it was usually admitted or known) but whether he was right in doing it; that is to say, was he *in his Law?* Was he acting upon a state of facts whereon the unwritten law gave the right of reparation or vengeance into his own bands? If not, he was out of law, *outlaw;* that is, he had lost his right to law as against anyone molesting him in person or property. p. 24. The common law sounds in damages. Thus, the earliest codes of statutes merely fix a scale of penalties. The notion of compelling a freeman to do something or to abstain from doing something was foreign to Anglo-Saxon ideas of liberty. Like the doctrine of free will carried to its extreme, a freeman was lord of his own acts; only liable for the consequences of same, to the person injured; later, only to the Crown if a criminal act, and to the individual injured if a private wrong. Even when the judgment of the court went against him, the defendant was never compelled to do a thing, or even, in ordinary cases, to make restitution, as in the Oriental system of rendering justice. This principle must never be lost sight of, for it explains many things noted in local history and in popular prejudice. Probably the power of the chancellor to issue injunction writs went as far towards prejudicing our ancestors against the courts of chancery and the Star Chamber (which was merely its criminal side) as the absence of the jury and the local county court. Repeated attempts to limit or do away with this jurisdiction are found in the States of the Realm, and the general prejudice against chancery courts came to our ancestors by direct inheritance. As is known, some States, notably Massachusetts, for some time withheld chancery jurisdiction entirely, and when adopted it was in a limited and tentative way Bearing in mind firmly the principle that the English law sounds only in damages, and that the notion of ordering or even forbidding any act (except under a criminal statute) is utterly foreign to its system; and the cardinal principle that no fact can be found without the intervention of the petit jury; we shall be able to understand both the historical reason and the present meaning of the objection of the American people to the injunctive powers of chancery and ex parte sentences for contempt made by the judge who issued the injunction and upon the facts found by him showing the infringement of the same Many further authorities can be cited to sustain this position; but these are sufficient to establish the general principle that the injunction process and contempt in chancery procedure, as well as chancery jurisdiction itself, is looked on with a logical jealousy in Anglo Saxon countries as being in derogation of the common law."

7. In "THE AMERICAN CONSTITUTION AS IT PROTECTS PRIVATE RIGHTS" by Frederic Jesup Stimson, Scribner's, New York, 1923, p. 22.:

"The Anglo-Saxon people have a genius for ruling themselves. Their laws are the most ancient of modern law, they extend in unbroken line from Ethelbert, the first Christian king of Kent. p. 59. Chancery jurisdiction rested originally on the royal powers as wielded by the King through his Chancellor (in civil matters) or Justiciar (in criminal). These high officials were usually clerics, hence familiar with canon or Roman law rather than the Anglo-Saxon common law, which they probably despised. The common law knew only one remedial process, punishment for doing wrong; it could not, as a priest might do, order a litigant to do right From the Chancellor grew his court of chancery and all our courts of equity. Mitigating or supplementing the somewhat clumsy and uncompromising common law was well and good; but the Chancellor also shared this extraordinary, un-English, Norman and tyrannical power of ordering a free citizen to do something that he did not wish to do For what we may call the Continental notion, derived from the Roman, is that all law rests on the order of a sovereign to his subject, couple with a threat of punishment if he does not obey; to make a man do something or not do something. This is still more the Oriental notion But this notion had absolutely no place in the common law of England. An Englishman was a freeman, responsible for his acts; he could be punished for them by the state, or made to pay damages for them by the individual; but he could not be ordered to do anything else. In the earliest days of all, when in Saxon tribes each man executed his own law, the 'courts,' i.e. the assembly of his neighbors, only tried the question whether he was in his right in so doing, and if not, he paid a regular fine, at first fixed by custom, later, and most elaborately, by the earliest written laws we have preserved in England so no one was ever ordered to do anything by court process."

WHEREFORE, defendant claims the right to a jury hearing of this action.

The federal judge finally dismissed my suit without argument, on the incredible grounds that "It appears that the plaintiff attempted to claim a deduction for business tosses on the ground that the annual inflation rate exceeded his 7% return on investments. Accrued interest, of course, should have been reported as gross income on the plaintiff's income tax return, USC 26 sec 61, and the failure to do so constituted a legitimate basis for IRS review."

The judge's opinion proved his total incompetence. I had fully reported all interest income on my tax return (it was interest on a savings account of $2100, and amounted to less than $200); the judge, or his clerk, became confused by the fact that I had filed a Motion for an Injunction to halt the Collection of Income Tax on Savings Interest Income. He apparently thought that this meant I had refused to report it, although my suit had stipulated that I had filed and reported all sources of income. The judicial error was so flagrant that I had no doubt, on appealing it to the notorious "Rocket Docket," the leftwing U.S. Court of Appeals for the 4th Circuit, that they would find in my favor. In my appeal, I explained in detail the error of the judge. On April 3, 1981, the appellate court stated "Mullins maintains he fully reported his interest income. Even if Mullins' statement is correct, the district court did not err in granting the government's motion for summary judgment."

Note the brilliant legal scholarship flaunted in the observation "Even if Mullins' statement is correct." This is a bold admission that the appellate court did not even bother to ascertain whether

I had told the truth about reporting the interest income. Such sloppy judicial work, showing a callous disregard for the appellate rights of the citizen, leads one to wonder what sort of actual judicial work would be done if I were appealing a death sentence.

On Nov. 20, 1987, 1was advised to send Certified to the Department of Justice a brief record of the circumstances leading to the denial of income from my writings. I sent the following notarized statement, which was also sent to the Internal Revenue Service. There was no response.

AFFIDAVIT OF EUSTACE C. MULLINS

I, the undersigned, Eustace C. Mullins, residing at 126 Madison Pl. Staunton Va. 24401 hereby swear and affirm the following facts:

On or about 15 June, 1953, I was being driven from my Manhattan apartment by Charles Smith (Smetonius) to his office in Union, N.J., where he managed Common Sense, an anti-Communist paper. During this drive, Smith informed me that his employers (he was a double agent working for the American Jewish Committee and the Anti-Defamation League of B'nai B'rith) were upset by my articles circulating widely. They authorized Smith to make this offer: I would continue to write whatever I wished, but all articles would be submitted to Smith and his employers prior to publication. In return, I would be paid handsomely. If I refused this offer, Smith's employers would see to it that I never received any further income from my writing. I declined the offer, because I wished to be independent, and I could not believe any group had power to deny me all income from my work. Smith then issued 100,000 copies of my book, The Federal Reserve Conspiracy, without payment of royalties. Other publishers also began to issue large printings of my books, which continues to the present. I filed two suits with the U.S. Court of Claims, because federal agents were active in these printings, but these suits were never argued in court. I complained to federal agencies continually since 1953 and in every case was rebuffed. I filed suits in federal courts but the judges refused to uphold Title 17 USC, copyright law, even though I held valid copyrights. In thirty-four years, I have suffered approximately $25,000,000.00 loss of income from my books because of a criminal conspiracy to violate the laws of the United States, and a criminal conspiracy to violate my civil rights by a private government which regards itself as being beyond the reach of due process, composed of the above-named groups, and in which federal agents and federal agencies have played an active role to deny me all income from my writings. You are duly notified.

CHAPTER 14

THE TAXING POWER

" The power to tax is the power to destroy." so spoke the Supreme Court, in the early days of the American Republic. However, the power to destroy not only carries a like power to refrain from destroying, but its punitive power has the obverse role of granting privileges and immunities, otherwise known as rewards. The political genius of the secretive Canaanite mechanism reached its apogee in 1913. Not only did it award control of the money and credit of the people of the United States to its most trusted henchmen; it also carried the admiralty powers conferred by the Sherman Anti-Trust Act, carefully phrased to protect the monopolies, by making new and rival monopolies illegal, to a new high with the 16th Amendment to the Constitution. This "income tax" amendment achieved the enviable goal of turning anyone who opposed the regime into a "criminal," while it simultaneously erected a vast bureaucratic maze in which the criminals could forever conceal themselves, immune from any punitive action. The nineteenth century political observer, Lysander Sqooner, wrote,

> "Whoever desires liberty should understand that every man who puts money into the hands of a 'government' (so called), puts into its hands a sword which will be used against himself, to extort more money from him."

1913 was the year in which Americans handed over to the international financiers control of their money and credit, and also allowed the passage of a tax amendment which in operation would allow the government to say who is a criminal and who is not. The result is that millions of law-abiding, hard-working, productive Americans are now toiling on a treadmill of taxation which seizes by extortion from fifty to eighty per cent of their earnings and assets each year. Lenin laid down the dictum, in "The Threatening Catastrophe," 1917, that "concealment of income will be punished by confiscation of assets." This became the official program of the Internal Revenue Service. The tax billions which are hauled in by the IRS from working Americans are immediately trucked to the nearest Federal Reserve Bank - not to the U.S. Treasury! Any minor league IRS agent has the power to declare any American a criminal, and to seize his money and property. The legal redress against such declarations is almost nil. The majority of the assessments for "deficiencies" are figures which would cost the taxpayer as much or more to dispute by hiring a lawyer. As a bargaining figure, the IRS usually claims a deficiency at least four times greater than any possible amount "owed." The *Washington Post* noted, April 16, 1989, that in 1988, the IRS, with all of its seizure power and totalitarian tactics, recovered only 26 per cent of the total deficiencies it had claimed it in vases that were closed." These were claims that were actually settled. In many cases, the IRS claims astronomical sums from taxpayers, claims of millions of dollars against citizens whose net worth may be ten or fifteen thousand dollars. The IRS knows that this money will never be collected, but it is a useful figure to bring before Congress. Budget increases are based upon such claims; the IRS can state that it has ten billion dollars in outstanding claims for deficiencies; Congress votes additional funds, so that the IRS can hire more people to collect the money, having no idea that two-thirds of the figure is mere hot air, with no possibility of its ever being collected.

The Post quotes Chief Judge Arthur L. Nims, "They (the IRS) set up some big numbers once in a while, totally unjustified." However, these are the numbers which are religiously quoted in the media, as "evidence" that many Americans are "evading" billions of dollars in income taxes. In fact, the IRS is collecting every dollar it can claim, using techniques of seizure, garnishee, and outright theft. IRS abuses led Congress to pass a Taxpayers Bill of Rights. Such a bill was totally unnecessary, because we already had a Bill of Rights. The IRS violations of the Bill of Rights caused Congress to pass a measure enormously popular with the voters, which promised to get the IRS "off their backs." In fact, the bill was an absolute fraud. Paul des Fosses, a former

IRS agent, who now leads the National Association of IRS Whistleblowers, revealed in an interview in the Post, April 29, 1989, that the Taxpayers Bill of Rights was passed by Congress as a tongue in cheek measure. The Congressmen accepted the gratitude of their constituents for passing it, while at the same time notifying the IRS to ignore it. Des Fosses stated that

> "The reality is quotas (of tax collection) are still being maintained and enforced, and the problem lies in the fact that IRS is under tremendous pressure from Congress to provide the funds Congress needs."

One of the most forceful warnings against the 16th Amendment came from Richard E. Byrd, Speaker of the Virginia House of Delegate, on March 3, 1910. Father of the political leader, Senator Harry Byrd, Richard E. Byrd warned,

> "It (the 16th Amendment) means that the state must now give up a legitimate and long established source of revenue and yield it to the Federal Government. It means that the state actually invited the Federal Government to invade its territory, to oust its jurisdiction and to establish Federal dominion within the innermost citadel of reserved rights of the commonwealth. This amendment will do what even the 14th and 15th Amendments could not do it will extend the Federal power so as to reach the citizens in the ordinary business of life. A band from Washington will be stretched out and placed upon every man's business; the eye of a Federal inspector will be in every man's counting house. The law will of necessity have inquisitorial features, it will provide penalties. It will create a complicated machinery. Under it businessmen will be hauled into courts distant from their homes. Heavy fines imposed by distant and unfamiliar tribunals will constantly menace the taxpayer. An army of Federal inspectors, spies and detectives will descend upon the State. They will compel men of business to show their books and disclose the secrets of their affairs. They will dictate forms of book keeping. They will require statements and affidavits. On the one band the inspector can blackmail the taxpayer and on the other, he can profit by selling his secret to his competitor. When the Federal Government gets a stranglehold on the individual businessman, state lines will

exist nowhere but on the maps. Its agents will everywhere supervise the commerce of the states."

Note that State Senator Byrd speaks only of the businessman. The original propaganda for the income tax amendment suggested that it would only apply to businessmen, who would be required to maintain tax records. Senator Byrd would have found it beyond the wildest imagination that Federal tax inspectors would require newsboys and scrubwomen and waitresses to record every nickel earned by their toil, and band over more than half of it to the Leninist tax inspectors. Another of the five points of Lenin's 1917 program, which swept him into power in Russia, was "the abolition of commercial secrets." This goal could easily be attained by the tax agent program of the IRS. Although Lenin could hardly have foreseen it in 1917, another great benefit of the tax program has been the steady stream of U.S. taxpayers' funds which have been collected by the IRS and turned over to the Soviet Union. This is obviously illegal, because no government agency has any constitutional power to tax an American citizen for the benefit of a foreign power. The engines of government, most of which have been in existence for less than fifty years, are dedicated to maintaining their flow of fuel, that is, tax money. Some of the revenues are taken from one group of citizens and given to another group; this is the famed policy of "redistribution of wealth" which originated on the gaming tables of Europe. Much of the revenue is spent by the agencies on themselves, and on their further self-aggrandizement, or on programs which have been created deliberately to spend these revenues. Such programs have only one basic requirement, that all the expenditures he wasted.

Few Americans realize that the basis of "wasteful government," as well as its oppressive policies, is our debt money system, which can be traced back to the cult of Baal and the Babylonian money system. Money is created from debt; the payment of the debt extinguishes the money. Therefore, the sole purpose of our present manipulated government is to create inextinguishable debt, and to maintain the debt money machine. They continually waste this money in boondoggles whose creators live only for today, hoping in vain that tomorrow will never come.

One cannot understand the "income tax" or what sort of tax is being laid on what type of income, without knowing the history of the tax. A tax on incomes was demanded by reformers after the Civil War, to supplement the revenues raised by the tariff; the tariff revenues were more than sufficient for the government expenditures of that period, but the reformers wanted a government which would exercise more direct control over the people. Congress imposed an income tax on all incomes above $4,000 per year on Aug. 28, 1894. This was the equivalent of $60,000 a year in today's dollars. On May 20, 1895, the income tax law was declared to be unconstitutional by the Supreme Court in Pollock v. Farmers Loan & Trust, 1895. The Court ruled that 1. Taxes on real estate being indisputably direct taxes, taxes on the rents or income of real estate were equally direct taxes. 2. That taxes on personal property or on the income of personal property were likewise direct taxes. The whole act was declared unconstitutional and void.

Despite this precedent, an income tax was enacted by constitutional amendment in 1913, although many scholars have noted that the amendment was never properly ratified by most states. It was a necessary measure, required to fund the financing of the First World War by the United States. The European nations were already bankrupt and had no money to finance the war. Thus the income tax was properly a "war tax," a fact which became more obvious during the Second World War, when the withholding tax on incomes was passed by Congress as a temporary wartime measure. Forty-five years later, it is still in effect, having been regularly renewed by Congress to feed its insatiable appetite for public funds. The Federal Reserve Act of 1913 was a scrip act, establishing a privately owned bank, which was not federal, which had no reserves, and which was not a "System," but a criminal syndicate. The Act authorized the central bank, which was thereby established to issue interest-bearing scrip. This was done by book-keeping entries, thereby creating money out of nothing, as King William m had authorized its predecessor, the Bank of England, to do in 1694.

The Federal Reserve Act further authorized the use of "elastic currency," that is, currency which could be expanded, in the great economic tradition of the rubber check. However, this elastic currency, illimitably expanded, had to be periodically retrieved, or the entire Ponzi scheme would collapse. The salvage agency which was created to handle this problem was the IRS. This agency has the task of sopping up the flood of elastic currency, known as counterfeit, or frauds, because it has nothing but paper backing, being backed by paper bonds.

The salvage operation was not wholly successful until Congress passed the Current Tax Payment Act of 1943, now known as the withholding tax. It has never been a "withholding" but it is an illegal garnishee of wages. A garnishee is a legal notice served as a writ of attachment to attach the wages of a debtor. Withholding named you as the debtor, and the government as the creditor. However, the tax is not collected by a legal notice, or by a writ of attachment. Second, no debtor-creditor relationship exists. The IRS makes the unfounded claim that the withholding system establishes "the liability at the source." However, no debt is established until the end of the year, long after the withholding has been collected.

In collecting the withholding tax for the government, the employer commits an illegal act against the employee. He executes a lien, although this has never been allowed in U.S. law. U.S. v. Hooe, 3 Cranch 73, established the legal precedent that "The United States, in the mere character of a creditor, have no lien on the real estate of the debtor. The priority to which the United States were entitled, did not partake of the character of a lien on the property of a public debtor. If the priority existed from the time the debt was contracted, and the debtor should continue to transact business with the world, the inconvenience would be immense." Not only does the employer have no authority to collect taxes; he collects taxes as a condition of your employment; both functions are illegal. The withholding tax plan originated during World War II, ostensibly as the creation of the chairman of the Federal Reserve Bank of New York, Beardsley Ruml, a longtime Rockefeller Foundation employee. He boasted to a New York interviewer that the withholding tax plan had been devised at a luncheon meeting at the exclusive Plaza Hotel in New York, by himself and some "fellow intellectuals," whom be refused to identify.

Because of the strong arm methods of its agents, the IRS is frequently accused of violating the Constitution. However, the IRS does not operate under any provision of the Constitution, just as the Mafia does not operate under any provision of the Constitution. The IRS operates under the principles of the law merchant. Its victims are brought before the Tax Court, which is an equity court. Because of their law merchant framework, IRS agents seize property without legal authority, conduct trials without juries, and harass citizens until they die of heart attacks. American citizens facing "tax charges" are never told that Constitutional safeguards do not apply. The jurisdiction of these admiralty courts is based upon the alleged "contract" which citizens enter into when they obtain a Social Security number, or when they use Federal Reserve scrip. However, such a contract cannot be valid if the party of the second part, the citizen, has never been advised of its provisions. Similarly, any conviction handed down in an admiralty court proceeding can be overturned because the judge failed to issue a Miranda warning to the defendant that he would be allowed no Constitutional safeguards. In many tax cases, judges have sternly warned defendants not to cite Constitutional safeguards.

The IRS frequently goes public with its basic principle that the Constitution does not apply in tax cases. In August of 1988, Rosemary Campbell, a spokesman for the IRS, appeared on Denver radio station KOA. She was asked by the interviewer, Gary Tessier, if IRS agents were not required to abide by the same rules as police officers in making a search. "We aren't protected by the Constitution (in income tax cases)?" Tessier asked. "That's correct," Campbell replied, going on record for the IRS.

The motto of the IRS is the ancient cry of the English highwayman, "Stand and deliver." Robbery is their aim, and the admiralty courts uphold their methods. Citizens are frequently horrified and angered by the callousness and brutality shown by IRS agents against the public. This brutality is explained by the underlying desperation which inspires every action of the agents. They must recover the Federal Reserve scrip from the citizens; this allows for the issuance of more "elastic currency," and makes it possible to continue payments to the Bank of England (which controls the Federal Reserve System through five New York banks, who own 53% of the Federal Reserve of Bank of New York stock).

THE TAXING POWER   457

DEPARTMENT OF HEALTH & HUMAN SERVICES   SOCIAL SECURITY ADMINISTRATION

Refer to:

706 E 41st Street
PO Box 1710
Sioux Falls SD 57117
January 10, 1986

Jerome T. Schiefen
RR 1 Box 149
Hudson, SD   57034

Dear Mr. Schiefen,

Your recent letter to the Attorney General's office has been forwarded to us to answer.

Social Security is a voluntary system in that no one is required to get a number. However, programs which use social security numbers for control purposes might not allow a person without a social security number to participate.

The Internal Revenue Service uses social security numbers as taxpayer identification numbers. P.L. 87-397 was passed on October 5, 1961 requiring each taxpayer to furnish an identifying number for tax reporting purposes. Because of this, employers must have the social security numbers of their workers to legally report their earnings. They could not continue to employ an individual for whom they could not legally report earnings.

A bank or lending institution is not governed by social security rules but I doubt very much if they would refuse a loan simply because the applicant had no social security number. However, a person with no social security number would have no taxable income (see paragraph above) and I am sure this fact would have a bearing on their decision.

An inheritance large enough to be taxable would require the recipient to have a social security number for IRS purposes. The person leaving the inheritance would not be required to have a social security number just for this purpose.

I hope this helps answer your question. If you need any further information, you may call us at 1-800-952-0100.

Sincerely,

Penny Payton
Claims Representative

I hereby certify that the above letter from the Department of Health & Human Services to Jerome T. Schiefen, #RR1. Box 149. Hudson. South Dakota 57034. dated January 10. 1986.

is a true and correct copy of the original.   John Haller   2/25/86
                                                      NOTARY

My commission expires   5/24/87

Former IRS agent Mike Klein is preparing an explosive revelation of the tactics used by the IRS in their dealings with American citizens. When Klein joined the IRS, he was stunned to hear agents boasting about how they threatened people. One agent declared that he loved to "bust chops," others were openly vicious. After talking to a citizen, an agent would brag, "Boy, did I make that guy jump. I had that woman crying when I told her I'd put her out on the street with her kids." Another agent was asked by a taxpayer how he expected him to pay the tax after he had padlocked his business. The agent rudely told him, "Go get your wife to peddle her".

The number of citizens who have died of heart attacks in IRS offices is not available, but it is believed to be in the hundreds. Many of those targeted for investigation are what the IRS terms "easy marks," that is, elderly people, in poor health, who can be easily intimidated. Klein cites the fate of one such taxpayer who was ordered to appear for an audit. After a lengthy and exhausting interrogation, he collapsed in the office and died of a heart attack. "They shoved the body into a vacant office, and threw a blanket over it." An audit is probably the most stressful ordeal any American can undergo. A citizen comes in, knowing that he may lose his business, his home, and all of his assets. The agent is also under tremendous strain; he must produce more revenue, because his career depends on how much money he can bring in.

One Criminal Investigation Division agent for the IRS was a lifelong sadist. He was so brutal to his wife and children that his son and daughter finally shot him. Despite the fact that the circumstances were widely aired on television, a judge sentenced the children to long prison terms.

Alarmed by the unconstitutional acts of the IRS agents, many Americans were faced with a serious dilemma--could they in good conscience continue to support a government which had now exceeded the worst abuses of King George III two centuries earlier? Some of them began to protest against the confiscation of property a la Lenin, without legal process. They thereby exposed themselves to immediate retribution, not only by the IRS, but also by other government agencies, and by the admiralty courts. One "conservative" group took an uncompromising stance-the John Birch Society thundered that "good Americans" were bound to pay all taxes assessed. They denounced any tax resistance. However, this move was said to have been forced upon them by their longstanding ties with the Council on Foreign Relations and other internationalist conspiracy groups.

The 1913 tax seemed a modest one, calling for a tax of 1% for couples with incomes over $4,000. By 1919, the minimum income for filing had been lowered to $1000, and the tax was increased by 77%. During the Great Depression, few Americans had to pay any income tax, because most of them were unemployed. By 1943, wartime employment made it imperative for the criminal syndicalists to enact a measure which would allow them to seize income "at the source," through the withholding tax. Although the Leninists' tax program was in full swing, few citizens remembered that an inalienable right of citizenship is the right to own property. It is the great distinction between our Republic and the Marxist nations, which forbid the ownership of private property. Property stems from the word "proper," deriving from the Latin "proprios, one's own, belonging to oneself," and from the French verb "proprier," to have in possession. Thus it is right to own property; one is not a proper citizen unless one owns property. The Founding Fathers required property ownership as a requisite to voting. Those who were not proper, who owned nothing, could not be expected to vote in a responsible manner.

We fought the Revolutionary War as a tax protest; no taxation without representation. Most colonists regarded themselves as good Englishmen; they had no desire to separate themselves from the British Empire. Indeed, slightly more than one-half of the colonists remained loyal to England throughout the war, the numerous Tories. Taxation was the bone of contention, although the admiralty courts and the denial of jury trial were also sources of unrest. Today, we have both excessive taxation and the admiralty courts, yet popular opposition is not nearly so great.

America's first tax revolt took place in 1632. The inhabitants of Watertown, Mass. were outraged when the directors of the Massachusetts Bay Co. levied funds for the fortification of

Cambridge. The revolt was ended when the settlers agreed to the popular election of selectmen, who then levied the taxes. Americans accepted taxation if it was done by a representative government. The present Congress is loyal only to the monopolists, and to foreign governments.

President Andrew Jackson, who incurred the undying enmity of the international bankers by his battle against their central bank, the Second Bank of the United States, was so averse to taxation that in 1836, be reduced Internal tax receipts to less than $500. In his Farewell Address, President Jackson said, "Congress has no right under the Constitution, to take money from the people unless it is required to execute some one of the specific powers entrusted to the Government; and if they raise more than is necessary for such purposes, it is an abuse of the power of taxation and unjust and oppressive." William Gladstone observed that "I believe an Income Tax does more than any other tax to corrupt the people." In the face of this declaration, the House of Representatives noted in the Congressional Record, July 12, 1909, "The income tax is the most just because (it) takes from the backs of the masses of the people some of the burden of taxation and lays it upon the pockets of those who do not bear their just share of the burdens of the government (i.e. the very wealthy)."

Congress' 1909 claim that the income tax takes from the backs of the masses should now read "takes from the pocketbooks of the masses." The principal victims of forcible IRS collections are newsboys and scrubwomen, waitresses and elderly widows. Contrast the treatment of scrubwomen by the IRS with the lengthy courtroom battles fought by media moguls such as the Newhouse family. Their newspaper empire is now worth $5.2 billion; the IRS seeks an estate tax of $609 million, later upped to $914 million. The Newhouses claim that the actual tax owed is $47 million. Insiders, according to Business Week, believe they will eventually pay some $50 million, plus several million in fees to their attorneys. The elder Newhouse was an autocrat who believed he would live forever; consequently, he refused to discuss estate planning. Now the heirs must bluff and cajole the IRS. One observer comments, "Don't shed any tears for the Newhouse boys. They will finally plant some trees in Israel, and the IRS will accept the lowest figure for a settlement."

The Philadelphia Inquirer recently published a series, "The Great Tax Giveaway," documenting that thousands of Americans have received tax write offs of billions of dollars through Congressional special tax "laws." One Californian received a tax break excusing him from paying millions of dollars in taxes; he then applied for a second private tax law to garner millions more. These provisions were incorporated into TEFRA, the notorious "Tax Reform Act" of 1986, passed by Congress in September of that year. The Act closed off long established tax deductions for most Americans, but extended them for a favored few. There was no altruism involved; the recipients of these multi-million dollar tax breaks were those who had previously donated to political campaigns. A donation of a few thousand dollars could inspire gratitude amounting to millions of dollars in tax breaks. The 1986 tax law gave one company a $20 million tax break, even though it had filed for Chapter II bankruptcy in 1981 and no longer existed. It was disclosed that a New York lawyer is now reaping this $20 million tax break. Two paragraphs inserted into the 1986 law allow certain companies to avoid payment of hundreds of millions of dollars in federal income taxes. One company was able to avoid payment of a half billion dollars because of the special provisions incorporated into the "Tax Reform Act."

While opening the sluice gates of special refunds and tax breaks for chosen individuals and firms, the tax agents are steadily tightening the screws on the wage-earning population. Michael Milken can "earn:" $500 million in 1988 through "junk bond" deals, but a $100 a week waitress must disclose every dollar she receives in tips. Only the prostitutes can still scoff at the tax laws.

However, the IRS toughest crackdown is scheduled for the nation's children. New IRS guidelines have decreed that every child over the age of five must have a Social Security number. Most American children are now issued a Social Security number when their parents register them for their birth certificates. The teen-agers who mow lawns during the summer, babysit or deliver newspapers in order to save money for their college tuition must now report and pay taxes and/or penalties on every nickel they receive; otherwise, they become "tax evaders." The "kiddie tax" provision is an essential part of the Congressionally drafted and enacted TEFRA, Tax Reform Act of 1986, the same "tax reform" act which contains so many special multi-million dollar write offs for the chosen few.

It has long been obvious that the income tax code is the greatest weapon of the monopolists. Not only is it the spoils system refined to an incredible degree, and, as such, the most lucrative gold mine for politicians and their favorite lobbyists; it is also the principal weapon against the productive American middle class. Not only are the children of this class (in a supposedly "democratic" government in which class distinctions do not exist) taxed and penalized because they wish to save money for their tuition-being "middle class," they are not eligible for the many tuition giveaways which are available to children from "special interest" families-but they are also prevented from engaging in "capitalist accumulation," as Karl Marx termed it, that is, saving money to finance any profit-making venture. The greatest problem facing any of the monopoly corporations is the march of time; the replacement of buggy whips by automobile horns. This explains why the monopolists funded and gave political backing to the world Communist movement. Under Communism, economic development will remain frozen in time, as the cryogenic economy of the world. People will be driving reproductions of the 1938 Packard for the next three hundred years, as the Soviets have been doing since that year. To prevent the Henry Fords of the future from building a better automobile in a rickety packing shed, the monopolists intend to see that they will never be able to "accumulate" the couple of hundred dollars they will need for tools and supplies. The IRS obligingly fulfills this vital function, seeing to it that the American worker remains restricted to the "bare subsistence wage." Under this dictum of David Ricardo, the worker will never be paid more than the minimal amount which he needs for himself and his family. There would be no possibility of saving any money from this limited income. Ricardo (1772-1823) was the third son of one Abraham Israel, a wealthy member of the Amsterdam banking community which had financed the Cromwell execution of the

King of England, and the "Glorious Revolution," which put William of Orange on the throne of England, and resulted in the chartering of the Bank of England in 1694. Israel emigrated to England as part of the chosen influx of the Glorious Revolution. He soon became a prominent member of the London Stock Exchange. His son David worked closely with Nathan Rothschild, and amassed a large fortune, which qualified him to become an economist. He not only authored the infamous "subsistence wage" theory, but also provided that if it became absolutely necessary to increase the wages of the workers, for some reason, then the government must step in and increase their taxes by a corresponding amount. Ricardo's slave labor theories of wages and labor were enthusiastically received by the more sinister elements of the capitalist community, not the least of whom was Karl Marx, a "scholar" who subsisted off of donations from wealthy entrepreneurs. Marx adopted Ricardo's theories, which became the guidelines by which the workers of Soviet Russia are enslaved today. Marx is even more renowned in the United States for his invention of the progressive income tax, which was first aired in his Communist Manifesto of 1848. The Marxist tax was enacted into law in the United States during the Civil War, shortly after Marx had authored it. A second version of Marx's tax was enacted in 1894, but was promptly declared unconstitutional by the Supreme Court. The monopolists were forced to take a new approach; they put the tax through as an amendment to the Constitution.

Ricardo's dictum, which became known as "the iron law of wages," became a standard feature of economists' proposals throughout the world. His descendant, Rita Ricardo, came to Washington in 1980 as part of the "Reagan Revolution," which was intended to be a re-enactment of the Glorious Revolution of England. She promptly assumed the post of Reagan's adviser on social security payments and workers' pensions.

As the KGB of Ricardo's iron law of wages, the IRS not only works to maintain the monopoly corporations in power throughout the United States; it also protects the Marxist government establishment by routinely delaying any criminal investigations of other government agencies, and thus plays a vital role in Drug, Inc., the international machine of the drug czars and organized crime. Reader's Digest noted in an article, in 1981, "How the IRS Helps the Mob," that a key provision of the aforementioned TEFRA reform act of 1986 was its special pronunciamentos purporting to protect the right of privacy. The Digest noted that these provisions have proven to be so protective of criminal rights that TEFRA is now known as "The Organized Crime Relief Act." Government agents who were investigating a narcotics case in Cleveland requested IRS help in deciphering numerous financial records which they had seized in their raids. They were told to send the documents to the IRS. Months later, the IRS informed the agents that not only would they refuse to discuss the case any further, but that the records which had been sent to them bad now been classified as "confidential tax information," and they could not be returned!

Meanwhile, IRS agents continue to be the subject of an ongoing House Government Operations Subcommittee on Commerce, Consumer and Monetary Affairs, chaired by Georgia Representative Doug Barnard Jr. In their investigation of IRS violations of civil and criminal statutes, the Committee found that when the IRS learned that senior employees were using their offices for private gain, and of other examples of misconduct, little or no punitive action was taken against the guilty parties. William Duncan, former Criminal Investigative Division agent of the IRS, testified that be felt like he had been "in the Twilight Zone." He had been ordered by superiors not to disclose information to the committee, and he was told to lie to the Congressmen if certain matters were brought up, including a money laundering operation. He then quit. Fred Goldberg, the Internal Revenue Service commissioner, sent a prepared statement to the Committee that he's not ready to make a quick judgment about the IRS Internal security system. Duncan quit the IRS after 17 years of service. IRS Manual on Revenue Procedure, 64-22 states, "It is the duty of the Service to carry out that policy for raising revenue by correctly applying the laws enacted by Congress... not to adopt a strained construction in the belief that he is protecting the revenue." The IRS agents are in fact forced to take a "strained construction" if they are to protect their jobs; careers and promotions depend on the amount of extra money they can bring in. On p. 145, the manual states that there is no set definition of 'substantial compliance' on producing records." Here again, the agent plays it by ear.

The citizen be is auditing will not have a copy of this manual in front of him, and must do whatever the agent demands. The Committee has publicized some notorious examples from its investigations, including the incidence of criminal conspiracy to obstruct the tax laws in the Los Angeles office of the IRS. The former chief of the LA CID IRS was "persuaded" by Guess Jeans to investigate a tax fraud against a competing designer jeans firm, Jordache. The IRS official delivered the investigation, and then went to work for Guess.

He was later found to have "deterred or impeded" two other tax investigations while he was head of the CID.

IRS agents have frequently played a crucial role in political campaigns, intervening on behalf of one candidate against another. The most famous victim of such abuse was Congressman George Hansen of Idaho. IRS tactics not only defeated him for re-election, but later sent him to prison on flimsy charges of "ethics violations." It was proven that he had followed House guidelines in filling out the new forms, but he was convicted and imprisoned in a political vendetta. When his wife announced that she would run for his Congressional seat, she was immediately threatened by IRS agents. They informed her that if she would not turn over lists of her campaign contributors, she too would be sent to prison. Her campaign supporters then came under fire from the IRS, and she was forced to abandon her race for Congress. All of these acts are forbidden by law; they constitute illegal interference with the electoral process, and at least five or six other criminal acts. Nothing has been done.

For those Americans who still believe that they have some Constitutional rights left, the *Washington Post* carried a demurrer on Feb. 26, 1989. The Post cited a Jan. 20, 1989 decision by Judge Larry McKinney, who handed down a ruling that there is no Constitutional right of privacy for bank accounts. (Raikes v. Bloomfield State Bank). The decision gives the IRS complete authority to continue its longtime practice of furtive examination of citizens' private bank accounts. The McKinney decision is merely part of a nationwide campaign to tighten the screws on all Americans by the tax collectors. Paul Craig Roberts noted in his syndicated column, Feb. 7, 1989,

> "Ever since Reagan and a handful of outsiders lifted the oppressive tax burden on the American people, Washington insiders and the capital's coterie of special interests have been trying to hike taxes."

Andy Melechinsky touched upon this problem when he recently stated,

> "Any person who lives by the Bill of Rights today, is 'at risk' of being caged, and even worse, by a powerful, ruthless, and insidious tyranny such as the world has never before known."

Melechinsky points out the vital distinction between "rights" and a "privilege" for those who depend upon their "rights" when they go into an American court.

> "I should point out that Fifth Amendment RIGHTS are not *privileges* in a court of law (as opposed to equity). Only in a court of equity do rights become privileges, and no one can be lawfully brought into a court of equity unless he knows exactly what he is getting into, and wants to be there."

Few Americans realize that if they elect to go into the Tax Court, they are walking into an equity court whose judges are chosen by the government taxing authorities. Under President Carter, the Tax Court Nominating Commission for judges was chaired by Robert Mundheim, the General Counsel of the U.S. Treasury Dept. Second in command was Jerome Kurtz, director of the IRS. The other commissioners had like backgrounds.

One of the more outspoken critics of the IRS has been Virginia scholar and activist, Kenneth White, who has for years headed the Virginia Taxpayers Association. White has given documented evidence on IRS abuses before Congressional committees and state legislatures. He has cited under oath specific IRS violations of 26 USC 7214 (extortion); 18 USC Sec 1001 (false and fraudulent documents); 18 USC 241 (conspiracy to injure, oppress, threaten and intimidate), and 18 use 1341 (mail fraud). White has also filed two criminal complaints with former

Atty Gen Edwin Meese ID against Raymond Keenan, director of the Memphis IRS Center, and against other IRS employees for using false and fraudulent documents.

American citizens such as Kenneth White are routinely vilified by government propagandists, and their names placed on special blacklists. They are given the derogatory term of "tax protester" because they have dared to document criminal activities by IRS agents. A citizen who voices a complaint or registers a document stating that a crime has been committed against him or against any other citizen is not a "protester"; he is merely complying with the law. Statutes define one who fails to file information about a crime known to him is guilty of "misprision," that is, of failing to notify the concerned authorities about a crime which to his knowledge has been committed. Like other concerned Americans, Kenneth White is trying to clarify matters which have never been satisfactorily defined-such as "Who is actually required to file and pay an income tax?" "In what medium of exchange should such a tax be paid?" and whether the U.S. government is empowered to lay and collect taxes on American citizens for the benefit of foreign governments. Atty Lowell H. Becraft Jr. of Huntsville Ala. points out that the legal tender powers of Congress are valid only in "its jurisdiction." He cites the Revised Statutes, Title 39, Sec; 3588, the act which made U.S. notes a legal tender,

> "United States notes shall be lawful money, and a legal tender in payment of all debts, public and private, within the United States, except for duties on imports and interest on the public debt."

The last U.S. notes authorized to be printed in the United States were authorized by President Kennedy, shortly before his assassination in Dallas. On June 30, 1963, Kennedy signed Exec. Order No. 11110, further amended E.O. Mo. 10289, Sept. 1951, thereby giving the President authority to issue the currency. He thereupon ordered the issue of $4,292,893,815.00 in lawful American money, which was not interest bearing currency, as are the Federal Reserve notes. The printing order was rescinded as one of President Lyndon B. Johnson's first official acts after he succeeded Kennedy. At least he knew why he had ascended to the Presidential chair. Despite the fact that the Federal Reserve notes are issued by the privately owned Federal Reserve banks, they are still promissory notes, obligations or promises to pay by the American taxpayer. When the present writer was sent the dread summons to appear at the IRS for a tax audit (unknown to him, the order had been sent at the instigation of an attorney who had been unable to defeat me in a lawsuit) I promptly sued the agent for $350,000 for terrorism. The case was filed in a state circuit court, but was immediately remanded by the government to federal court, whereupon the plaintiff filed a motion to have it remanded back to state court, citing numerous precedents and stipulations from the U.S. Code. The case dragged on for many months, during which time the plaintiff filed thirty-eight motions, not one of which was ever answered by the government, or allowed to be argued in court. Plaintiff also filed Written Interrogatories with the IRS which were never answered. "Question 8. Plaintiff has charged the IRS with racial discrimination. Does the IRS practice racial discrimination against white taxpayers such as plaintiff, while allowing black political leaders to avoid paying income taxes because of these black leaders' threats to organize riots in the black communities if they are forced to pay taxes? Question 9. Why did an IRS official tell Drew Pearson that "We accept noncompliance from black political leaders because this is the price that Americans must pay to maintain racial peace in American cities?" Pearson printed this dialogue verbatim in his Washington Merry Go Round column.

Not only does the IRS function as a "vigorish" or collection arm for the Black Hand, as the Mafia operation called the Federal Reserve System is known to insiders; not only does the IRS function as the enforcement arm of Karl Marx's program calling for a graduated or progressive income tax; not only does the IRS function to maintain monopoly corporation power throughout the United States, preventing American citizens from competing by developing their own businesses under our alleged "free enterprise" system; the IRS also functions as the single largest negative force on the U.S. economy. Michael Evans, in his ground breaking work, "Let's Abolish the Income Tax," records that during the year of 1986, Americans spent a total of 5.3

BILLION hours in maintaining financial records, documents, and the preparation of income tax returns at the command of the IRS. If the average income of these American taxpayers is computed at a reasonable figure of $20 per hour, because most persons who earn less than $10 an hour pay little or no income tax, we have a dead loss to the American economy of more than $100 billion a year, a figure which could significantly reduce our national deficit. In 1988, the progressive or graduated income tax of Karl Marx brought in some $400 billion of tax revenue to the government from individuals, as compared to only $100 billion collected in corporate income taxes.

If we examine the aforesaid loss of $100 billion a year from nonprofit activity of American citizens, from an economist's view of the phenomenon known as "velocity of circulation," with an average turnover of five times per year in velocity of circulation, we arrive at the true figure of a loss to the American economy of $500 billion a year - to say nothing of the psychological stress under which Americans are placed as they toil over their income tax returns, knowing that as an error of a few dollars may cost them everything they own, in penalties and confiscations a la Lenin.

Because the IRS system itself has been for years on the point of total collapse, Americans need not fear that they will have to continue spending five billion hours per year on their income tax returns. The IRS now has a 25 year plan under which IRS agents will eventually fill out all tax forms.

They will compute your tax as a "simplified service" for taxpayers. In view of the fact that 60% of all IRS advice given to taxpayers about filling out their income tax forms has been shown to be erroneous, and is so faulty that the IRS itself will not allow the advice of its own agents to be used as a legal excuse for filing a faulty or incomplete tax return, we can only shudder at the chaos which will result when the IRS agents prepare everyone's tax form, and notify the citizen the amount he is expected to pay. The IRS 25 year plan also calls for "pay equality," an IRS refinement of the ancient Marxist precept of "comparable worth," which sets down guidelines for paying taxes from each according to his worth and handing the proceeds out to each according to his needs. Under the IRS plan, hardworking Americans will be forced to accept "pay equality," that is, reductions in pay, disguised as higher taxes, while favored special interest groups will get special bonuses. Any challenge to such IRS decrees would be interpreted as "Criticism of the state," or by the accepted term in Soviet Russia, "Slandering the State," and would be punished accordingly. The contemplated IRS plan would permanently enthrone it as the KGB of America, an all seeing, all powerful secret police which would inflict the maximum punishment on anyone who dares to criticize Big Brother in our 1984 Socialist State. It is Orwell's vision of the jackboot being stamped into the citizen's face, forever. Although few Americans have expressed alarm at the spectacle of some of the most notorious leftwing Congressmen hastily departing Washington only hours ahead of summonses and indictments, the exodus may have greater import than those revelations afforded us by the servile press.

The hegira of these professional politicians, although boding well for the future of the Republic, may not have been altogether inspired by the prospect of lengthy ethical hearings followed by the usual slap on the wrist. For some time, there have been rumors about a disturbing memorandum drawn up by the Department of Justice, which outlines a strong possibility that one or more of the Arab nations may request the indictment of a number of our more prominent Congressional leaders on war crimes indictments. The Department of Justice memorandum cites the public activity of these Congressmen in sponsoring and passing numerous appropriations bills for the State of Israel, these funds then being used to massacre Palestinian women and children in the vain efforts of the Zionist terrorist leaders to crush the desire of the captive Palestinians for freedom from their oppressors.

The memorandum makes it plain that these Congressmen, by their own admission, have become liable under the Nuremberg trials guidelines for the "massacre of thousands of civilians, including many women and children," for "confining thousands of political prisoners in concentration camps, under extremely inhumane conditions prohibited by the Geneva Convention," and for "plotting and waging aggressive war" against civilian populations.

The legal basis for the indictments is that these Congressmen have provided all of the military and economic aid to Israel which has made the Israeli occupation possible, which has paid for every bullet fired into the body of each Palestinian victim of Zionist atrocities, and which has paid all of the expenses of the Israeli occupation government. Under the Nuremberg guidelines, the Israeli government qualifies as a military occupation force equivalent to Nazi occupation governments in European countries in which they had set up satellite states. Many officials of these occupation governments were subsequently convicted and executed by decision of the Nuremberg tribunals, Although, in many cases, the evidence of their liability was much less than that of U.S. Congressmen in the sponsorship of the Israeli government actions.

The Department of Justice memorandum was prepared in response to an inquiry from a Congressional staff member about the possibility of war crimes charges being brought against one or more members of Congress. Its conclusion is that

> "We regret to inform you that, from the overwhelming amount of evidence readily available for prosecution, that defense against such a charge would be extremely difficult, if not impossible. Even though conviction of charges of war crimes would not necessarily result in the imprisonment or other punishment of those charged, due to the absence of an international force capable of carrying out such a sentence, the mere airing of such war crimes charges would be very damaging to the continuation of present United States foreign policy commitments, and might well result in extensive rethinking of and revision of our outstanding commitments to the State of Israel."

The memorandum went on to describe the "deleterious propaganda value of such war crimes charges," because the United States government would find it difficult either to defend the accused or to cooperate in their prosecution.

Another Department of Justice legal position recently surfaced which has even more alarming potentialities. It suggests that great obstacles now exist to further prosecution of American citizens who are indicted on charges of failure to file or failure to pay income taxes, because of the possibility that they can mount an unbeatable defense by citing the First Amendment, (1791),

> "Congress shall make no law respecting an establishment of religion, or prohibiting the free exercise thereof;"

For some years, I had pointed out that Congress, by enacting into law numerous appropriations bills which gave billions of dollars to the State of Israel, were in violation of the First Amendment. My argument had been that because the State of Israel is publicly known as a theocracy, that is, as a religious state with an openly religious government, and which excludes from office members of other religions who are nevertheless resident in and paying taxes in that nation, the Congress is thereby guilty of violating the First Amendment, that Congress shall make no law respecting an establishment of religion." I had not yet had the opportunity to introduce this argument in a legal action, but had long been hoping for the chance to place a federal judge on the spot, forcing him to admit that it was impossible to extort by force funds from American citizens, when those funds were then appropriated by act of Congress to be sent to a theocratic state, for the purpose of maintaining a religious entity as a sovereign nation among the family of nations. Indeed, the State of Israel seems to be the only world power at the present time which is openly and acknowledgedly a theocratic state, the tendency in modern history having been for several centuries against theocracy in government, and favoring governments which were open to members of all religious beliefs, as in the United States. Support for my legal argument emerged last year when the hero of the Congressional political show trials of the Iran Contra debate, which has finally resulted in the conviction of Col. Oliver North on vague charges of having "obstructed Congress," a charge, which if true, should cause him to receive a medal from the American people, said hero, Senator Daniel K. Inouye (D. Hawaii), who was then chairman of the Senate foreign operations subcommittee, aroused a controversy by yielding to the command of one of his campaign contributors that he appropriate eight million dollars from the U.S. Treasury to build religious schools for North African Jews in France. Inouye, who had been notorious for his vicious attacks on Col. North throughout the Iran-Contra hearings, eagerly agreed to violate the Constitution of the United States by giving the eight million dollars to the Zionist agitprop group, the Ozar Hatorah organization. There was a brief discussion of the appropriation in the servile media, although no mention was made of the fact that it was a flagrant violation of the First Amendment. Congressmen, like our judges, look upon the Constitution as an outmoded document which, in any case, has been totally replaced by admiralty law or the law merchant. Under the law merchant, there is no legal stigma or prohibition against U.S. taxpayers' funds being spent for Jewish religious instruction, as the law merchant observes no Bill of Rights. Most of the bills enacted into law by the United States Congress base their legal validity upon the principles of the law merchant, the most notorious being the enactment of the Federal Reserve Act into law by Congress in 1913. The Federal Reserve Act openly violated the Constitutional provision that only Congress should have the power to coin money, regulate the value thereof (Art I. Sec.8), and may be said to have enthroned the law merchant as the new and regnant law of the United States.

The problem of funding Jewish religious schools is once again raging in Washington, as a headline in the *Washington Post* of July 18, 1989, duly noted, "AID Funding of Israeli Religious Schools Hit" "Lawmakers Decry 'International Pork Barrel.' "The story revealed that the Agency for International Development (AID) has earmarked $3.5 million for the construction of two orthodox Jewish religious schools in Israel and a teacher-training institution for Jewish settlements in the Israeli-occupied West Bank. AID deputy administrator Mark Edelman is now fielding protests about the "apparent increased politicization" of AID's $35 million ASHA program-American Schools and Hospitals Abroad. The story goes on to condemn the ASHA program as "an international pork barrel for pet projects of key pro-Israeli senators and their Jewish fundraisers." AID is also paying out one and a half million dollars in construction funds to the Sha'alvim Teachers College in Ayalon, Israel, to build dormitories for Israeli students, who will then work as teachers in West Bank Jewish settlements. The teachers college, founded in 1976, is described as "a center for the teaching of Jewish culture." Also scheduled for AID funds is the Machon Alte Institute in Safed, Israel, part of a network of Jewish centers run by the Chabad Lubavitcher Movement, an extremely orthodox Hasidic sect which is headquartered in Brooklyn, and which is well known for sponsoring local vigilante groups in Hasidic neighborhoods. It also has one and a half million dollars earmarked by AID for the construction of dormitories. AID also has set aside $500,000 for the Or Machayim Girls College in Bnei Brak, Israel, whose stated purpose in its AID application is "to raise the economic and cultural levels of Israel's Sephardic population." The Israel Arts and Science Academy in Jerusalem is also scheduled to get $1.5 million from AID this fiscal year, and an additional one million next year for dormitory construction. Its American sponsor is Robert H. Asher, who, coincidentally, is also the chairman of Washington's most powerful political lobby, the American Israel Public Affairs Committee, or AIPAC. With such influential backing, it is understandable that the Agency for International Development would be appropriating such large sums to institutions in the State of Israel, even though its dedication to these goals might lead some Americans to think that AID stands for the "Agency for Israeli Development." Nevertheless, Asher denied that AIPAC had any part in obtaining these multi-million dollar appropriations for his ideological homeland.

Several Congressmen have called for a review of these appropriations, not from excessive zeal in protecting the American taxpayer from such outrageous exploitation on behalf of a foreign theocratic power, but from fear that, as AID becomes more identified in the public mind as an agency of AIPAC and other Zionist lobbies in Washington, it could endanger their multitudinous other pork barrel projects, public revulsion against such wholesale raiding of the U.S. Treasury leading to cutbacks in many other government funded operations.

CHAPTER 15

MULLINS ON EQUITY

The law merchant exists primarily to assure equitable dealings in commerce. Or so we are told. In fact, the law merchant exists to subvert all other legal systems in the world, and all governments. It is primarily an instrumentality of plunder.

Frederic Bastiat writes, in "The Law,"

> "Legal plunder can be committed in an infinite number of ways; hence, there are an infinite number of plans for organizing it. Tariffs, protection, bonuses, subsidies, incentives, the right to employment, the progressive income, tax, free education, the right to profit, the right to wages, the right to relief, the right to the tools of production, interest free credit, etc. etc. And it is the aggregate of all these plans in respect to what they have in common, legal plunder, that goes under the name of SOCIALISM."

Communism's offer to "redistribute the wealth" is the ultimate in political demagoguery. In "*The World Order,*" the present writer traced the origin of Communism to international bankers who were embarked upon a universal program of "levelling," that is, of reducing all things to a single manageable standard. Former Secretary of the Treasury William Simon writes that "The redistribution of wealth from the productive citizen has become the principal government activity." Of course the "redistribution" of wealth means taking it from producers and giving it to non-producers, in order to buy the political support of the nonproductive element of society. Samuel Adams, one of the Founding Fathers, wrote,

> "The utopian scheme of leveling, and a community of goods, are in our government, unconstitutional."

Adams pinpoints the fundamental problem in America today, that the law merchant and its communistic program of redistribution and leveling are forbidden by our Constitution; the syndicalists are therefore dedicated to removing and destroying the Constitution as the principal obstacle in their path. This is why the battle now comes to a bead in American courts; the law merchant has insidiously wreaked its will for many years, and it is finally exposed as an alien fraud and the final subverter of the legal system which was guaranteed to the American people by our Constitution.

In the Oxford English Dictionary, we find the law merchant defined under "1856 H. Broome. Common Law. Lord Campbell remarks that the general lien of bankers is part of the law merchant. (*lex mercantoria*)."

Now, this seems innocuous enough. A banker may be justified in obtaining a lien to protect his loan, or his interest. In practice, however, this means that the ability of the central bank to issue and create money creates a maelstrom which inevitably draws all property and all persons into its suction; it creates a lien on everything within the state. It is now widely believed that our central bank, the Federal Reserve System, holds at the present time a lien on all property in the United States. This means that there really is no personal property, and that therefore we have arrived at the Communist ideal, in which private individuals own nothing.

Black's Law Dictionary defines lex mercatoria, the law merchant, as part of the common law. It may be present in our courts, but not as the common law. It is the antithesis of the common law, because it is the vehicle of equity. The pernicious presence of equity in our legal system is a hoary relief of Oriental despotism, of autarchy, and of the abuses of unbridled power and the loss of individual rights. Equity is the Star Chamber of the Middle Ages, and the legal system of Babylonian absolute power; it is also the cult of Baal, the legacy of Nimrod, and the personification of the stealthy Masonic power. It is not accidental that the law merchant is enshrined in the Masonic rites; in the Ancient and Accepted Rite, the 31st degree is closely associated with equity; as is the 16th degree, the Princes of Jerusalem. It also is accepted as the Grand Defender, the 31st degree of the Ancient and Primitive Rite.

To the average citizen, the law merchant simply means the original principles of commerce, the law of negotiable instruments, contracts, partnership and trademarks. There is nothing sinister in these precepts. The law merchant contemplates good faith and credit among those dealing in commerce; again, there is no quarrel with such precepts. The Oxford English Dictionary defines a contract as "to enter mutual obligations, from Latin contractus, or agreement; an agreement enforceable by law, an agreement which affects a transfer of property, a conveyance 1588. A.King tr. Canisius Catech 39, Ali unlauchful usurping of othir mens geir be theft usurie, inust winning, decept and other contracts." The Law merchant upholds agreements between contracting parties. This too is acceptable; if a disagreement over the terms develops, it can be settled in a court. However, Blackstone developed the theory that court judgments themselves become "Specialties," contracts of the highest sort. The judgment of the court itself, in issuing an Order of Execution for the forcible payment of a judgment, creates a special "contract" which then must be fulfilled. It has been said that law looks to the past, but equity looks for the future. What this means is that law is that fixed understanding, developed by our traditions, which guides us, while equity looks to the future and a managed economy which is actually a return to the darkest period of man's history, the era of absolute despotism. Equity, or chancery, as it was known in the Middle Ages, stems from the duties of the secretaries (that is, secret emissaries), of the emperor. To give them authority to carry out his wishes, the emperor made them chancellors, that is, cancellors of sins to those who were favored by the emperor, from whence came the designation, chancery, and chancery court.

From its inception, chancery court proceedings were shrouded in secrecy and overshadowed by conspiratorial forces. Because of their dictatorial nature, they were also known as "Star Chamber" courts, a term which originated after William the Conqueror invaded England. From J. R. Green's "Short History of England," we learn that "A royal justiciary secured law to the

Jewish merchant, who had no standing ground in the local courts; his bonds were deposited for safety in a chamber of the royal palace at Westminster, which from their Hebrew name of 'stars' gained the title of the Star-Chamber. The famous Star-Chamber court system of England came from this arrangement."

Under the Federal Reserve System and its collection agency, the Internal Revenue System, the United States has now returned to a feudal system of the Middle Ages. The IRS originated in Italy as the Black Hand, which carried out demands for extortion for the Princes of the Black Nobility. Under our present feudal system, we live on the "lord's land" as "villeins," having title to nothing, and remaining as tenants at the lord's pleasure. The "lord," of course, is the central banker, who exercise control through the Federal Reserve System. It was not accidental that the secret conclave which drafted the Federal Reserve Act met clandestinely at Jekyll Island Ga., a millionaires retreat, whose members at that time controlled one-fourth of all the wealth of the world (Secrets of the Federal Reserve, by Eustace Mullins). The IRS maintains an Inquisition which was originally developed by the Jesuits in Spain; this inquisition pays a tithe to informants, and is seldom countermanded by the legal system, which exists merely to enforce its demands.

The central bank itself is the ultimate corporation, the final weapon of the conspiratorial Black Nobility and their World Order. Chief Justice Marshall noted in the famous case of Dartmouth v. Woodward: "a corporation is an artificial being, invisibly intangible, and existing only in contemplation of law. Being the mere creature of law, it possesses only those properties which the charter of its creation confer upon it."

Corporations were well known in Roman law, and were copied from the laws of Solon. They were private companies which were entitled to function as long as they did nothing contrary to the public law. The fundamental problem presented by corporations is that corporations and free persons cannot coexist in the same nation. The Constitution was written for free individuals, each being one person; the corporation cannot be one person, but is an aggregate person. The corporation is something which has attained immortality, something which is denied to all free individuals. The corporation ordains perpetual succession; it can be sued and it can sue; it can purchase gold, lands, and chattels; it can have a common seal; and it can make bylaws and appoint or remove members.

Because a corporation is not a person, it cannot have citizenship in a nation, or exhibit loyalty to a nation. A corporation therefore has no national loyalties, or any allegiance to national boundaries. However, the fundamental problem of the corporation is that because it is not a person and because it can go to court to sue or to be sued, this creates a situation in which legal positivism develops as a logical outgrowth of social activism, the Holmesian concept of law. As Roscoe Pound wrote, "There are no objective, God-given standards of law; since God is not the author of law, the author of law must be men." This is the dominant theory of our legal system God has nothing to do with the law - the Ten Commandments were never delivered - and the law is no longer concerned with persons, except as they come into conflict with the nonperson of the international law merchant - the corporation. When an American citizen goes into court, he arrives there as a creature of God and as a beneficiary of the Constitution.

He is met by the mercenaries of the law merchant, who function solely to enforce the admiralty court procedures of the nonperson, the corporation, as epitomized by the ultimate corporation, the world central bank, against that American person. It is this fundamental conflict which has never been stated in the court. The corporation's legal representatives, the judges and the lawyers, are aware of who they represent, but they never inform the citizen that they are functioning on the principles of the law merchant, while the citizen expects to be defended under the principles of the Constitution. The respected legal scholar, Bruce Fein, states, "It is very disturbing if you have a secret law that is known only to the judge or the government." *Washington Post*, April 18, 1989. The entire purpose of this work is to inform you, the American citizen, of the existence of this secret law. Thus it is no longer a secret, and you can mount an adequate defense.

The basic problem of the law merchant is that the free born individual, as a creature of God, comes into court to defy the corporation, a non-person which has been artificially created by the Black Nobility as a creature of Satan, and as upheld by ancient Oriental despotism, typified by the Babylonian monetary and court system. Sanford Levinson's book, "Constitutional Faith" treads gingerly around this problem. As a present day advocate of the latest version of Holmesian social activism in the legal system, Levinson treats the concept of "post-modernist thought." As described by Levinson, postmodernist legal thought is inspired by the anti-rationalist philosophies of Nietzsche and Heidegger, and by more recent "deconstructionist" epigones, Derrida, Foucault, Barthes, de Man and Richard Rorty. "Constitutional Faith" is intended as the final epitaph for constitutional traditions in our legal system, as Levinson intones, "The death of 'constitutionalism' may be the central event of our time, just as the death of God was that of the past century (and for much the same reason)."

In fact, the "death of God" was the desperate philosophical attempt of the corporationists to deny a God which had played no part in the creation of their corporation; the "death of the Constitution" will prove to be as much of a shibboleth. Levinson defines constitutionalism as a misguided faith in "timeless moral norms" ; that is, law as a fixed force as it is defined in its most ancient understanding, and law as a moral force emanating from the Presence and Power of God. Levinson tells us that "Popular sovereignty as a motif emphasizing the energy and moral authority of will (and willful desire) rather than the constraints of a common moral order to which the will was bound to submit, has become the view emphasized today at most major law schools." Is this surprising? The law schools train students to uphold the law merchant, and to subvert the Constitution. "Popular sovereignty" represents the sovereignty of the individual as a creature of God; it will always be the enemy of the corporation. Levinson tells us that "Law is stripped of any moral anchoring political institutions thus become the forum for the triumph of the will." Levinson evokes "political visions of a civil religious persuasion" in which "it is doubtful that logical argumentation plays a crucial role." He creates new philosophical substantiation for the Harvard School of "deconstructionism" which maintains the view of legalism as a Marxist weapon to combat "bourgeois society and its oppression of the masses." Levinson apparently believes in the nineteenth century concept of Communism as a great wind which will blow away all the outmoded trappings of the old bourgeois society, leaving in its place a community lacking in ornamentation, with clean bright buildings which have little or no furnishings, in short, a hospital room or a jail cell, as the ideal home of the future. Levinson declares that "Social life as we know it is being challenged and may even be dissolving in an ever greater Heraclitean flux." Levinson paints a scenario of the Supreme Court's participation in a "constitutional abolition of private property in the name of a proletarian dictatorship" as an imaginary development; in fact, he describes just what the Supreme Court has been doing for years, gradually expropriating the private property of the American people, and turning it over to the world corporation through our Federal Reserve System. This program can be overturned; we have the weapons; we can go into court and challenge the law merchant because we are individual creatures of God who are protected by the Constitution as our inheritance of God's law. Not only is the corporation against God, as a nonperson created to subvert God's Presence on this earth; it is also the antithesis of God's law as the national will. The corporation is international, and functions throughout the world as admiralty or maritime law. Admiralty jurisdiction extends over land and sea, beyond all national boundaries. The corporation itself is a violation of the Constitution, because each corporation in practice becomes a New State. An entity which exercises authority in more than one state, the corporation itself becomes a state. As chartered by the government, the corporation becomes an arm of the government which is not only multi-state; it is also multi-national. Thus, a New York corporation exercises authority in Virginia, or in China. It also creates money, which is a function of state sovereignty. Art. IV sec 3 of the Constitution says, "no new State shall be formed or erected within the Jurisdiction of any other State." The corporation sets up new States as "Districts" or federal operations of the admiralty courts. Thus the Federal Reserve System divides the United States into Federal Reserve

Districts; the Internal Revenue Service divides the United States into Districts; the legal system divides the United States into areas of "U.S. District Courts"; and each corporation divides the United States into its own sales districts, manufacturing districts, and districts of opportunity.

Because of the existence of the corporations, the law merchant, or marine law, is not part of the law of any particular country, but is part of the law of all nations. A bottomry bond may be issued in London, as a loan on a ship and its freight, or as a respondentia bons, a loan on pledge of the cargo. This itself is not only a security, or adhesion, contract; the loan or mortgage becomes a security in itself, or new money, which may be traded, discounted, or sold as a "security"; hence our bonds and shares sold on Wall Street. The Constitution, Art. VI, states that "the Constitution shall be the supreme law of the land," but Statute l, Sec. 9, p. 77, line 26, 1st Session of Congress Sept. 24, 1789, says,

> "And the trial of issues in fact in the district courts, in all causes except in civil causes of admiralty and maritime jurisdiction, shall be by jury."

Thus we are to have jury trial, except in admiralty cases. How does this square with the fact that we now have admiralty procedures in our courts? Quite easily. We can still have a jury, but the jury is nullified by the judge's instructions to the jury, which are straight from the law merchant. Thus the common law meets the maritime-admiralty law in our courts and is soundly defeated. Admiralty comes into the nation by the power of contract. We find that "The Admiralty court is a maritime court instituted for the purpose of the laws of the seas. There seems to be ground, therefore, for restraining jurisdiction, in some measure, within the limit of the grant of the commercial power; which would confine it, in cases of contracts, to those concerning navigation and trade of the country upon the high seas and tide-waters with foreign countries" New Jersey Steam Nav Co v. Merchants Bank, 6 How 392 (1848).

It is known that most insurance is a tontine scheme, and is therefore forbidden by law. Although insurance is basically a private enterprise rather than government, when the government became a corporation (National Recovery Act etc. in the FDR administration), the government then became involved in private and commercial enterprise. The commerce clause Art 1. sec. 8, which gives Congress the power to regulate commerce between the States, also invokes admiralty law as "the Law of Nations) on Land and Water." Yet the 1st Continental Congress itself had entered a complaint against England "which extend the powers of the Admiralty courts beyond their ancient limits." When the government embarked on its nationwide tontine scheme, the Social Security Administration and its accompanying "insurance policies," the courts of the nation were thereby converted into Admiralty courts. "A policy of insurance is a maritime contract, and therefore of admiralty jurisdiction." De Lovio v. Boit, 7 Fcd.Chs. No 3.7766 (1815).

Title 28, USC sec 1333, "Admiralty, maritime and prize cases; The district courts shall have original jurisdiction, exclusive of the courts of the United States, of: (i). Any civil case or admiralty or mmj. time jurisdiction, saving to suitors in all cases all other remedies to which they are otherwise entitled." And what are these remedies? The Fed. Statutes Anno. v 9, p. 88, says, "... saving to suitors in all cases, the right of a common law remedy, where common law is competent to give it" Home Ins Co v. North Packet Co., 3I 1a.242 (1871).

However, an American citizen's claim to common law citizenship is thought by some authorities to be compromised by Social Security (FICA) subjecting of said citizen's persona to the maritime jurisdiction of the U.S. District courts through an insurance claim: "The Court will not pass upon the constitutionality of a statute at the instance of one who has availed himself of its benefits." Gt Falls Mfg. Co v. Atty Gen. 124 U.S. 581. Thus the citizen who seeks common law remedy may be forced against his will into an equity jurisdiction through the "contract" of the Social Security Ponzi scheme, on the grounds that equity law carries out the law of contract, or the law merchant. What, then, is its effect on the rights, privileges and immunities guaranteed a citizen by the protection of the Constitution of the United States? Many persons have been stating their belief that anyone participating in this equity contract or a similar government Ponzi scheme thereby loses those rights, privileges and immunities. In so stating, they are merely echoing the claims of the equity courts themselves.

However, it is only natural to claim that your brand is right, because this is your claim to power, and your claim to your share of the market. The Federal Laws of Civil Procedure themselves are merely codes of equity.

Thus we are told that a citizen of the United States, that is to say, of a State of the United States (without getting into the present inquiry as to whether there are not actually two separate United States at this time), who handles a Federal Reserve note, or has a driver's license, or has a Social Security number, has thereby entered into an equity contract with the government, and have thereby lost the rights, privileges and immunities as a citizen of the United States. Certainly this is a most pernicious doctrine. Not only does it ignore the law of contract itself - a contract must stipulate an offering, a consideration and an acceptance of the parties, whereas those who teach this doctrine merely focus on the acceptance the acceptance of a number, or of a stipend from the insurance sham but where is the offering? Where is the consideration of the parties detailed? Such a claim could be substantiated only if the citizen has executed a form and signed it, as follows, "I, _____ born a citizen of the United States and presently enjoying the rights, privileges and immunities thereby, do, in order to obtain a Social Security number (or birth certificate, or driver's license), do knowingly and willingly renounce said rights, privileges and immunities." This is a contract. Anything less is not a contract. To claim that there are hidden codes, secret agreements and carefully disguised meanings, none of which are spelled out, in the act of obtaining a Social Security number etc. is to offend the law of contract.

As for the handling of a Federal Reserve note, a promise to pay, or promissory note against the citizens of the United States, the handling of such a note actually opens the door for the citizen to sue the Federal Reserve System for conspiracy. The Federal Reserve Act was written as a conspiracy, enacted into law as a conspiracy, and still fonctions today as a secret conspiracy whose deliberations are forbidden to the public, and to the Congress of the United States! (*Secrets of the Federal Reserve*, by Eustace Mullins).

We do not wish to gloss over the fact that thousands of American citizens are presently languishing in our government concentration camps, having been convicted of some equity violation of said alleged contracts. However, these prisoners were convicted of having challenged the totality of equity jurisdiction, which is assigned the duty of protecting every aspect of the corporation central bank's operations; these prisoners have challenged Marxism, the supreme authority of the state as commissioned by the corporation. These prisoners, as we have previously stated, were convicted on an "information" of having violated a court injonctive order as an overt act. They were convicted and sentenced in violation of the Constitution, and can be freed only by a Constitutional Revolution.

Equity law cannot challenge or supersede Constitutional law; it does bypass it, refusing to confront what began as God's law, His Covenant or contract, codified in the Bible as an Affidavit from God, that is, with the three and a half million Israelites, from Jacob only, and continued in the Twelve Tables of Roman Law. By 900 B.C., as the Canaanites, who now called themselves Phoenicians (later Venetians, which developed into the Black Nobility), a second form of law, set up by the Phoenician international traders for their own convenience and purposes, appeared on the Isle of Rhodes. This second form of law became known as the law merchant, our present law of contract. This form of law constitutes the statutory civil law of the United States. Meanwhile, God's Covenant persisted as the English common law, which Alfred the Great codified as Alfred's Dooms, in 872 A.D., the continuation of His Contract with the people of Jacob, or Israel. It was known as the common law of England, not because it was a law for the common people, but because it was common to all people, rich and poor alike.

William Avery correctly states that the first defense of an American citizen who is charged with a violation of equity law is "inability to perform." You are charged with failure to deliver when you were never informed that you should deliver. In fact, the charge is "stand and deliver," the ancient cry of the English highwayman. If a policeman tells you he is going to give you a ticket for parking in a No Parking Zone, and you reply that you didn't see the sign, he charges you anyway, because you are pleading a failure of vision. When the state charges you with failure to perform under equity law, such as failure to pay a "tax," your response is that you are unable to perform because you were not informed of the obligation. Some citizens have been requesting that the IRS send them "a letter of delegation of authority," that is, a letter from their superior delegating to them the authority to conduct an audit or to investigate you. Usually, the agents either refuse to produce such a letter or are unable to obtain one from their superior. Should they actually produce such a letter, the next step would be to demand a copy of the contract under whose provisions you are being charged with failure to perform, with itemized claims of whatever you have failed to deliver. The conventional response of the IRS agent has been to cite some provision of the IRS code. However, this does not itemize what you have failed to deliver, nor does your 1040 form, if you have filed one, itemize such information, since it contains what you have declared, not what they claim you didn't declare. The 1040 form itself is really an estimate; in equity, it is difficult to hold anyone to the amounts of an estimate, and under Constitutional Law, it is absolutely inadequate.

The 1040 form itself is a listing of promissory notes, that is, of promises to pay, the Federal Reserve notes. This is interest-bearing currency which is only paper, and which is backed only by paper bonds, even though it claims to be backed by the faith and credit of the Government of the United States, or the people of the United States. This is paper issued against interest bearing "government" bonds held by the privately owned Federal Reserve System. This System, like many other economic entities which have been created under express authority of equity jurisdiction rather than under Constitutional Law, is actually a criminal syndicalist operation. As such, it works closely with other criminal syndicalist operations in the United States, such as the Rockefeller Foundation and the other major tax-exempt foundations, and other monetary schemes chartered under equity law.

American citizens who are charged with "violations" in our equity courts are usually faced with the uphill task of defending themselves against vague claims that they have "failed" to cooperate in one or more of these criminal syndicalist operations. Because the IRS is merely a collection agency for the Federal Reserve System, an IRS charge is based on your "inability to perform" some task allotted to you by the Federal Reserve System. The proper defense here is that no American citizen who is a law abiding person can fulfill any performance demanded by a criminal syndicalist operation without becoming a criminal himself. Thus, tax analysts have stated for years that no American can file a 1040 form without committing a criminal act. Also, our citizens are often charged, under equity, with "willful failure" to become a criminal. A criminal syndicalist operation is always disturbed by any person existing within its sphere of operations who has not yet become a criminal himself. The goal of any criminal system is that everyone must become a criminal. The very nature of "majority rule" demands that a small minority of non-criminals residing within an area which has a large, active majority of criminals is willfully failing to conform, and that they must give in to the majority and join in the criminal operations. However, the principle of majority rule applies only to a lawful government, not to a criminal one. If the citizens residing within a criminal sphere of influence refuse to collaborate with "the system," they must rely upon common law principles to protect them from the exigencies of equity law.

The real purpose of equity law is to convert equities or financial assets into debt, and to deprive holders of real property of their lawful possessions through the principle of legal plunder, by forcing them to accept a less valuable or worthless substitute in exchange for their real property. At its inception, the law of contract was developed to protect the interests of parties engaged in trading endeavours, so as to make certain that they would receive proper payment. Each party was informed of the offering and the consideration, and accepted the requirements. Because of the international nature of trade, the traders often verged upon piracy, or upon some form of government "cooperation" to carry on their trading activities. This might be as temporary as the bribery of officials, or it might engage other government powers, such as the deployment of armies or navies, and most particularly, the use of the courts to implement their programs. Thus equity became synonymous, early on, with crime, particularly as it applied to international operations.

This seems antithetical, because the original meaning of "equity" was fairness. An equitable contract was one which was equally fair to both parties. Equity in law was intended to mean absolute equality under the law. In practice, equity, as the outgrowth of chancery, or the emperor's chancellors, became the vehicle for the wielding of influence and power, as well as legalized theft. The worldwide tendency towards socialism would not have been possible without the illegal profits conferred by equity decisions. The criminal syndicalism of such operations as the Federal Reserve System and the Rockefeller Foundation has always demanded more and more government controls, and a corresponding decrease in individual liberties.

Thus we find that criminal syndicalism never considers itself safe until it has converted the government into the vehicle for its criminal syndicalist operations; that is, the government becomes the Great Satan, the focus and the center of criminal operations. How does this work in actual practice? You may have a small business which you wish to expand. You advertise for workers, and you hire the most likely applicant. However, the government notifies you that its regulations require that you hire a handicapped lesbian mulatto whose origins should be defined as being one-third black, one-third Hispanic, and one-third Jewish. The government then notifies you that you have failed to fulfill this requirement, which means that you must now undergo a lengthy prosecution, you must hire a person fulfilling the requirements of the government regulation, and you must also pay her a penalty of $200,000, plus fines and other penalties. You are now bankrupt, and your business is closed. Such travesties are inevitable because the government has set up conditions which no one can meet and still stay in business. Second, your bankruptcy means that your business has been stolen from you by anyone with funds, a bank or a broker. Third, the government ensures that no individual will be able to open and operate an independent business under the conditions which have been set up.

These conditions originated because of Congressional concerns for "compassion" and "caring," showing a commendable dedication to the handicapped, the minorities and the deprived. In effect, government socialism as dictated by government social activists now lays down the conditions, and the only conditions, under which an American business can operate. Then we hear recriminations because we can no longer compete in the world economy with nations such as Japan, and Korea, which do not have such restrictions on their business operations. A welcome development for the international bankers was that the United States, because it could not compete, began to accrue an enormous deficit and an unpayable debt, on which it now pays huge interest. Japan now owns one-third of our national debt, and is collecting the interest. Does anyone believe it is accidental that our economy has been destroyed, and that we are now at the mercy of Japan, a nation which we defeated in World War II, and which may now be exacting its revenge? Whether Japan has devised this program or not, the fact is that it could not have taken place without the dictates of equity law. As James J. Kilpatrick wrote in the *Washington Post*, Jan. 14, 1989, commenting on "the right to vote freely for legislators,"

> "Over the past thirty or forty years both Congress and the federal courts hundreds of times have ordered legislators to vote in particular ways or suffer the consequences. Congress has conditioned the grant of federal funds upon the enactment of specific state or local legislation. These conditions center on coercion to pass bills concerning speed limits, rights of homosexuals, AIDS patients, minority rights etc."

Under the color of "a law," that is, the legal enforcement of equity contracts in favor of minorities or other special interest groups who are pawns in the drive for world socialist power, equity, originally the fairness doctrine, has been converted into an instrument of debt creation, legalized monopoly, financial theft, and the imposition of tyrannical strictures upon all citizens of the United States.

Consider the claims that are now made by equity law; that a check is a maritime contract, and that its use either as a writer or recipient places you under the jurisdiction of admiralty law; that a marriage license or a birth certificate gives title of your life to the state; that the Social Security number establishes an irrevocable contract with the state to pay income tax; that a debt can be paid, but not discharged, under equity law. Who is secretly responsible for the fastening of such dictatorial manifestoes upon the people of the United States? We have already mentioned the crucial dates, 1688, 1694, and 1714. When King George III, spurred on by the demands of the stockholders of the Bank of England, began to lay unconscionable additional taxes upon the American colonists, they responded with the Declaration of the First Continental Congress, May 14, 1774,

> "the British Parliament, claiming a power of right to bind the American people by statute in all cases whatsoever, bath, in some acts expressly imposed taxes upon them, and in others, under various pretexts but in fact for the purpose of raising revenue, bath imposed rates and duties payable in these colonies which extend the powers of the Admiralty courts beyond their ancient limits, deprive the American subjects of trial by jury and are subversive of American rights."

Note that the Continental Congress still referred to the colonists as "subjects," and, in a sentiment common to most Americans of that time, maintained that they were still loyal subjects of the Crown, who were finding it difficult to exist under the stringent conditions being imposed by the King. It is important to remember that the British people, despite the great profits which were being raked in by the stockholders of the Bank of England, did not themselves benefit from these profits. The lot of the average Briton, prior to the Revolutionary War, was much worse than that of the average colonist. Nor were the Britons greatly disposed to fight the Americans; King George III had to make a deal with a German prince, the Elector of Hesse, to obtain mercenary soldiers who would fight the colonists, a contract which became the basis of the Rothschild fortune.

Much of the world's commerce has been conducted on the principle of a fair trade, that is, the exchange of a substance for a substance. If the party had no substance to trade, then be had to make payment in coin. The sale itself is commerce, which is public business in motion through negotiable instruments of exchange, rather than a common law transaction. It was this existence of trade itself as an entity which was not covered by the common law, which gave rise to the body of the law merchant, as an instrument for governing trade. Those engaged in trade found that debts were extinguished by the delivery of goods and services, or by paper representing such goods and services. It was found that extinguishing debt deprived the debt holder of the power and a pertinent influence which accompanied the continued holding of the debt. Consequently, for centuries the law merchant has moved continuously towards the creation of inextinguishable debt, which, in tum, confers inextinguishable power, a goal of the Canaanites or Black Nobility. Thus the Federal Reserve System issues a currency which is based upon government bonds, using the money and credit of the people of the United States, and creating debt or monetizing debt as a private corporation. As the owner of the negotiable instrument of exchange, the Federal Reserve becomes the "owner" of all property in any transactions in which negotiable instruments of exchange are used. However, the Federal Reserve wisely does not take actual possession, allowing the purchaser to use the property, in the mistaken belief that he is now the actual owner. The Federal Reserve reserves the power to call in its property whenever it wishes to do so, as a final measure of control, or as a step in the carrying out of other programs.

The equity courts fonction to administer "a law" as instrumentalities of the criminal syndicates which operate under their jurisdiction within the United States. This is defined in sec. 9. "The district courts (federal courts) as courts of admiralty and as courts of equity, shall be deemed always open for the purpose of filing and any pleading, of issuing and returning mesne and final process, and of making and directing all interlocutory motions, orders, rules and other proceedings preparatory to the hearing, upon their merits, of all cases pending therein." 36 Stat. 1088 (1911).

Under the equity, or admiralty law, a citizen of the United States who has received any "benefit" from a government program thereby is said to "lose" his constitutional rights! Legal precedent for this equity ruling is found in the decision of Great Falls Mfg. Co. v. Atty Gen. 124 U.S. 581, "The Court will not pass upon the constitutionality of a statute at the instance of one who has availed himself of its benefits." Also cited by Wall v. Parrot Silver & Copper Co. 244 U.S. 407, 411-12; St. Louis Malleable Casting Co. v. Prendergast Constr. Co. 260 U.S. 469; Alexander v. TVA, 297 U.S. 288,346 (1935).

Thus, anyone who has "benefitted from such government program" not only is denied the right to challenge it in court, but also loses his Constitutional right to defend himself from further government action. This is the basis for imprisoning numerous American citizens who have "failed" to handle the Federal Reserve scrip as prescribed by equity law.

The ratification of the Constitution of the United States meant that the people chose this instrument to defend their rights. Admiralty law, like the King's writ, ended at the saltwater mark; the land was under the jurisdiction of Constitutional principles. However, this principle was overthrown in 1838. "When the doctrine was held that the admiralty jurisdiction in cases purely dependent upon the locality of the act done was limited to the sea and to tide waters as far as the tide flows, and that it did not reach beyond the high water mark, it was said that mixed cases do arise, and indeed do often arise, where the acts and services are of a mixed nature, as where salvage services are performed partly on tide waters, and partly on the shore, for the preservation of the property saved, in which the admiralty jurisdiction has been constantly exercised to the extent of decreeing salvage." U.S. v. Combs, 12 Pet 75 (1838). The performance of mixed services was eventually interpreted in equity that the Federal Reserve System could "salvage" its flood of paper money, backed by nothing more than paper bonds, with which it had inundated the United States! This salvage operation had to be continuous, as the flood of "new" money was continuous, in order for the System to maintain its profits and its influence over the economy. Consequently, when the Federal Reserve Act was enacted into law by Congress in 1913, during that same year, the 16th Amendment to the Constitution was enacted to legally authorize the Federal Reserve's salvage operation, in which a new unit of the criminal syndicate, the Internal Revenue Service, was created as an essential salvage service to enforce the admiralty principles of salvage upon all the people of the United States.

The equity court remains the linchpin of the criminal syndicalist movement throughout the United States, because the equity court is the court of conspiracy; it is the court of legalized theft and plunder; and it is the court of monopoly. In 1890, the monopolists enacted the Sherman Anti-Trust Act to protect their monopolies by establishing conditions which made it illegal for anyone to set up a competing business. The Act states that "Every contract, combination, in the form of trust or otherwise, or conspiracy, in restraint of trade or commerce among the several States, or with foreign nations, is hereby declared to be illegal." Henceforth, anyone whose business operations presented a threat to the monopolists could be convicted of "illegal restraint of trade." The monopolists had now enshrined their monopolies as creatures of the state, or state trusts, as in their later creation, Soviet Russia. The created corporations had now taken over their creator, the State. The Sherman Act also extended greater controls over every citizen, by making every citizen a merchant, because it established controls making citizens liable for illegal restraint of trade for engaging in any transaction which was not controlled by the manufacturing monopolies. Citizens are also considered merchants under the commerce clause of the Constitution. The 1842 decision in Swift v. Tyson declared that mercantile law is now the common law of the United States. The Interstate Commerce Act of 1887 extended the power of the monopolies to pervert the processes of government to their private purposes, as was later finalized in the Sherman Act. Justice Story declared in Swift v. Tyson, 16 Peters 19, "The law respecting negotiable instruments may be truly declared in the language of Cicero, adopted by Lord Mansfield in Luke v. Lyde, (2 Burr R.883-887) to be in great measure not the law of a single country only, but of the commercial world. It is observable that the law merchant and the maritime law are not generally distinguished from each other, but are frequently used indiscriminately. The only real difference is in the sanction. When viewed as a part of the municipal law the rules are called the law merchant; when regarded from the standpoint of international law, the same rules are the law maritime." It was necessary to impose the admiralty law on the citizens of the United States, because the income tax cannot exist under common law; income tax assessments and judgments are enforced upon statutes in equity by summary judgments of the executive, or writs of assistance. The income tax is enforced as a tax on a franchise for doing business under the law merchant. A general income tax would be a direct tax on property. The 16th Amendment establishes a tax on a franchise, the privilege of doing business in a corporate capacity, as well as the privilege of perpetual existence, perpetual succession, and limited liability for debts under the law; that is, the 16th Amendment converts private citizens of the United States into corporations. A natural person, who is not a corporation, cannot be subjected to the regulations of the Internal Revenue Service, nor can they be made to inform upon themselves by the IRS.

In Wheaton v. Peters, 8 Peters 659, we find that,

> "It is clear there can be no common law of the United States The judicial decisions, the usages and customs of the respective states, must determine how far the common law has been adopted and sanctioned in each."

The FRS and IRS tax scheme was grounded in the commerce clause, Art. 1, Sec 1.C13, which allows Congress to "regulate commerce with foreign nations, and among the several states, and with the Indian tribes." The Supreme Court then held, in Gibbons v. Ogden, 1824, that commerce "comprehends traffic, trade, navigation, communications, the transit of persons, and the transmission of messages by telegraph-indeed, every species of commercial intercourse."

This was later expanded by the United Nations Treaty of 1945, under which every human on earth has become a "merchant" by partaking in any commercial transaction under the law merchant, a strictly voluntary law and unwritten, as well as the law of negotiable instruments, insurance, sales, etc. The person becomes a "merchant" by accepting bills of exchange as "money." The Federal Reserve notes issues of 1963, and 1969, were then legalized as "lawful tender" on March 18, 1968, as well as promissory notes or irredeemable perpetual annuity bonds for government securities, and for checks.

Sir Edward Coke stated that "A corporation is a body politic established by prescription, by letter of patent, or by Act of Parliament:" In the U.S., this became "by Act of Congress in the United States, such as the establishment of the Federal Reserve System in 1913. However, such corporations were created in violation of the Supreme Court precedents, such as Osborn v. the U.S. Bank, 9 Wheaton, 859, 860, in which the Supreme Court admitted that Congress could not create a corporation for its own sake, "or for private purposes." The Federal Reserve System was created for private stockholders, but was disguised by a "quasi-public" intent. Its "profits" were to be paid to the U.S. Treasury. In fact, the owners of Federal Reserve bank stock were less interested in the sums earned by the System than in the control which the Act conferred upon those stockholders, the control of the money and credit of the American people. They now exercise control of the daily quantity of money and the price of money throughout the United States. This power gives them the opportunity to make enormous profits in stock issues, market operations, and other monetary operations.

Thomas Jefferson foresaw these abuses in his powerful argument raised against the first Bank of the United States. As a sleeper agent of the Bank of England and the Rothschild interests, Alexander Hamilton had delivered an extensive argument on Feb. 23, 1791, declaring that "the right of erecting corporations is one inherent in, and inseparable from, the idea of sovereign power that the power to erect corporations is not to be considered an independent or substantive power, but as an incidental and auxiliary one, and was therefore more properly left to implication than expressly granted that the incorporation of a bank is a constitutional measure." However, Jefferson had delivered a more detailed argument on Feb. 16, 1791: "The bill for establishing a national bank in 1791, undertakes, among other things - 1. To form the subscribers into a corporation. 2. To enable them, in their corporate capacities, to receive grants of land; and so far, is against the laws of mortmain. 3. To make alien subscribers capable of holding lands; and so far is against the laws of alienage. 4. To transmit these lands, on the death of a proprietor, to a certain line of successors; and, so far, changes the course of descents. 5. To put the lands out of the reach of forfeiture, or escheat; and so far, is against the laws of forfeiture and escheat. 6. To transmit personal chattels to successors in a certain line; and so far, is against the laws of distribution. 7. To give them the sole and exclusive right of banking, under the national authority; and, so far, is against the laws of monopoly. 8. To communicate to them a power to make laws paramount to the laws of the states; for so they must be construed, to protect the institution from the control of the state legislatures; and so probably they will be construed.

... The incorporation of a bank, and the powers assumed by this bill, have not, in my opinion, been delegated to the United States by the Constitution."

The struggle to foist upon the people of the United States a national, or central, bank, to be operated for the benefit of alien interests, is the untold story of the 19th century. In 1913, the financiers finally achieved their goal by the enactment of the Federal Reserve Act. The central bank, a machine to create perpetual and inextinguishable debt, was now in place. Today, 12 U.S. Code 412 allows currency to come into circulation on the basis of U.S. debt obligations, that is, government bonds which have been issued by the private stockholders of the Federal Reserve System. This law was scheduled to sunset on July 30, 1945, during World War II at the close of the business day. Just before that hour, a measure was passed to allow the United States to assume U.S. debt obligations in perpetuity. However, in their haste, the manipulators overlooked the loophole which allows alternative means of issuing currency, including 12 USC 347c. This establishes the legal basis for issuing credit cards, for redeemable coupons, food stamps, and such currency as the American Express Co. notes, and other company notes. Under the Federal Reserve monopoly, fractional pieces of credit are turned into circulating media.

Since 1913, the Federal Reserve System and the IRS have formed a universal debt-credit franchise, in which private individuals are compelled to inform upon themselves as "merchants." Forced withholding from wages began on July 1, 1943. In 1945, the United Nations Treaty turned all U.S. courts into trading pits, and courts of the staple, because of the merchant practice. Under the courts of the staple, merchants had met under the protection of the crown to implement their own law among their own members. The Magna Carta had given merchants, in Article 48, the right "to buy and sell, according to their ancient customs, among themselves." Every private individual has the right to contract upon his services, talents, labor and endeavours, and to profit therefrom; he can then be assessed a direct truce, but he cannot be compelled to inform on himself, under the protection of the 4th and 5th Amendments to the Constitution. The courts of the staple, as the District of Columbia equity courts are now known and positioned throughout the United States, enforce the merchants' law on all private citizens. The conspirators then enacted the 25th Amendment to the Constitution in order to set up the presidency of the United States as a chancellorship in executive equity, controlled by the corporation America, and its directors.

HJR 192 further legitimized the Federal Reserve monopoly by making Federal Reserve bank credit legal tender. A Treasury note of 1890, before the enactment of the Federal Reserve Act, read "This note is legal tender at its face value in payment of debts public and private except when otherwise stipulated in the contract." This was phrased to include the possibility that the contract might stipulate payment in gold, silver, or other payment. The Federal Reserve note now reads, "This note is legal tender for all debts public and private." This establishes its function to pay the United States debt owed to the bankers, which makes all such notes promissory notes intended to continue payments on the bank-created and inextinguishable debt. However, it is made clear that the Federal Reserve notes are only for the payment of debt, and thus can be superseded by money intended for any other purpose. Harvard professor Barry Fell wrote a book, "America B.C." which contains a picture of the Bourne Stone, found in Massachusetts, which in effect annexes the land to Hanno, a Suffete of Carthage. A similar stone was found in South America. As was pointed out in *The Curse of Canaan* [8], by Eustace Mullins, the Carthaginians were the Phoenicians, who had changed their name from Canaanites, and who became the Black Nobility which has foisted their monetary schemes upon the world. Thus the Bourne Stone may be the secret deed by which the Canaanites have laid claim to the title of all property in the Americas, and which the equity courts are now acting to uphold. Law is grounded in or derived from guaranteed allodial land titles. Equity is the enforcement of "natural rights" not necessarily found in common law. Law deals in substance; equity deals in the potentiality of the substance. If an existing title is the basis for the present practice of equity law, then the person not informed of such allodial title cannot obtain a fair and impartial hearing.

Until 1913, "lawful money" was based on whatever comprised the reserves of a National Bank, gold, silver, gold or silver certificates, Treasury Notes, and U.S. Notes. The Federal Reserve Act allowed banks to count commercial paper as bank reserves, and thereby changed the basis of our monetary system. HJR 192 legitimized the process by making Federal Reserve bank credit legal tender, and by substituting the language governing payment of debt. "Payment of debt" was altered into a new phrase, "discharge of obligation." Henceforth, debts could be paid, but they could not be discharged. They could not be legally held to be paid, because they had not; they were merely exchanged for other forms of debt. One banker exposed the scheme by stating, "If one bill of exchange goes through and in fact is paid with a cashier's check, the ball game is over for Federal-type banking." Such a payment would put the lenders of credit out of business. A specter is indeed haunting American business, but it is not the famed specter of Communism; it is the specter that someone may someday pay a debt.

---

[8] *The Curse of Canaan, a demonology of history,* Omnia Veritas Ltd, www.omnia-veritas.com.

American citizens remain uninformed of the difference between the payment at law, and discharge at Equity, and, even more important, the difference between voluntary payment at Law, and compelled performance in Equity. Payment at Law means meeting the requirements of the rights, privileges and immunities accruing to a citizen of the United States as guaranteed by the Constitution. Discharge at Equity, or compelled performance in Equity means that court orders are issued for compelled performance in equity against citizens of the United States by judges and lawyers, who maintain an active alliance with the limited liability corporations through the American Bar Association. The fractional reserve banking corporations thus grant Titles of Nobility, in violation of the Constitution, by ordering Bills of Attainders against U.S. citizens, which is also forbidden by the Constitution. This unholy alliance has resulted in the looting of the American people by international interests, through mergers, acquisitions, leveraged buyouts, and management buyouts. This process was made possible by the ascension of Lord Mansfield as Chief Justice of the Kings Bench in 1756. Lord Mansfield transformed the Civil Law by allowing it to supersede the common law. Actions of assumpsit for debt now became equitable action. Lord Mansfield began denying trial by jury on writs of assistance, a procedure which forced the colonists into open rebellion.

The investment banking bouse which launched the present tidal wave of buyouts is Drexel, Bumham Lambert of New York. This firm, now known as the king of junk bonds, is the New York representative of the Rothschild Bank, Banque Bruxelles Lambert of Brussels. The Lambert of this firm, Baron Lambert, is the Belgian branch of the Rothschild family. Because of this firm's influence, Brussels is now the capital of the world. NATO is headquartered there, as is the World Computer Network, another Rothschild enterprise. Lord Carrington, the head of NATO, is also a member of the Rothschild family. The first Lord Carrington was Archibald Primrose; his son, Viscount Rosebery, married Hannah Rothschild, daughter of Mayer Rothschild. The present Lord Carrington is not only director of Rio Tinto Zinc, one of the three firms which comprise the base of the Rothschild fortune; he is also a director of Hambros Bank. During World

War II, Sir Charles Hambro was the director of Britain's Secret Intelligence Service; in that capacity, he supervised the organization of its American branch, the OSS, which is now known as the CIA. In 1982, Lord Carrington merged his business interests with those of Henry Kissinger, in Kissinger Associates. Lord Carrington's cousin, David Colville, became the first partner of N. M. Rothschilds Sons, London, who was not an immediate member of the Rothschild family. Kissinger Associates furnished the backbone of the Reagan and Bush cabinets. President Bush has named It. Gen. Brent Scowcroft, of Kissinger Associates, to the critical National Security Council, and Lawrence Eagleburger, president of Kissinger Associates, to the post of Deputy Secretary of Defense.

Because of Bush's close ties with the Bank of England through his family banking bouse, Brown Bros. Harriman, Bush was named head of the CIA. The recent imbroglio over the appointment of Sen. John Tower as Secretary of Defense, for which he was defeated, hinged upon the fear that Kissinger Associates might not be able to control Tower. They envisioned a scenario in which Tower would spend his time in night clubs, living up to Dryden's dictum that "None but the brave deserve the fair," but at the last minute changed their minds in favor of a more malleable choice.

Drexel Burnham Lambert waged a three year battle to take over the major American corporations for the Rothschild interests from 1985 to 1988, when a $650 million fine was levied against the firm for illegal activities in stock trading. During this period, some $300 billion in stock was retired through mergers. During the same period, corporate debt in the United States increased by $360 billion, meaning that these firms must be paying some $36 billion a year to the creators of inextinguishable debt in interest payments, which effectively removes them from the burden of paying taxes on their corporate income. Such Rothschild operations have produced huge government deficits, reduced the status of the United States to that of a Balkan republic, and ranked the nation as a Third World Banana Republic in the international order. Now the United States faces a bleak future as a bankrupt nation, whose people are being informed they must "make sacrifices," while they face increased taxation, inflation, and food and fuel crises. These pressures will result in (and are probably intended to) force a rebellion, with military dictatorship and civil war in the United States before the criminal syndicalists are finally brought to justice.

These developments are inherent in the nature of the problems which we face. The Erie Railroad decision of 1938 took the law merchant out of the common law (nullifying the 7th Amendment) and put it into Equity to be "judicially noticed" in any jurisdiction. The Law Merchant is Summary Judgment, whereas the Law of Nature is, in the final analysis, the law of tooth and claw. "Law" means the Law of the State; the Rules of Equity are the Law Merchant. The Federal Reserve notes are intended to, and are so doing, confiscate in equity, through summary judgment, all private landed property by the agents of the international commercial interests. Although no federal law can outlaw the cash basis of the law imposed on the States by Art. I, sec. 10, and the federal government cannot touch allodial land titles in the states, this is being circumvented by the inherent profit in the Federal Reserve notes; they discriminate against real property, because real property is not personality -(chose-in-action). They discriminate against holders of allodial land titles in favor of the merchants and merchant bankers because of the ten to one, to sixteen to one, return on bank deposits. Thus equitable paper is worth from ten to sixteen times as much as real property or substance, and in time will swallow up, or "buy" all allodial land. Thus our law, which is grounded in or derived from allodial land titles, is thereby subverted by the financiers and their international conspiracy, as executed through equity courts, the courts of conspiracy.

American citizens are brought before these courts of conspiracy, their rights, privileges and immunities guaranteed them by the Constitution are duly denied, and they are tried and sentenced as Artificial Persons, or corporations. When they claim to be real, when they claim to exist, they affront the equity court, and face further imprisonment for their "contempt". Although the court sentences the Artificial Person, it is the real American citizen who is subsequently carted off to prison.

Because equity law has as its goal the creation of inextinguishable debt, and the subsequent transferring of all real property from its legal allodial possessors to Artificial Entities, which have been created by the state, who are primarily banking corporations, debt has assumed a major role in equity law. Thus we find in the 14th Amendment not merely the enshrinement of public debt, as an entity whose very existence cannot be questioned, but also the defining of "unacceptable debt," that is, debt incurred by any entity which has not been chartered by the state, or which is seen as inimical to the state. The 14th Amendment states, in that capacity,

> "The validity of the public debt of the United States, authorized by law, including debts incurred for payment of pensions and bounties for services in suppressing insurrection or rebellion, shall not be questioned. But neither the United States nor any state shall assume or pay any debt obligation incurred in aid of insurrection or rebellion against the United States, or any claim for loss or emancipation of any slave; but all such debts, obligations and claims shall be held illegal and void."

Thus the public debt of the United States is placed on a pedestal, beyond attack, but the obligations of the southern states, incurred as the result of the states battling for their rights against the international power of the criminal syndicalists, "shall be held illegal and void."

The public debt today consists of bookkeeping entries in the ledgers of the Federal Reserve System; those who purchase Treasury bills do not receive so much as a flimsy piece of paper; instead, the purchase exists only as a blip on a computer screen. The 14th Amendment thus requires that the blip on the computer screen shall not be questioned, nor the right of the Federal Reserve System to issue government bonds as Lord Rothschild's magical money-making machine. Because the 14th Amendment was enacted under martial law, it has had no validity since 187, when martial law was ended in the southern states, and Federal troops were withdrawn. Martial law is supreme, and overrides all state and local governments, but only during the period of military occupation. The 14th Amendment was ratified in 1868, ten years before martial law was ended in the southern states. The 14th Amendment can only be valid if it is maintained that the entire United States is still under martial law. This is not legal pettifogging; it is a serious legal question, which must be resolved in the courts. The federal, or equity, district courts might have little difficulty with this problem; they could simply declare that the states are only legal fictions, which exist at the pleasure of the federal entity, just as the citizens of the several states, through Social Security law and income tax regulations, have been transformed into Artificial Persons.

The scrip issued by the privately owned Federal Reserve Banks, functioning as colonial banks under the aegis of the Bank of England, has been variously described as "Communist slave scrip," "beggar's alms," or as stock certificates in a joint stock company. It may be all three. "Scrip," in Old French dialect, meant the bag for alms which was publicly carried by pilgrims or beggars. Scrip, in its general derivations, is usually a derogatory term, carrying a connotation of scoffing or jeering. In 1676, C. Hatton wrote, in Hatton's Chronicles, "I punish myself yet I may revenge myself upon you for your little scrips of paper." By 1820, scrip had become a term for a stock certificate, when G. Carey wrote in his "Guide to Public Funds," "When the loan is in progress the separate parts are called Scrip." In its 1828 edition, Webster's Dictionary defines scrip as "A certificate of stock subscribed to buy a bank or other company or of a share of other joint property, is called in America a scrip." The Federal Reserve notes issued by the private stockholders of the twelve Federal Reserve Banks were used to finance the Bolshevik Revolution in Russia in 1917, and were further used to maintain the Soviet Government since that time. In 1918, at a time when the Bolshevik government was already bankrupt, three directors of the Federal Reserve Bank of New York came to their rescue; George Poster Peabody, William Boyce Thompson, and William Laurence Sanders. Sanders was also the chairman of the business equipment firm, Ingersoll Rand.

Thompson had also pledged one million dollars of his personal funds to spread Bolshevik propaganda in the United States. Because Federal Reserve notes have served as the mainstay of the Soviet Government since 1918, it is proper to term them "Communist slave scrip"; it is also issued to the slaves in the United States.

Walt Mann has written of the 14th Amendment that it is the legal basis of the injunctive power which the government has used against our citizens since 1868. It lays down an injunction against questioning the validity of the public debt. Our citizens are then sentenced for violating injunctive orders which stern from this as a basic injunction. This sentencing power also stems from the admiralty court procedure. Because the 14th Amendment stems from martial law, and admiralty procedures also are based upon martial law, the power of the captain to command a military ship of the line while it is at sea, the judge of the equity court fonctions as a military commander, exercising the power of martial law over citizens of the United States.

It is this power which brings into question the claim that participating in a contract volunteers oneself into admiralty jurisdiction. However, this jurisdiction violates the right, privileges and immunities which are guaranteed us by the Constitution. Martial law may be the pretext by which these guarantees have been suspended. We find the Admiralty Court defined as follows:

> The Admiralty Court is a maritime court instituted for the purpose of administering the law of the seas. There seems to be grounds, therefore, for restraining jurisdiction, in some measure, within the limit of the grant of the commercial power, which would confine it, in cases of contracts, to those concerning trade and navigation of the country upon the high seas and tide-waters with foreign countries. N.J. Steam Nav Cov. Mchts Bank, 6 How 392 (1848).

The fixing of Admiralty jurisdiction in the United States is said to lie in the commerce clause, Art. I, sec. 8, "The Congress shall have Power To regulate commerce with foreign Nations, and among the several States, and with the Indian tribes." In effect, this separates Admiralty jurisdiction from Internal jurisdiction. The federal courts overcame that distinction by becoming courts of equity. The problem with the Social Security system is that it poses as an insurance policy, but collects its premiums through the compulsory taxing process. The forced payment of said insurance premium violates the following precept:

> "The individual, unlike the corporation, cannot be taxed for the mere privilege of existing. The corporation is an artificial entity which owes its existence and charter powers to the state, but the individual's right to live and own property are *natural rights* for the enjoyment of which an Excise cannot be imposed." Redfield v. Fisher, 292 P 813, p. 819 (1930).

Construction of the term "natural right" as opposed to the employment of the Law Merchant against citizens of the United States may be clarified by the following excerpt from Colin Blackbum's "Contract of Sale," published by T & W Johnson, Phil. 1847:

There is no part of the history or English law more obscure than that connected with the common maxim that the Law Merchant is part of the law of the land.

In the earlier times it was not a part of the common law as it is now, but administered in its own courts in the staple, or else in the Star Chamber. The Chancellor, in the 13 Edw. 4, 9, declares his view of the law thus: "This suit is brought by an alien merchant who is come by safe conduct here, and he is not bound to sue by the law of the land, to abide the trial of twelve men, and other forms of the law of the land; but he ought to sue here (in the Star Chamber) and it shall be determined by the law of nature in Chancery, and he may sue from hour to hour for the dispatch of merchants; and he said further that a merchant is not bound by statutes, where the statutes are *introductiva novae legis;* but if they are *declarativa antiqui juris* (that is to say of nature &c). And since they have come into the kingdom, the king has jurisdiction over them to administer justice, but that shall be *secundum legem naturae,* which is called by some the Law Merchant, which is the law universal of the world." And the justices being called on, certified that the goods of this plaintiff were not forfeited to the crown as a waif (though those of a subject would have been) because he was an alien merchant. It is obvious that at that time the law merchant was a thing distinct from the common law. This accounts for the very remarkable fact that there is no mention whatever of bills of exchange, or other mercantile customs in our early books; not that they did not exist, but that they were tried in the staple, and therefore were not mentioned in the books of the common law; just as the matters over which the Courts of Admiralty, or Ecclesiastical Courts, have exclusive jurisdiction, are at this day never treated as part of the common law. But as the courts of the staple decayed away, and the foreign merchants ceased to live subject to a peculiar law, those parts of the law merchant which differed from the common law either fell into disuse, or were adopted into the common law as the custom of merchants, and after a time began to appear in the books of common law. How this great change was brought about does not appear; but though bills of exchange were in common use among merchants in the 13th century; the first mention of one in an English report is in Cro. Jac., in. the beginning of the 17th century; and though the right of *rei vindicatio* must have prevailed in the continent from the time of the revival of the Civil Law, the first mention of it in our books is as late as 1690. It seems quite impossible that such matters should not have been the subject of litigation in some shape or other in England for centuries before those times.

Blackstone, whom internationalists prefer to quote over Lord Coke, classified the Law Merchant as one of the "customs" of England, and so a part of the common law; but it is not properly a custom, as it is not restricted to a single community, and is not the municipal law of a single country, but regulated commercial contracts in all civilized countries. The body of mercantile usages which compose this branch of law, having no dependence upon locality, does not need to be established by witnesses, but judges are bound to take official notice of it. The principal branches of the law merchant are the law of shipping, the law of marine insurance, the law of sales, and the law of bills and notes. The feudal law, which grew up in a time when property consisted chiefly of land upon whose alienation great restraints were laid, was found inadequate for the needs of the mercantile classes who were coming into prominence. The courts, when commercial contracts were brought before them, adopted from merchants the rules which regulated their business dealings and made them rules of law. Many of these rules were in direct contradiction to the common law. Magna Charta contained a special provision guaranteeing to merchants, among other things, the right "to buy and sell according to their ancient customs," and many later statutes were enacted for their special protection. As the custom of merchants began to encroach upon the common law, there was a determined effort on the part of lawyers to resist it. It was attempted to make the custom of merchants a particular custom, peculiar to a single community, and not a part of the law of the land. It was finally decided in the reign of James I (1603-1625) to be a part of the law of the realm. An attempt was then made to restrict the application of the law merchant to persons who were actually merchants, but the courts, after considerable variance, held that it applied to the same contracts between parties and merchants.

We quote further from The American Universal Cyclopaedia, on Mercantile Law, v. IX NY 1884, S. W. Green's Son:

> Mercantile law is the only branch of municipal law which, from the necessity of the case, is similar, and in many respects identical, in all the civilized and trading countries of the world. In determining the relations of the family, the church, and the state, each nation is guided by its own peculiarities of race, of historical tradition, of climate, and numberless other circumstances which are almost wholly unaffected by the conditions of society in the neighboring states. But when the arrangements for buying, selling, and transmitting commodities from state to state alone are in question, all men are very much in the same position. The single object of all is that the transaction may be effected in such a manner as to avoid what in every case must be sources of Joss to somebody, and by which no one is ultimately a gainer-viz., *disputes and delay.* At a very early period in the trading history of modern Europe, it was found that the only method by which these objects could be attained as by establishing a common understanding on all the leading points of mercantile, and more particularly of maritime law. This was effected by the establishment of those maritime codes, of which the most famous, though not the earliest, was the *Consolato del Mare.* It is sometimes spoken of as a collection of maritime laws of Barcelona, but it would seem rather to

have been a compilation of the laws and trading customs of various Italian cities-Venice, Pisa, Genoa, and Amalfi, together with those of the cities with which they chiefly traded-Barcelona, Marseilles, and the like. That it was published at Barcelona towards the end of the 13th century, or the beginning of the 14th, in the Catalonian dialect, is no proof that it originated in Spain, and the probability is that it is of Italian origin. As commerce extended itself to the northwestern coasts of Europe, similar codes appeared. There was the *Guidon de la Mer,* the *Roles d'Oleron,* the *Usages de Damme,* and most important of all the ordinances of the great Hanseatic League (Deutsche Hansabund). As the central people of Europe, the French early became distinguished as cultivators of maritime law, and one of the most important contributions that ever was made to it was the famous ordonnance of 1681, which formed part of the ambitious and in many respects successful legislation and codification of Louis XIV. AH these earlier attempts at general mercantile legislation were founded, as a matter of course, on the Roman Civil Law, or rather on what that system had borrowed from the laws which regulated the intercourse of the trading communities of Greece, perhaps Phoenicia and Carthage, and which had been reduced to a system by the Rhodians.

From the intimate relations which subsisted between Scotland and the continent of Europe, the lawyers of Scotland became early acquainted with the commercial arrangements of the continental states; and to this cause is said to be ascribed the fact that down to the period when the affairs of Scotland were thrown into confusion by the rebellions of 1715 and 1745, mercantile law was cultivated in Scotland with much care and success. The work of Lord Stair, the greatest of all the legal writers of Scotland, is particularly valuable in this department."

The role of the government in functioning with the individual is proscribed by the principle of joint tenancy, according to the following excerpt from John William Smith's "Mercantile Law":

For the most distinguishing incident of joint tenancy is the *jus accrescendi,* by which, when one joint tenant dies, his interest is not transmitted to his heirs, in the case of descendible property, nor to his personal representatives, in the case of personal effects or chattels, but vests in the survivor or survivors; this right of survivorship being admitted equally in regard to personal chattels, as in estates of every denomination. Now if stock in trade were subject to the same claim, one of two evils might ensue: either the family of a deceased partner might be left destitute; or men's fear of employing a considerable part of their property in these undertakings might check the spirit of commerce. It is therefore, the established law of merchants, that among them joint tenancy and survivorship do not prevail. (Co. Li. 182a; Snon. 2 Browne. 99; Anon. Noy. *55; Hall v. Hujfam,* 2 Lev. 188; Annand v. *Honiwood,* 2 Ch. C. 129).

This right of survivorship Sir William Blackstone apprehends to be the reason why neither the king nor any corporation can be a joint tenant with a private person. (2 Comm. 184). But the rule is more extensive: for two corporations cannot be joint tenants together (Litt. S. 296; Co. Li. 189b, 190a).

The citizen's defense in an admiralty court begins with his denial that he is under martial law, or that the punitive injunctive power of the 14th Amendment, which is founded on martial law, can be applied to him. Because the admiralty court powers derive from the captain of the ship being given the power of an admiral (there not being enough admirals to place one on every ship), the captain then functions under the military power of the King of England. The captain's authority extends to the passing and imposition of a death sentence, as was frequently carried out in death by keelhauling. The offending sailor was dragged under the ship until he had been drowned or tom into pieces by the knife-like barnacles growing on the ship's bottom.

There are only two criminal jurisdictions: common law jurisdiction and international jurisdiction. How did it come to pass that the citizen of the United States could be held to appear under an international jurisdiction? In 1938, because of the enormous debt which President Franklin D. Roosevelt had borrowed from international bankers, to finance his New Deal, the common law, which does not compel performance, was merged with equity procedures, which do compel performance. However, the criminal syndicalists discovered that equity compelled performance has no criminal penalty, but only civil. No jail sentence can be handed down. This was remedied by bringing in the admiralty court procedures, with their power of life or death sentencing. This was made possible by the claim that the debt, owed to international bankers, thus became an international contract. A contract made under the law of nations brings the nation under international law. Because of this development, since 1938, the Congress could pass no more "Public Laws." Instead, they now pass "Public Policy Statutes," which are measures designed to bring relief to the nation's international creditors. Because Congress no longer passes "Public Laws," they have done away with the common law; all laws passed by Congress are now in equity, and conferring equity jurisdiction. Thus the federal district courts function only as equity courts under equity Rules of Procedure, which are nevertheless published under the title, "Federal Rules of Civil Procedure."

Congress, prior to 1939, had also passed private laws, as opposed to Public Laws. In 1913, the income tax amendment and the Federal Reserve Act were passed as private laws. The federal agents are aware of the difference, although they usually refuse to inform the citizen of this significant factor. Title 28 USC is public law, but the IRS operates under Title 26, which is private law, a contract between you and the United States. The corporation excise tax of 1909 became the income tax law of 1913 under the commerce clause of the Constitution, maintaining that the citizen was using corporate paper in an equitable manner, creating a contract consideration. However, no constitutional right is applicable to the filing of an income tax. In tax matters and other government prosecutions, the federal judges are informed that the defendant is a juristic person bankrupt under the terms of the international contractual obligations, and take silent judicial notice of this fact. Citizens are held and charged because of the default on an international contract and its incumbent obligations.

The citizen's defense in this equity procedure, in which he faces admiralty court punishment, is that he must state at his arraignment, after the court asks, "Do you understand the charge?" The defendant then answers "No." Under the 6th Amendment he now has the right to ask both the nature and the cause of the accusation. The defendant then states, "Let the record of this court show that this is a criminal action." The defendant must make this plain, because the defense of a civil action is different from defense of a criminal charge. If the court does not respond fully, the defendant then states, "Let the record of this court show that the defendant asked the nature and the cause of the accusation under his right as guaranteed by the 6th Amendment, and that the court has failed to inform the defendant of secret jurisdiction which is known only to licensed attorneys."

The defendant must make this point because of the fact that both the state and local chapters of the American Bar Association and the International Bar Association are under the direction and control of the international bankers. They must maintain this control in order to continue to use equity jurisdiction to enforce the collection of their international debts. The judge will then state that the defendant is to be tried under statutory jurisdiction. The defendant will then request that he be furnished a copy of the rules of criminal procedure under statutory jurisdiction. The court cannot comply, because there are no such rules.

Having made this point, the defendant will then request the court to state whether it is operating under admiralty jurisdiction. Because no American court will admit that it is actually operating under admiralty jurisdiction, this should be sufficient to win a dismissal, because the court cannot proceed until an admission is made, or a denial, that the court is operating under admiralty procedures. The defendant should then state,

> "Let the record of this court show that it is a criminal court which is operating under an admiralty judge."

American courts cannot convict under admiralty jurisdiction unless a valid international contract is in existence, and unless a copy of said contract can be brought into the court. The court faces the task of proving whether the defendant is a party obligated under such contract. The court must prove jurisdiction by proving an interest in the debt, and must prove it is a valid contract. No court can enforce an invalid contract, which means that the validity of the contract must be proven beyond a shadow of a doubt. The defendant must challenge the validity of the contract, because the law merchant code establishes the difference between a valid and an invalid contract; the invalid contract cannot be enforced. The defendant is actually being charged under the terms of a debt which was created by a bank and which therefore has no substance. Law is concerned with substance. To be convicted at law, the defendant must be shown to have been concerned with a matter of substance. The bank now has no interest in substance, and substance must be proved if the contract is to be enforced. The admiralty jurisdiction under which American courts try defendants is maintained by silent judicial notice. Once the issue of admiralty jurisdiction is brought into the open, it is no longer a secret, and the judge can no longer operate under the secret code which he maintains with his fellow members of the bar association, the prosecutor as well as the defense attorneys, licensed members of the bar, who appear before him. Because he is participating in a secret jurisdiction, the judge assumes judicial immunity to protect himself in the admiralty court. Under the Constitution, he has taken an oath to uphold the Constitution, which is binding upon him in a common law court, but which is not binding in the admiralty court; hence the doctrine of judicial immunity behind which the judges exercise their equity and admiralty procedures.

CHAPTER 16

OUR LEGAL FUTURE

The reader may have noted in the samples of legal briefs reprinted in the foregoing pages, that there were no references to admiralty law. I did cite sources on chancery and equity law, but during the forty years that I was representing myself in American courts, I had not yet researched the cause of our legal dilemma, that our Constitutional courts, as authorized in the Constitution, had stealthily been replaced by equity courts operating on the stern military principles of admiralty punishment. That I managed to survive in these courts without the protection of the knowledge which is freely offered in this work, is less likely due to the benevolence of the judges and lawyers, as it is to their constant fear that in my ongoing and continuous legal researches in preparing my briefs, I would discover their guilty secret. I could then have mounted a serious challenge to their secret fraternal power. The one time that the Masonic connection was mentioned during a lawsuit in which I was engaged, the judge beat a hasty retreat, and immediately granted my motion. Even that connection was cited, not by myself, but by one of my supporters. This indicates the vulnerability of those who have conspired to oppress and deceive us.

When an American citizen goes into court, he can say, as Christ said in Luke 22:53, "this is your hour, and the power of darkness." We are on the verge of dispelling the power of darkness in our courts. We must now turn on the lights full force, and see hordes of cockroaches scuttling frantically towards a dark comer. There are a number of encouraging developments throughout the United States; first, a growing awareness of the absolute corruption of the legal process; two, there is little that most lawyers will do for you except to take your money; and, three, your awareness of the true condition of the legal morass is your best protection. I often tell my audiences,

> "Go into any American prison, and look down the rows of cells. In each of those cells sits a prisoner; and each of those prisoners had a lawyer; and each of those prisoners paid a lawyer."

Several television documentaries have exposed the frantic efforts of the legal profession to halt the growing tendency of Americans to use paralegals for routine legal documents, such as deeds and wills.

In Louisiana and Florida, paralegals have been arrested and their offices closed down, because they tried to help citizens caught in the spider's web of legal procedures. The statutes are vague about "the practice of law"; it is generally interpreted as forbidding persons who have not been granted a license to practice law from representing anyone in court.

However, the paralegals who were arrested and fined never represented anyone in court. Instead, they presented a threat to the lucrative aspects of the legal monopoly, in which legal secretaries do all the work of preparing wills, deeds, and other documents, but the lawyer charges the full lawyer's fee for the work which is done by unlicensed members of his staff.

One of the organizations which continues to do important groundbreaking work in exposing the legal monopoly is HALT. Based in Washington, D.C., HELP ABOLISH LEGAL TYRANNY notes that

> "Our 150,000-plus members are desperate for reliable, no-nonsense information the national movement that's afoot to do away with the unnecessary lawyer monopoly that keeps those prices unconscionably high. As the only national nonprofit group that represents the users of our legal system, HALT has been leading that movement. From Maine to California, citizens are demanding and winning more do-it-yourself forms, streamlined and simplified procedures, and-above all-a free market in which to shop for legal help The estimated 100 million Americans whose legal services now go unserved deserve nothing Jess."

Richard Hebert, Communications Director, HALT, an organization of Americans for Legal Reform, Washington, D.C. Letter to Wall Street Journal, May 18, 1989.

It is certainly important that Americans should no longer be gouged for such everyday legal forms as deeds and wills. It is even more important that every American should know just what is going on in our courts. We must be aware of what has happened to our legal guarantees which were written down in our Constitution. We must be able to challenge the stealthy takeover of our judicial system by furtive conspirators, hiding behind the international allegiances of the law merchant, the Star Chamber procedures of the equity courts, and the secret fraternal associations which dictate judicial decisions diabolically opposed to the interests of our citizens and our nation.

OTHER BOOKS BY EUSTACE MULLINS

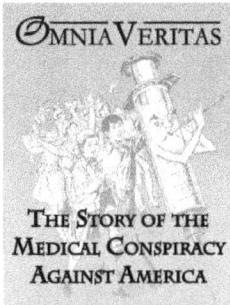

Omnia Veritas Ltd presents:

MURDER BY INJECTION

by

EUSTACE MULLINS

THE STORY OF THE MEDICAL CONSPIRACY AGAINST AMERICA

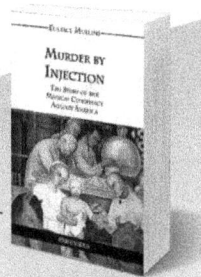

The cynicism and malice of these conspirators is something beyond the imagination of most Americans.

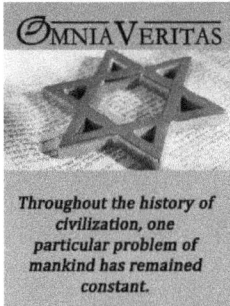

Omnia Veritas Ltd presents:

NEW HISTORY OF THE JEWS

by

EUSTACE MULLINS

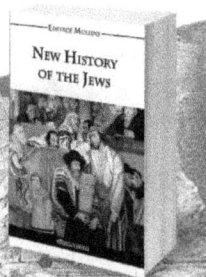

Throughout the history of civilization, one particular problem of mankind has remained constant.

Only one people has irritated its host nations in every part of the civilized world

Omnia Veritas Ltd presents:

THE CURSE OF CANAAN

A demonology of history

by

EUSTACE MULLINS

Liberalism, more popularly known as secular humanism, can be traced in an unbroken line all the way back to the Biblical "Curse of Canaan."

Humanism is the logical result of the demonology of history

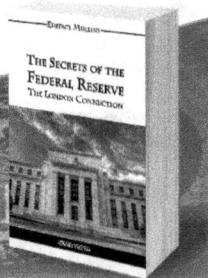

www.ingramcontent.com/pod-product-compliance
Lightning Source LLC
Chambersburg PA
CBHW052103230326
41599CB00054B/3707